canadian
macroeconomics

problems and policies

seventh edition

canadian
macroeconomics

problems and policies

seventh edition

brian lyons

Sheridan Institute of Technology and Advanced Learning

PEARSON

Prentice
Hall

Toronto

National Library of Canada Cataloguing in Publication

Lyons, Brian

Canadian macroeconomics : problems and policies / Brian Lyons. — 7th ed.

Includes index.
ISBN 0-13-120123-9

1. Macroeconomics. 2. Canada—Economic conditions. I. Title.

HB172.5.L96 2004   339'.0971   C2003-901416-9

ISBN 0-13-120123-9

Vice President, Editorial Director: Michael J. Young
Acquisitions Editor: Gary Bennett
Marketing Manager: Deb Meredith
Developmental Editor: Meaghan Eley
Production Editor: Marisa D'Andrea
Copy Editor: Susan Marshall
Proofreader: Laurel Sparrow
Production Coordinator: Andrea Falkenberg
Page Layout: Christine Velakis
Art Director: Julia Hall
Interior/Cover Design: Amy Harnden
Cover Image: Digital Vision

2 3 4 5   08 07 06 05 04

Statistics Canada information is used with the permission of the Minister of Industry, as Minister responsible for Statistics Canada. Information on the availability of the wide range of data from Statistics Canada can be obtained from Statistics Canada's Regional Offices, its World Wide Web site at http://www.statcan.ca and its toll-free access number, 1-800-263-1136. The Statistics Canada CANSIM II database can be accessed at http://cansim2.stat-can.ca/cgi-win/CNSMCGI.EXE.

Printed and bound in Canada.

For Barb, Amber, Marnie,
Brent, Dylan, and Liam

BRIEF TABLE OF CONTENTS

TABLE OF CONTENTS

Chapter 6 Booms, Recessions, and Inflation 121

Chapter 7 Stabilizing the Economy: Government Monetary and Fiscal Policies 148

Chapter 10 The Canadian Dollar in Foreign Exchange Markets   218

Chapter 11 The Global Economy 242

Chapter 12 Canada in the Global Economy 266

"In the News" Boxes

"You Decide" Boxes

Preface

Introduction

This book is an introductory macroeconomics text that addresses itself to the major economic opportunities and challenges facing Canada today and the policy choices for governments in dealing with these issues. It is not oriented toward rigorous, abstract or elegant economic theory, nor to a mathematical approach to economics—students of introductory economics neither want nor need these. Rather, its approach tends to be practical and pragmatic, introducing theory not for its own sake so much as to contribute to an understanding of the issues being discussed.

The text is ideally suited for a student's first course in macroeconomics and is used in this role at the secondary school, community college, and university levels. For the seventh edition, this book and its companion book are again being published in separate volumes only and not in the combined text as was done previously.

New to This Edition

The revisions for this seventh edition were undertaken with the following goals in mind in addition to the usual updating:

1. To improve the flow of the material, both within and between chapters.
2. To add current and interesting material, through

    - various new *In the News* and *You Decide* items;

    - new end-of-chapter questions that add interest and relevance to the material; and

    - many new margin boxes with examples and colourful facts.

3. To increase interactivity of students with the text, through not only new In the News and You Decide items, but also through more references to websites, with questions inviting students to update information in the text.

Various efforts have been made to make the material current and relevant and to keep it so. In addition to the usual updating of information, more questions in the various boxes and at the end of chapters have been added that involve students in updating of statistics and information in the text and in interpreting the updated information. To this end, sources of current data have been suggested, and URLS have been provided for various organizations and sources of information referred to in the text.

Past users of the text will notice updatings of not only its content, but also its structure. The intended result of these changes is a text that is not only more current, but also flows more smoothly from chapter to chapter.

The main *structural* update is the reduction of the number of chapters from 14 to 13, which results from the consolidation of the previous edition's chapters 8 and 13. The coverage of the dangers of *inflation* and *government deficits and debt* (previously in Chapter 13) has been moved into Chapter 8. The rationale is that these topics have shifted from being recent and important events to the sort of "caveats and cautions" that fit better into Chapter 8, which covers various real-world problems and pitfalls relating to economic stabilization policy.

This change led to another shift of material that had some fortuitous effects: to make room in Chapter 8, the material on the various types of unemployment and the idea of "full employment" were moved to Chapter 2, which consolidated the material on unemployment into one chapter. The fortuitous aspect of these changes was that the coverage in Chapter 2 of the idea of "full employment" being an unemployment rate of around 7 percent made the concept of "capacity output" in Chapter 3 more concrete and meaningful—"capacity" is reached when producers have sufficient problems obtaining additional workers. This represents a considerable improvement in Chapter 3, which now presents a clearer impression of what "capacity" means in the real world. It also supports the coverage in Chapters 4, 6, and 8 of the interaction between the demand side and the supply side of the economy, in which the concept of capacity plays an important role.

The overall result of these changes is stronger coverage of key concepts earlier in the text, which supports an improved flow of the material in subsequent chapters.

The most noteworthy *updating of content* involves the related topics of deflation and the sharp decline in the international value of the U.S. dollar in the spring of 2003. These are covered in Chapter 11 on globalization, as part of a review of the state of the global economy as of mid-2003, including the United States, Japan, and Europe. The topic of deflation is introduced in the context of Japan's experience with deflation and concerns about deflation in Europe and the USA. And the related matter of the long-awaited decline of the U.S. dollar occurred just (barely!) in time to be included in this seventh edition. More details of the revisions to Chapter 11 are provided in the chapter-by-chapter review of updates that follows.

In Chapter 2, information has been added on what is regarded as "good" for each of the three economic statistics covered. This adds real-world significance to these statistics and gives students better benchmarks for economic performance earlier in the text/course. Also, the fact that the unemployment rate seldom goes below 7 percent sets up and strengthens the explanation of "capacity output" in Chapter 3.

In Chapter 3, the meaning of "capacity output" in the real world is explained as being mostly the result of shortages of qualified labour that arise when the economy is in a boom. This explanation is linked back to the more thorough coverage of employment and unemployment in Chapter 2. Chapter 3 also includes an update of Canada's weakness re: productivity growth and the projected consequences of this problem, bolstered by some excellent material from the Centre for the Study of Living Standards.

In Chapter 4, the latter parts have been reorganized so as to improve the flow of the material, and the addition of an *In the News* item on demand trends in recent years adds relevance and provides interesting insights into the changes that have occurred in the Canadian economy during and since the 1990s. Also, coverage of cuts to federal taxes on personal and business incomes over the 2001-05 period has been added.

In Chapter 5, the coverage of the money-creation process has been expanded and made clearer.

Chapter 7 includes a rewriting of the section on monetary policy that provides clearer explanations, supported by more illustrations and examples to which students can relate. Also, the material on time lags in the effects of monetary policy has been shifted from Chapter 8 to Chapter 7, making Chapter 7's coverage of monetary policy more complete.

Chapter 8 now includes the limits that are imposed upon monetary and fiscal policy by the need to keep inflation and government debt under control, which had been covered in Chapter 13 of previous editions. This change consolidates all of the "real-world" problems and pitfalls associated with macroeconomic stabilization policy into this single chapter.

Chapter 9's content is basic in nature and seldom changes much. To add a little spice and relevance, several margin boxes with interesting information have been added. In addition, there is new coverage of services and more coverage on Mexico.

In Chapter 10, coverage of the connection between interest rates and the exchange rate is strengthened, and the idea that a floating Canadian dollar can act as a "shock absorber" for the economy in the event of a recession is introduced. This was one reason for the Bank of Canada's scepticism concerning the growing proposals for "dollarization" that accompanied the dollar's decline in 2001-02.

Chapter 11 has been updated extensively. It includes a review of the state of the global economy as of mid-2003, with emphasis on the role of capital flows as a key driving force behind exchange rates. In the United States, capital inflows are explained as the reason for the strong U.S. dollar, which was related to the growth of U.S protectionism and the embroilment of the USA in trade disputes. In the first half of 2003, outflows of capital were the driving force behind the sudden decline of the U.S. dollar. The coverage of Japan has been expanded considerably, owing to its experience with deflation, which is introduced as a topic in this chapter. Coverage of Europe is also increased, with stress on how the risk of deflation is increased by the EU's own rules for budget deficits and inflation targets, which limit governments' use of monetary and fiscal policies to stimulate their economies. The increase in the exchange rate of the euro against the U.S. dollar is likely to place these arrangements under growing strain.

In addition to the coverage of deflation in Japan, there is a new and separate section on deflation that explains why deflation is considered to be a potentially serious problem, why deflation concerns were growing in 2003, and why there were concerns that it might spread.

Chapter 12 continues the saga of the Canadian dollar, with emphasis on the role of capital flows in its decline through 2002, and the implications (both positive and negative) for Canadians. In 2002, the continuing decline of the dollar generated the debate over "dollarization," so Chapter 12 also looks at the pros and cons of Canada adopting the U.S. dollar as its currency.

The sharp increase in the exchange rate of the Canadian dollar in the spring of 2003 occurred too late to be covered in the main body of the text; however, there was (just!) time to add a question at the end of Chapter 12 that noted this development and asked about its effects on Canadians. The *causes* of the surge in the Canadian dollar are to be found mostly in Chapter 11's coverage of how capital flows affected the international value of the *U.S.* dollar, since the key factor was the decline of the U.S. dollar.

Chapter 13 provides the "wrap-up" that was previously in Chapter 14. The addition of material from the former Chapter 13 makes this chapter a more complete review of the changes that have taken place in Canada over the past decade and are the backdrop to the current economic situation. The result is a more complete and effective concluding chapter.

Features

According to both students and teachers, a major feature of this book is its readability, which helps considerably in the learning and teaching of a subject that has an (undeserved) reputation of being rather formidable. Other aspects of the text include:

- **Organization** The material is organized in a manner that students find logical and easy to follow.
- **Structure** The reduced number of chapters fits well into most schools' programs, and if time is short, Chapter 13 can be omitted, bringing the number of chapters to 12.
- **Interactiveness** The boxes described above, together with the discussion questions at the end of each chapter and in the Study Guide, provide extensive opportunities for students to interact with the material, both in groups and on their own.
- **Pedagogical Tools** Learning Objectives, *You Decide* boxes, *In the News* boxes, and end-of-chapter questions all help students focus on and apply the important points in each chapter.

Organization

For the main body of the book, the updates have created a more focused and cleanly-flowing presentation of macroeconomics. Following the introductory material in the first two chapters, the supply side of the economy is presented, followed by the demand side, providing a structured overview of the economy on a macroeconomic scale at an earlier point in the text. Money and banking are then covered, expanding on the coverage of the demand side and providing a link to the major topic of economic instability in Chapter 6. In the next chapter, the monetary and fiscal policies used to stabilize the economy are covered, followed by a chapter on the realities that limit what can be achieved by these policies in the Canadian context.

Chapter 9 introduces international trade, emphasizing the importance of trade in the Canadian economy and the basic principles concerning trade and trade restrictions. Chapter 10 deals with exchange rates and government exchange rate policy, and the relationship of these to trade performance. In Chapter 11 the globalization of the world economy is addressed, using the two main themes of international agreements concerning the topics of Chapter 9 and 10: trade (the GATT/WTO) and exchange rates (the IMF). In addition, Chapter 11 reviews recent major developments in the world economy, including the threat of deflation. Chapter 12 focuses on Canada's involvement in this globalized world economy, stressing Canadian trade policy, NAFTA and its effects on Canada, international investment flows and Canada's foreign debt, and Canada's exchange rate.

Chapter 13 summarizes Canada's economic position and government policy directions for the future with respect to trade, productivity, and monetary and fiscal policy. With respect to the latter, the coverage of government finances has been updated to provide details of how the federal government turned its budget deficits into surpluses, followed by a discussion of the alternative ways in which these surpluses might be used.

Supplements

The following supplements are available for this text:

- Instructor's Resource Manual and Transparency Masters: includes the answers to all end-of-chapter questions, assignment questions and answers for each chapter, answers to boxed questions in the text, and Transparency Masters for all figures and tables in the text.

- Test Item File: includes over 1500 multiple choice, fill-in-the-blanks, and essay questions with difficulty ratings and page references.

- Pearson TestGen: includes all the contents of the Test Item File in a computerized format, which enables instructors to view and edit the existing questions, add questions, generate tests, and print the tests in a variety of formats. Issued on the Instructor's Resource CD-ROM, the Pearson TestGen is compatible with both Windows and Macintosh systems.

- Study Guide: includes a review of central themes, self tests with multiple choice, true/false, fill-in-the-blank, short answer, problem, and case study questions, and answers for all self-test questions.

- Companion Website: includes valuable student resources such as, self-assessment quizzes, and links to related websites. Visit the site at **www.pearsoned.ca/lyons**.

Acknowledgments

Anyone undertaking a project of this magnitude and duration feels indebtedness to many people. In particular, I would like to express my gratitude to Bill Trimble, who said I should do it, Len Rosen, who refused to let me say I wouldn't, and all those teachers and students who used the first six editions and offered helpful comments and suggestions. I would also like to thank the people whose reviews of all six editions of the manuscript were so helpful: for the first edition, Ray Canon, Gord Cleveland, Ward Levine, Jim Thompson and Ian Wilson; for the second, Alan Idiens and Chuck Casson; for the third, Linda Nitsou, Bo Renneckendorf, Gord Enemark, L.W. Van Niekerk, Stephen Wise and Ann Dunkley; for the fourth, Carol Ann Waite, Izhar Mirza, John Parry and Byron Eastman, and for the fifth, Valerie Beckingham, Michael Loconte, Pauline A. Lutes, Peter J. MacDonald, Karen Murkar, John Parry, Don Pepper, Judith Skuce, Don Wheeler, and Peter Young; for the sixth edition, to Peter Peters of University College of the Cariboo, Karen Murkar of DeVry Institution of Technology, Ian Wilson of St. Lawrence College, Don Wheeler of College of the North Atlantic, Jean Cormier of New Brunswick Community College, Martin Moy and Bill Gallivan of University College of Cape Breton, Terri Anderson of Mohawk College, and Jane Taylor of Nova Scotia Community College. And finally, many thanks to the reviewers of this, the seventh edition, Worku Aberra of Dawson College, Frances Ford of New Brunswick Community College (Moncton), Carl Graham of Assiniboine Community College, Donald Howick of St. Clair College, Al Idiens of College of New Caledonia, Peter J. MacDonald of Cambrian College, Raimo Marttala of Malaspina College, Martin Moy of University College of Cape Breton, A. Gyasi Nimarko of Vanier College, John Pirrie of St. Lawrence College, and Charles Walton of Nova Scotia Community College.

Finally, I want to express my appreciation to my family—Barb, Marnie, and Amber—who have provided support and understanding over unduly long periods of time.

I have no doubt that there are many improvements that can be made to this book, and welcome suggestions from teachers and students. Please write to me at Sheridan Institute of Technology and Advanced Learning, 7899 McLaughlin Road, Brampton, Ontario L6V 1G6, or e-mail me at **brian.lyons@sheridanc.on.ca**.

Brian Lyons
2003

A Great Way to Learn and Instruct Online

The Pearson Education Canada Companion Website is easy to navigate and is organized to correspond to the chapters in this textbook. Whether you are a student in the classroom or a distance learner you will discover helpful resources for in-depth study and research that empower you in your quest for greater knowledge and maximize your potential for success in the course.

Companion
Website

[www.pearsoned.ca/lyons]

PEARSON
Prentice
Hall

Jump to...   http://www.pearsoned.ca/lyons   Home Search Help Profile

Companion
Website

Home >

Companion Website

Canadian Microeconomics: Problems and Policies, Seventh Edition, and *Canadian Macroeconomics: Problems and Policies,* Seventh Edition, by Lyons

Student Resources

The modules in this section provide students with tools for learning course material. These modules include:
- Chapter Objectives
- Destinations
- Quizzes
- Net Search
- Glossary

In the quiz modules students can send answers to the grader and receive instant feedback on their progress through the Results Reporter. Coaching comments and references to the textbook may be available to ensure that students take advantage of all available resources to enhance their learning experience.

Instructor Resources

The modules in this section provide instructors with additional teaching tools. A downloadable Instructor's Manual will be available in this section. Where appropriate, this section will be password protected.

Chapter 1

What Is Economics?

Learning Objectives

After studying this chapter, you should be able to:

1. Explain why scarcity is regarded as the basic "economic problem."

2. Explain the meaning and the significance of the terms *productivity*, *efficiency*, and *effectiveness*.

3. Explain the three basic questions of economics.

4. Explain how a market system economy provides answers to each of the three basic questions of economics.

5. Explain how profits and the profit motive contribute to the effective and efficient use of economic resources.

6. Explain how competition contributes to the effective and efficient use of economic resources.

7. State three types of problems that tend to occur in market system economies.

8. Explain why Canada's economic system is described as a "mixed free-enterprise" system, and describe three major types of roles played by government in the Canadian economy.

What is "economics"? To the householder, economics is the difficult task of balancing the family budget, so that there is not too much month left over at the end of the money. To the business leader, economics is the problem of producing a product at such a low cost that it can be marketed profitably in competition with the products of other producers. To a government leader, economics means difficult policy choices between goals that too often conflict with each other, making it impossible to please everyone and difficult to ensure re-election. To the general public, economics is usually associated with incomprehensible and often contradictory pronouncements of people called "economists," who many people suspect were created in order to make weather forecasters look good.

Each viewpoint, representing a particular group (business leaders and government leaders), is only one aspect of the real meaning of economics. To the economist, however, economics deals with the broader question of how well a society's economic system satisfies the economic needs and wants of its people.

Economics, then, is about many matters both small and large. On a small scale, *microeconomics* (after the Greek word *micro*, meaning small) focuses on various *parts* of the economy, such as consumers, business, labour, and government. These topics and other issues are covered in the companion text, *Canadian Microeconomics: Problems and Policies*.

On a wider scale, *macroeconomics* (after the Greek word *macro*, meaning big) deals with broader matters pertaining to the performance of the economy *as a whole*, such as recessions, unemployment, government finances and debt, inflation, interest rates, and international trade and finance. This book deals with matters such as these.

The Varied Nature of Economics

Some aspects of economic issues raise *philosophical questions*; for instance, should the government provide Employment Insurance benefits to people who earn considerable income through seasonal work? Other aspects of economics, however, involve more *technical economic analysis*. For example, if the Bank of Canada reduces interest rates, by how much could we expect unemployment to decrease? In many cases, also, economics becomes involved with *value judgments*. For example, suppose that economic analysis estimates that if the government restricts imports of eggs in order to protect jobs on Canadian farms, higher egg prices in Canada will cost consumers roughly $120 000 for every job saved through this policy. Is this a worthwhile price to pay for the jobs that are saved? This question involves a value judgment, in the sense that even people who agree about the economic analysis of the issue may disagree on what policy the government should follow. One person may be more concerned about the effect of job losses, while another may place greater emphasis on the higher prices that Canadian consumers will have to pay for eggs.

The Limitations of Economic Analysis

Because it deals with the behaviour of people (consumers, workers, businesspeople, government policy-makers), economics is not a precise science such as mathematics. And with respect to important economic policy issues, economic analysis does not provide clear and simple *answers*, such as "reduce interest rates by 1.25 percentage points." However, economic analysis can greatly *clarify the choices* to be made, through the estimation of the consequences of reducing (or not reducing) interest rates. So while economic analysis does not *provide us with* decisions, it does provide us with a much better *basis for making* decisions.

Can Economists Agree on Anything?

"Ask five economists what should be done about a problem and you'll get six different recommendations" is a jibe frequently directed at economists. Given the disagreements among economists (and others loosely described as such) on important matters, it is easy to get the impression that the field of economics involves more unsubstantiated opinion than systematic analysis.

In fact, however, economics is in considerably better condition than seems to be generally supposed. First, to add controversy to news coverage, the media often seek out dissenting opinions on economic issues, giving even illogical opinions an undeserved appearance of legitimacy. Second, many public pronouncements on economic matters are made not by economists, but rather by politicians whose goal is not to discuss economic issues rationally, but rather to score (or obscure) points politically. Most disagreements among economists arise not from *economic analysis* of issues but rather from differences concerning *policy recommendations* (value judgments) that arise from that analysis. In fact, there are many generally accepted facts, concepts, and theories that constitute a sort of "mainstream" of economic thought that is less publicized but much more important than disagreements between individual economists. This book attempts to build around this mainstream of thought, while considering the major alternatives to it where these are important.

Isn't This All Terribly Difficult?

Not really. Probably the most insightful observation ever made about economics as a field of study is that it is a *complex* subject but not a *difficult* one. Unlike nuclear physics or differential calculus, there is little in economics that many people find conceptually difficult. Rather, economics deals with people and their behaviour and decisions as consumers, workers, businesspeople, and government policy-makers. Much of this behaviour is already known to the student of introductory economics; what needs to be done is to organize these fragments of knowledge into a framework for analyzing and understanding economic events. This book attempts to do this in a way that does not require abstract theories and complex mathematics, and focuses instead on developing an understanding of real and relevant Canadian macroeconomic issues in a readable and, hopefully, enjoyable way. Before examining these issues, however, we will consider the basic problems of economics and the nature of Canada's economic system.

The "Economic Problem": Too Many Wants, Not Enough Resources

The fundamental problem of economics—so basic that it is known as *"the economic problem"*—is the simple fact that we cannot have everything that we would like. And because of this reality, we are forced to make some difficult decisions.

All too often, however, this and other key economic realities become lost in the confusing complexity of our modern economy. A modern economy can seem very bewildering, because it consists of a myriad of factors, such as consumers, small businesses, big businesses, ebusinesses, labour unions, and governments. In addition, there are external factors such as exports, imports, trade policy, and the international value of the Canadian dollar. And a modern economy generates seemingly countless statistics concerning output, employment, unemployment, the money supply, interest rates, prices, government tax revenues and spending, consumer spending and saving, banks, profits, stock markets, and many others. Furthermore, each of these factors is related to the others in ways that are often subtle and complex. Such complexities often make understanding an issue difficult because they obscure the basic economic principles of the issue.

In order to better understand an economic situation, it is helpful to eliminate the many complexities associated with a modern economy, so that we can focus on the basic economic principles involved. As an example of eliminating complexity, suppose that a group of people is stranded on a deserted island. With none of the complexities of a modern economy to distract them, this group must come to grips with the most basic economic problem: the people in the group have *economic needs and wants*, but there are only certain *economic resources* available to them. The group needs and wants things such as food, shelter, clothing, security, and so on. To produce these things, the group has three basic types of **economic resources**, or **inputs**— the skills of the people in the group, the equipment they have, and the natural resources of the island.

economic resources Labour, capital equipment, and natural resources that are used to produce goods and services.

inputs Are the same as economic resources.

labour The largest single productive input available to any economy, labour includes all of the productive talents of the people of a society, mental as well as physical.

The Skills of the People ("Labour")

The largest and most important single economic resource available to any society is the skills of its people, which economists refer to as **labour**. Labour includes all types of skills: manual labour, skilled work, management, and professional services. In our island mini-society, people will have various useful skills, such as hunting, fishing, farming, building, planning, and managing.

Capital Equipment

Another vitally important economic resource is society's stock of **capital equipment** (also simply called **capital**), by which we mean its tools, equipment, machinery, factories, computers, and so on. Capital equipment is crucially important because it increases **output per worker** (per hour), or *productivity*. And when each worker produces more, the society can enjoy more economic prosperity, or a higher **standard of living**—more goods and services per person. Figure 1-1 illustrates the importance of capital equipment.

capital equipment The tools, equipment, machinery, and factories used to increase production per worker, and thus improve living standards.

output per worker The goods and services produced by a worker using productive inputs.

FIGURE 1-1 The Importance of Capital Equipment

Capital Equipment		Higher Output per Worker per Hour (productivity)		Higher Potential Standard of Living (goods + services per person)

standard of living A measure of the economic prosperity of the people of a society, usually expressed in terms of the volume of goods and services consumed per person per year.

While a modern industrial economy possesses a vast array of factories, machinery, equipment, and computers, our island mini-society will only have a few basic tools, such as spears, fishnets, and plows. As a result, productivity will be low, and the people of the mini-society will have relatively few goods to enjoy. So in order to increase their productivity and their standard of living, they might, for example, build more capital equipment.

land Short form for all the natural resources available to a society's economy as economic inputs.

Natural Resources ("Land")

The third economic resource available to a society is natural resources, which economists refer to as **land**. In our island mini-society, these natural resources would likely be few and simple—waterways, fish, land, trees, plants, and so on. In a modern economy, natural resources are often much more complex. For example, using energy resources such as oil, natural gas, and atomic energy involves sophisticated technology.

People tend to think of natural resources as depletable (and depleting), but this is not always the case. Some natural resources, such as forests and fish, can be renewable if managed effectively, while technology is capable of creating entirely new resources, such as oil, natural gas, and nuclear power. For example, until the development of nuclear reactors, uranium could not reasonably be considered an economic resource. In a similar way, improvements in technology made the Athabasca Tar Sands of Northern Alberta into a major energy resource. So while some natural resources are becoming depleted, new resources can be developed through technology.

"If you were asked to choose just one test of an economy's performance, one of the strongest candidates would be growth in productivity. In the long run, increases in productivity—that is, in output per worker—are the only way for a country to raise its living standards."

The Economist

The Task of an Economic System

The task of the economic system of any society is to organize and use these economic resources, or productive inputs, to produce goods and services (**output**) of the types and quantities that will best satisfy the needs and wants of the people of the society. This process is shown in Figure 1-2.

In our island mini-society, the process shown in Figure 1-2 would be quite simple: people with various skills would use simple tools such as spears, nets, and plows to produce products to satisfy basic needs such as food, shelter, and security. In a modern economy, this process is much more sophisticated, involving a wide range of skills and "high-tech" equipment and resources to produce a tremendous volume and variety of both goods and services. However, the basic task is the same in both economies: to use our economic resources to our best advantage.

The Basic "Economic Problem" of Scarcity

Using our economic resources to our best advantage is particularly important because we do not have enough economic resources to produce everything that we would like to have. This is the basic "economic problem" of **scarcity**: the economic resources (inputs) on the left side of Figure 1-2 are in limited supply, while the amounts of goods and services wanted by people on the right side of Figure 1-2 seem to be unlimited. Since we cannot have everything that we want, we are forced to *make choices*, some of which might be difficult.

output The goods and services produced by a society using its productive inputs.

scarcity The problem that, while economic inputs (and thus potential ouput) are limited in availability, people's wants and needs are apparently unlimited.

FIGURE 1-2 The Basic Operation of Any Economic System

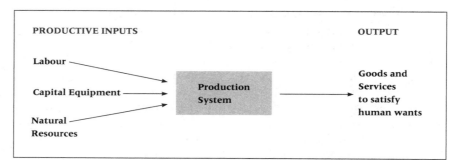

The island mini-economy illustrates this reality particularly clearly because the choices are so limited. Suppose there are ten people available for work, and the group decides to use five of them for getting food, three for getting fuel, and two for taking care of security by maintaining fences and standing watch against certain threatening creatures that roam the island. If the group finds that they don't have enough food, they can increase food production by 20 percent by adding another person to the "food team." However, this addition would require removing that person from the subgroups who are either getting fuel or providing security. While the group would be better fed, it would have either less comfort or less security. So having more of any one of these items means having less of another, forcing the group to make difficult choices.

These are the same issues that Canadian households face in managing their budgets. Since your income can't buy everything that you would like, you have to make choices about what you will have and what you will forgo. Taking that dream vacation would be wonderful, but it will mean that you cannot buy the car that you really want. See the "You Decide" box for a look at the concept of opportunity cost in making choices.

YOU DECIDE   OPPORTUNITY COST

Economists use the term **opportunity cost** to describe the choices that scarcity forces upon us. That is, opportunity cost refers to what you *could have had* if you had used your resources for something else.

Questions

1. Suppose that in the island mini-economy you had four people working: two people catching a total of six fish per day and two others picking a total of 8 kg of fruit per day. If you decided that you wanted to have three more fish each day, what would be a reasonable estimate of the opportunity cost of that decision?

    As a consumer in a modern economy, your economic resources consist of the money available to you. Suppose that you had only $150 and your mother was expecting a Mother's Day gift (tickets to a Rolling Stones concert) that cost $150; however, your car had just broken down, and it would cost $150 to repair it.

2. What would be the opportunity cost of buying your mother the gift?
3. What would be the opportunity cost of getting your car fixed?

> **opportunity cost** The concept that the real economic cost of producing something is the forgone opportunity to produce something else that could have been produced with the same inputs.

And an entire nation, through its government, must come to grips with the same problems. The public wants the best health-care and education systems as well as other government services, but governments lack the tax revenues to provide the ideal levels of all services. Since using more tax resources for one service would leave less for other services, we must accept less than ideal levels of all services.

So the basic economic problem of scarcity is a universal one, affecting all societies. In the following sections, let's consider some of the implications of the problem of scarcity.

Effectiveness and Efficiency

Because we cannot have everything that we would like, it is very important that we use our scarce economic resources wisely, by producing as much as we can of things that are needed and wanted. This brings us to the concepts of *effectiveness* and *efficiency,* which are the two most basic measures of the performance of any economic operation, from an individual business to a nation's entire economy.

effectiveness A measure of how well an economy performs in terms of producing goods and services that meet the needs and wants of people.

efficiency A measure of how well an economy performs in terms of producing high volumes of goods and services at a low cost per item.

Effectiveness refers to producing goods and services that are *needed and wanted*. If an economic system achieves these goals, it is said to be "effective." **Efficiency** refers to using the economic resources available to you to produce a *high volume of output* at a *low production cost per unit*. One common measure of efficiency is "productivity," or output per worker per hour. Societies with efficient economies that produce a high volume of goods and services per worker tend to have a high standard of living, or consumption per person.

To recap, it is important that an economy be *both* effective *and* efficient. The more efficiently and effectively a society uses its economic resources, the more successful it will be in making available to its people larger volumes of goods and services that are needed and wanted and at lower prices. As a result, its people will enjoy a higher standard of living.

The Three Basic Questions of Economics

As we have seen, the task of any economic system is to use its scarce economic resources efficiently and effectively in order to best satisfy the needs and wants of its people. Since economic resources are scarce and we cannot have everything that we want, we are forced to make certain very basic choices:

- What goods and services will we produce?
- How should we produce these goods and services?
- How will we divide up our output of goods and services among ourselves? That is, who will get how much?

These are the three most basic economic questions that every society must face, regardless of its stage of development or the nature of its economic system.

What to Produce?

Because economic resources (or productive inputs) are scarce, no society can have all the goods and services it would like to have. Instead, it must *make choices*, or set priorities. For example, the people in our island mini-society would have to decide whether to produce fish, vegetables, shelter, fuel, security, or more equipment to make their work more efficient.

What makes such choices difficult is that they involve deciding not only what *will* be produced, but also what *will not* be produced. If the group decides to use six people to farm vegetables, those six people will not be available to gather fuel or build shelter. So, a decision to produce *more* of one thing necessarily means accepting *less* of other things. This type of decision forces us to set priorities, or decide what is most important to us. Obviously, making such decisions relates to the goal of *effectiveness*, as discussed in the previous section, because the priorities we set will reflect our needs and wants, or how much we value each product.

Consumer Goods or Capital Goods?

One of the most basic what-to-produce decisions that must be made is whether *consumer goods* or *capital goods* will be produced. Consumer goods (such as food and fuel) can be enjoyed *in the present*, but are used up quickly and do not contribute to longer-term economic prosperity. Capital goods (such as tools and equipment), on the other hand, cannot be consumed and enjoyed *today*, but they will increase our productive efficiency *in the future*. In this way, capital goods will contribute to our future production and prosperity, by increasing our productivity for the many years that they will last. Figure 1-3 illustrates this choice.

FIGURE 1-3 Consumer Goods and Capital Goods: The Choice

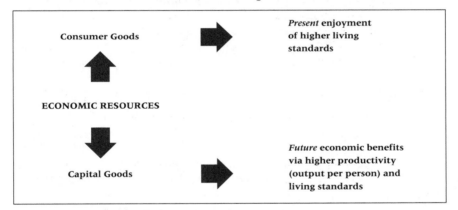

These decisions will have a crucial influence on the prosperity of a society both in the present and in the future. If our island mini-society emphasizes the production of consumer goods, its people will enjoy a higher standard of living in the present. However, if they emphasize consumer-goods production to the point of neglecting capital-goods production, they will enjoy less prosperity in the future. On the other hand, if the people are willing to do with fewer consumer goods in the present in order to build more capital goods, they can look forward to higher levels of economic prosperity in the future. In the second half of the twentieth century, the greatest economic improvement was experienced by nations that stressed the production of capital goods, such as Japan and Germany.

How to Produce It?

Once we have decided *what* we want to produce, we must decide *how* each product or service is to be produced. This is a question of production methods: How should we combine our scarce inputs of labour, capital equipment, and natural resources for use in production?

As a simple example, suppose our island mini-society has decided to produce (cultivate) vegetables. The next question is, How should the group do this? Should people cultivate by hand? Or use simple tools such as hoes? Or use more sophisticated equipment such as plows? Before the vegetables that the group wants can be produced, the group will have to decide how to produce them.

Generally speaking, our goal will be to develop production methods that result in *higher efficiency* in order to increase our economic prosperity. However, the decision becomes more complicated if we need to use economic resources to build capital equipment in order to increase output per worker. If the amount of capital equipment we can build is limited, would it be better, for example, to build a plow for cultivating vegetables or a net for fishing? This decision would be easier to make if we could find a way to measure the *costs* of using the plow and the net (in terms of the hours, materials, and equipment needed to build each of them) against the *benefits* of each (in terms of the increased output each would bring).

Obviously, in deciding the answer to this question, we are pursuing the goal of *efficiency*, as discussed earlier. By being efficient, we avoid wasting our scarce economic resources, and so increase our economic prosperity.

Who Gets How Much? (Dividing the "Economic Pie")

The last of our three basic questions is, How we will divide up our output of goods and services among our people? Who will receive what share of what we have produced?

Should everyone receive an equal share? Or should some people receive more than others? If some are to receive a larger share, why should they get more, and how much more should they get?

We have seen that a society will prosper economically if the work of its people is *effective* and *efficient*. This consideration argues in favour of inequality, with a larger "piece of the pie" providing incentives for people to work more effectively and efficiently. If everyone knew that they were going to receive the same share as everyone else, why should anyone make an extra effort or contribution?

In addition to effectiveness and efficiency, however, there is the goal of *fairness*. How wide a gap between the rich and the poor are we prepared to accept? What if some people cannot produce enough to live decently without help from the others? Should the most productive people give up some of what they have produced (earned) in order to help the less productive ones? And if our answer to this question is "yes," how much should the better-off people give up in order to help the less fortunate (or less capable)?

This question of how to divide up the economic pie is certainly the most controversial of the three basic economic questions. In a modern economy such as Canada's, a person's share of the "economic pie" depends on his or her *income*. If an accountant's income (after taxes) is twice as large as a labourer's, the accountant's share of the economic pie will be twice that of the labourer.

But by what standards should we *decide* who gets higher incomes and a larger share of the pie? Should hockey players receive a larger share than doctors? Should lawyers have a larger share than social workers? Should firefighters get a larger share than that of day-care workers? Somehow, every society has to work out the question of how to divide up the economic pie.

Answering the Three Questions

In this section, we have considered the three basic questions of economics that every society must answer—what to produce, how to produce it, and how to divide it up. Different societies answer these questions in very different ways. In the next section, we will consider how Canada's economic system deals with these most basic questions.

Canada's Economic System

We have seen that the basic economic problem of scarcity forces upon every society the need to address three questions: what to produce (and not produce), how to produce it, and how to divide it up among the people of the society. To deal with these questions, a society has to organize its economic resources (labour, capital equipment, and natural resources) in order to use them both effectively (produce things that are needed and wanted) and efficiently (produce them in high volume and at low cost and price), thereby generating economic prosperity for its people.

Effective and efficient organization of resources is no small task. The Canadian economy—the eighth largest in the world—includes over 31 million consumers with their own wants and needs, over two million business enterprises producing millions of different goods and services, and a labour force of about 17 million people with a wide variety of skills. How, then, does the Canadian economy organize all these economic resources to produce over $1 trillion ($1 000 000 000 000) of goods and services annually, and in the process manage to provide its people with one of the highest standards of living in the world?

The Market System

Most of Canada's economic system is organized according to a *market system*. In the **market system** (also known as the *free enterprise system*), privately owned businesses (*free enterprises*) produce goods and services in response to the demand of buyers and for a profit. Nearly 80 percent of the total output of the Canadian economy is produced by such businesses, which are collectively known as the *private sector*. In the private sector, the key economic decisions are made by consumers and businesses.

market system An economic system in which economic decisions are made mainly by consumers and privately owned producers in a decentralized manner.

In addition to its private sector, the Canadian economy has a substantial *government sector*, in which the key decisions are made by governments. The government sector accounts for about 20 percent of the output of the economy, consisting mostly of public services such as health care, education, and public security. In addition, governments play a number of other important roles in the economy, which we will examine later.

First let's examine what a market is and how it operates, and how a market system functions.

What Is a "Market"?

Simply stated, a *market* is where buyers and sellers come together to exchange goods and services for money, or to buy and sell things. Figure 1-4 illustrates this concept a little more formally, using the market for candles as an example. Figure 1-4 shows that the market for candles consists of:

(a) a number of sellers offering to sell candles, in competition with each other (economists call this side the *supply side* of the market), and

(b) many buyers offering to buy candles, in competition with each other (economists call this side the *demand side* of the market).

FIGURE 1-4 The Market for Candles

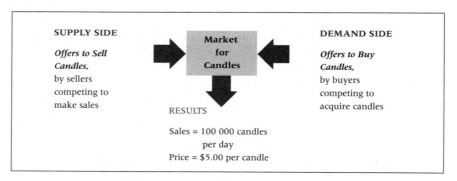

The interaction between buyers and sellers in the marketplace determines the *price* of candles ($5.00 each) and the *sales* of candles (100 000 per day). If the willingness of buyers to buy candles or the willingness of sellers to sell them were to change, the price and sales of candles would also change.

How Do Markets Work?

Markets respond to changes in buyers' demand. For instance, if the demand for candles increased (because there were more buyers, or buyers had more money, or they just liked candles better than before), the increased demand would cause the *price* of candles to increase, say, from $5 to $7. This higher price, together with higher sales, would make it more profitable to produce candles. Because of this potential for higher profit, more candles would be produced and offered for sale, perhaps 110 000 per day instead of 100 000.

In the same way, if the demand for candles were to fall, then the price would fall, making candle production less profitable. With lower prices and lower sales, producers would produce fewer candles, in response to the lower demand of consumers.

The "classic" form of market is a farmers' market or a flea market, where many producers and consumers come directly together to buy and sell various products. However, markets take many other forms. To most people, the most familiar form of market is at the retail level, where consumers buy goods and services from retailers. In addition, there are: wholesale markets and commodity markets, where the buyers are businesses that bid for the products in an auction environment); labour markets, where people's time and skills are purchased, and the price paid is a wage rate or salary; capital markets (or markets for loans), where the use of someone else's money is purchased, and the price paid is the interest rate; and stock markets, where the shares of corporations are bought and sold.

Some markets (such as the market for baby-sitters) are extremely local in nature, while others (such as the market for wheat or oil) are worldwide in scope. Regardless of its particular form, however, any market consists of a supply side and a demand side, as pictured in Figure 1-4.

Because demand is the most basic force in markets, the market system is sometimes said to be *demand-driven*. And because of the key role played by prices and price changes in adjusting production to demand, the market system is sometimes referred to as the *price system*.

Some markets are conducted over the internet. For examples, visit www.autotrader.ca and www.expedia.ca.

How a Market System Is Organized

Figure 1-5 illustrates the operation of a market system. The upper flows in Figure 1-5 represent consumers buying goods and services from businesses.

FIGURE 1-5 The Operation of a Market Economy

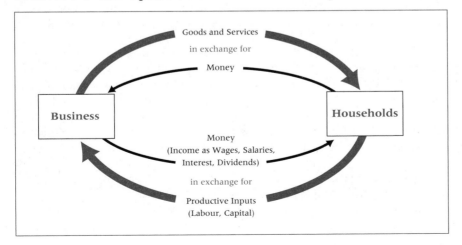

These flows represent many thousands of markets for specific goods and services, in which millions of consumers buy these items at the prices and in the quantities determined in the marketplace.

In other words, the upper flows would consist of the market for hamburgers, the market for jeans, the market for apartments, the market for laptop computers, the market for haircuts, and all of the other markets for all of the other goods and services that consumers buy. And in each of these markets, a *price* is determined for the product or service involved.

The lower flows in Figure 1-5 represent a different side of the economy in which businesses buy the inputs for producing the goods and services shown in the top flows.

So the lower flows would include markets for factory workers, for computer programmers, for retail clerks, for professional athletes, and for all of the other job skills that the economy needs. And in each of these markets, a price—in the form of a wage rate or salary level for that type of skill—is established.

The operation of a market system such as that shown in Figure 1-5 involves billions of individual decisions by consumers, business firms, and workers about consumer purchases, production levels, prices, the numbers of workers to be employed, wage rates, capital investment, and so on. It is through these decisions, made in countless markets, that the answers are developed to the three basic questions of what to produce, how to produce it, and how to divide it up.

How the Market System Answers the Three Questions

What to Produce?

Consumers play the largest role in deciding what will be produced. Since the basic goal of business is to earn a profit, businesses will produce those goods and services that are in demand. This process is described by the phrases "consumer sovereignty" (meaning that the consumer is viewed as "king of the marketplace") and "dollar votes," (meaning that, by buying a product, a consumer is in effect casting a vote in the marketplace for the production of that product).

At Glen Abbey golf course in Oakville, Ontario, the fee for an 18-hole round of golf in 2002 was $235.

Prices provide an important link between what buyers want and what businesses produce. For instance, if the demand for golfing increases, the price of golfing will increase. The increase in price will make operating golf courses more profitable, creating an incentive for businesses to create more golf courses. In the same way, a reduction in the demand for red meat would depress its price, making its production less profitable and creating an incentive to reduce its production. "Price signals" such as these are also transmitted through the labour markets, as shown at the bottom of Figure 1-5. For instance, if the higher demand for golfing led to an increase in the demand for greens-keepers, the wages of greens-keepers would rise, attracting more people into working in that field.

How to Produce It?

The decision of how to produce a product is made by producers, or private businesses, who will strive for the most efficient possible production method. Lower production costs not only mean higher profits; in a highly competitive industry, they may be the key to survival.

Prices also help to decide the production methods for producing goods and services. In determining the most efficient production methods, it makes obvious economic sense to minimize the use of the most scarce inputs. Prices help to minimize using scarce inputs because the more scarce an input is, the more costly it will be for producers to buy. For instance, if lumber is scarce, its price will be high. Since it is such a costly input, producers will minimize waste and will substitute other less costly materials. So in order to maximize their profits, businesses have to manage society's scarce economic resources carefully, economizing the most on the use of the most scarce resources.

How to Divide up the Economic Pie?

A person's share of the economic pie depends on his or her *income*. For instance, if computer programmers take home (after taxes) five times as much pay as day-care workers, their share of the economic pie will be five times as large as that of day-care workers.

And since your income is really the *price* of your productive skills, prices play a major role in deciding the question of how to divide up the economic pie. Like other prices, people's incomes (or salaries or wages) are mostly determined by the interplay of supply and demand—in this case, the supply of and the demand for your productive skills. For example, if tool and die makers are in short supply but in great demand, their incomes (and their share of the economic pie) will be quite high. On the other hand, if there is a large supply of day-care workers relative to the demand for them, they will have low incomes and a small share of the pie.

How Does the Market System Organize the Use of Economic Resources?

As we have seen, organizing the vast and varied economic resources of an economy such as Canada's into the effective and efficient production of millions of goods and services is an enormous task. On the face of it, the market system might appear to be ill-suited to such a complex task. The market system seems to lack any organizing or coordinating forces; rather, it looks more like an economic "free-for-all" in which people buy whatever they want, produce whatever they want, and work wherever they want. Economic decision-making is spread among millions of consumers and producers in a decentralized and apparently uncoordinated manner, rather than organized according to a centralized plan. Nevertheless, the market system has in practice proven to be the best system for achieving both the effective and efficient use of economic resources and for providing a high standard of living for its people.

What, then, are the forces within the market system that enable it to mobilize economic resources so effectively and efficiently? The two key features of the market system that promote effectiveness and efficiency are the *profit motive* and *competition*.

The Profit Motive

profits Those funds left from a business's sales revenues after all expenses have been paid; such funds are therefore available (after taxes have been paid) for dividends to shareholders and reinvestment in the business.

Profits are those funds from a business's sales revenues that are left after all expenses and taxes have been paid. Profits are therefore available for reinvestment in the business or to be paid out as dividends to the shareholders who own the business.

The *profit motive* plays two vital roles in the operation of a market system. First, profits provide incentives for businesses to use economic resources both effectively and efficiently. By producing goods and services that consumers will buy—that is, by using economic resources *effectively*—a business will increase its sales and profits. And by producing those goods and services at the lowest possible production cost—that is, by using economic resources *efficiently*—a business will also increase its profits.

The second important role of profits is that they provide funds for the *purchase of capital equipment*. Each business purchases capital equipment to improve its own efficiency and profitability. But when *many* businesses do this, the result is improved productivity across the economy, which is the basic source of higher living standards for society generally. So, reinvestment of profits by business makes an important contribution to a society's economic prosperity.

In addition, many Canadians have a large stake in the profitability of corporations. In 2002, 46 percent of adult Canadians owned shares of corporations, many of these in mutual funds and registered retirement savings plans. In addition, about three dollars of every eight in *pension funds* in Canada are usually invested in corporate shares, so many people who do not think of themselves as shareholders have a stake in the success of Canadian corporations. Thus, millions of Canadians have billions of dollars invested in shares. These people not only receive part of the corporate profits as dividends, but also they are counting on the prosperity of those corporations for financial security in their retirement.

Nonetheless, there is a great deal of misunderstanding among the public concerning profits. The very word "profit" evokes for many people images of exploitation of workers and consumers. One misconception concerns the *level* of profits. Surveys indicate that the public believes that manufacturers' profits amount to 30 or 40 cents per dollar of sales, whereas before-tax profits are actually about 7 to 10 cents per dollar of sales, and after taxes, most manufacturers' profits amount to only 4 or 5 cents per dollar of sales. Ironically, the public believes 20 cents per dollar of sales to be a "fair" profit, indicating that there is a great deal of confusion regarding the matter of profits.

The public also has misconceptions concerning the *uses* of profits, which are often regarded as being hoarded away in corporate coffers or being paid out in lavish dividends to wealthy shareholders. In fact, between two-fifths and one-half of business profits goes to taxes, and most of the remainder is reinvested by businesses in capital equipment. Dividends to shareholders generally amount to a modest return on their investment, and these "capitalist" shareholders include not only the wealthy, but also many ordinary Canadians who directly or indirectly own shares, as described above.

Competition

Competition, which is the other key element in a market system, plays three vitally important roles in a market economy. First, competition forces businesses to produce what consumers want, in order to increase their sales and profits. In this sense, competition *promotes effectiveness* in the use of economic resources. Second, competition *promotes efficiency* in the use of economic resources. To prosper in a competitive marketplace, a producer must be as efficient as possible. And third, competition forces producers to *keep prices as low as possible*, in order to compete successfully for business. So, competition ensures that the advantages of higher efficiency and lower production costs are passed along to the consumer, allowing the maximum possible number of people to enjoy them.

Competition is closely linked with *information* in the effective functioning of markets. A free marketplace provides a wide variety of goods and services, of various qualities and at different prices. If consumers are well-informed about what items are available and at what prices, they will be better able to take advantage of the opportunities offered by a free and competitive marketplace. By contrast, poorly informed consumers will be more likely to get poorer value for their money.

Suppose a corporation has annual sales of $600 million, profits after taxes of $24 million, 4000 employees, and $300 million of shareholders' capital invested in the company.

From the viewpoint of the employees, it might seem that they are being underpaid. If the $24 million of profits were divided among them, each would receive $6000 more ($24 million ÷ 4000).

From the viewpoint of consumers, $24 million in profits might seem to indicate that they are being overcharged for this company's product. Realistically though, the total elimination of the manufacturer's profits would only reduce prices by 4 percent ($24 million ÷ $600 million).

From the viewpoint of the shareholders of the company, their capital invested in the company is earning a rate of return (after tax) of only 8 percent ($24 million ÷ $300 million). Compared to other investments, this might not be an attractive rate of return. So while employees and consumers and politicians might be complaining about this company's high profits, investors could very well be deciding to sell their shares in the company.

In summary, a highly competitive marketplace pushes private profit-making producers to serve the interest of consumers by being effective and efficient and by keeping prices down. By contrast, in situations in which there is little or no competition, producers tend to be less responsive to consumers' preferences (less effective), to be less efficient than they could be, and to charge excessive prices to consumers.

Together, the two incentives of profits and competition tend to push producers to use economic resources both effectively and efficiently. The ability of the market system to automatically coordinate the decisions of millions of businesses and individuals in response to changes in consumer demand has been referred to as "the miracle of the market."

Figure 1-6 summarizes the market system's powerful incentives for efficiency and effectiveness, which contribute greatly to productivity and prosperity. Figure 1-6 also shows how the basic concepts of effectiveness and efficiency relate to the income statement and the profits of a business. A business that is *effective* in the sense of producing what buyers want will enjoy a *high sales income*. If that business is also *efficient*, it will have *low production costs* and other expenses. So the more effective and efficient the business, the more profitable the business.

FIGURE 1-6 Incentives in a Market System

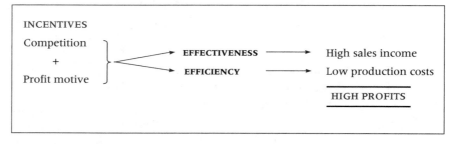

The Market System in Perspective

About four-fifths of the Canadian economy—the private sector—is organized as a market system. How well does this sector of the economy perform?

According to the criteria of *effectiveness* and *efficiency*, the market system performs very well. With respect to effectiveness, there is no economic system that is more responsive to consumer demand than the market system, which is marvelously flexible in adjusting its production automatically in response to changes in consumer preferences. And with respect to efficiency, no system provides greater incentives for efficient use of economic resources than the combination of the profit motive and competition.

However, the market system also has certain weaknesses. For instance, there is good reason to doubt that private enterprise is the best way to deliver certain *public services*, such as health care and education. These services might be provided by government-operated schools and hospitals, funded by the taxpayers in order to make them accessible to everyone.

market power The ability to raise one's price; usually associated with a dominant or monopolistic position in a market.

A problem that can develop in a market system is **market power**, or monopoly-like power in some markets. Sometimes, producers may be able to band together and agree to limit competition among themselves and charge higher prices. In a similar manner, some workers may be able to band together into labour unions that achieve essentially the same result—less competition and higher prices (wages) for their members. In both cases, an organized group (of businesses or workers) reduces competition in the marketplace for its own benefit, at the expense of others.

And while free markets for labour provide strong incentives for people to acquire skills that are in demand and to work efficiently, it is also true that, in a market system, there is a tendency for great *inequality in incomes* to develop, as some people enjoy very high incomes, while others live in poverty.

While the profit motive provides strong incentives to be effective and efficient, it also provides incentives to do things that are less beneficial to society, including using unfair competitive practices, misleading consumers, unfair treatment of vulnerable employees, and polluting the environment.

On a larger, macroeconomic scale, another fundamental problem with the market system is *economic insecurity*. Market economies tend to slump into periodic **recessions**, during which the economy's output falls and unemployment rises. During a typical recession in Canada, the number of unemployed people rises by more than half a million.

These weaknesses of the market system have led governments to take corrective action of various sorts, as we will see when we complete our description of Canada's economic system.

recessions Situations in which the economy is producing considerably less than its potential output, and unemployment is high. Formally defined as two consecutive quarters (a quarter being three months) of declining real output.

The "Mixed" Economic System of Canada

Canada's economic system can best be described as a *mixed free-enterprise system* because while our economy is basically a market system, it also includes a large government sector and a great deal of government involvement in the private sector.

The Private Sector

As we have seen, about 80 percent of the total annual output of the Canadian economy is produced by the private sector. In this sector, in which the vast majority of Canadians are employed, businesses produce goods and services in response to market demand and for a profit, and economic decisions are made by households (or consumers) and businesses.

The Government Sector

In the government sector, the key economic decisions are made by governments. The government sector accounts for about 20 percent of the annual output of the economy, most of which consists of public services such as health care and education. In broad terms, governments play three major roles in the economy.

http://canada.gc.ca

First, governments are major *providers of public services*. From health care, education, and law enforcement to traffic control, public transit, and postal service, Canadian governments provide the public with a wide range of services. In most cases, such as health care, police protection, and elementary and secondary education, the public pays for these services with its tax revenues. In effect, then, the government is buying these services collectively on the public's behalf, from the government's own employees (such as teachers) and from others (such as doctors) who provide the services. In some cases, governments *operate enterprises* that provide services, including Crown corporations (such as Canada Post and the Canadian Broadcasting Corporation) and public commissions that provide services (such as public transit and hydroelectricity). In many cases, including public transit and post-secondary education, governments *subsidize public services*. **Subsidies** use tax revenues to pay part of the cost of the service, making the cost to the user lower. The grand total of these government-provided services is impressive—when the

subsidies Government financial assistance to a firm or industry, through measures such as grants, loans, or special tax treatment.

services of all government employees are counted as government purchases, Canadian governments account for over 20 percent of all the goods and services produced by the economy. In 2002, this portion amounted to over $243 billion, or over $7700 for every Canadian man, woman, and child.

Second, governments *regulate* in many ways the operations and practices of businesses. For example, government laws or agencies set standards for many products, regulate advertising practices, set employment standards such as minimum wage rates and safety standards, set rules for the conduct of employer–union relations, regulate the competitive practices of businesses (including the prohibition of monopolistic practices), and set environmental protection standards. In the case of some farm products, government marketing boards regulate the amount that farmers can produce. In addition, many prices are regulated by government, including electrical rates, tobacco and alcohol prices, some transportation rates, and apartment rents in some areas.

The third major area of government involvement in the economy is the *redistribution of income* through programs that transfer income from people with higher incomes to those with lower incomes. Such programs include Employment Insurance, welfare, old age security allowances, assistance to farmers and other groups, and various features of the income-tax system (tax credits) that reduce the taxes payable by those with lower incomes. In 2001, government transfer payments to persons (mostly through Employment Insurance, welfare, and pensions) amounted to $117 billion, or nearly $3800 per Canadian. This figure includes only *government payments* to Canadians; it excludes government assistance to lower-income Canadians through *tax credits* that reduce their income taxes and/or entitle them to tax refunds, such as the GST tax credit refunds received by many students.

Taken together, these government programs amount to a great deal of government involvement in the Canadian economy. In 2002, the grand total of spending by Canadian governments (on goods and services, transfer payments to persons, and interest on government debt) amounted to 40 percent of Canada's **Gross Domestic Product (GDP)**, which measures the total of goods and services produced and incomes earned in Canada in any one year. When the many government regulations of economic activity as described earlier are added, the Canadian economy is accurately called a "mixed" system—still mostly "market" in nature, but with a large amount of government involvement.

Gross Domestic Product (GDP) A measure of the total value of goods and services produced and incomes earned in a country in one year.

Chapter Summary

1. The fundamental economic problem is *scarcity*: whereas society's economic resources are limited in quantity, people's wants and needs are apparently unlimited; thus, not all wants and needs can be satisfied. (L.O. 1)

2. Because of the scarcity problem, it is important that economic resources be used both effectively and efficiently. (L.O. 2)

3. The problem of scarcity requires that the following three questions be answered:
   (a) what to produce,
   (b) how to produce it, and
   (c) how to divide it among people. (L.O. 3)

4. A market system operates through markets. In these markets, what to produce is decided by consumer demand, how to produce it is decided by producers, and the division of the economic pie is decided by people's incomes. (L.O. 4)

5. Profits provide incentives for the efficient and effective use of economic resources and are a major source of funds for capital investment, which contributes to economic prosperity by increasing output per worker. (L.O. 5)

6. Competition keeps prices and profits down and pushes producers to be both efficient and effective (responsive to consumers). (L.O. 6)

7. The main weaknesses of the market system are its tendency toward periodic recessions, a lack of competition in some markets, and a tendency for incomes to be distributed unevenly. (L.O. 7)

8. Canada's economic system is called a "mixed" or "mixed free-enterprise" system: while it is basically a market or free enterprise system, it includes significant elements of government involvement in the economy. Major aspects of government involvement in the Canadian economy are the provision of various public services, the regulation of economic activity, and the redistribution of income from those with higher incomes to those with lower incomes. (L.O. 8)

Questions

1. Explain how each of the following decisions would be intended to affect *effectiveness* and/or *efficiency*:
   (a) A plan whereby a company's sales representatives provide feedback and suggestions to management based on their experience with customers.
   (b) The introduction of a piece-rate incentive plan under which workers are paid according to the number of products they produce.
   (c) A quality-control program under which finished products are inspected more thoroughly in order to ensure that they meet quality standards.
   (d) A profit-sharing plan under which a portion of the company's profits above a certain level will be shared with the employees.
   (e) The use of industrial robots that are programmed to perform production tasks repetitively and with great precision.

2. In some of the situations in Question 1, a conflict could arise between effectiveness and efficiency; that is, a decision that increased efficiency would decrease effectiveness, or vice versa. Which are these decisions, and why could such a conflict occur?

3. How could having an internet website improve the *effectiveness* and the *efficiency* of a firm's operations?

4. Suppose that a manufacturer is selling two products (product A and product B) for $100 each, and is making a profit (before taxes) of 7 percent of the selling price of each product.
   (a) If strong demand increases the price of product A by just 2 percent, by what percentage will the profits on product A rise?
   (b) If weak demand for product B causes its price to fall by just 1 percent, by what percentage will the profits on product B decline?
   (c) Given these facts, what should the management of the company decide to do?

5. Three of the following are essential to the operation of a free-enterprise market economy. Which one might such an economy operate *without*?
   (a) the profit motive
   (b) markets
   (c) corporations
   (d) prices

6. Explain how a development in communications technology, such as the internet, could improve the way in which some markets function.

7. When the government subsidizes a service, it uses taxpayers' money to reduce the cost of that service to the people who use it. What might be the justification for using taxpayers' money to subsidize:
   (a) users of the Toronto Transit Commission?
   (b) students taking post-secondary education?
   (c) users of campsites at provincial parks?
   (d) a city's symphony orchestra?

Chapter 2

Introduction to Macroeconomics

Learning Objectives

After studying this chapter, you should be able to:

1. Describe the five key factors on the supply side of the economy and the four components of its demand side.

2. Explain the characteristics of the supply side and of the demand side of a market economy that is functioning smoothly.

3. State what the Gross Domestic Product measures, list the four major components of GDP, and show how GDP is calculated.

4. Explain the difference between money GDP and real GDP.

5. State what the Consumer Price Index measures, explain how the CPI is constructed to achieve this purpose, and calculate the rate of inflation from the CPI for two consecutive years.

6. State the purpose of the Labour Force Survey, describe the main statistics in this survey, and calculate the unemployment rate from Labour Force Survey data.

7. Describe each of the four basic types of unemployment.

8. Explain why changes in the unemployment rate should be interpreted carefully.

9. Explain how the economic statistics discussed in this chapter can be used to monitor the condition of the economy (boom, inflation, and recession).

Figure 2-1 shows the operation of a market system economy, such as we saw in Chapter 1. The upper flows in Figure 2-1 represent markets for countless goods and services. In most such markets, the products or services are bought by millions of consumers and sold by many producers. Microeconomics studies the market for *each particular* good or service—computers, or automobiles, or restaurants—in this upper flow, and its price and the amount purchased. Macroeconomics deals with similar matters, but on a much broader scale— the *grand total* of all goods and services produced in the economy, and the *average level* of the prices of these. In other words, macroeconomics deals with the *total size* of the upper flow of goods and services in Figure 2-1, on an *economy-wide scale*.

FIGURE 2-1 The Operation of a Market Economy

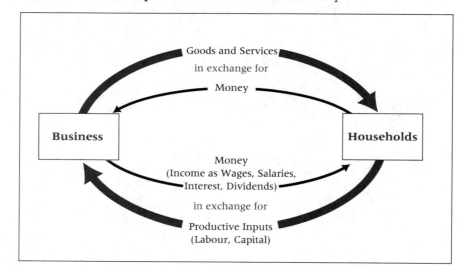

Similarly, the lower flows in Figure 2-1 show producers, or businesses, obtaining the productive inputs that they need in order to produce the goods and services in the top flows. The most important of these inputs is labour, ranging from unskilled workers to skilled trades workers to professionals. The lower flows in Figure 2-1 show this wide range of productive skills being "sold" to businesses by the people who possess those skills, in exchange for wages and salaries. Microeconomics examines the market for *each* of these skills, and also the wage rate and the number of workers employed in each market. For instance, in microeconomics, we might study the market for part-time student labour, for computer programmers, or for professional hockey players. Again, in macroeconomics, we are concerned with similar matters, but on a much wider scale—the levels of *total employment (and unemployment) and total incomes* in the economy as a whole, or the *total size* of these flows in the lower loop, on an *economy-wide scale*.

Markets on a Microeconomic Scale

Before considering these larger macroeconomic matters, let's review how markets operate on a microeconomic scale. In Chapter 1, we described markets for individual goods and services as consisting of:

- a demand side, or offers by buyers to purchase a good or service, and
- a supply side, or offers by sellers to sell the good or service as shown in Figure 2-2.

demand side The purchasers of society's output of goods and services.

supply side The ability of the economy to use its productive resources efficiently to produce goods and services.

FIGURE 2-2 A Microeconomic Market

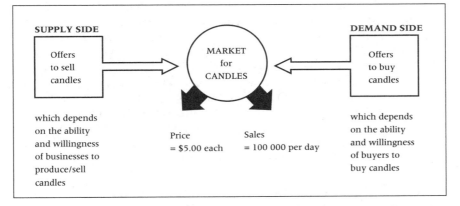

Let's use the market for candles as an example. The key to the demand side of this market is *the ability and willingness of buyers to purchase candles*, and the key to the supply side of this market is *the ability and willingness of businesses to produce candles and offer them for sale*. And it is the interaction of the demand side of the market and the supply side of the market that determines the price and the sales of candles, or any other good or service.

In one sense, the most basic factor is the supply side's ability and willingness to *produce* candles. If society is to *have* the volume of candles that it needs or wants, the candle industry must be able to *produce* this volume of candles at a price per candle that will allow the industry to pay the production costs and earn a profit. This ability to produce will depend upon the labour, capital equipment, and other inputs available to the candle industry.

On the other hand, the demand side of the market is equally important. The key on the demand side is the ability and willingness of people to *buy* candles. If the demand for candles is low, production and prices will be low, with the result that candle workers will be laid off. Higher demand for candles would cause higher production, and more workers would be employed. And, if the demand for candles were so high that the producers could not keep up with it, the price of candles would rise rapidly.

Markets on a Macroeconomic Scale

Macroeconomics is concerned with how the economy operates on a much larger scale; that is, the *grand total* of all the goods and services produced in the whole economy. However, the general approach to analyzing macroeconomic matters is the same as that used in analyzing markets on a microeconomic scale. In both cases, the basic economic forces are supply and demand.

As with microeconomic markets, we can divide the economy on a macroeconomic scale into a *supply side*, in which the key is the ability and willingness of the nation's producers as a whole to produce goods and services and offer them for sale, and a *demand side*, in which the key is the ability and willingness of all buyers in total to purchase goods and services. These are the same "supply side" and "demand side" forces that we saw in our microeconomic analysis, but on a much larger, economy-wide scale.

On the *supply side*, we will consider the ability and willingness of the entire economy—*all* producers, large and small, private and government—to produce goods and services efficiently. Our analysis of the supply side will lead us to consider the factors that make a nation productive—the skills of its labour force (including management), the quantity and quality of its capital equipment, incentives to be efficient, such as competition and economic gain (the "profit motive"), and various other factors. These factors are summarized briefly in Figure 2-3; we will consider them in detail in Chapter 3.

FIGURE 2-3 Macroeconomic Supply Side Factors

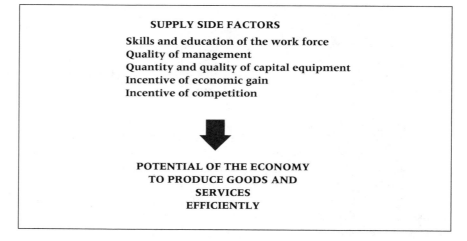

SUPPLY SIDE FACTORS
Skills and education of the work force
Quality of management
Quantity and quality of capital equipment
Incentive of economic gain
Incentive of competition

**POTENTIAL OF THE ECONOMY
TO PRODUCE GOODS AND
SERVICES
EFFICIENTLY**

And on the *demand side*, on a macroeconomic scale we have to take into account the total of *all* spending on goods and services in the entire economy, by *all* buyers. We can divide these buyers into four basic groups: consumers, businesses, governments, and foreign buyers. The total spending on goods and services by all of these groups is known as "aggregate demand." The components of aggregate demand are summarized in Figure 2-4; we will consider these factors in detail in Chapter 4.

FIGURE 2-4 Macroeconomic Demand Side Factors

DEMAND SIDE FACTORS

Consumer spending on goods and services
+ Business investment spending on capital goods
+ Government spending on goods and services
+ Foreign spending on Canadian goods and services

**TOTAL SPENDING ON
("AGGREGATE DEMAND" FOR)
GOODS AND SERVICES**

The Operation of the Economy on a Macroeconomic Scale

Figure 2-5 shows these "supply side" factors and "demand side" factors as part of a "model" of the economy.

FIGURE 2-5 The Economy on a Macroeconomic Scale

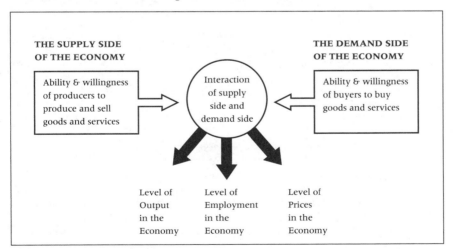

THE SUPPLY SIDE
OF THE ECONOMY

THE DEMAND SIDE
OF THE ECONOMY

Ability & willingness
of producers to
produce and sell
goods and services

Interaction
of supply
side and
demand side

Ability & willingness
of buyers to buy
goods and services

Level of
Output
in the
Economy

Level of
Employment
in the
Economy

Level of
Prices
in the
Economy

While it is much larger and considerably more complex than the market for a single item, the macroeconomic model of the economy shown in

economic boom A condition of higher demand in the economy as a whole, bringing output and employment to high levels.

inflation An increase in the general level of the prices of goods and services.

Figure 2-5 operates in the same way that the microeconomic markets covered earlier do. For instance, if demand in the economy were low, output would be low and employment would be low, and there would be a recession. If demand were to increase, output and employment would rise to higher levels, and there would be an **economic boom.** Finally, if demand were to rise to such high levels that output could not keep up with demand, prices would rise rapidly, and there would be **inflation.** Each of these situations is covered in much more detail in the chapters that follow.

An Illustration of a Smoothly Functioning Market System

Figure 2-6 shows a market system that is operating ideally on a macroeconomic scale. On the supply side of the economy, there is a strong ability to produce efficiently the goods and services that are in demand. The economy possesses all of the productive inputs needed to produce goods and services efficiently: a capable labour force, good capital equipment, and ample natural resources or raw materials. In addition, the economy provides producers with strong incentives to use these inputs as efficiently as possible, in the form of the "carrot" of profits (after taxes) and the "stick" of competition. In short, the supply side of the economy is capable of efficient and effective production. However, for the supply side to be able to achieve its potential, there has to be an appropriate level of demand.

FIGURE 2-6 A Smoothly Functioning Market System

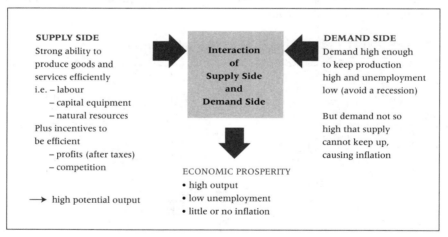

capacity output The maximum real output that the economy is capable of producing in any given year.

On the demand side of the economy, what is a "healthy" level of demand? This level depends on the volume of goods and services that the supply side is capable of producing, or its **capacity output.** If demand were well below this level, low sales would cause producers to reduce output and lay off workers. The economy would be producing below its capacity output, factories and equipment would be idle, and workers would be unemployed— and there would be a recession. On the other hand, if demand grew too rapidly, the output of the supply side would be unable to keep up with demand. This imbalance would cause the prices of goods and services in general to rise rapidly—and there would be inflation.

We have learned through hard experience that both recession and inflation can cause economic hardship. Ideally, then, the level of demand would be neither too low nor too high relative to the ability of the supply side to produce goods and services. In other words, the demand side would generate high enough spending to prompt the supply side to produce as much output as it could, but not so much spending that the supply side could not keep up with demand, which would result in rapid inflation.

If the economy has a strong ability to produce goods and services, and demand is neither too low nor too high *relative to capacity output*, the results will be as shown at the bottom of Figure 2-6:

- high output of goods and services (i.e., at or near the economy's capacity, or potential output),
- high levels of employment (or low unemployment), and
- little or no inflation.

Of course, market economies do not always perform as well as in the ideal situation portrayed in Figure 2-6. There are three basic types of problems that a market economy can develop on a grand macroeconomic scale (excluding international problems, which are covered later):

- *weaknesses on the supply side* that prevent it from producing goods and services efficiently, such as a poorly trained labour force or inadequate capital equipment,
- *inadequate demand for goods and services* on the demand side, which will cause unemployment and a recession, and
- *excessive demand for goods and services* on the demand side, which will cause inflation, or rapid increases in prices.

Supply-side problems are covered in Chapter 3. The problems of inadequate demand and recessions and those of excessive demand and inflation are dealt with in Chapter 6.

Our Economic Goals and How We Measure Them

Figure 2-6 shows a smoothly operating economic system that generates prosperity as measured by three criteria—high output, low unemployment, and little or no inflation. In the following sections, let's take a closer look at each of these performance standards, and see just what each involves. Then, in the remainder of this chapter, we will see how to track how well the economy is performing in these areas.

High Output of Goods and Services

As we saw in Chapter 1, the most basic task of any economic system is to provide its people with a *high standard of living*, by producing a high volume of goods and services. One key to reaching this goal is to achieve high levels of *productivity*, or output per worker. A related goal is a *stable* level of output, in the sense of avoiding downturns in output. Such downturns or recessions threaten both living standards and jobs, as outlined in the next section.

Low Unemployment

full employment The lowest rate of unemployment that can be achieved without generating unacceptable inflation in the economy.

Another fundamental economic objective is **full employment**, which means the lowest possible level of unemployment. High unemployment means economic hardship for many people, and that a significant proportion of the economy's most important economic resource—its people—is being left unused. Ever since the Great Depression of the 1930s, minimizing unemployment has been a high-priority economic objective for governments.

Little or No Inflation

If the 1930s established low unemployment as a basic economic objective, the experience of the 1970s and 1980s established the dangers of allowing inflation to become too rapid, as we will see later. Since this experience, the goal of minimizing inflation, or keeping prices as stable as possible, has gained considerable importance for governments.

Economic Statistics

The purpose of economic statistics is to track how the economy is performing with respect to output, employment, inflation, and a variety of other criteria. By providing up-to-date information regarding the performance of the economy and economic trends, these statistics can be very helpful to policy- and decision-makers in business and government. Many economic statistics (relating to output, employment/unemployment, prices/inflation, money supply and interest rates, productivity and costs, wage rates, government finances, exports and imports, flows of capital between nations, and the value of nations' currencies) are used to monitor the performance of the economy. In subsequent chapters, some of these statistics will be introduced as we look into different aspects of the economy. However, in this chapter, we will consider only those that measure the economy's success in achieving the three broad objectives referred to earlier. These are:

* *Gross Domestic Product*, which measures the economy's output of goods and services,
* *the Consumer Price Index* and *the rate of inflation*, which measure the performance of the economy with respect to prices and inflation, and
* *employment statistics* and *the unemployment rate*, which measure the extent of the economy's success in providing jobs.

The Task of Gathering Economic Statistics

We have seen how markets work, as businesses produce the supply of goods and services to meet the demands of consumers. This economic activity produces macroeconomic flows of spending, goods, and services between the business sector and the household sector of the economy, as shown by the upper loops in Figure 2-1. In addition, this activity generates employment and investment and flows of income (wages, salaries, interest, dividends) arising from these, as shown in the lower loops in Figure 2-1. Obviously, the more economic activity that is occurring in the economy, the more output will be produced, the more jobs there will be, the more income will be earned (and spent), and the greater the economic prosperity of the society will be. The flows of goods, services, and incomes in Figure 2-1 will grow, and the economic statistics used to keep track of these developments will reflect this growth.

Monitoring the performance of the economy in this way is not a simple task—it involves tracking the production and sale of over a trillion dollars' worth ($1 000 000 000 000) of millions of types of goods and services and the prices of these goods and services, as well as the activities of a labour force consisting of about 17 million people. This important function is performed by *Statistics Canada*.

www.statcan.ca

Measuring Output: Gross Domestic Product

Measuring the total flows of output and income in an economy is a massive task. The statistic that measures these total flows is called the **Gross Domestic Product**, or **GDP**.

The Gross Domestic Product measures the grand total of economic activity across Canada. It is an estimate of the annual output of all the sectors of the nation's economy—consumer goods and services, capital goods, government goods and services, and exports. These sectors include a tremendous volume and diversity of goods and services. The only way to add together such a variety of goods and services is to add up their values, or prices, expressed in dollars. The grand total figure that results is the Gross Domestic Product, which is defined as *the market value of the total annual output of final goods and services produced in the nation.* A simpler definition of GDP is "the sum of the price tags of all final goods and services produced in the country in that year."

Why are only "final" goods counted? Suppose that:

- farmers produce $0.30 of wheat, which
- millers make into flour worth $0.70, which
- bakeries make into $1.20 worth of bread.

At first, it looks as though this process has added $2.20 of production to the GDP ($0.30 + $0.70 + $1.20). But closer examination shows that the real addition to GDP is only $1.20—the value of the bread that is the final good in this process. The wheat and flour are *intermediate* products in the production of the bread. The $1.20 price of the bread *includes* the value of the wheat and flour, as part of the cost of producing the bread. If we had included, or "counted," the values of the flour and wheat in the GDP, we would have overstated the GDP, because we had "double-counted" some items. To avoid double-counting, the GDP is calculated in such a way as to include only the final goods and services produced: in our example, only the value of the bread would be included.

Gross Domestic Product (GDP) A measure of the total value of goods and services produced and incomes earned in a country in one year.

Subdivisions of Gross Domestic Product

The Gross Domestic Product consists of a vast number of diverse goods and services—all of the automobiles, televisions, haircuts, entertainment, houses, factories, machinery, roads, military equipment, police services, education, wheat, minerals, lumber, and other goods and services that are produced in one year. To help understand and analyze these statistics, we can classify them according to the four basic types of purchaser: consumers, businesses, governments, and foreign buyers.

Consumption (C)

This category consists of all *consumer goods and services* purchased by households. This includes a wide range of items, from nondurable goods that are used up quickly (such as food and clothing), to durable goods (such as cars and appliances) that last several years, to services (such as travel and entertainment). In recent years, consumption has amounted to about 60 percent of GDP.

Investment (I)

Investment includes all additions to society's stock of privately owned capital equipment, buildings, and inventories of products. The largest part of the investment category is business spending on plant and equipment—factories, offices, stores, machinery, equipment, vehicles, computers, and so on. The investment statistics also include additions to business inventories of products and new housing construction.[1] Together, these types of investment have comprised 17 to 18 percent of GDP in recent years.

Government (G)

Governments (federal, provincial, and local) constitute another major purchaser of goods and services. Most of what governments purchase consists of services, the two largest of which are health care and education. Some government purchases, such as health care, are described as *current consumption*. Other purchases, such as schools and roads, are really *capital investment*, in that they are assets that provide social benefits over long periods of time. The government sector of the economy, which is also known as the "public sector," has accounted for about 21 percent of GDP recently.

Net Exports (X – M)

So far, we have accounted for all goods and services produced for Canadian households (consumption, or **C**), business firms (investment, or **I**) and

---

[1] If a manufacturer's inventory of finished products increases by $2 million over last year's inventory, this increase represents $2 million of production that must be included somewhere in the GDP statistics. It cannot be counted as "consumption," since it has not yet been purchased by consumers, so we add it to the "investment" statistics instead. Newly constructed housing will be purchased by households, but its value is included in the investment statistics, mainly because of its nature as a long-term asset.

governments (government spending, or **G**). Now we must account for two facts arising from Canada's trade with foreign nations:

- Products and services produced in Canada and sold to foreign buyers (Canada's exports) must be added to our figures. These exports have amounted to 41 to 43 percent of GDP in recent years.
- Some of the Canadian purchases (C + I + G) that we have recorded include purchases of imports of foreign-made goods. While these were *purchased* in Canada, they were not *produced* in Canada. So these imports, which have amounted to 37 to 40 percent of GDP recently, should not be included in Canada's GDP, which measures Canadian production.

To correct our GDP figures to allow for these effects of foreign trade, we must *add* to our C + I + G total the value of all Canadian exports (X) and *deduct* from our C + I + G total the value of all imports (M) purchased by Canadians. By making these adjustments, we ensure that we are measuring what was *produced* in Canada, as distinct from what was *sold* in Canada. The net effect of these adjustments (X − M) is called *net exports*. The net effect of foreign trade will be an increase in GDP if exports are larger than imports, and the net effect will be a decrease in GDP if imports are larger than exports.

Calculating GDP Statistics

GDP measures the total amount of economic activity in Canada in any given year, which can be viewed as the *total output* produced or the *total income* received. So there are two different approaches to calculating GDP statistics: the expenditures approach and the incomes approach.

The expenditures approach calculates GDP by adding up all the *spending* by consumers (C), businesses (I), governments (G), and the net exports (X − M) on goods and services. The result is expressed in the equation

$$GDP = C + I + G + (X - M)$$

This approach is illustrated in Table 2-1.

The incomes approach, the second approach, is based upon the fact that expenditures and incomes are simply two different sides of any transaction. That is, every dollar that is *spent* on goods and services becomes an *income* to someone—mostly the people and businesses involved in the production and distribution of the goods and services, but also to governments, whose taxes are sometimes included in the price of the goods and services. So GDP statistics can be calculated either by adding up all *expenditures* on goods and services, or by adding up all the *incomes* received in any given year. The incomes approach is illustrated in Table 2-2.

www.statcan.ca/english/
Pgdb/econ04.htm

TABLE 2-1 GDP Statistics—Expenditures Approach

	($ Billions)	2002
Consumption		
Consumer expenditure on goods and services		651.2
Investment		
Business investment in plant and equipment	134.4	
Residential construction	63.1	
Addition to inventories[1]	2.7	
Total investment		200.2
Government		
Government expenditure on goods and services		243.4
Exports and Imports		
Exports of goods and services	470.1	
Imports of goods and services	423.1	
Balance		+47.0
Gross Domestic Product		1142.1

Note: Totals do not always add up correctly because of statistical discrepancies.

[1] Includes government.
Source: Statistics Canada, adapted from *National Income and Expenditure Accounts*, Catalogue 13-001, 2002.

www.statcan.ca/english/
Pgdb/econ03.htm

TABLE 2-2 GDP Statistics—Incomes Approach

	($ Billions) 2002
Wages, salaries, and supplementary labour income	595.3
Corporation profits before taxes	125.5
Government enterprise profits	10.8
Interest and miscellaneous investment income	49.7
Accrued net income of farm operators from farm production	2.1
Net income of non-farm unincorporated business including rent	71.9
Inventory valuation adjustment	−3.0
Indirect taxes less subsidies	137.6
Capital consumption allowances	152.6
Gross Domestic Product	1142.1

Note: Totals do not add up due to statistical discrepancies.

Source: Statistics Canada, adapted from *National Income and Expenditure Accounts*, Catalogue 13-001, 2002.

Real GDP Versus Money GDP

If your take-home pay increased by 3 percent due to a pay raise, it would *seem* that you were 3 percent better off economically. However, if the prices of consumer goods and services had risen by 2 percent, you would *in fact* be only 1 percent better off. Your *money income* (in dollars) would be 3 percent higher, but your **real income** (in terms of purchasing power, after inflation) would only be 1 percent higher.

A similar "money illusion" occurs with GDP figures whenever prices increase. For example, GDP measured in dollars might have increased by 5 percent, but real production might have increased by only 3 percent, with higher prices (inflation) accounting for the other 2 percent.

This problem arises because GDP statistics can increase for two very different reasons:

- *Increased production of goods and services (higher real output)*. If the economy's *output* of goods and services increases, GDP will increase. This increase is called "real economic growth," because there is a larger output of goods and services.
- *Higher price levels*. If the *prices* of goods and services rise, GDP will also rise because it is stated in terms of current market prices. For instance, suppose that real output were exactly the same as last year's, but the prices of all goods and services were 3 percent higher—in such a case, the GDP would register a 3-percent increase over last year. This increase is obviously not "real economic growth"; in fact, real output has not increased at all. But because the GDP statistics are boosted by higher prices, it *looks like* the economy has grown.

We call these inflated GDP statistics "GDP at market prices," or "**money GDP**." The problem with such statistics, as we have seen, is that they are not particularly meaningful. For instance, a 6-percent increase in money GDP could mean that:

(a) real output has risen by 6 percent and prices have not risen,

(b) prices have risen by 6 percent and real output has not risen, or

(c) *both* real output and prices have risen, with the combined effect of a 6-percent increase.

The key to interpreting money GDP figures is to know how much prices have risen—then we could readily estimate the increase in real output. Suppose that money GDP increased by 6 percent and prices increased by 2 percent. Of the 6-percent increase in money GDP, higher prices would account for 2 percentage points, leaving a 4-percent increase in real output. The 4-percent increase in real output is a much more accurate representation of the growth of the economy than is the 6-percent increase in money GDP.

So by adjusting money GDP statistics to eliminate the effects of price increases, we can develop a much more accurate statistic that measures how the real output of the economy is changing. This adjusted statistic is known by several names, including "**real GDP**," "GDP in constant dollars," and "GDP in 1997 dollars," which means that the GDP figures are calculated as if prices were the same as they were in 1997.

Figure 2-7 shows money GDP and real GDP (in 1997 dollars) since 1985. Note how real GDP has grown more slowly than money GDP, which is inflated by rising prices. The 1990–91 recession provides a good example of

real income The purchasing power of income (as distinct from its dollar value).

money GDP GDP in current dollar terms; that is, including any price increases due to inflation.

real GDP GDP statistics that have been adjusted to eliminate the effects of price increases, the result being a statistic that measures only changes in real output. Also called "GDP in constant dollars" or "GDP at 1992 prices."

the difference between money and real GDP statistics. From 1990 to 1991, money GDP increased by 0.8 percent, while real GDP *decreased* by 2.1 percent.

FIGURE 2-7 Money GDP and Real GDP (in 1997 dollars), 1985–2001

www.statcan.ca/
english/Pgdb/
econ05.htm

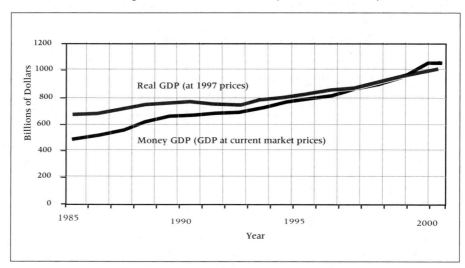

Source: Statistics Canada, adapted from *National Income and Expenditure Accounts*, Catalogue 13-001, 2002, and *Canadian Economic Observer*, Catalogue 11-010, 2002.

In reading and interpreting economic statistics, you should know whether the statistics have been adjusted for the effects of inflation or not. Generally, the adjusted (real) statistics are more useful because they reflect what *really happened* to the economy's output of goods and services.

Other Limitations of GDP Statistics

Even after adjustments for inflation, GDP statistics do not represent the "final word" on the economic prosperity of a nation's people. Rather, they are only an estimate of one aspect of economic prosperity—the total production of the country's economy.

One limitation of GDP statistics is that they omit a considerable amount of economic activity. For example, housework, volunteer work, and food grown for home consumption are not included in the GDP, because they are not purchased and are therefore not reported as sales. Also not counted are goods and services sold in the "underground economy," in which people avoid paying income tax and sales taxes by buying and selling goods and services for cash and not reporting their income. The underground economy is especially active in areas such as residential repairs and food service (tips). The size of the underground economy is unknown, but believed to be considerable—the Auditor General of Canada has estimated it to be 4.5 percent of GDP, which would be around $50 billion per year.

www.underground
economy.ca

GDP does not measure the standard of living of the people of a nation. A better measure of living standards would be personal income or consumption per person, rather than the GDP's grand total output of all types of goods and services, many of which are not for the enjoyment of consumers.

GDP does not pretend to measure the "quality of life." All that it provides is a measure of the total quantity of goods and services produced; $1000 of health food, $1000 of medical care, $1000 of cigarettes, $1000 of handguns, and even $1000 of economics texts—each counts for $1000 in the GDP.

In fact, sometimes a higher quality of life might mean accepting a *lower* GDP. Consider leisure time. In the twentieth century, the average work week declined from over 60 hours to less than 40 hours. By working less, Canadians have accepted that they are producing—and consuming—less goods and services (real GDP) than they could. However, they willingly choose this increase in leisure because they value it more highly than the higher GDP per person that they could have by working longer hours. In effect, they have decided that higher consumption per person is not everything. So GDP is not a measure—much less *the* measure—of human welfare, but only a useful estimate of material production, which is one part of that welfare.

> For a broader measure of the quality of life, see the United Nations measure of human welfare at http://hdr.undp.org. (Click on *Statistics.*)

Interpreting GDP Statistics

Is a real GDP of $700 billion "good"? That evaluation depends on the size of the economy's *capacity output*, which is an estimate of the economy's maximum potential output. If the economy's capacity output were $710 billion, a real GDP of $700 billion would indicate a major economic boom, in which the economy's production is very close to capacity. But if capacity output were $900 billion, the same $700 billion GDP would indicate a recession, with the economy operating more than 20 percent below its potential.

Another "benchmark" for interpreting real GDP is how much it has increased from the previous year; this benchmark measures how much the economy has grown. From 1990 to 2002, real GDP grew at an average rate of 2.7 percent per year, with the rate of growth ranging from a low of −2.1 percent in 1991 to a high of +5.1 percent in 1999.

> In most years, an increase of 3 to 3.5 percent in real GDP is considered a healthy rate of growth. We will examine what "healthy" means in Chapter 3.

Finally, real GDP statistics are used to determine when the economy has entered a recession. If real GDP decreases for two consecutive quarters (three-month periods), a recession is considered to be underway, a matter that we will consider further in Chapter 6.

Measuring Prices: The Consumer Price Index

Statistics Canada also keeps track of inflation by monitoring prices and how rapidly prices are increasing. Since there are too many prices to monitor all of them, Statistics Canada keeps track of only representative samples of prices, which are known as *price indexes*. There are indexes for various types of specific prices, such as farm prices, food prices, and housing prices. But the price index

Consumer Price Index (CPI) A weighted average of the prices of a "basket" of goods and services purchased by a typical urban family.

with which people are most familiar is the **Consumer Price Index (CPI)**, which measures the prices of consumer goods and services in general.

The Consumer Price Index is an average of the prices of some 600 goods and services bought by representative or typical urban households. The CPI is also described as the cost of a "basket" of goods and services bought by a typical household. As the prices of these goods and services rise, so does the CPI.

To determine the CPI for each month, Statistics Canada actually records the prices of the 600 goods and services in the "basket" in various centres across Canada. Then the average of these prices is calculated, and this average becomes the CPI for that month, for each province and for Canada as a whole.

The calculation of the CPI takes into account that consumers spend more on some items in the "basket" than on others. For instance, consumers spend much more on rent than on milk. To recognize this reality, each item in the "basket" is given a *weight* in the CPI, based upon the proportion of the typical household's income that is spent on it. So if a typical household spends 50 times as much on rent as it does on milk, rent would be given a "weight" in the index 50 times as large as the weight given to milk. As an example, a 10-percent increase in rents would have 50 times the impact on the CPI as a 10-percent increase in the price of milk. Figure 2-8 shows the weights assigned to each broad category of items in the CPI, such as housing, transportation, food, and so on. However, it is important to remember that *within* each of these categories, there are dozens of individual goods and services, each with its own weight. For instance, the transportation component of the CPI includes car prices, gasoline prices, insurance rates, public transit fares, airline and train fares, and so on.

FIGURE 2-8 Weights of the Major Components of the CPI, 2001

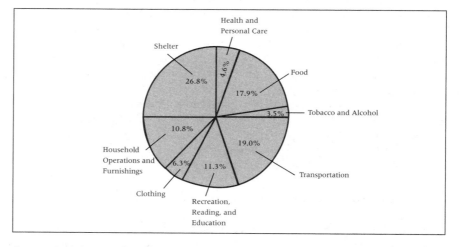

Source: Statistics Canada, adapted from *The Consumer Price Index,* Catalogue 62-001, 2002.

The CPI does not express the cost of the "basket" of goods and services in terms of dollars and cents. Instead, the CPI is expressed in terms of how much it has changed from a *base year* (1992 at the time of writing) in which the CPI was 100.0. This is illustrated in Table 2-3, which shows not only the CPI in general ("all items"), but also the various major components of the CPI. In the base year of 1992, the CPI and each of its components are 100.0. By following each column down, you can track how rapidly prices have risen, both in general ("all items") and for each component. For instance, the fastest-rising component of the CPI from 1992 to 2002 was transportation, with a 34.4-percent increase, from 100.0 in 1992 to 134.4 in 2002.

TABLE 2-3 The Consumer Price Index by Categories, 1992–2002

(1992 = 100) Year	*All items*	*Food*	*Shelter*	*Household operations and furnishings*	*Clothing and footwear*	*Trans- portation*	*Health and personal care*	*Recreation, education and reading*	*Alcoholic beverages and tobacco products*	*Goods*	*Services*
1992	100.0	100.0	100.0	100.0	100.0	100.0	100.0	100.0	100.0	100.0	100.0
1993	101.8	101.7	101.4	101.0	101.0	103.2	102.7	102.4	101.6	101.6	102.1
1994	102.0	102.1	101.8	101.2	101.8	107.8	103.6	105.5	85.0	100.5	103.8
1995	104.2	104.5	102.9	103.1	101.7	113.4	103.5	109.5	84.9	102.4	106.4
1996	105.9	105.9	103.1	105.3	101.4	117.8	104.1	112.1	86.6	104.0	108.1
1997	107.6	107.6	103.3	106.6	102.7	121.5	105.9	114.9	89.3	105.6	109.9
1998	108.6	109.3	103.7	108.2	103.9	120.5	108.1	117.5	92.6	105.8	111.9
1999	110.5	110.7	105.1	109.1	105.3	124.5	110.2	119.6	94.5	107.7	113.8
2000	113.5	112.2	108.8	110.0	105.5	130.7	112.0	122.5	97.6	111.1	113.9
2001	116.4	117.2	112.8	112.2	106.0	130.8	114.2	124.3	105.1	113.9	119.3
2002	119.0	120.3	113.8	113.8	105.2	134.4	115.5	126.3	123.6	115.8	122.8

Source: Statistics Canada, adapted from *The Consumer Price Index*, Catalogue 62-001, 2002.

The Rate of Inflation

This brings us to the rate of inflation. The Consumer Price Index measures *how high* prices are, while the rate of inflation tells us *how rapidly prices are rising*. For instance, the CPI was 116.4 in 2001, then increased to 119.0 in 2002, an increase of 2.2 percent over the year, calculated as follows:

$$\frac{\text{This year's CPI} - \text{Last year's CPI}}{\text{Last year's CPI}} \times 100 = \text{Rate of Inflation}$$

To calculate the rate of inflation for the year 2001, substitute the appropriate values into the above equation and calculate.

$$\frac{119.0 - 116.4}{116.4} \times 100 = \frac{2.6}{116.4} \times 100 \doteq 2.2 \text{ percent}$$

So the rate of inflation of 2.2 percent for 2002 simply means that the cost of the "basket" of goods and services increased by 2.2 percent in 2002. And because the "basket" is representative of what consumers buy, the inference is that consumer prices in general increased by about 2.2 percent in 2001.

A rate of inflation between 1 and 3 per-cent per year is con-sidered "acceptable." We will discuss this aspect in more detail in Chapter 8.

Figure 2-9 summarizes how statistics concerning the Consumer Price Index and the rate of inflation are gathered and calculated. Figure 2-10 shows the results of those calculations—the CPI and the rate of inflation from 1961 to 2002. It shows that the rate of inflation has varied very widely over this period, from as high as 12.4 percent in 1981 to as low as 0.2 percent in 1994.

FIGURE 2-9 Calculation of the Rate of Inflation

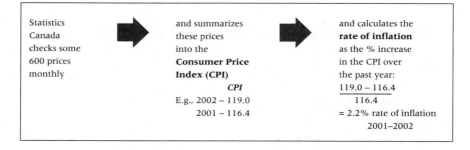

Statistics Canada checks some 600 prices monthly ➡ and summarizes these prices into the **Consumer Price Index (CPI)**
CPI
E.g., 2002 – 119.0
2001 – 116.4
➡ and calculates the **rate of inflation** as the % increase in the CPI over the past year:
$$\frac{119.0 - 116.4}{116.4}$$
= 2.2% rate of inflation 2001–2002

These variations reflect major changes in the basic economic forces driving the economy that will be considered in Chapter 6. In this chapter, we have been concerned only with how inflation is measured. In Chapter 8, we will consider what drove inflation to such high rates, the damage that such rapid inflation can do to the economy, and what can be done to control it.

Measuring Employment and Unemployment

A key aspect of the performance of the economy is its success in *providing jobs* for Canadians. To monitor employment and unemployment, Statistics Canada must deal with the complex task of keeping track of a workforce of about 17 million people.

To gather this information, Statistics Canada conducts its monthly Labour Force Survey of about 50 000 representative households across Canada. The survey asks a number of questions that are designed to classify respondents as "employed," "unemployed," or "not in the labour force," according to the following definitions:

Employed: all persons who, during the survey week, did any work at all or had a job but were not at work due to their own illness or disability, personal or family responsibilities, bad weather, a labour dispute, or vacation.

Unemployed: those persons who, during the survey week,
(a) were without work, had actively looked for work during the past four weeks, and were available for work,
(b) had not actively looked for work in the past four weeks but had been on layoff for 26 weeks or less and were available for work,
(c) had not actively looked for work in the past four weeks but had a new job to start in four weeks and were available for work.

FIGURE 2-10 The Level and the Rate of Increase of the Consumer Price Index, 1961–2002

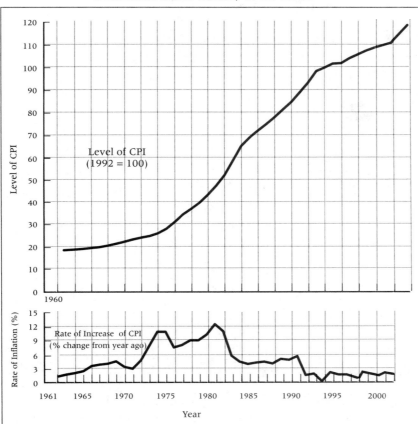

Source: Statistics Canada, adapted from *The Consumer Price Index*, Catalogue 62-001, 2002.

Labour Force: that portion of the civilian non-institutional population 15 years of age and over who are employed or unemployed. People who are not looking for work are not counted as employed or unemployed, and are therefore not included in the labour force.

Figure 2-11 uses 2002 statistics to show how the data from the Labour Force Survey are organized into statistics on employment and unemployment. There were 24 946 000 Canadians of working age, of whom 66.9 percent, or 16 689 000, participated in the labour force by either working or seeking work. Economists describe this 66.9 percent as the labour force **participation rate**. Of the **labour force** of 16 689 000, 15 412 000 were employed (12 528 000 full-time and 2 884 000 part-time), leaving 1 278 000 unemployed. This 1 278 000 represented 7.7 percent of the labour force of 16 689 000, and 7.7 percent is the **unemployment rate**. By gathering these

participation rate The percentage of the population of working age that is working or seeking work.

labour force Those Canadians who are either employed or are unemployed and both available for work and seeking work.

unemployment rate The percentage of the labour force that is unemployed.

statistics monthly—not only for Canada as a whole, but also for regions within Canada—Statistics Canada can monitor developments in employment and unemployment across the country.

FIGURE 2-11 Employment Statistics, 2001

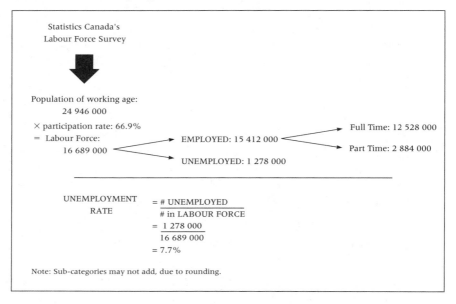

Source: Statistics Canada, adapted from *Historical Labour Force Statistics*, Catalogue 71-201, March 2001.

Figure 2-12 shows the unemployment rate from 1950 to 2002. The recessions of the early 1980s and early 1990s are clearly visible in the graph, as are the economic recoveries from these recessions in the second half of each decade. What is also evident is that the lowest unemployment rate since 1974 was the 6.8 percent that was reached in 2000, and that the unemployment rate was seldom below 8 percent. In Chapter 8, we will consider why the unemployment rate has been so high, even during economic booms.

Behind the Statistics: Types of Unemployment

One reason for such high unemployment rates is that there are various reasons why people become unemployed, and remain unemployed even when there is an economic boom.

Cyclical unemployment arises from the periodic recessions associated with economic cycles, when the unemployment rate increases by about 4 percentage points. These recessions cause the periodic peaks in the unemployment rate that are evident in Figure 2-12. And as Figure 2-12 also shows, when recessions end, the unemployment rate falls as cyclical unemployment

cyclical unemployment
Unemployment that is caused by periodic cyclical weaknesses in aggregate demand associated with recessions.

FIGURE 2-12 Unemployment Rate, 1950–2002

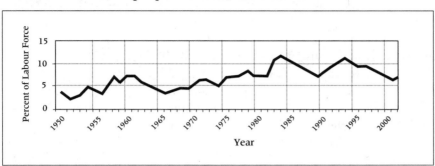

www.statcan.ca/english/
Pgdb/econ10.htm

www.statcan.ca/english/
Subjects/Labour/LFS/
lfs-en.htm

Source: Statistics Canada, adapted from *Historical Labour Force Statistics,* Catalogue 71-201, March 2001, and *Canadian Economic Observer*, Catalogue 11-010, 2002.

decreases. However, there are other types of unemployment, and these keep the unemployment rate relatively high, even in economic booms.

Frictional unemployment is due to people being temporarily out of work because they are changing from one job to another. Most frictional unemployment is quite brief and is considered to be a normal and healthy process in a free and dynamic economy in which people frequently change jobs.

Government income-security programs can add to frictional unemployment. For instance, the availability of Employment Insurance (EI) benefits encourages some claimants to prolong their job search, lengthening the duration of their unemployment and adding to the unemployment rate. The incentive to find work is also reduced by the fact that if a recipient of EI or welfare earns more than a certain income by working, his or her welfare benefits are often reduced by so much that working more brings little or even no economic gain.

Seasonal unemployment is also short-term. In seasonal industries such as agriculture, fishing, forestry, and construction, unemployment increases in the winter and decreases in the summer. Seasonal unemployment is highest in Eastern Canada, where seasonal industries account for a higher proportion of employment. Like frictional unemployment, seasonal unemployment is an inevitable aspect of Canadian labour markets; however, it has declined over the past 20 years or so.

Structural unemployment is a much more serious problem because of its longer-term nature. Structural unemployment arises from a mismatch between the skills required by employers and those possessed by unemployed workers, which can make it very difficult for the unemployed to find work.

The major causes of structural unemployment are changes in *production technology* or *product demand*. Changes in product demand can cause the decline of entire industries, and changes in technology can leave laid-off workers or those entering the labour force with inadequate or outdated skills.

Frictional unemployment
Unemployment arising from people being temporarily out of work because they are in the process of changing jobs.

Seasonal unemployment
Unemployment arising from seasonal downturns in employment in some industries.

Structural unemployment
Unemployment arising from a mismatch between the skills required by employers and those of unemployed people.

Due to the existence of frictional, seasonal, and structural unemployment, the unemployment rate remains quite high even in booms, when cyclical unemployment decreases to minimal levels.

Interpreting Changes in the Unemployment Rate

An unemployment rate of 7.0 to 7.5 percent is considered to be good. The lowest the unemployment rate has reached in the last 25 years is 6.7 percent, and in a recession, it can exceed 11.0 percent.

An increase in the unemployment rate might seem to definitely indicate layoffs, lost jobs, and deteriorating economic conditions, such as a recession. But this is not always the case, as Table 2-4 shows.

In year 20X1, the labour force is 100 000, 91 000 of whom are employed and 9000 of whom are unemployed, making the unemployment rate 9.0 percent. Suppose that, in year 20X2, the unemployment rate rises to 10.0 percent. This could mean fewer jobs and a recession, as shown in case (a), in which employment has fallen by 1000 to 90 000 and unemployment has risen by 1000 to 10 000. However, as case (b) shows, it could also mean that there are more people looking for work. In case (b), the number of people working is still 91 000, the same as in 20X1; however, 1100 more people are looking for work and not finding it. As a result, the labour force increases to 101 100 and the number of unemployed rises to 10 100, pushing the unemployment rate up to 10.0 percent. In both cases, the unemployment rate increases from 9.0 percent to 10.0 percent; however, in the first case this is due to *fewer jobs*, while in the second case it is due to *more job-seekers*.

TABLE 2-4 Two Different Reasons for the Same Increase
in the Unemployment Rate

Year	Labour Force	Unemployed	Employed	Unemployment Rate
20X1	100 000	9 000	91 000	9.0%
20X2 (a)	100 000	10 000	90 000	10.0%
20X2 (b)	101 100	10 100	91 000	10.0%

When the economy is recovering from a recession, the number of jobs may be increasing quite rapidly, as economic conditions improve. But as the job market improves, more people become interested (again) in working, increasing the number of job-seekers, which keeps the unemployment rate high and makes economic conditions appear to be worse than they are. Conversely, in some months during recessions, the unemployment rate goes down, not because there are more jobs, but because some people give up looking for work.

People who give up looking for work are called "discouraged workers." These people want to work, but have given up looking for work because they believe jobs cannot be found. Such people are not counted as "unemployed" because the Labour Force Survey records them as not seeking work.

The result is **hidden unemployment**—unemployed people who are not counted in the statistics. It has been estimated that during recessions, when discouraged workers are more numerous, hidden unemployment could amount to as much as 2 or 3 percent of the labour force. Hidden unemployment is higher in regions such as the Atlantic provinces, where chronically high unemployment generates more discouraged workers.

hidden unemployment
People who are unemployed but are not counted in the unemployment statistics because they have given up looking for work.

Conclusion: Using the Statistics

The economic statistics described in this chapter allow us to continually "take the pulse" of the Canadian economy. During a typical economic boom, real GDP and employment will rise more rapidly than usual, and the unemployment rate will decrease. Later, an increase in the rate of inflation might be a sign that the boom is approaching its end, as output is having difficulty keeping up with rising demand. During a recession, real GDP actually falls, employment will probably decrease, and the unemployment rate will rise. An increase in real GDP, followed by increased employment, would signal the end of a recession. Because they show economic trends, these and other economic statistics are watched closely by the business and financial communities, as well as by policy-makers in governments.

In addition, the statistics tell us not only about the performance of the economy as a whole, but also about strengths and weaknesses in particular parts of the economy and regions of the country. GDP statistics provide information about the total output of the economy *and* its *components*: that is, important trends in consumer spending, business investment spending, government spending, exports, and imports. CPI statistics keep track of the overall rate of inflation, and also *which types* of prices (housing, food, transportation, etc.) are rising more or less rapidly. And labour force statistics tell us a great deal about trends in employment and unemployment, not only for the nation as a whole, but also for its various regions and for subgroups of the labour force, such as young people, women, and men. Taken together, these and other statistics can help government and business leaders to gain a clearer picture of not only where the economy is, but also where it may be going.

In this chapter, we have looked at *what* economic statistics tell us about the economy. In the next few chapters, we will consider the *reasons why* economic developments actually occur.

Chapter Summary

1. On a macroeconomic scale, the economy consists of:
    (a) a supply side, in which the key is the ability and willingness of producers to produce goods and services and offer them for sale, and

(b) a demand side, in which the key is the ability and willingness of buyers to purchase goods and services. (L.O. 1)

2. A smoothly functioning economy on a macroeconomic scale will have:

(a) a supply side that is capable of high productivity and high capacity output, and

(b) demand that is high enough to keep production high and unemployment low, but not so high that supply cannot keep up, causing inflation. (L.O. 2)

3. The Gross Domestic Product, which measures the total output of the economy, consists of four components: consumption (C), investment (I), government (G), and net exports (X – M). (L.O. 3)

4. The Gross Domestic Product can increase either because the output of goods and services is higher or because their prices have risen. These inflated "money GDP" statistics can be adjusted to eliminate the effects of increased prices, the result being "real GDP" statistics that are more meaningful because they measure only real output. (L.O. 4)

5. The Consumer Price Index is the most common and well-known measure of prices. It is a weighted average of the prices of goods and services bought by a typical urban family. The percentage increase in the CPI from year to year is called the rate of inflation. (L.O. 5)

6. The Labour Force Survey gathers data on the number of people who are employed and unemployed, and calculates the unemployment rate. (L.O. 6)

7. There are various types of unemployment: cyclical, frictional, seasonal, structural, and voluntary. (L.O. 7)

8. Because the unemployment rate is affected not only by the number of people who are unemployed but also by the number who are seeking work, it is necessary to interpret unemployment rate statistics carefully. (L.O. 8)

9. Statistics on output, employment, and inflation can be used to determine the condition of the economy (recession, boom, or inflation) and the direction in which it is moving. (L.O. 9)

Questions

1. Use Statistics Canada's website to update the statistics in Table 2-1 and in Figures 2-7, 2-10, 2-11, and 2-12. What do your updates of these data indicate about the direction of the economy? What seem to be the causes of these trends?

2. (a) If money GDP has increased by 5.3 percent over last year's level, can we conclude that the economy's production of goods and services has risen?

(b) If the general level of prices has risen by 3.2 percent over the same period, what can we conclude about the economy's production of goods and services?

(c) If the general level of prices increased by 6.3 percent over the same period, what has happened to the economy's output of goods and services?

3.

Year	Consumer Price Index	Annual Rate of Inflation
1994	102.0	_____
1995	104.2	_____
1996	105.9	_____
1997	107.6	_____
1998	108.6	_____

(a) Calculate the rate of inflation for each year from 1995 to 1998.

(b) Draw on a graph the Consumer Price Index over the 1994–98 period.

(c) Draw on a graph the rate of inflation over the 1995–98 period.

(d) What explains the different trends shown by the two graphs?

4. Table 2-3 shows that from 1992 to 2002 the prices of *services* rose more rapidly than the prices of *goods*. Can you explain why this relationship would be normal and expected?

5.

Year	Population of working age	Partici- pation Rate	Labour Force	Employ- ment	Unemploy- ment	Unemploy- ment Rate
1989	20 968 000	67.5%	14 151 000	13 086 000	1 065	7.5%
1995	23 027 000	64.8%	14 928 000	13 506 000	1 422	9.5%

Use the participation-rate data in the table to estimate how much "hidden unemployment" increased from 1989 to 1995. (That is, how much higher would unemployment and the unemployment rate have been in 1995 if the participation rate had not decreased from 1989 to 1995?)

6.

Year	Population of Working Age (millions)		Partici- pation Rate (%)	Labour Force (millions)	Employed (millions)		Unem- ployed (millions)	Unem- ployment Rate (%)
20X1	20.0	60.0		12.0	10.8	1.2	10.0	
20X2	21.5	61.5			11.2			

In 20X1, the population of working age is 20 million, 60 percent of whom participate in the labour force, making the labour force 12 million. Of these, 10.8 million are employed and 1.2 million, or 10 percent of the labour force, are unemployed.

Suppose that, in 20X2, the following developments occur:

(a) Employment grows quite rapidly (by 4 percent), to 11.2 million.

(b) The population of working age increases to 21.5 million.

(c) The participation rate increases to 61.5 percent.

Calculate the unemployment rate for 20X2.

7.

Year	Labour Force (000)	Employed (000)	Unemployment Unemployed (000)	Rate (%)
1992	14 482	12 842	_____	_____
1993	14 663	13 015	_____	_____
1994	14 832	13 292	_____	_____
1995	14 928	13 506	_____	_____
1996	15 145	13 676	_____	_____

(a) Calculate the number of unemployed Canadians and the unemployment rate in each of the years shown.

(b) In 1993, the number of *unemployed* people increased, but the unemployment rate *fell*. Why?

(c) In 1996, the number of employed people increased by 170 000, but the unemployment rate *increased*. Why?

8. Many people believe that the source of unemployment rate statistics is the number of people claiming Employment Insurance benefits. Why would this not be a good source of statistics on unemployment?

Chapter 3

Sources of Economic Prosperity: The Supply Side

Learning Objectives

After studying this chapter, you should be able to:

1. Explain why high productivity is considered to be the basis of economic prosperity.

2. State six factors that influence productivity, and explain how each factor affects productivity.

3. Write an account of three possible explanations for the productivity slowdown that occurred in many nations after the late 1970s.

4. Describe Canada's productivity performance, explain two reasons why it is of concern, and explain six possible reasons for this performance.

5. Explain how government policies could improve productivity performance by strengthening each of the six factors in Learning Objective 2.

6. State the approximate percentage annual increase in the Canadian economy's potential output in recent years, and explain the combination of factors that generates this increase.

supply side The ability of the economy to use its productive resources efficiently to produce goods and services.

productivity A measure of productive efficiency, usually measured by output per worker-hour or output per worker.

Why are some nations so much richer than others? This question is very complex, involving differences in economic and social systems, technology, education and skills, natural factors such as resources and climate, and many other factors. However, societies that have achieved a high standard of living do tend to have one thing in common: a strong **supply side** to their economies. That is, they have the ability to produce goods and services efficiently.

The key to a strong supply side is the ability to make efficient use of economic inputs (labour, capital equipment, and natural resources) in order to achieve high levels of **productivity**, or output per worker. High levels of *output per person* are the key to enjoying high levels of *consumption per person*, or a high standard of living. Also, nations that are efficient tend to have lower production costs that enable them to be more successful in international competition. For a country such as Canada, with both exports and imports that represent a high proportion of its GDP, being internationally competitive is a very important consideration.

The Nature of Productivity

Productivity is not a word with a single simple meaning. In its broadest sense, it refers to the efficiency with which all three productive inputs (labour, capital equipment, and natural resources), work together to produce goods and services. However, the most common definition of productivity—and one that is easier to understand—is labour productivity, or *output per worker per hour*. A similar measure of productivity (and one that is easier to estimate) is *real GDP per employed person*.

"Labour productivity is probably the most telling measure of economic performance. Unless productivity grows, living standards stagnate."

The Economist

www.economist.com

Productivity is the key to the supply side of the economy. As the output of an average worker increases, the economy's *capacity output* (its maximum potential output) grows.

Factors Affecting Productivity

Defining productivity in terms of output per worker (per hour) seems to imply that productivity depends mainly on how hard people work. This is not the case—productivity is more strongly influenced by several other factors, which are summarized in Figure 3-1 and explained in the following sections.

As Figure 3-1 shows, the major factors that influence productivity are (a) capital equipment, (b) education and skill levels of the labour force, (c) management, (d) size of market and scale of operations, (e) the incentive of after-tax gain, and (f) the incentive of competition. In the sections that follow, we will explain each of these factors. We will then review Canada's performance regarding productivity, and consider government policies that can improve productivity performance.

FIGURE 3-1 The Supply Side of the Economy

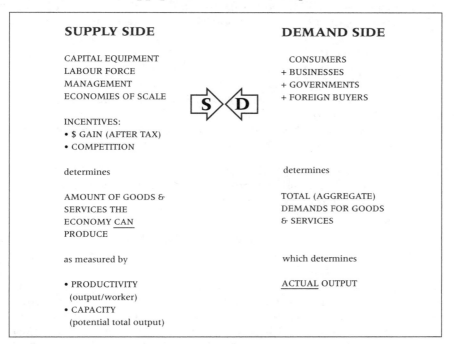

SUPPLY SIDE	DEMAND SIDE
CAPITAL EQUIPMENT	CONSUMERS
LABOUR FORCE	+ BUSINESSES
MANAGEMENT	+ GOVERNMENTS
ECONOMIES OF SCALE	+ FOREIGN BUYERS
INCENTIVES:	
• $ GAIN (AFTER TAX)	
• COMPETITION	
determines	determines
AMOUNT OF GOODS & SERVICES THE ECONOMY CAN PRODUCE	TOTAL (AGGREGATE) DEMANDS FOR GOODS & SERVICES
as measured by	which determines
• PRODUCTIVITY (output/worker)	ACTUAL OUTPUT
• CAPACITY (potential total output)	

Capital Equipment and the Saving–Investment Process

The amount—and quality—of capital equipment per worker is a key factor in determining workers' productivity. Generally, the more and better capital equipment that workers have to work with, the higher output per worker and living standards can be. So a fundamental factor influencing productivity is the amount of *capital investment* by a society in plants, equipment, and machinery. But a more basic question is this: What does it take for a society to *obtain* this capital equipment?

Building capital equipment: The saving–investment process The process by which a society acquires capital equipment is so fundamentally important that we will examine it in detail. To emphasize the basic economic concepts involved in the process of capital investment, we will use a simple illustration. Suppose you are alone on a deserted island and must find food to survive. The most accessible food is fish from a nearby stream, so you set out to catch some.

You have no capital equipment at all. So you use your hands, with only limited success, and find that you are able to catch two fish per day. This is just enough to feed you for a day, but to catch two fish takes the entire day—all of your available labour. You have no time available for any other productive activities, such as cultivating vegetables or building a shelter. Your low productivity is limiting you to a subsistence-level standard of living.

Before long, you decide that you have to become more efficient at catching fish, so you set out to build a spear. But building a spear has an opportunity cost: the time that you spend building the spear cannot also be spent catching fish. In other words, to obtain the capital good (the spear), you will have to do without, or sacrifice, some consumer goods (fish). It takes an entire day—leaving you very hungry—but you are able to fashion a spear.

Now you have a piece of *capital equipment* to help you produce consumer goods (catch fish). Using the spear, you can now catch six fish per day—a significant improvement. This piece of capital equipment has increased your productivity, and by doing so, it has widened your economic choices considerably. Because you can catch enough fish to feed yourself in less than half a day, you have in effect freed up your time (labour) *to do other things*. You could use your freed-up time to:

- produce other *consumer products*, such as shelter or other types of food,
- produce more *capital goods,* such as a net, or a plow, or traps, so as to increase your efficiency further, or
- enjoy some *leisure time*.

Suppose you decide to build a net. This is a more complex two-day project, but because you can now catch all the fish you need in a few hours each day, you can spread the building of the net over a period of four half-days. You could have caught 12 fish in this period of time, but you have decided instead to acquire another piece of capital equipment—a net. Using the net, you are able to catch enough fish to feed yourself for a whole day in about half an hour. Your productivity in fishing is now so high that you have a great deal of free time to do other things. You then use this available time to fashion some primitive tools—a hammer, a saw, a knife, and so on, with which you can construct more capital equipment. After a few weeks, you have a ladder for picking fruit from trees, traps for catching animals, a bow and arrows for hunting, a plow for cultivating vegetables, a house for shelter, and a boat for transportation—not to mention several hours per day of leisure time and a comfortable hammock in which to spend it.

Your standard of living has increased tremendously from its original subsistence level. The key to this process is, of course, the capital equipment that has increased your productivity. But how was this capital equipment obtained? To make the spear, you had to do without one day's consumption of fish—the two fish you could have caught instead of working on the spear. Making the net also involved a sacrifice of consumption: the things you could have produced in the two days' time it took to make the net. Similarly, to acquire all the other pieces of your capital equipment, you had to *forgo consumption*—that is, *forgo present enjoyment*. This is the concept of *opportunity cost* explained in Chapter 1. The opportunity cost of building capital equipment to increase your prosperity in the future is reduced consumption of goods and services in the present.

You were willing to do this because the capital equipment would *increase your future consumption*, by increasing your productivity. So you made the decision to trade off a lower standard of living *in the present* against a higher standard of living *in the future*. Each time you made a piece of capital equipment you were in effect saying, "I'll accept less consumption than I could have had today so that I can have more in the future." At first, this process was quite painful—you had to go a full day without food. Later, as your productivity increased, the sacrifices in the present became less harsh, because you could produce your daily food quite speedily and build more capital equipment in the remaining time each day.

Consumption, saving, and investment These basic ideas are so important that we will define them carefully. **Consumption** refers to consumer goods and services that are produced to be used up by consumers for *present* enjoyment. Consumption includes things such as food, clothing, cars, and entertainment. The production of capital goods, which will make possible greater production of goods and services *in the future*, is called **investment**.

But the basic economic problem of scarcity forces upon us a choice: the *more* of our output we devote to *investment* (for future prosperity), the *less* of our output will be available for *consumption* (for present enjoyment). This basic concept of doing without (forgoing) consumption is known as **saving**. Saving is obviously very important because saving is essential if there is to be the investment necessary for economic progress. Figure 3-2 shows this key relationship between consumption, saving, and investment, and how it generates higher productivity.

consumption Consumer goods and services that are used up by consumers for present enjoyment.

investment The production of capital goods that make possible increased production in the future.

saving Doing without (forgoing) consumer goods; disposable income not spent on consumption.

FIGURE 3-2 The Relationship Between Consumption, Saving, and Investment

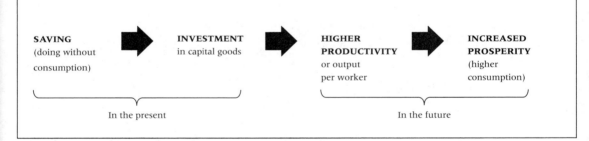

The saving–investment process in a modern economy The deserted islander scenario has the advantage of illustrating the realities of the saving–investment process as clearly as possible. The islander did without some consumption (fish) in the present in order to build a capital good (spear) to increase productivity and standard of living in the future. This is shown in the top half of Figure 3-3.

In a modern economy such as Canada's, the saving–investment process is somewhat more complex than on the island, but it is essentially the same process. As the bottom half of Figure 3-3 shows, people save some of their income; that is, they don't spend it on consumption. They *do without some consumption* that they could have had, in the same way that the islander did without fish. These savings can be used to buy shares and bonds issued by businesses. These decisions are often made by professional financial managers of mutual funds, pension funds, or financial institutions. In any case, the savings can be made available to businesses. The businesses can then use these funds for the purpose of buying or building *capital goods*, which will *increase productivity* in the economy, making higher living standards possible.

In both the deserted island situation and the modern economy, the basic economic realities of the saving–investment process are those shown in the middle of Figure 3-3: saving makes investment possible, which leads to higher living standards.

FIGURE 3-3 The Saving-Investment Process

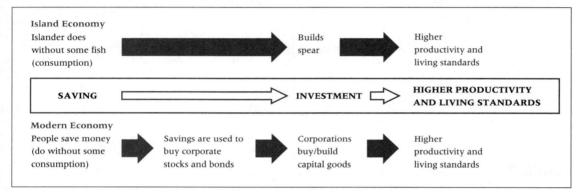

Education and Skills of the Labour Force

"If you think education is expensive, try ignorance."

Derek Bok, former president, Harvard University

"Increasingly, educated brainpower—along with the roads, airports, computers, and fibre-optic cables linking it up (to the rest of the world)—determines a nation's standard of living."

Robert B. Reich, "The REAL Economy," in *The Atlantic Monthly*.

Obviously, the better-educated and more highly skilled the nation's labour force is, the more likely it will be that its workers—and the nation—will be highly productive. Over the course of the twentieth century, economic activity shifted steadily away from the physical work associated with agriculture and factories and toward service industries and high-technology industries that employ large numbers of well-educated and trained "knowledge workers." These changes, which have been accelerated in recent years by advances in computer technology, have made it essential for a modern society to have a well-educated and highly skilled labour force.

In addition to changes in technology, recent changes in the international economic environment have added to the importance of Canada's having a highly qualified labour force. In today's "globalized" world economy, business investment capital flows more freely than ever between nations, seeking the most attractive location. And given the importance of "knowledge workers" in modern business, an educated and skilled labour force can be a powerful attraction to multinational corporations.

In the past, a nation's prosperity might have depended mainly on its natural resources or its massive investments in facilities to process resources into manufactured goods. In the future, prosperity will be much more dependent upon the education, training, and skills of a nation's labour force, which can in turn attract the business investment needed for prosperity. This is why spending on training and education is regarded as a key strategic investment in the economic future of a nation, and it is often referred to as an "investment in human capital."

www.hrdc-drhc.gc.ca

Management

The quality of management is an important contributor to productivity because management is ultimately responsible for the efficiency with which productive resources are used to produce goods and services. This involves management skills well beyond the traditional skills of planning, organizing, directing, and controlling work activities. In a sophisticated economy that utilizes many knowledge workers, the abilities to communicate effectively, to lead people, and to solve problems are critically important management skills. Furthermore, the quality of employer–employee relations, much of which depends on management, influences employee morale and productivity.

Size of Market and Scale of Operations

Sometimes, as the size of a production operation increases, its production costs per product fall. With larger-scale production, mass-production techniques involving more sophisticated and specialized capital equipment and workers can be used. The increased efficiency is attributable to what economists call **economies of scale**.[1]

Economies of scale are more important in some industries than in others. In many service industries, such as restaurants and barbershops, production methods are labour-intensive, and there are few if any efficiency advantages to huge operations. But in manufacturing and resource industries, large-scale capital equipment and mass-production techniques can bring substantial gains in efficiency and production costs per unit.

In many manufacturing industries, firms must be able to produce on a very large scale in order to be competitive. To sell such volumes of output, they must have *access to large markets*, either domestically or through international trade. Economists estimate that, in many such industries, producers need access to markets of at least 100 million people in order to operate on a scale that will generate the efficiency that makes their production costs and prices internationally competitive.

Capital equipment, quality of the labour force and management, and size of market are all *physical* factors that *make it possible* for a nation to be efficient. In order to *actually achieve* this potential productivity, there must be *incentives* that push people and businesses to become more efficient. Two basic incentives are *economic gain* and *competition*.

economies of scale The achievement of increased efficiency as a result of larger-scale productive operations and reductions in production costs per unit made possible by large-scale production.

----

[1] Economies of scale are reductions in production costs per unit that are made possible by higher volumes of output; these are usually achieved through mass-production technology.

The Incentive of After-Tax Economic Gain

Economic gain is a key incentive for both producers and individuals to improve productivity. For businesses, this economic gain is the *profit motive*, which creates incentives for efficiency in at least two ways. First, higher productivity means lower costs and thus higher profits. Second, higher productivity can also make lower prices possible, which can help to increase sales and the growth of the enterprise. On an individual level, managers and employees will be more inclined to improve productivity if there is personal economic gain for themselves in doing so, in the form of pay raises or bonuses based on productivity or profits.

It is important to note that economic gain refers to the *after-tax* gain of the businesses or people involved. If tax rates are too high, the incentive to improve efficiency will be reduced, because the after-tax gains from doing so will be smaller. So government taxation policies can have important effects upon incentives, and upon a nation's productivity and prosperity.

marginal tax rate The percentage of any *additional* income received that goes to taxes; an important factor influencing incentives to work, save, and invest.

The key to economic incentives is the **marginal tax rate**, which is defined as the percentage of any *additional* income (over and above one's present income) that is taken by taxes. If Fred earns a salary of $40 000 per year for working in a library and pays $8000 in income taxes on this salary, he is paying a 20-percent tax rate on his income. This percentage is his tax rate on his *total* income, whereas his marginal tax rate is the percentage of any *extra* income that he earns that would be taken by taxes. For instance, if Fred earns an *extra* $10 000 as a semi-professional wrestler in the evenings and he must pay $4000 in income taxes on this $10 000 of additional income, his *marginal tax rate* is 40 percent ($4000 ÷ $10 000). His marginal tax rate will be an important factor affecting Fred's incentive to do such additional work. If the marginal tax rate is too high, Fred's extra work will provide him with so little extra income after taxes that he may decide that the additional work is not worth doing. High marginal tax rates can discourage people from working to earn additional income in various ways such as second jobs, bonuses, profit-sharing plans, overtime, and pay raises for promotions. See the "You Decide" box below for an interesting look at the effects of high marginal tax rates in Great Britain.

YOU DECIDE   THE "TAXMAN"

Under the tax system of socialist British governments, the Beatles paid a marginal tax rate of 95 percent on much of their income. This is the origin of the lyrics of their song "Taxman," which refers to nineteen pounds going to the taxman and one to the Beatles, who had earned the money. The Rolling Stones, like many other higher-income people, left England to escape British taxes.

Question

1. What lesson should governments learn from this?

High marginal tax rates can also undermine the all-important *saving–investment process*. If high marginal tax rates reduce the after-tax returns to savers/investors on their income from interest, dividends, and capital gains too much, people will be discouraged from saving, and less capital will be available for business investment. Similarly, high tax rates on business profits can discourage capital investment—not only by leaving business with less funds for capital investment but also by reducing the profit incentive for businesses to invest in plant and equipment.

Finally, if a nation's tax rates on profits and investment income are too high relative to tax rates in other countries, there is a risk that investment funds will relocate to countries where taxes are lower. This is a particularly important consideration for Canadian tax policy, due to the opportunities for investment in the United States.

In conclusion, in establishing their taxation policies, it is essential that governments take into account not only their need for tax revenue, but also the effect of marginal tax rates on incentives to work, save, and invest.

The Incentive of Competition

The other main incentive in a market system is *competition*. Both theory and experience indicate that strong competition pushes producers to become more efficient. Generally, competition is stronger in industries in which there are many competing producers (including foreign competitors), and it is relatively easy for new producers to start up.

On the other hand, when there are only a few firms in an industry and their government protects them from foreign competition, the lack of competition tends to cause the industry to fall behind in efficiency.

The Productivity Slowdown

Since the mid-1970s, the growth of productivity has slowed in most industrialized countries. There is a lack of consensus regarding the causes of this important development. In fact, only about one-half of the productivity slowdown can be explained with reference to known factors. This has left the other half of this problem open to speculation, of which there has been no shortage.

Many observers believe that the *growth of service industries* has contributed to slower productivity growth. Generally, it is easier to apply productivity-increasing technology to the production of *goods* than to *services*. For instance, mass-production technology can be readily applied to produce goods such as food and appliances, whereas the provision of services such as restaurants, health care, legal counsel, and education are less easily "automated." As the world's industrialized economies have grown wealthier, a rising proportion of consumer demand—and thus output and employment—has been for services, such as restaurants, entertainment, travel, health care, education, and so on. This expansion of the service sector, in which productivity growth tends to be slower, is seen by many as an underlying cause of slower productivity growth in the economy as a whole. A contributing and related factor could be the *growth of part-time employment* associated with some service industries, such as retail trade and food service, which cater to periods of peak demand. Simply because they work fewer hours per week, part-time workers drag down statistics about the average output per worker (but not statistics about the output per hour). Other economists believe that one cause of the productivity slowdown *was a weakness in business capital investment spending*, as inflation and high interest rates in the 1970s and 1980s depressed business investment spending by making borrowing more expensive.

Finally, some economists question whether productivity growth *really has* slowed down as much as the statistics indicate. Measuring productivity in goods-producing industries is easy—if the number of pencils per worker-hour rises by 5 percent, the productivity increase is 5 percent. However, the largest part of modern economies' output consists not of goods but of services, and it is more difficult to measure productivity in services accurately, especially when the quality of the service is also improving. For instance, how do you measure the productivity gain when new communications technology generates a small increase in the *quantity* of communications processed, but a large improvement in its *quality* in terms of speed, interactiveness, and other aspects?

Canada's Productivity Performance

Experts agree that there are real difficulties in measuring productivity, and that it is especially difficult to compare the productivity statistics and performance of different countries. However, there is broad agreement concerning certain aspects of the productivity performance of the Canadian economy.

Productivity Performance

First, the *level* of productivity in Canada is relatively high—Canada is included among the high-productivity nations in the world. However, there are areas of concern about Canada's productivity performance:

- The rate of productivity *growth* in Canada has been among the slowest of the major industrialized nations.
- Canada's productivity is significantly lower than productivity in the United States, our major trading partner—nearly 20 percent lower in 2001, according to the Centre for the Study of Living Standards.
- Productivity in Canada's manufacturing sector is especially weak, averaging some 30 to 32 percent below U.S. levels in 2001, as compared to a gap of only 12 percent as recently as 1994 (Centre for the Study of Living Standards).

www.csls.ca

So, in the key area of productivity, Canada has been falling farther behind the United States, with output per worker-hour slipping from 85 percent of the U.S. level in 1989 to 81 percent in 2001. Meanwhile, other nations have been gaining on Canada in productivity, and passing us.

Consequences

Such weak productivity performance can only have negative effects on the living standards of Canadians. During the 1990s, the living standards of Canadians slipped from third place to ninth among members of the Organization for Economic Cooperation and Development (OECD), a Paris-based research agency. In late 1998, an OECD report warned that if there were no change in Canada's economic performance, Canadians' living standards could fall from their current level of 10 percent above the average of OECD nations to 15 percent *below* that average in about 20 years. And in 2002, the Conference Board of Canada warned that the gap between the incomes of Americans and Canadians would double by 2010 if current trends continued.

oecd.org

oecd.wash.org

Poor productivity performance also undermines the ability of Canadian firms to compete internationally, an important matter for a nation that exports over 40 percent of its GDP. This concern is especially strong regarding the manufacturing sector, since Canadian productivity there is particularly weak and so much of world trade is in manufactured goods. Furthermore, an economy in which productivity is stagnant is less likely to attract its share of the international business investment and skilled people that are two keys to success in the globalized world economy.

> "In 1990, Canada had the fourth highest standard of living within the OECD economies. By 1999 we had sunk to seventh as Japan, Norway and Denmark overtook us."
>
> Charles Baillie, CEO, TD Bank,
> February 26, 2001.

For these reasons, many economists regard poor productivity performance as the most fundamental weakness of the Canadian economy. However, determining the *reasons* for this productivity performance is no simple matter, because productivity depends upon the complex interactions of various factors. While productivity is *measured* in terms of output per worker-hour, the *cause* of high or low productivity is not simply the performance of workers—factors such as capital equipment, management, economies of scale and incentives are key contributors to productivity. In the following sections, we will look at some of the possible reasons for Canada's weak productivity performance. The discussion of these factors is necessarily in general terms only, which may or may not apply to particular industries or firms. We will also consider some more specific research relating to the manufacturing sector of the Canadian economy, which accounts for much of the lag in Canada's productivity.

Capital Investment

Investment by Canadian businesses in machinery and equipment in the 1990s was about 30 percent below the pace set by their U.S. counterparts. In addition, the share of foreign business investment—which brings with it up-to-date technology—decreased at this time. The largest Canadian firms, such as the auto companies, do have world-class technology, but many Canadian manufacturers, especially small and medium-size ones, have been slower than their foreign competitors to adopt up-to-date production technology, such as robotics and computer-assisted design and manufacturing (CAD/CAM). Also, Canada ranked 15th among OECD nations in expenditure on research and development (R&D), which contributes to productivity growth.

Education and Skills of the Labour Force

As a percentage of GDP, Canada spends more on education than most other major industrialized nations, and Canadians' high average levels of educational attainment reflect this fact. However, many secondary-school graduates lack the required literacy and numeracy skills to function effectively in today's modern economy. Employers have often noted the shortages of people with middle-level technical, business, and managerial skills—the skilled tradespeople, technicians, technologists, and operations managers who contribute to productivity in the day-to-day operations of enterprises of all sorts.

Furthermore, Canadian businesses have not filled these gaps with training programs of their own. Canadian employers spend considerably less on training than their foreign counterparts do—by some estimates, Canada ranks only 15th in the world in employee training. Also, apprenticeship programs in Canada often do not meet the needs of Canadian employers for skilled workers, in large part because employers and governments have, until recently, found it easier and cheaper to import skilled workers rather than train people in Canada.

Management

As noted earlier, management skills are particularly important to the development of high productivity. Canada has sufficient university graduates in business and management to fill *senior* positions, but many observers believe there is a shortage of well-trained, practical, and competent *middle managers* to handle the management of *day-to-day operations*, which is often the key to efficiency.

Canadian managers have also been criticized for being slow to adapt to the rapid changes in the world economy, particularly the growth of international trade and competition known as "globalization." According to the Swiss-based World Economic Forum, a weakness in Canada's international competitiveness has been the lack of "outward orientation" of Canadian management. It is believed that this deficiency may be related to the smaller size and domestic orientation of many Canadian manufacturers, and to Canada's historical government policy (until recently) of protecting them from foreign competition, as discussed in the next two sections.

Scale of Operations and Size of Market

Especially in manufacturing, larger producers enjoy economies of scale that allow them to achieve higher levels of productivity. And, as noted earlier, a market size of 100 million is necessary in order for many manufacturers to realize the full benefits of economies of scale. But Canada's domestic market is small, and much of Canadian industry has consisted (and still consists) of smaller-scale and less efficient firms. These firms were, until recently, protected from foreign competition by a government policy of tariff protection. While this protection helped Canada's manufacturing sector to survive and grow, it did not help this sector to become efficient. And even after the adoption of free-trade policies, many Canadian firms remained relatively small and oriented to the small Canadian market. We will further explain this issue later in this chapter in the section on manufacturing, and also in Chapter 12.

The Incentive of After-Tax Economic Gain

By the late 1990s, many observers argued that high taxes were limiting Canada's economic progress. Canada's overall tax burden (total taxes as a percent of GDP) was comparable to the average tax burdens for major industrial countries; however:

- Canada's tax burden of 37 percent of GDP was considerably higher than the 29 percent of GDP tax burden in the United States,
- Canada's personal and corporate taxes were considerably higher than those in the United States, and
- Canada's tax burden had slipped from 8th-lowest among OECD nations to 17th-lowest.

In the view of some observers, Canada's high taxes on corporations were one reason for the relatively low level of business investment in Canada (including Canada's declining share of international business investment). This view was supported by the *Global Competitiveness Report* of the World Economic Forum, which listed high taxes as one of the weaknesses of the Canadian economy.

www.weforum.org

The Incentive of Competition

Productivity in the Canadian economy has until recently suffered from a lack of strong competition for several reasons. First, there has been Canada's *tariff policy*, as discussed earlier, which, for over a century, protected many Canadian producers from foreign competition. Second, many Canadian industries have been dominated by only a few large firms. In such industries, known to economists as *oligopolies*, it is possible that the dominant firms will agree to limit competition among themselves in order to earn comfortable and secure profits. Obviously, such a situation reduces the competitive pressure to continually improve productivity. Finally, various Canadian industries have historically been subject to a variety of *government regulations*. Some of these regulations restrict how many firms can operate in a particular field (such as taxis and airline routes), and some restrict how much producers can produce (such as farm marketing boards), or establish prices, often in a way that guarantees producers a certain rate of profit (such as cable television). Many of these government restrictions have the side effect of *restricting* competition and the incentive to improve productivity in parts of the Canadian economy.

The Widening Productivity Gap in Manufacturing

www.csls.ca

According to the Centre for the Study of Living Standards (CSLS), Canada's output per worker-hour in manufacturing slipped from 88 percent of the U.S. level in 1994 to only 68 percent in 2001. Over the 1994–2000 period, U.S. manufacturing output per worker-hour grew by a reported 4.9 percent per year, compared to only 1.1 percent in Canada. This widening gap in manufacturing productivity is very significant, as it accounted for two-thirds of the widening of the overall productivity gap between the United States and Canada.

CSLS estimates that one-eighth of the increase in the manufacturing productivity gap is the result of measurement problems. Because the U.S. statistics for manufacturing employment exclude temporary workers, output per worker is overestimated. But what accounts for the rest of the large growth of the productivity gap after 1994?

According to CLSC, both Canadian and U.S. manufacturers increased their output considerably after 1994, but Canadian firms did so mostly by *hiring workers*, while American firms did not hire more workers—instead, they invested in *capital equipment* that increased output *per worker*. One reason for this difference might have been that in Canada, the *cost of labour* was increasing more slowly than in the United States, due to Canada's higher unemployment rates. At the same time, the *cost of capital equipment* in Canada was increasing faster than that in the U.S. Much of the capital equipment purchased by Canadian businesses is imported from the United States, and as the international value of the Canadian dollar decreased (by about 25 percent in terms of U.S. dollars over the decade!), this equipment became more and more costly. CSLS also mentions a number of other factors that could have created a less favourable climate for business investment in Canada, including higher taxes than in the U.S., more government regulation, higher rates of unionization, and the sluggish Canadian economy for much of the 1990s.

Differences in the *industrial structure* of Canada and the United States also contributed strongly to the widening productivity gap in manufacturing. In the United States, the "high-tech" sector of the economy (which produces high-technology products such as machinery and electrical and electronics products) accounts for 35 percent of U.S. manufacturing output, as compared to only 17 percent in Canada. So in the late 1990s, when both output and productivity in this sector increased sharply, the impact on overall (average) U.S. manufacturing productivity was much greater than in Canada. According to CSLS, the high-tech industries' larger share of manufacturing output accounted for 71 percent of the widening productivity gap between the United States and Canada from 1994 to 2000.

Finally, *plant size* is believed to have played a role in Canada's lagging productivity performance. According to CSLS, a higher proportion of Canadian manufacturers are smaller enterprises than in the United States.

Smaller firms accounted for 77 percent of manufacturing employment in Canada and 65 percent in the United States in 1994, when the gap in manufacturing productivity between the two nations began to widen rapidly.

Some observers believe that the widening of the Canada–U.S. productivity gap that occurred in the 1990s will prove to be a temporary phenomenon arising from different economic conditions in the two countries and the exceptional surge in the size and productivity of the U.S. high-tech sector that occurred during this period. It will take several years before we know whether this is the case or not.

Government Policies to Strengthen Productivity and the Supply Side of the Economy

While government policies sometimes weaken productivity, they can also help to improve productivity, prosperity, and the international competitiveness of a nation's industries. In the following sections, we will consider some policy directions that have been taken and could be taken to improve the productivity and competitiveness of Canadian industry.

Regarding Capital Investment

By providing tax incentives that make it financially attractive for people to save and invest money (such as Registered Retirement Savings Plans) and for businesses to invest in capital equipment, governments can promote the *saving–investment process* that is the key to capital formation. Additional support for technological improvements can come from government support for *research and development* (R&D), in the form of tax allowances or other financial support.

Regarding Education and Skills of the Labour Force

Given the importance of human capital in a modern economy, governmental education and training policies have become very important to a society's economic prosperity. Most observers believe that the education system should place more emphasis on basic skills and should be linked more closely to the needs of the workplace in which graduates must function. In addition, there should be more emphasis on science programs and the development of middle-level technical, business, and management skills and on apprenticeship programs, and employers should devote more resources to employee training and retraining. Finally, governments have shown increased interest in reforming social welfare programs by linking unemployment and welfare benefits to training or retraining, either by requiring benefit recipients to undertake training or by providing financial incentives for them to do so.

Regarding Management

At the strategic level, government export programs can help managers to shift their focus toward the global economy, and to understand how trends and developments in the international economy provide both opportunities and challenges for their firms. At the operational level, Canada's educational system and business community need to develop more well-trained middle managers who are capable of managing for the increased productivity that is needed by both businesses and the economy at large.

Regarding Market Size and Scale of Operations

Without access to larger foreign markets, many Canadian producers would be unable to achieve the economies of scale needed to be competitive internationally. From this perspective, Canada's signing of the Canada–U.S. Free Trade Agreement of 1989 and the North American Free Trade Agreement of 1994 is very important. In the 13 years following the signing of the Canada–U.S. Free Trade Agreement, Canada's exports in real terms increased by 123 percent, as compared to 38 percent growth for the economy as a whole.

Regarding the Incentive of After-Tax Economic Gain

capital taxes Taxes levied on the amount of a corporation's assets, or its capital.

As noted earlier, by the late 1990s, it was believed that high taxes were undermining Canada's economic growth. In 2001, the federal government made the first of a five-year series of cuts to personal and corporate income taxes that would total about $100 billion from 2001 to 2005. There were also proposals to reduce **capital taxes**, which are levied on the assets of large corporations and are believed to discourage business investment. According to the federal Department of Finance in 2001, capital taxes added the equivalent of 3.6 percentage points to the tax rate of large taxable corporations.

Regarding The Incentive of Competition

Probably the most important steps taken by the federal government to increase competition in the Canadian economy were the signing of the Canada–U.S. Free Trade Agreement of 1989 and the North American Free Trade Agreement (NAFTA) of 1994. Under these agreements, the degree of import competition has increased substantially: during the 13 years following the signing of the Canada–U.S. Free Trade Agreement, imports into Canada in real terms increased by 97 percent, as compared to 38-percent growth for the economy as a whole.

Another step toward promoting competition had been taken in 1986, with the passage of new competition legislation (the Competition Act) that provided stronger measures against anticompetitive practices by corporations, such as price-fixing and mergers of firms in order to dominate a market or an industry.

Finally, as noted earlier, government regulation of industries often has the effect of reducing competition. In recent years, governments have "deregulated" (to varying degrees) various sectors of the economy, including oil and gas, airlines, communications, and financial services, thus promoting increased competition, higher productivity, and lower prices.

The Supply Side of the Economy in Review

We have discussed six factors that influence the productivity, or the production potential—the *supply side*—of the economy:

- Capital equipment and the saving–investment process
- The labour force (size, education, and skills)
- Management
- Scale of operations and size of market
- The incentive of after-tax gain
- The incentive of competition

Together, these factors determine not only the efficiency with which the economy can produce goods and services but also its potential total output, or the "capacity output" of the economy.

Growth of the Supply Side (of Capacity Output)

Ultimately, the capacity output of the economy depends on two factors:

- the size of the labour force (the *number of workers* available), and
- productivity (average *output per worker*)

Both of these factors increase gradually over time. The size of the labour force grows due to population growth and immigration. Output per worker increases due to various factors such as improvements in technology and skills. In recent years, the size of the labour force has grown by about 1.6 percent per year, and output per worker has increased by about 1.4 percent per year. The combined result of these factors has been that the potential output of the economy has risen by roughly 3 percent per year, as reflected in Figure 3-4. These are average figures for the past few years, and can change to some degree from year to year. For instance, if productivity growth were to become faster, the potential output line in Figure 3-4 would rise more rapidly, and vice versa. Notwithstanding this, the impression conveyed by Figure 3-4— that the supply side of the economy grows at a fairly slow and steady pace— is reasonably accurate.

But what actually *determines* the "*capacity*" output of the economy as shown in Figure 3-4—what is it that prevents output from increasing beyond the level shown by the dotted line in the figure? In practical experience, the factor that limits the growth of output tends to be *the availability of qualified labour*. We saw in Chapter 2 that the unemployment rate seldom goes below 7 percent of the labour force, even in a strong economic boom. So, in a boom, the obstacle that producers encounter when they seek to increase output further is a shortage of labour in general, and of skilled labour in particular. This obstacle also helps to explain why in the later stages of a boom, wage rates and labour costs per unit produced often increase, as employers compete for the limited number of qualified workers available. This brings us to the last section of this chapter—the aggregate supply curve.

FIGURE 3-4 The Growth of the Supply Side of the Economy

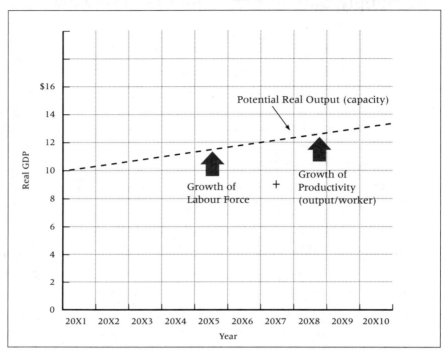

The Concept of Aggregate Supply

aggregate supply curve
A graphical representation of the supply side of the economy showing how production cost per unit changes as the level of output is increased toward its potential.

The supply side of the economy can be represented by an **aggregate supply curve**, as shown in Figure 3-5, which shows how the level of total output ("aggregate supply") is related to the cost per unit of producing that output.

When operating at *capacity* (that is, at its highest production level), this economy is capable of producing 100 units of output per week. The farther we move to the right on the aggregate supply (AS) curve, the closer we get to this capacity output. The higher the curve goes, the more costly it is to produce goods and services. Up to about 80 or 90 units of volume, we can increase output without experiencing increases in production costs per unit because the economy has plenty of inputs (labour, capital, and resources) available or unemployed. It should, therefore, be possible to obtain more inputs without having to pay higher wage rates or prices to attract them. Beyond this level, however, it is no longer possible to increase output further without some increases in production costs per unit.

In some industries, production *bottlenecks* will occur due to shortages of labour, production capacity, or other inputs. Output can be increased, but only by means that will also increase production costs per unit: higher wages

FIGURE 3-5 Aggregate Supply Curve

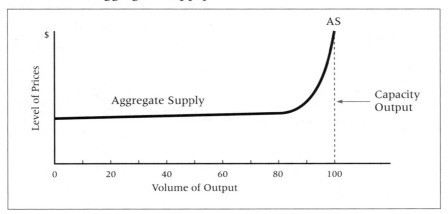

for overtime, extra shifts, higher prices for increasingly scarce materials or other inputs, and so on. In Figure 3-5, this relationship means that we can move to higher levels of production, but only by accepting higher costs per unit, as shown by the AS curve sloping upward.

The closer we get to the economy's capacity output, the more severe these problems of shortages and production bottlenecks become, and the faster the AS curve rises. Finally, at its capacity output of 100 units per week, the economy is simply not capable of producing at a faster pace, and the AS curve becomes vertical. The economy is using all of its inputs and the pace of production cannot be increased further, even at sharply higher costs per unit.

Changes in the AS Curve

Figure 3-5 represents the AS curve at a particular point in time. If the economy's *potential to produce* were to increase next year as its labour force and stock of capital equipment grew, the AS curve would shift to the right, as shown by AS_1 in Figure 3-6.

AS_1 reflects the fact that the economy is now capable of producing a higher volume of output (110 units) than last year, at about the same cost per unit. Efficiency (productivity) has not improved, as shown by the fact that production costs per unit are the same as last year, but the greater volume of inputs available makes possible a higher volume of total output.

If *overall productivity* in the economy were to improve so that it was using its inputs more efficiently, not only would its potential (capacity) output rise, but production costs per unit would also fall. This relationship is shown in Figure 3-7, in which AS_2 represents the new situation, with production costs per unit lower than before and capacity output higher than before.

When combined with the aggregate demand curve that we will introduce in Chapter 4, the aggregate supply curve will be a useful tool for analysis.

FIGURE 3-6 AS Curve Illustrating Increased Production Potential

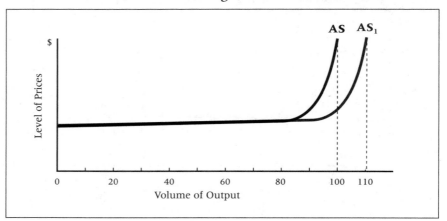

FIGURE 3-7 AS Curve Illustrating Increased Overall Productivity

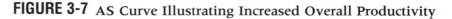
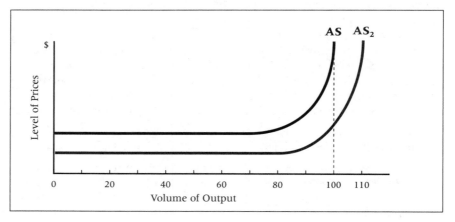

Can Saving Be *Too* High? A Preview of the Demand Side of the Economy

In this chapter, we have stressed the importance of the *supply side* of the economy—its ability to produce goods and services efficiently. Without this ability to achieve high productivity, economic prosperity is not possible. Furthermore, we have stressed the desirability of saving, which makes possible the investment that increases the economy's productive potential. However, productive capability *alone* is not enough to ensure prosperity. If this productive capacity is to be *used*, there must be sufficient *demand* for its output. This raises the possibility that saving could be too high—that excessive saving by households could depress consumption spending (demand), leaving business with low sales and little or no incentive to invest in new plant and equipment.

Ideally, then, there would be a *balance* between consumption spending and saving. Saving would be sufficiently high to finance adequate levels of capital investment, while consumption spending would be sufficiently high to provide business with an incentive to invest in additional plant and equipment. Such a balance between spending and saving is essential for economic progress.

In summary, economic progress and prosperity depend on the interaction between the *supply side* and the *demand side* of the economy. Not only must the economy have the ability to produce efficiently, but also there must be sufficient demand for its output to ensure that the economy will actually produce to its fullest possible capabilities. In Chapter 4, we will consider the demand side of the economy more fully.

Chapter Summary

1. A key to economic prosperity is high productivity or output per worker-hour. (L.O. 1)

2. The main factors affecting productivity are:

    (a) capital equipment and the saving–investment process that builds it; this requires forgoing current consumption in order to build the capital goods that will increase productivity (and consumption) in the future,

    (b) the education and skills of the labour force,

    (c) management,

    (d) size of market and scale of operations,

    (e) the incentive of after-tax economic gain, and

    (f) the incentive of competition. (L.O. 2)

3. Most nations experienced a slowdown in productivity growth after the late 1970s. The reasons for this slowdown are believed to include a shift in output and employment from goods-producing industries to service industries, a slowdown in business capital investment, and the difficulty of measuring productivity in services industries. (L.O. 3)

4. After the late 1970s, productivity growth in Canada was slower than in its major trading partners, with productivity in the manufacturing sector a particular concern. This caused concerns about Canadians' future living standards and the international competitiveness of Canadian producers. (L.O. 4)

5. This slow productivity growth is attributed to various factors, including a small domestic market, slowness to adopt up-to-date production technology, weak R&D, a labour force (including managers) inadequately

educated and trained to match the economy's needs, government regulations that reduce competition, and high personal and corporate income taxes. (L.O. 4)

6. Government policies that could help to improve productivity include policies to encourage saving, investment, and R&D; education more attuned to the needs of the economy; agreements to gain/secure access to larger markets, such as the Canada–U.S. Free Trade Agreement; reducing marginal tax rates on business and personal income; and policies to strengthen competition, such as freer trade, stronger competition legislation, and less government regulation of business. (L.O. 5)

7. In recent years, the potential output (supply side) of the Canadian economy has been growing at about 3 percent per year. This is the result of a combination of labour-force growth and productivity growth. (L.O. 6)

Questions

1. (a) Donna teaches accounting in a community college for a salary of $60 000 per year, and she pays income tax of $15 000. The average percentage of Donna's income paid to income tax is, therefore, ___ percent; this is Donna's average tax rate.

    (b) If Donna teaches night school, she will earn an additional $2000. The income tax payable on this additional income will be $750. The marginal tax rate paid by Donna on her additional income is ___ percent.

    (c) How would Donna's incentive to work be affected by a significant increase in her:

    (i) average tax rate?

    (ii) marginal tax rate?

2. Fill in the remaining average and marginal tax rates.

Income	Income Tax	Average Tax Rate	Marginal Tax Rate	
$30 000	$5000	16.7%	————	
31 000	5300	17.1%	30.0%	($300/$1000)
32 000	5650	————	————	
33 000	6050	————	————	

3. People who are working overtime sometimes say that they work "the first two hours for the government, then the next three for themselves." Use the concept of the marginal tax rate to explain what they mean by this.

4. As an illustration of how a recession can affect labour productivity (output per employee), consider the following case: You are the owner/manager of a small firm that produces candles, with the following labour force:

    • 1 president/manager (you)

- 2 office staff: your secretary/receptionist and a bookkeeper/clerk
- 1 sales representative
- 1 plant supervisor
- 20 plant workers

The total number of employees is 25, and presently you are producing 5000 boxes of candles per week, for an average productivity of 200 boxes of candles per person employed.

Suppose a recession cuts your sales, causing you to reduce output by 20 percent to 4000 boxes per week.

(a) How many employees will you probably lay off?

(b) What will "labour productivity" (output per employee) be after the layoffs?

(c) What is the percentage change in labour productivity, and why has this change occurred?

(d) When the recession ends and sales and production increase again, what will happen to productivity?

5. Suppose a mini-economy has 200 workers whose productivity is, on average, 200 units of production per year in 20X1.

(a) The capacity output of this mini-economy in 20X1 would be ___ units of output per year.

Suppose that next year (20X2):

- the labour force grows by 1.5 percent, and
- average worker productivity increases by 1.5 percent.

(b) The capacity output of the economy in 20X2 will be ___ units of output per year.

(c) The percentage increase in capacity from 20X1 to 20X2 will be ___ percent.

6. In 2001, 13 percent of Canada's population was over 65 years of age. It was forecast that by 2030, the over-65 group would be 22 percent of the population, and by 2050, 42 percent.

(a) What explains these forecasts?

(b) What are the implications of these forecasts for the living standards of Canadians?

(c) What could the government do to alleviate the effects in (b)?

7. During the 1990s, it was found that in some computer-based service industries such as communications and many internet "ebusinesses," companies could achieve greatly increased sales and output *without* having to invest in costly expansion of plant capacity. What would the implications of not having to invest in additional equipment be for productivity growth and the operating costs (per unit of output) in such enterprises?

8. The graph below shows the aggregate supply curve for an economy that can produce a maximum (capacity) output of 100 units per week. Explain how the AS curve would be changed if:
   (a) the economy had 20 percent more of all productive resources, which could be utilized with the same efficiency as its existing resources.
   (b) the efficiency with which the economy's existing productive resources could be utilized increased by 20 percent.
   (c) the economy had 20 percent less of all productive resources.
   (d) the efficiency with which the economy's existing productive resources could be utilized decreased by 20 percent.

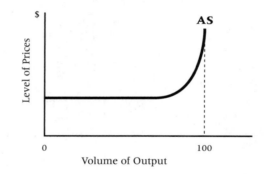

9. Capital taxes are taxes on businesses that are calculated as a small percentage of the assets of a business. In Canada, capital taxes are often four times as high as in the United States. Why are such high capital taxes particularly inappropriate for a country that is suffering from low productivity?

10. If a group of farmers store away some food to eat during the winter, they could be said to be "saving" that food. Is this the same idea as was discussed in the text with respect to saving and investment?

11. Some people believe that the productivity slowdown that has occurred since the mid-1970s is largely the result of the decline of the "work ethic." Do you agree that Canadians are becoming lazier?

12. Has the gap between Canadian and U.S. productivity continued to widen, or has it narrowed? Search the website of the Centre for the Study of Living Standards, (www.csls.ca) for updates concerning productivity trends.

Chapter 4

Sources of Economic Prosperity: The Demand Side

Learning Objectives

After studying this chapter, you should be able to:

1. List the four components of aggregate demand and express each as a percentage of GDP.

2. Explain three factors that have an important influence on the amount of household consumption spending and saving.

3. Explain the two main factors that influence the amount of business investment spending.

4. Explain why saving can be viewed as both an opportunity for economic progress and as a threat to the economy.

5. Using a supply-side/demand-side graph of the economy (or an aggregate demand/aggregate supply graph), explain how and why an increase in aggregate demand would affect output, employment, and the rate of inflation in the economy:
   (a) if output were well below capacity.
   (b) if output were near capacity.
   (c) if output were at capacity.

6. Summarize what would constitute an ideal balance between the demand side and the supply side of the economy, and the results of that balance.

In Chapter 3, we considered the supply side of the economy, or the factors that determine the economy's ability to produce goods and services. These factors determine the *potential* output (capacity output) of the economy, but they do not decide how much output *actually will* be produced. In a market system, output will only be produced if there is a demand for it. So the *actual* output of the economy—the Gross Domestic Product—will be decided by the *level of total spending on goods and services* in the economy, or what economists call the **demand side** of the economy.

demand side The purchasers of society's output of goods and services.

The level of total spending on goods and services (**aggregate demand**) is critically important to the performance of the economy on a macroeconomic scale. If aggregate demand is too low, there will be a *recession*, with output well below its potential level and high unemployment. Rising aggregate demand will generate higher levels of both output and employment, or an *economic boom*. But if aggregate demand becomes too high, output will be unable to keep up with demand and *inflation* will occur, as prices rise rapidly. Figure 4-1 summarizes the demand side and the supply side of the economy, and shows the need for a reasonable balance between them.

aggregate demand Total spending on goods and services, consisting of consumption spending, investment spending, government spending, and net exports (C + I + G + X − M).

FIGURE 4-1 The Demand Side and the Supply Side

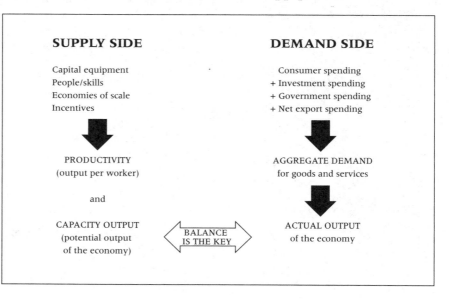

Aggregate Demand: Purchasers of the Economy's Output

We can divide aggregate demand into the same four categories into which we divided Gross Domestic Product in Chapter 2.

(a) *Consumption spending.* This is spending by households on consumer goods and services; it usually buys about 60 percent of the economy's output.

(b) *Investment spending.* The largest component of this category is business spending on capital goods, which usually purchases 10 to 12 percent of GDP. This category also includes investment by households in new housing, which is generally an additional 5 to 6 percent of GDP.

(c) *Government spending.* Government spending on goods and services has been about 21 percent of GDP in recent years. Current spending on goods and services (such as health care and education) has been about 19 percent of GDP, with spending on capital projects accounting for the rest.

(d) *Net exports (exports minus imports).* Purchases of Canadian exports by foreign buyers adds to aggregate demand in the Canadian economy, while purchases of imports by Canadians reduces demand for Canadian

FIGURE 4-2 Aggregate Demand, 2002

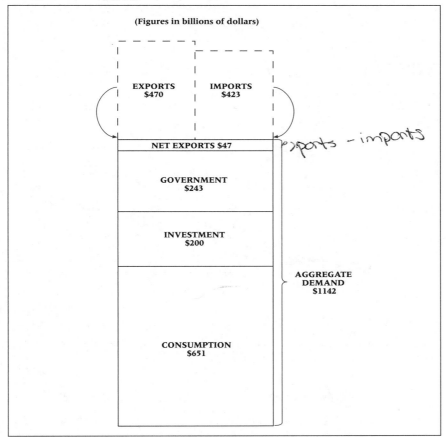

Source: Statistics Canada, adapted from *National Income and Expenditure Accounts,* Catalogue 13-001, 2002.

output. So the *net effect* of international trade on demand for Canadian goods and services can be calculated as *exports minus imports*. In recent years, exports have exceeded imports, so the foreign trade sector has boosted demand and output in Canada.

Figure 4-2 on the previous page illustrates these components of aggregate demand, using 2002 statistics. In the following sections, we will examine each of these components of aggregate demand in more detail in order to better understand the demand side of the economy.

Consumption Spending by Households

consumption spending
Spending by households on consumer goods and services.

Consumption spending is defined as spending by households on consumer goods and services. This spending can be divided into three categories: *non-durable goods*, such as food and clothing, which are used up quite quickly; *durable goods*, such as cars and appliances, which last considerably longer; and *services*, such as entertainment, medical services, and travel. Consumption spending is the "workhorse" of the demand side of the economy in the sense that it is by far the largest single purchaser of the economy's output. As Figure 4-3 shows, consumption spending buys about three-fifths of the goods and services produced by the economy.

FIGURE 4-3 Consumption Spending and GDP, 1961–2002

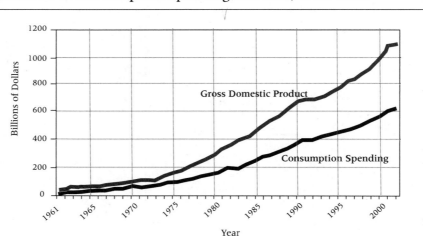

www.statcan.ca/english/Pgdb/econ04.htm

Source: Statistics Canada, adapted from *National Income and Expenditure Accounts,* Catalogue 13-001, 2002.

What Determines the Level of Consumption Spending?

www.statcan.ca/english/Pgdb/famil6a.htm.ca

The amount of consumption spending done by an *individual* household in any given year may be influenced by various factors peculiar to that household. However, when we consider the level of *total* consumption spending in the economy as a whole in a given year, a few key factors stand out.

The most important factor influencing total consumption spending in the economy is total **personal disposable income** (personal income less personal taxes), which is the amount of money households have available to spend. As Figure 4-4 shows, consumer spending increases as personal disposable income increases.

Another important factor influencing consumption spending is **consumer confidence**, or the degree to which consumers feel optimistic—or pessimistic—about their future economic prospects. If consumers feel confident about their job and income prospects, they will be inclined to spend more of their disposable income and save less. More importantly, they will be willing to *borrow more* to make larger purchases such as houses, cars, furniture, appliances, and vacations that are difficult or impossible to finance out of current disposable income. On the other hand, when their confidence is

personal disposable income Personal income less personal taxes, or after-tax personal income; may be spent or saved.

consumer confidence The degree to which consumers feel optimistic (or pessimistic) about their future economic prospects.

www.conferenceboard.ca

FIGURE 4-4 Consumer Income and Consumer Spending, 1971–2002

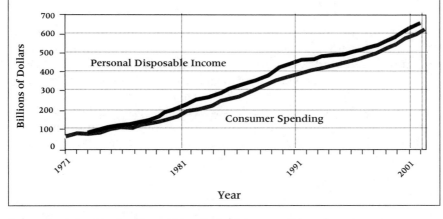

Source: Statistics Canada, adapted from *National Income and Expenditure Accounts*, Catalogue 13-001, 2002.

low, consumers will borrow and spend less, and they may reduce their consumption spending so as to pay off their debts. Figure 4-5 shows consumer confidence as measured by the Conference Board Survey of Consumer Attitudes. Figure 4-5 shows how consumer confidence fluctuates considerably from year to year. During recessions, when unemployment is a concern, consumer confidence tends to be low. During booms, when job and income prospects are good, confidence tends to increase considerably.

Interest rates also affect consumer spending. Low interest rates encourage borrowing and spending, especially on "big-ticket" items such as houses, cars, appliances, and furniture. On the other hand, high interest rates make borrowing more costly, and so depress spending on big-ticket items.

interest rates Percentages of borrowed money paid by a borrower (and received by a creditor) annually.

FIGURE 4-5 Conference Board of Canada's Index of Consumer Attitudes, 1979–2002

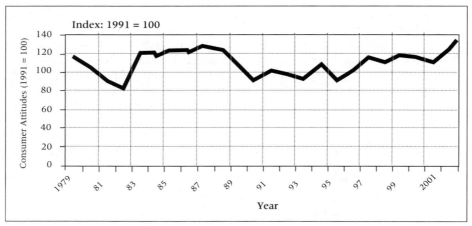

Source: The Conference Board of Canada.

consumer indebtedness
Consumer debt as a percentage of disposable income; affects consumers' willingness to spend.

A related factor affecting consumers' willingness to spend is the level of **consumer indebtedness**. Consumers with heavy debts are less likely to spend aggressively, especially by borrowing. If they are sufficiently concerned about their debts, they may even reduce their consumption spending in order to pay down their debts. A similar (but opposite) effect can occur regarding *households' assets*—an increase in the value of consumers' assets such as stocks can make consumers feel that they can afford to spend more and save less.

Saving by Households

personal saving
Personal disposable income not spent on consumption.

Households do not spend all of their disposable income; they save some of it. **Personal saving** is defined as personal disposable income not spent on consumption. For instance, if Fran's disposable income is $2600 per month and she spends $2200 of it on consumer goods and services, her monthly *saving* is $400. Whether she puts this $400 into a savings account or uses it to buy stocks, this $400 is still *saving* because it is disposable income that was not spent on consumption. The same concept applies on a national scale—in 2002, Canadians' disposable income was $696 billion and they spent $665 billion on consumer goods and services (including interest), so their personal saving was $31 billion.

Saving by households takes many forms. Much of it is done through banks, in the form of savings accounts and guaranteed investment certificates. Some people prefer bonds or mortgages because they pay higher interest, or corporate stocks or mutual funds because their value may increase.

personal saving rate
The percentage of personal disposable income that is saved.

How much do Canadians save? The best measure of saving is the **personal saving rate**, which is the percentage of personal disposable income that is saved. For example, in 2002 personal saving was $30.9 billion and disposable income was $695.9 billion, so the personal saving rate was 4.4 percent ($30.9/$695.9). As Figure 4-6 shows, the personal saving rate of Canadians has fluctuated considerably over the years. In the 1960s, the personal saving rate was only 5 percent. In the 1970s, it rose into the 10– to 12-percent range. In the 1981–84 period, it peaked in the 15– to 18-percent range and then settled at about 10 percent through 1993. After that, the personal saving rate decreased again, to 5 percent.

FIGURE 4-6 The Personal Saving Rate, 1961–2002

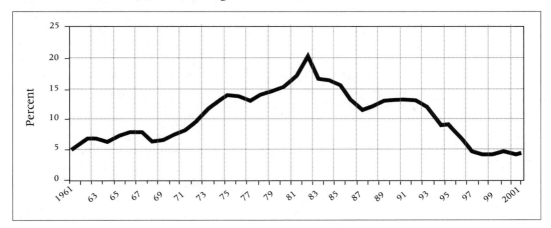

Source: Statistics Canada, adapted from *National Income and Expenditure Accounts*, Catalogue 13-001, 2002.

What Determines the Level of Personal Saving?

People's saving is influenced by the same factors that influence their consumption spending. As their *disposable income* rises, people not only spend more, but also save more. *Consumer confidence* plays a role—if confidence is high, consumers tend to spend more, and save less. Consumer confidence is influenced not only by the economic outlook and job security but also by the level of *household wealth*—in the late 1990s, the rapidly rising value of their investments in stocks led many people to feel less of a need to save from their current income. Conversely, higher levels of *debt* tend to make people reduce their spending in order to pay off some of their debt. In addition, *interest rates* affect saving. Higher interest rates discourage borrowing and spending, which increases saving. Lower interest rates tend to decrease saving by encouraging borrowing and spending. In addition, *habit* is a factor in saving, as many people budget to save a certain amount regularly—for security or for a "rainy day." Also, *government taxation policies* can influence the saving decisions of households. For instance, the introduction of registered retirement savings plans, which allowed tax deductions for saving for retirement, led to a large increase in the personal saving rate of Canadians. Finally, *demographic factors* can influence the personal saving rate—as the baby boomers approach retirement, their saving is expected to increase, pulling up the saving rate for the country as a whole.

How Canadians Invest Their Savings

Many people think of "savings" in terms of bank deposits, guaranteed investment certificates, and Canada Savings Bonds, or investments in stocks and bonds. However, people save in large amounts in two other ways that are less visible—*pension fund contributions and mortgage payments*. People who contribute to a pension fund save for their retirement by having part of each paycheque (often 6 percent) deducted and paid into a pension fund. These savings are invested (mostly in bonds and stocks) for the purpose of providing retirement incomes for members of the pension fund. In 2002, $580 billion was invested in such pension funds. Repayments of the *principal*[1] on mortgage loans are also counted as saving because they also represent income that is not spent on consumption, but rather is used to pay down the loan that was made to buy a house (i.e., a mortgage). For many people, their major assets later in life consist of their pension entitlements and their home, which they obtained by saving in the ways described above.

When Canadians' savings are invested in stocks or bonds, they become available to businesses, which can then invest the funds in capital equipment—the *saving–investment process* that we saw in Chapter 3. This is one of the key economic roles of saving, and brings us to the next component of aggregate demand—investment spending by business.

Investment Spending by Business

Investment is defined as spending by business firms on capital goods, which includes all types of capital goods—factories, machinery, equipment and tools, computers and office equipment, and so on. Investment spending includes both additions to society's stock of capital goods and replacements for capital goods that have become obsolete, or worn out or depreciated.

The term "investment" sometimes causes confusion because many people associate the word with purchases of stocks and bonds. The two meanings are obviously related, because companies often finance their purchases of capital goods ("investment") by issuing stocks or bonds (in which the public "invests"). However, when the term "investment" is used in this text, it will refer to business spending on capital goods unless otherwise specified.

Business investment spending on plant and equipment amounts in most years to about 10 to 12 percent of GDP—much less than consumption spending. However, business investment spending is a particularly important

---

[1] On the other hand, the interest component of mortgage payments is not considered to be "saving." It accumulates no assets, and is more like a current consumption item—payment to the lender for the current use of the funds, similar to paying rent for the use of a car.

economic process because capital goods increase output per person, or *productivity*, making possible a higher standard of living and improving the international competitiveness of Canadian producers.

What Determines the Level of Business Investment Spending?

Two factors that influence investment spending by business are: (1) expectations regarding the profitability of investments, and (2) interest rates.

> To monitor and forecast investment spending, the federal government twice yearly conducts a survey of business investment intentions. From this survey of a sample of businesses, the government can estimate the future trend of business investment spending in the Canadian economy.

Expectations regarding the profitability of investment projects Business investment decisions are future-oriented. Since the plant and equipment involved are costly and will typically last for many years, they must earn a sufficient profit to justify the investment. So the *expectations* of businesses regarding the future financial performance of such investments are very important. If the outlook for the future of investment projects is favourable, investment spending will be high, but if it is uncertain or unfavourable, investment spending can be quite low.

Probably the most important considerations underlying business investment decisions in general are:

- how high sales and production are relative to production capacity, and
- whether sales are expected to increase in the future.

If production is at or near capacity levels and sales are expected to rise further, there will be pressure on businesses to expand through capital investment spending projects. On the other hand, if sales are expected to be stagnant or to fall, capital investment spending is likely to be quite low. So *economic forecasts* play a significant role in business investment decisions—if good economic conditions are forecast and rising sales are expected, investment spending tends to increase, and vice versa.

Various other considerations can influence business expectations and investment decisions. Will competition increase or diminish? Will our present production facilities have to be upgraded with new equipment in order to remain competitive? Will government trade policy change, bringing new competition from imports or new opportunities in export markets? Will taxes change? Will construction costs increase next year? (If so, maybe we should build now.) Will interest rates fall next year? (If so, maybe we should wait, and borrow money then.) Do government programs provide tax reductions or other incentives that encourage investment?

Because they are specific to firms and industries, expectations are difficult to analyze in detail on a macroeconomic scale. Still, they are the most important factor influencing the level of investment spending. Figure 4-7 shows the Conference Board of Canada's Index of Business Confidence, which is based on surveys of Canadian business firms.

Interest rates Frequently, capital investment projects are financed with borrowed money, which the company usually raises by selling bonds to the public. To be profitable, an investment project (say, a plant) must *earn* a higher

FIGURE 4-7 Conference Board of Canada's Index of Business
Confidence, 1979–2002

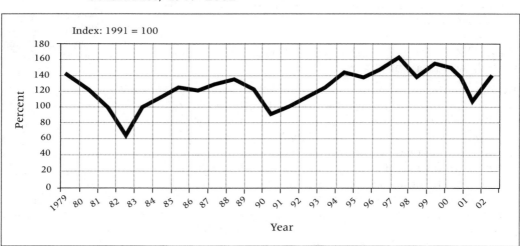

Source: The Conference Board of Canada.

rate of return on the money invested in it than the rate of interest that the
business must *pay* on the borrowed funds. For instance, if a company must pay
a 6-percent annual interest rate on money borrowed through a bond issue, it
would be quite profitable to borrow money to build a plant that earned a
10-percent-per-year rate of return. However, if the company had to pay a
10-percent interest rate, the same investment project would not be profitable.
So lower interest rates encourage investment spending by businesses, while
higher interest rates discourage borrowing and capital investment.

Financing Capital Investment: The Saving–Investment Process Revisited

In Chapter 3, we used the illustration of fishing on the deserted island to
show the saving–investment process that builds capital equipment. We saw
that in order to invest in capital goods (spears) that would increase their
future prosperity, people had to "save" in the sense of doing without
consumer goods (fish). Investment was the key to economic progress, but it
was not possible without *saving*.

This basic economic principle also applies to a modern economy such as
Canada's. In the early 2000s, Canadian businesses were investing nearly
$140 billion per year in plant and equipment, which means they must have
access to about $140 billion of savings to finance these investment projects.
These savings come mainly from three basic sources: *personal savings, business
savings,* and *foreign savings.*

Personal savings are one source of funds for business investment. These savings can be made available for business investment when they are used to buy stocks and bonds issued by businesses. Some of these stocks and bonds are purchased directly by households, but for the most part this is done on their behalf by pension funds and financial institutions (such as banks and mutual funds), which invest the savings of households.

Another source of funds for capital investment is **business savings,** or **retained earnings.** These are profits retained in the business after taxes have been paid and dividends have been paid to the shareholders. Table 4-1 shows a simplified illustration of the calculation of the retained earnings of a business. In this example, after all expenses, taxes, and dividends have been paid, $4 million of additional retained earnings becomes available for reinvestment into the business in the year shown.

As Figure 4-8 shows, profits and retained earnings are a *quite variable* source of savings, rising rapidly in some years but actually falling in others. The most important factor influencing the overall level of profits is the state of the economy itself—in periods of rapid economic growth, profits rise rapidly, while economic slowdowns usually bring declines in profits.

business savings Profits retained in a business after taxes have been paid and dividends have been paid to shareholders. (Also known as **retained earnings.**)

retained earnings Profits retained in a business after taxes have been paid and dividends have been paid to shareholders. (Also known as **business savings.**)

TABLE 4-1 Retained Earnings: An Illustration

	Sales income	$100	million
	Expenses	92	
=	Profits before tax	8	
−	Taxes	3	
=	After-tax profits	5	
−	Dividends to shareholders	1	
=	Addition to retained earnings	$ 4	

Canada has traditionally financed considerable amounts of capital investment by "importing" *foreign savings,* mainly from the United States. Foreign investors and firms have historically provided nearly 20 percent of the savings used for capital formation in Canada, if the profits of foreign-owned companies that are reinvested in Canada are included.

Business Investment in Canada in Recent Years

Figure 4-9 shows business investment spending in Canada in recent years. The graph shows that capital investment tends to *fluctuate* considerably more than consumer spending (compare Figure 4-9 with Figure 4-4) as business expectations and interest rates change.

FIGURE 4-8 Corporation Profits Before Taxes, 1961–2002

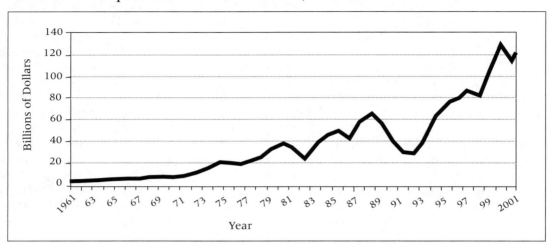

Source: Statistics Canada, adapted from *National Income and Expenditure Accounts*, Catalogue 13-001, 2002.

FIGURE 4-9 Business Investment Spending, 1961–2002

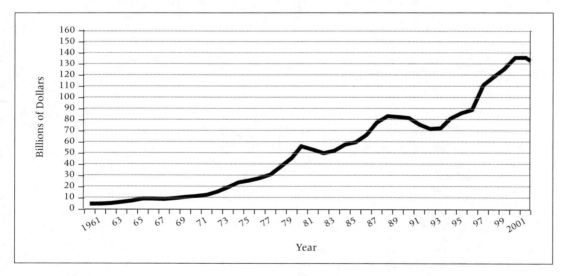

Source: Statistics Canada, adapted from *National Income and Expenditure Accounts*, Catalogue 13-001, 2002.

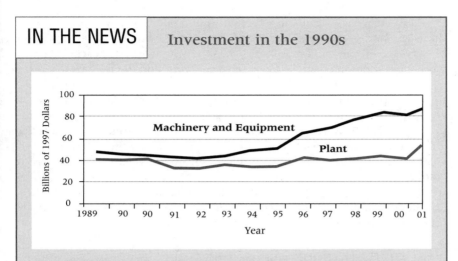

IN THE NEWS | Investment in the 1990s

Source: Statistics Canada, adapted from *National Income and Expenditure Accounts,* Catalogue 13-001, 2002.

Over the expansion period from 1993 to 2000, business investment spending on *construction* (of plant) increased by 42 percent in real terms. Over the same period, business investment in *machinery and equipment* increased by *108 percent.*

Question

1. What might explain why business spending on machinery and equipment increased so much faster than spending on plant construction?

Government Spending on Goods and Services

Another major purchaser of the economy's output is government. Purchases of goods and services by governments—federal, provincial, and municipal—have amounted in recent years to about 21 percent of Canada's GDP. Of this, the vast majority (about 19 percent of GDP) has consisted of current expenditures, with only a small amount (2 percent of GDP) going to capital expenditures.

Most current government expenditures on goods and services consist of the wages and salaries of government employees, who provide a wide range of services to the public (such as health care workers, teachers, social workers, law enforcement workers, civil servants, and the military).

Government spending decisions are made by elected leaders, and therefore could be said to be determined by political factors. However, government spending is limited by the government's tax revenues (and the public's willingness to pay taxes) and by the government's ability and willingness to borrow. Generally, government spending on basic public services such as health care and education tends to be relatively stable, rising gradually as the population grows. An exception was from 1993 to 1998, when very large budget deficits (government spending in excess of revenues) and high and rising debt forced governments to reduce their spending in order to balance their budgets.

Net Exports (Exports Minus Imports)

As we have seen, purchases of Canadian exports by foreign buyers constitute an important component of aggregate demand in the Canadian economy, amounting to over 40 percent of Canada's GDP in recent years. While export spending *adds* strongly to aggregate demand in Canada, Canadian purchases of imported goods and services have the opposite effect—they *reduce* the level of spending within Canada. So, to obtain the net effect of international trade, we must *add* to aggregate demand foreign purchases of Canadian exports and *subtract* Canadian purchases of imports. For instance, in 2002 Canadian exports were $470 billion and imports were $423 billion. So net exports (exports minus imports) were +$47 billion, and the net effect of international trade was to add $47 billion to aggregate demand in the Canadian economy. Conversely, if imports had exceeded exports, the net effect of international trade would have been to reduce aggregate demand in the Canadian economy.

Since about 85 percent of Canada's exports go to the United States, the condition of the U.S. economy is a key factor affecting Canadian exports. When the U.S. economy is in a boom, Canadian exports will be strong, while a U.S. recession will cut into Canada's exports. While the foreign trade component of aggregate demand is very important to the performance of the Canadian economy, it depends on complex international factors that are quite different from the other components of aggregate demand discussed in this chapter. Therefore, we will cover the international sector only briefly in this chapter, and we will return to it in more detail in Chapters 9 to 12.

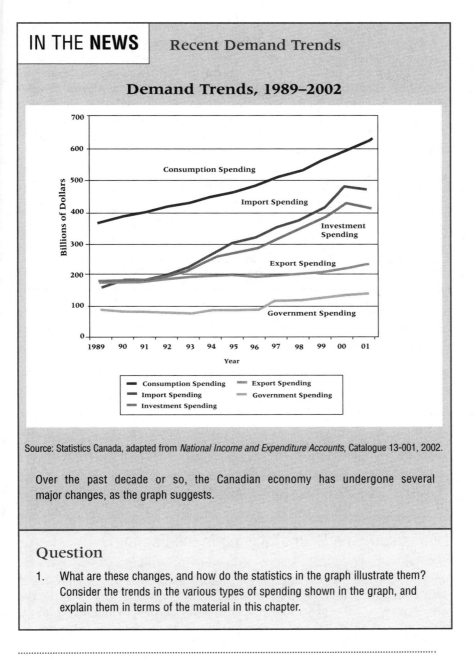

IN THE NEWS   Recent Demand Trends

Demand Trends, 1989–2002

Source: Statistics Canada, adapted from *National Income and Expenditure Accounts*, Catalogue 13-001, 2002.

Over the past decade or so, the Canadian economy has undergone several major changes, as the graph suggests.

Question

1. What are these changes, and how do the statistics in the graph illustrate them? Consider the trends in the various types of spending shown in the graph, and explain them in terms of the material in this chapter.

Summary of the Demand Side of the Economy

So far, we have examined each of the four components of aggregate demand *separately*. But what really matters on a macroeconomic scale is how these four components *combine* to determine the grand total level of spending on goods and services (aggregate demand) in the economy.

Figure 4-10 portrays the combined effect of the factors discussed in this chapter on the level of aggregate demand, which is represented by the thick line. The upward-pointing arrows represent factors that *increase* aggregate demand—these are simply the four types of spending discussed earlier in this chapter. The downward-pointing arrows reflect factors that *reduce* demand in the economy. Saving is income that is *not* spent (including profits retained by businesses), taxes reduce the ability of buyers to spend, and spending on imports removes demand from the Canadian economy.

FIGURE 4-10 Influences on Aggregate Demand

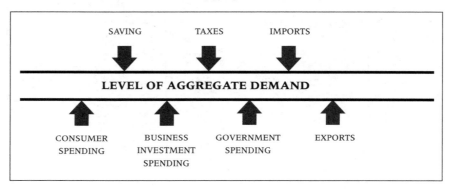

Anything that changes any of the factors in Figure 4-10 will affect the level of demand in the economy. For instance, if interest rates were to fall, consumer and investment spending would increase, saving would decrease, and aggregate demand would increase. An increase in personal income taxes (assuming no corresponding increase in government spending) would reduce aggregate demand by decreasing disposable income and consumer spending. Practise using this framework by answering the questions in the "You Decide" box on the next page.

Digression: The Role of Saving in the Economy

The role played by saving in the operation of the economy can be a confusing one. Chapter 3's coverage of the supply side of the economy presented saving as a key to economic progress, as the essential first step in the saving–investment process that generates higher productivity and economic prosperity. On the other hand, Figure 4-10 suggests that saving could lead to problems on the demand side of the economy. Too much saving could mean too little demand in the economy, which could lead to a recession. So does saving have a positive effect or a negative effect on the economy?

Suppose that Canadians increased their saving by $10 billion per year. Would this be beneficial or damaging to their economy? There is no simple answer to this question; the outcome would depend on whether or not the

---

---

additional savings found their way into investment spending. If they did not, aggregate demand would fall, and the economy would slow down. On the other hand, if these savings did get invested into capital goods, there would be two positive results. First, demand would not fall, and second, with more capital goods, the economy would become more productive, and living standards would rise.

To illustrate the role of saving in the economy, imagine two very different economies—one in which households and businesses saved a very large proportion of their income and another in which they saved none of it. The economy in which saving was very high would suffer from a serious shortage of spending. Without this demand to support current production, producers would have to reduce output and lay off workers. Such a high-saving economy would experience severe *demand-side* problems *in the present*.

The second economy, with no saving, would not have that problem—there would be no shortage of spending with a saving rate of zero! However, without saving, this economy could not invest in capital goods. It would not be able to increase its productive efficiency and total output—in short, it would experience *supply-side* problems that would severely limit its *future* prosperity.

Neither of the two scenarios above will result in good economic performance. What is required for good economic performance is an appropriate *balance* of consumer spending, saving, and investment. Consumer spending should be high enough (and saving low enough) to support output, employment, and prosperity *in the present*, while saving should be high enough to support sufficient capital investment to generate higher productivity and economic prosperity *for the future*.

....

The Demand Side and the Supply Side

Aggregate demand is the total of spending by the four sectors of the economy: the consumer sector, the business sector, the government sector, and the international (trade) sector. For example, if spending by each of these sectors were as shown in the illustration below, aggregate demand for that year would be $680 billion.

Consumption spending		$400 billion
Business investment spending	$80	
Residential construction	40	120
Government spending on goods and services		150
Exports of goods and services	170	
– Imports of goods and services	–160	
= Net exports		10
Aggregate demand		$680

In the illustration above, is $680 billion the "right" level of aggregate demand for the economy in this year? The answer to this question depends on the *supply side* of the economy, or how much the economy is capable of producing.

If the supply side were capable of producing $850 billion of goods and services and aggregate demand were only $680 billion, then production— and employment—would be 20 percent *below* their potential levels. The economy would be in a *recession*, and unemployment would be very high.

On the other hand, if the supply side were only capable of producing $600 billion of goods and services, aggregate demand of $680 billion would be *too high*. Supply could not keep up with demand. As a result, prices in general would rise rapidly, generating rapid *inflation*.

From these illustrations, we can see that, ideally, there would be a *rough balance* between the supply side and the demand side of the economy. That is, the level of aggregate demand would be close to the capacity of the supply side to produce goods and services, and not so low as to cause a recession nor so high as to generate serious inflation.

A Supply-Side/Demand-Side Model of the Economy

To understand the economy on a macroeconomic scale, we need to consider both the demand side and the supply side together. Figure 4-11 shows the two sides of the economy and the key factors that influence each side. But Figure 4-11 is only a *static representation* of the economy. It is the *dynamic interaction* between the supply side and the demand side of the economy that determines the performance of the economy regarding output, real GDP, employment, and prices. This interaction is shown in Figure 4-12.

FIGURE 4-11 The Supply Side and Demand Side of the Economy

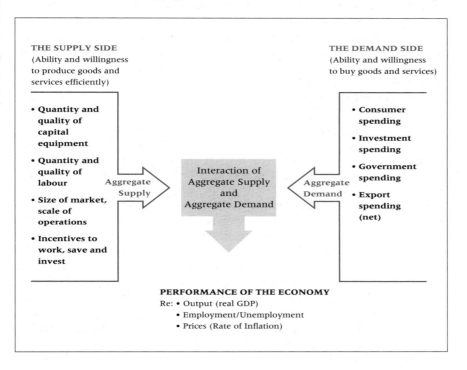

THE SUPPLY SIDE
(Ability and willingness
to produce goods and
services efficiently)

THE DEMAND SIDE
(Ability and willingness
to buy goods and services)

• **Quantity and
quality of
capital
equipment**

• **Quantity and
quality of
labour**

• **Size of market,
scale of
operations**

• **Incentives to
work, save and
invest**

Aggregate
Supply

Interaction of
Aggregate Supply
and
Aggregate Demand

Aggregate
Demand

• **Consumer
spending**

• **Investment
spending**

• **Government
spending**

• **Export
spending
(net)**

PERFORMANCE OF THE ECONOMY
Re: • Output (real GDP)
    • Employment/Unemployment
    • Prices (Rate of Inflation)

FIGURE 4-12 A Supply-Side/Demand-Side
Model of the Economy

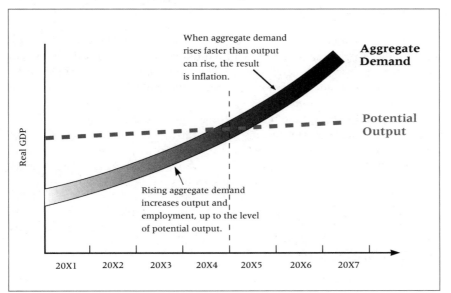

When aggregate demand
rises faster than output
can rise, the result
is inflation.

**Aggregate
Demand**

**Potential
Output**

Real GDP

Rising aggregate demand
increases output and
employment, up to the level
of potential output.

20X1   20X2   20X3   20X4   20X5   20X6   20X7

The dotted line in Figure 4-12 represents the economy's *capacity output*—the maximum potential output of the supply side of the economy. As we saw in Chapter 3, the economy's capacity output increases only gradually from year to year as the number of workers in the labour force and output per worker (productivity) both gradually increase. In recent years, capacity output has increased by about 3 percent per year, as reflected by the gradual rising trend of the dotted line.

This type of model is useful for illustrating the interaction between the demand side and the supply side of the economy as both sides change over a period of time. The wide solid line shows changes in aggregate demand, from year 20X1 to 20X7. In 20X1, the economy is in a recession. Aggregate demand for goods and services is well below the economy's capacity production level, leaving production and employment well below their potential levels.

As aggregate demand rises in years 20X1 through 20X4, output increases quite rapidly. Because production has been below capacity levels, it can temporarily rise by more than 3 percent per year, as previously unemployed labour and unused plant capacity are brought into production. In fact, when the economy is recovering from a recession, it is possible for output to rise by as much as 5 or even 6 percent per year.

Such rapid increases in output cannot continue indefinitely, however, because before long the economy's output will reach its capacity level, as shown by the dotted line. From this point forward, output can only increase as rapidly as the productive capacity of the economy increases, which we have seen to be about 3 percent per year. By the end of year 20X4, the economy has reached its potential output, and output cannot increase as rapidly as before. If aggregate demand continues to rise after year 20X4 as it has in the previous three years, output will be physically unable to keep up with demand—and demand will "outrun" supply.

In Figure 4-12, after year 20X4, the output of goods and services (which is limited to the amount shown by the dotted line) is unable to keep up with the rapidly rising demand (as shown by the solid line). As a result, the prices of goods and services in general will rise quite rapidly as they are bid up by the excess of demand over available supply—there will be a growing problem of *inflation* in the economy.

In the real world, the effects of rising aggregate demand on output and prices are not as separate and distinct as this analysis may suggest. Rising aggregate demand tends to cause *both* output *and* prices to rise, with the effect on prices being stronger, the closer the economy gets to its potential output. This relationship is shown by the grey area in year 20X4 in Figure 4-12: the darker the line, the more rapidly prices are rising as higher demand pushes the economy closer to its limits. So a period of economic expansion tends to be characterized not only by rising output and employment but also by inflation, and the closer output gets to capacity, the more rapid inflation is likely to become.

An Aggregate Demand/Aggregate Supply Model of the Economy

Another type of model of the economy uses aggregate demand and aggregate supply curves to illustrate the performance of the economy under different conditions, ranging from severe recession to rapid inflation. In doing so, it illustrates how and why inflation becomes more severe, the closer the economy moves to its capacity level of output.

YOU DECIDE | WHAT WILL HAPPEN?

State how each of the following events would probably affect *output*, *employment*, and *the rate of inflation* in the economy, and explain why these effects would occur.

1. Interest rates are reduced when the economy is in a recession.
2. Taxes are reduced when the economy is in a boom and output is very close to capacity.
3. Taxes are increased when the economy is in a recession.

Aggregate Demand Graphed

Figure 4-13 shows the relationship between aggregate demand (AD) and the *level of prices* in the economy. At high price levels (in the upper range of the AD curve), the quantity demanded is relatively low, while at low price levels (in the lower range of the AD curve), the quantity demanded is higher. These "opposite" relationships are mainly due to the fact that if the prices of Canadian products are higher, foreigners buy fewer Canadian products and Canadians buy more imports, with the combined effect of depressing the demand for Canadian products. On the other hand, if Canadian prices are lower, both Canadian and foreign buyers will purchase more Canadian goods and services. The level of prices could affect the purchasing behaviour of Canadians in another way: higher prices of goods and services may cause Canadians to postpone their purchases, holding aggregate demand down, while lower prices could have the opposite effect, increasing aggregate demand. The result of these factors is that the aggregate demand curve is shaped as it is in Figure 4-13, with the quantity demanded higher at lower levels of prices and lower at higher levels of prices.

We have seen that aggregate demand fluctuates, being low in periods of recession and high during periods of boom and inflation. These fluctuations are shown in Figure 4-14. AD is the same curve as in Figure 4-13, while AD_1 represents the low levels of aggregate demand typical of a recession. Note

FIGURE 4-13 Aggregate Demand

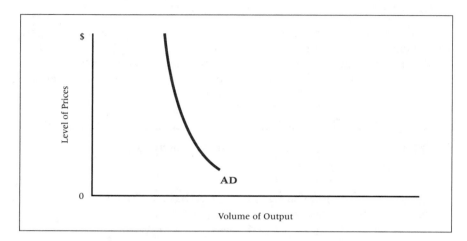

that, at any given price level, AD_1 indicates a lower quantity demanded than does AD. On the other hand, AD_2 represents a higher level of aggregate demand, with more output being demanded at any given price level.

FIGURE 4-14 Changes in Aggregate Demand

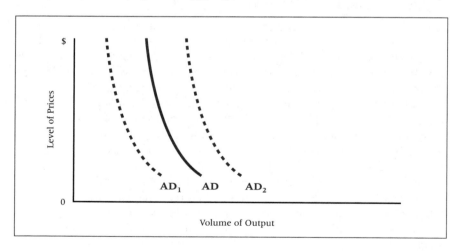

Aggregate Demand and Aggregate Supply Combined

Figure 4-15 adds the aggregate supply curve (AS) from Chapter 3. As we saw in Chapter 3, the AS curve shows that, up to an output of 80 units, output can be increased without significant increases in production costs and prices, because with output so far below the economy's capacity, the plant capacity, labour, and materials needed to increase output are readily available.

Businesses wanting to increase production will be able to obtain the labour and materials they need without having to pay higher wages and prices that would increase their production costs per unit and force prices upward.

FIGURE 4-15 Aggregate Demand and Aggregate Supply Combined

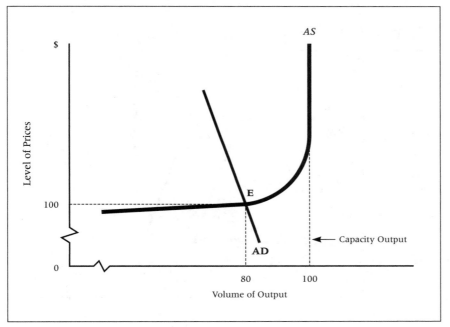

However, as output is increased beyond 80 units, production "bottle-necks" begin to appear in the form of shortages of labour, plant capacity, or materials that make it more difficult and costly to increase output. And the closer the economy gets to capacity production, the more severe and costlier these bottlenecks will become. As a result, increases in output beyond 80 units will come at a higher production cost—and price—per unit, and these increases in costs and prices will become greater as capacity output is approached. This relationship is shown by the upward swing in the AS curve as production nears its capacity level of 100 units.

Figure 4-15 shows the interaction of the aggregate supply curve from Chapter 3 and the aggregate demand curve from this chapter. With the AD and AS curves intersecting at E as shown, the level of output will be 80 and the level of prices will be 100: the economy is in a recession, with output well below its capacity level of 100 and unemployment quite high due to inadequate aggregate demand. With aggregate demand so weak, the level of prices is rising very slowly.

If aggregate demand were to increase to the level shown by AD_1 in Figure 4-16, output would rise to 95 and unemployment would be lower.

However, this higher level of demand would also bring more inflation, as the price level rises to 110. If aggregate demand were to move still higher, to the level shown by AD_2, the economy would be producing at capacity and unemployment would be minimal; however, AD_2 represents an *excessive* level of aggregate demand. Because demand exceeds the economy's capacity to produce, inflation becomes very severe, as shown by the movement to a price level of 150.

FIGURE 4-16 The Effects of Rising Aggregate Demand

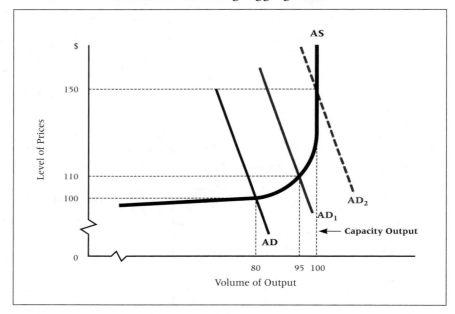

So, increases in aggregate demand can have quite different effects upon the performance of the economy (output, employment, and prices), depending on the circumstances. If the economy is operating well below capacity and unemployment is high, increased aggregate demand (up to the level shown by AD in Figure 4-16) will have mainly *beneficial* effects. Output and employment will increase considerably and prices will increase only slightly, as the summary in Table 4-2 shows.

If the economy is closer to its capacity level of output, a similar increase in aggregate demand (from AD to AD_1 in Figure 4-16) will have *mixed effects* on the economy. Output and employment will increase, but not as rapidly as before, while prices will rise more rapidly. If aggregate demand were to be increased further (from AD_1 to AD_2 in Figure 4-16), there would be only small gains in output and employment at the cost of rapid increases in prices, as the economy is *overheated* by aggregate demand that is so high that aggregate supply has difficulty keeping up with it. Beyond AD_2, further increases in aggregate demand cannot boost output and employment any higher and will result only in more severe inflation.

TABLE 4-2 The Effect of Increases in Aggregate Demand on the Economy Under Different Conditions

(See Figure 4-16 for graph)		
	Effect upon	
Increase in Aggregate Demand	*Output and Employment*	*Prices*
Up to AD	Major gains	Very small increases
AD to AD_1	Lesser gains	More rapid increases
AD_1 to AD_2	Quite small gains	Quite rapid increases
Beyond AD_2	No gains	Very rapid increases

In summary, it is the interaction between aggregate demand and aggregate supply that determines how well the economy functions regarding output, employment, and inflation. Aggregate demand can be too low relative to the economy's productive capacity, causing a recession and high unemployment. Rising levels of aggregate demand can bring worthwhile gains in output and employment, although they will also increase the rate of inflation. But excessively high levels of aggregate demand will generate much more severe inflation, and only small gains in output and employment, which makes it desirable to have a balance between aggregate demand and the economy's capacity to produce, or between the demand side and the supply side of the economy.

However, it is not always possible to maintain such a balance between the demand side and the supply side of the economy. In Chapter 6, we will examine how and why these two sides of the economy can get out of balance with each other, and we will look at the consequences that this imbalance can have on the performance of the economy. But before we do that, we need to consider one more key aspect of the demand side of the economy— the banking system and its effect on the economy, which will be the subject of Chapter 5.

Chapter Summary

1. Aggregate demand consists of consumption spending, investment spending, government spending on goods and services, and net export spending (exports minus imports). (L.O. 1)

2. Consumption spending, which purchases about three-fifths of GDP, depends mainly on the level of personal disposable income. It is also influenced by consumer confidence, household wealth or indebtedness, and interest rates. (L.O. 2)

3. Personal saving increases as disposable income rises. It is also influenced by the same factors as in 2 above. (L.O. 2)

4. Business investment spending on capital goods is usually 10 to 12 percent of GDP. Business investment, which is vital to prosperity, depends mainly on expectations concerning the future profitability of investment projects and on interest rates. (L.O. 3)

5. Government purchases of goods and services, which consist mainly of the wages and salaries of government employees who provide public services, amount to about 21 percent of Canada's GDP. (L.O. 1)

6. Exports have in recent years accounted for over 40 percent of the GDP; however, when Canadians' purchases of imports are deducted from exports, the net effect of international trade on aggregate demand in Canada is much smaller. (L.O. 1)

7. Saving can pose a threat to the economy because money that is saved by households and businesses does not buy goods and services; however, if savings are used by business for investment spending on capital goods, the economy can grow. (L.O. 4)

8. If aggregate demand is well below capacity output, increases in aggregate demand will cause output and employment to rise quite rapidly, but they will not generate much additional inflation. (L.O. 5)

9. As output approaches its capacity level, higher aggregate demand will still increase output and employment, although less rapidly than before, and will tend to generate more inflation than before. (L.O. 5)

10. If aggregate demand rises above the economy's capacity output, the result will be severe inflation. (L.O. 5)

11. Ideally, there would be a rough balance between the demand side and the supply side of the economy, with aggregate demand close to the economy's capacity to produce goods and services, and neither so low as to cause a recession nor so high as to generate too much inflation. (L.O. 6)

Questions

1. In 2001, the federal government made the first of a five-year series of cuts to personal income taxes. It has been projected that personal incomes taxes would be about $23 billion lower in 2005 than they would have been without the cuts. Estimate the impact of these tax cuts on the demand side of the economy in 2005.

2. One of the most variable components of consumer spending from year to year is spending on durable goods, especially new automobiles. Why do you think this is so?

3. Figure 4-5 shows that consumer confidence was low during the recession of the early 1990s. Make an argument that this low confidence was:
   (a) a *result* of the recession, and
   (b) a *cause* of the recession.

4. During an economic boom, when output is rising, why does the rising supply of goods and services not cause the prices of them to *fall*?

5. During an economic recession, when output is depressed, why does the depressed supply of goods and services not cause prices to *rise*?

6. Suppose that widespread rumours of a recession caused people to avoid borrowing, in an attempt to protect themselves against the event. What effect would this avoidance of borrowing have on the economy?

7. Suppose that rapid inflation caused people to reduce their saving and spend more, in anticipation of higher prices in the future. How would this increased spending affect the economy?

8. Suppose the economy is in the situation shown in the graph below, near its capacity level of output.

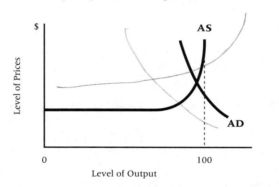

If a major increase were to occur in the price of imported oil which:

(a) reduced the level of aggregate demand by withdrawing large volumes of funds from the economy to pay for the oil, pushing the AD curve to the left, and

(b) raised production costs throughout the economy by making energy much more expensive, making it costlier to produce any given level of output, thus pushing the AS curve upward to higher levels of cost per unit,

draw the new AD and AS curves, and explain the effects of the new situation on the levels of output, employment, and prices in the economy.

9. In the graph at the top of the next page, the AS and AD curves represent the situation in 20X1, with output and prices both at levels of 100. AS_1 and AD_1 represent the situation in 20X3, two years later, when output is 120 and prices are at the same level as in 20X1.

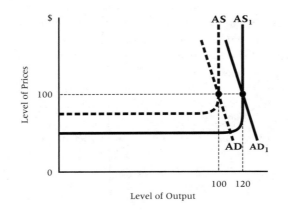

Ordinarily, such a rapid increase in aggregate demand and output would be accompanied by a significant increase in the price level. Why, in this example, has there been no increase in prices?

10. (a) At the level of aggregate demand represented by AD_1, the economy is operating at approximately _____ percent of its capacity output (potential GDP), and is in a condition of _____.

(b) AD_2 represents a(n) _____ in the level of aggregate demand that has brought the economy to approximately _____ percent of its capacity output. Describe the effect that this change in aggregate demand has on:

(i)   output and employment, and

(ii) the general level of prices,

and explain the reasons for these effects.

(c) To get the economy to 95 percent of its capacity output requires a level of aggregate demand as represented by AD_3. How does the effect of this change in aggregate demand differ from the change from AD_1 to AD_2, and why?

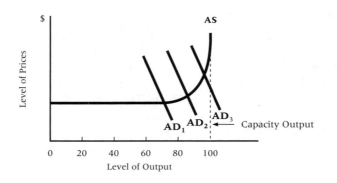

Chapter 5

Money and the Economic System

Learning Objectives

After studying this chapter, you should be able to:

1. Explain why the size of the money supply is very important to the performance of the economy.

2. State the three basic functions of money.

3. State the one characteristic that money must have, and four qualities that help to establish this characteristic.

4. State the three basic types of money in use in Canada today.

5. Write a brief summary of the different definitions of the money supply.

6. Explain how most money is created and why this process can create money to the extent that it does.

7. Given the cash reserves of a bank and its cash reserve ratio, calculate the potential amount of deposits the bank could support.

8. Explain why the banking industry is subject to a considerable degree of government regulation and influence.

In Chapter 4, we emphasized the importance of the level of *aggregate demand*, or total spending in the economy. If aggregate demand is too low, the economy will fall into a recession, while if aggregate demand outruns the economy's capacity to produce goods and services, inflation will result.

In this chapter, we examine *money* and the **money supply**, which is *the total volume of money in circulation*. The money supply is a very important factor in the performance of the economy. If there were too little money in circulation, the result would be low aggregate demand and a recession. On the other hand, an excessively large money supply would generate excess demand and inflation.

In Chapter 5, we will deal with two basic questions, What is "money"? and How is money created (or, Where does money come from)? Chapter 6 will explain why the economy fluctuates from recession to boom to inflation and back to recession again, and the role played by money and the money supply in this process.

In Chapter 7, we will examine how the government tries to keep the money supply at an appropriate size—neither too high nor too low, in order to avoid the extremes of recession and inflation.

money supply The total volume of money in circulation, defined variously as M1, M2, and M2+.

Part A: What Is "Money"?

Most basically, money is a *medium of exchange*—something that people use to *buy things*. That is, money is something that is generally accepted by people in exchange for (as payment for) goods and services.

Without money, transactions would have to be conducted by barter, which is the direct exchange of one product for another. In a barter system, a person who had an extra horse and wanted a cow would have to find another person who had a surplus cow and wanted a horse, making a direct exchange possible. Such a system is so awkward as to be unworkable, except in the most primitive economies where there are few goods for exchange, and few transactions are made. A barter system would be utterly incapable of handling the billions of daily transactions that occur in a modern economy.

Money also serves as a *standard of value*, or the yardstick by which we measure the value of a great number of diverse goods and services. If people were using a barter system instead of money, the value of each product would have to be expressed in terms of every other product for which it might be exchanged: a horse might be worth one cow, or four sheepdogs, or fifty bushels of apples, and so on. With money, the values of all items can be expressed in terms of one simple standard—the unit of currency, or the dollar. So a horse and a cow may each be worth $100, a sheepdog $25, a bushel of apples $2, and so on. Using money makes comparing the values of different goods and services easier.

Money also provides us with a *store of value*—a way to save, or store, purchasing power. Under a barter system, you must accept another good at the time you sell something; however, if you receive money, you can save it until some time in the future when you choose to spend it. Sometimes, purchasing power is stored for a very short period of time. For example, you might store enough money in a chequing account for only a few days to cover expenses until next payday. For some reasons, such as a vacation, it may be stored for longer periods of time, perhaps by making regular deposits into a savings account. And for other reasons such as retirement, purchasing power is stored for very long periods of time, in the form of various longer-term investments.

The Advantages of Money

We have seen that a barter system is an extremely awkward way of conducting transactions, whereas money is much more convenient. The person with the extra horse can sell the horse, say, for $100, then use the money to buy a cow from someone else. There is no need to find another person who has a cow and wants a horse. Clearly, then, money is a *great convenience* for people who engage in economic transactions.

However, the importance of money goes well beyond being a convenience. As we have seen, the key to a society's economic prosperity is its *productivity*, or output per worker. Generally, people will be more productive if they are *specialized* in a particular kind of work. And when people are specialized in this manner, the number of exchanges of goods and services that take place among them is tremendous, as each person produces only one product or service (or only one part of it) and buys everything else from others. By making it easy for people to exchange (buy and sell) goods and services, money makes such specialization feasible, which in turn makes possible higher levels of productivity and thus economic prosperity. So by serving as a medium of exchange, money actually contributes to our prosperity.

What Can Be Used as Money?

We have seen that the introduction of "money" into an economy can greatly benefit its people. Now we need to address the question of what people might actually *use* as "money."

The short answer to this question is that people can use *anything* as money, provided that other people are prepared to *accept* it as payment for goods and services. Different peoples, in different societies and at different times, have used as money things that seem quite strange to us, including shells, cattle, and heavy stone wheels. In prisoner of war camps in the Second World War, prisoners used cigarettes as money. These examples show that money can be *anything that people agree to use* and accept as a medium of exchange.

The one essential quality that something must have in order to function as money is *acceptability*: people must be prepared to accept it in exchange for goods and services. Certain characteristics help to make an item acceptable as money, including *scarcity* (which ensures value), *durability* (money that rots in your pocket is less than ideal), *portability* (so that you can carry it around with you), and *divisibility* (for making change when necessary). However, as some of the above examples show, not all these characteristics are essential as long as people will accept the item as money—neither heavy stone wheels nor cattle nor cigarettes are particularly portable, durable, and divisible, yet they have been used as money because people agreed to *accept* them as money.

The Evolution of Money

Most major currencies have developed in a similar manner, originating with precious metals and evolving into the more sophisticated forms of money that we use today.

Precious Metals

Many currency systems originated with gold or silver. Because they are naturally scarce, gold and silver have a naturally high value, which is sometimes referred to as *intrinsic value*, meaning that people intuitively associate such metals with value. It was this value of the precious metal itself that gave the earliest forms of money their acceptability—someone who was asked to accept "money" in exchange for something of real value (say, a horse) had to be confident that the money was as valuable as the horse. In the early days of money, gold and silver provided the necessary confidence.

Gold has always played a special role in people's perceptions of "value," and therefore in monetary systems. Gold's most basic quality is, of course, its *scarcity*—all of the gold ever mined in the entire world could be contained in a single cube with edges less than 20 metres long. In addition, gold is associated with *permanence*—gold is a very stable metal that never tarnishes or corrodes. The gold recovered from a sunken Spanish galleon of the 1500s still shines like new.

At first, pieces of gold and silver of varying sizes were used as money, making it necessary for them to be weighed when used in transactions. Later, gold and silver were made into coins of standard weights and values, which was more convenient.

In England, Henry VIII and his successor tampered with the currency so seriously that by 1551, one penny contained only one-sixth of the silver that it had contained in 1520.

Gold's scarcity made it very acceptable as money, but it also led to another problem—there was too little gold to provide the growing money supply that was needed as economies grew. This problem was solved (at least in part) by *debasement*—the addition of other or base metals to molten gold or silver. A king, needing money to finance a war or some other endeavour, would recall all of the currency, which consisted of pure gold coins. These would be melted down and re-minted into new coins. During the melting and minting, however, other metals would be added to the gold, so that *more* new coins could be minted. Then, all the pure gold coins that had been taken out of circulation could be replaced with "debased" coins that would be returned to the people who had owned them, *and* there would be surplus coins that the king could keep to pay for his war—a convenient, if not totally straightforward, way of raising revenues for the royal treasury.

The debasement of coinage in this way presents an interesting problem—while the *face value* of each coin remains the same, it contains *less gold* and has lost some of its intrinsic value. What will it now be worth? How much will it buy? The answers to these questions depend on whether people *accept* the coins at their face value in exchange for goods and services. If they do, the new coins will be worth their face value, and they will function as money just as well as the pure gold coins did, because people have faith that they can spend the coinage at its face value. This is the case with our coinage today: the metallic content of the coins that we use is far less than their face value, but they are accepted at their face value in exchange for goods and services. Rather than *possessing* value, they are *representative* of value.

Paper Bills (Bank Notes)

The use of paper bills (bank notes) as money originated with goldsmiths, who performed some of the earliest banking functions. The goldsmith would provide safekeeping facilities for people who would deposit their money (gold) with him. In return, the goldsmith would issue a receipt, or *bank note*, for the gold, as illustrated in Figure 5-1.

FIGURE 5-1 An Early Bank Note

> J.R. Goldsmith, Banker
> will pay to Fred Flintstone
> on demand
> Twenty Dollars ($20.00)
> in gold
> (Signed)
>
> *JR Goldsmith*
> J.R. Goldsmith

At first, when people wanted to buy things, they would return the receipt to the goldsmith/banker and withdraw their gold in order to make the purchase. However, as they became more familiar with the bank notes, they found it much more convenient simply to use the bank notes for buying goods and services—that is, to use these pieces of paper (bills) as money. Originally, a receipt, or bank note, was made out in the name of the depositor, who would then have to sign the note over to the person to whom it was being given. Later, however, a goldsmith or a banker would make the note payable "to the bearer" (that is, anyone who held the note). This form was more convenient for bills that would be used as money and exchanged from person to person.

In this way, paper bills, issued by private banks, came to be used as money. These paper bills were special, however, because they involved a *promise to pay* gold to the holder of the notes. It was because of the *gold backing* of bank notes that people would accept these paper bills as money—they were, as the saying went, "as good as gold." But as we will see later in this chapter, the gold backing did *not* mean that there was $1 of gold for *every* $1 of bank notes in circulation.

In 1996, the $2 bill was replaced by the $2 coin known as the "toonie" ("twonie"?) . The $2 coin cost $0.16 to make compared with $0.06 for the $2 bill; however, the coin's lifespan was 20 years as compared with only one year for the bill. At the time the $2 bills began to be phased out, there were about 245 million of them in circulation.

www.bankofcanada.ca

Later, when governments undertook to regulate currency more systematically, bank notes issued by private banks were replaced by bank notes issued by the government or, more correctly, by government agencies known as *central banks*. Originally, many countries maintained gold backing for the bank notes issued by their central banks in order to ensure the acceptability of their currency.

As time passed, however, this practice became unnecessary, as people became completely confident in the paper bills. As well, gold backing of bank notes became impossible as the volume of money needed by growing economies far outgrew the available stock of gold. Today, there is no gold backing behind the bank notes issued by Canada's central bank, the Bank of Canada.

Bank notes no longer involve a promise to pay but are instead *fiat money*, meaning that the government has simply *declared* them to be "legal tender," so that they must be accepted as payment for debts. This fact was officially recognized in the bank note issue of 1971: the new notes issued no longer said "Will pay to the bearer on demand," but rather simply declared "This note is legal tender."

Bank Deposits (Book Entries)

In many cases, people use *cheques* to make payments. Are cheques "money"? At first glance, the answer would appear to be yes. Money is used to buy things, and people do buy things with cheques.

In actual fact, however, cheques are not themselves "money." If cheques were money, everyone would be able to write their own money without limit. Also, the cheque shown in Figure 5-2 will not stay in Mr. Framish's possession—it will be returned by the bank to Ms. Stuk, for her records. Furthermore, the cheque is valueless if there are not sufficient funds in the account of the cheque writer (which one might suspect to be possible in the case of a cheque writer named "U. R. Stuk"). So the cheque itself is not money.

If you read the cheque carefully, you will see that it is really simply a *letter to the bank*, instructing the bank to pay $25 to Mr. Framish. Figure 5-3 illustrates this fact by showing the cheque rewritten in the form of a letter.

What, then, is the actual "money" to be paid to Mr. Framish? He may cash the cheque, in which case he receives bank notes and coins, which we have already discussed. The more interesting case is that he might deposit it into his own account—what does he receive then? He will receive a *deposit to his bank account*, in the form of *book entries* on the bank's records. When Mr. Framish deposits the cheque, the book entry in his account will be

FIGURE 5-2 A Typical Cheque

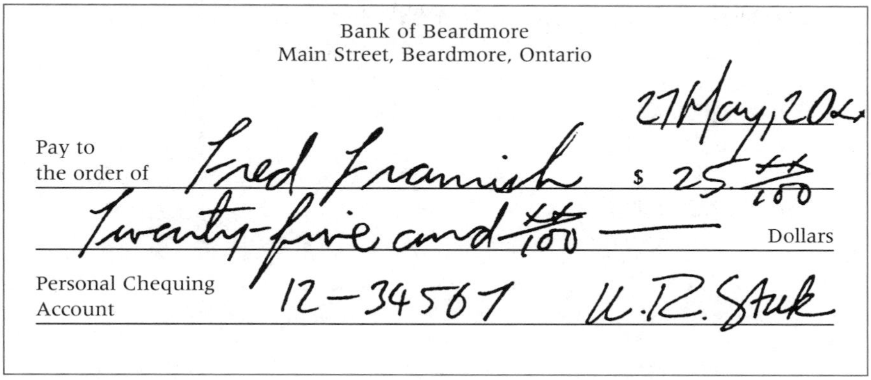

Bank of Beardmore
Main Street, Beardmore, Ontario

27 May, 20__

Pay to
the order of   *Fred Framish* $ *25 __*

Twenty-five and __ ——————— Dollars

Personal Chequing
Account   *12-34567*   *U.R. Stuk*

FIGURE 5-3 A Cheque is Really a Letter

Bank of Beardmore   May 27, 20XX
Main Street
Beardmore, Ontario

Dear Banker:
Please pay Mr. Framish $25 of mine. You will
find it in my account #12-34567.

Thank you,

U.R. Stuk

U.R. Stuk

increased by $25 and the book entry in Ms. Stuk's account will be reduced by $25. There is no cash involved in this transaction at all—just book entries.

Are these book entries in the bank's records "money" to Mr. Framish? This question can be answered simply by asking if he can *spend* them. Of course he can, by writing cheques on them, as Ms. Stuk did. So these bank deposits (book entries) are "money," and banks can transfer this money between people's accounts as instructed by cheques.

Credit cards, like cheques, are used to make purchases, but are not in themselves money. Credit cards give the cardholder access to *instant credit* (or instant loans) for the purchase of goods and services. However, when people *actually pay* their credit card accounts, they almost always do so with bank-deposit money.

Some people think that book entries represent cash deposits (bills and coins) and that bank deposits are not therefore a separate form of money. In fact, this is not true—total bank deposits (book entries) *far exceed* the total amount of bank notes and coins in the economy. Also, these book entries constitute a separate and very important form of money, through which more than 90 percent of the volume of transactions are made. For instance, Sara's cheque for a new cell phone is covered by her deposit of a paycheque written on her employer's account, into which have been deposited other cheques from customers, written on accounts into which people have deposited their paycheques, and so on. In none of these transactions is cash used. In Part B, we will examine the process by which these deposits are actually created.

Electronic Banking

The original (and traditional) way of transferring book-entry money between accounts has been through cheques, as described above. However, modern computer and communications technology has provided more convenient alternatives.

Telephone banking is one of the most-used alternatives. From home, a customer can check account balances, transfer funds between accounts, make deposits and withdrawals, pay bills, apply for a loan or mortgage, purchase a guaranteed investment certificate, and so on, 24 hours per day. With a personal computer linked to the bank through the internet, a customer can do all of these transactions in addition to buying stocks and creating financial reports for small businesses and professionals.

The other major innovation has been *direct payment (direct debit) cards* such as Interac. With a debit card, a merchant can be paid by electronically withdrawing the money from a customer's account at the point of purchase. In addition, Interac's CashBack program allows customers to obtain cash from participating merchants with high cash balances, such as supermarkets and liquor stores. Canadians are the world's biggest users of electronic banking services.

Some Things That Are Not Money

To improve our understanding of what money *is*, we will take a quick look at some things that are *not* money, and why they are not money.

Stocks (corporate shares) and bonds are transferable financial securities, but they are not money because they are not used as a medium of exchange. Because their value fluctuates, using stocks and bonds as money is too inconvenient.

Canada Savings Bonds do not fluctuate in value; they can always be cashed in for their face value (plus the interest that has built up to the time they are cashed). However, Canada Savings Bonds are not legally transferable from one person to another, so they cannot be used as money. Financial assets such as stocks and bonds are not money: they can be converted into money by simply selling them, but the same thing can be done with any asset, even a house or a car. Strictly speaking, *non-chequing bank deposits* (such as savings accounts) are not money, because they cannot be transferred either electronically or to someone else to pay for something. Of course, to use these deposits as money, the funds in this type of account could easily be *transferred*

You DECIDE

ELECTRONIC CASH?

The banks would like to extend the use of electronic banking in ways that *replace cash*. Cash is still the main method of payment for the many small transactions that people make daily; however, for banks, the handling of cash is a costly, labour-intensive function. While automated teller machines (ATMs) reduce the banks' costs by *dispensing* cash, there is also interest in using computer technology to *replace* cash.

This interest has taken the form of experiments with "electronic cash," using what are sometimes called "stored value cards." A stored value card is plastic, with a computer chip onto which cardholders can download "cash" from their accounts at an ATM or a specially-equipped telephone. The cardholder could then use the card for small purchases such as convenience store purchases, from any business or person with the required computer terminal. With each purchase, the balance of "cash" stored on the card would decrease, just as would the cash in one's pocket or purse.

Some people foresee the final step in the evolution of money as the "cashless society," in which there would be no cash whatsoever, and all transactions would be handled electronically. Each person would have a card for access to his/her accounts, and would use this card for any purchase.

QUESTIONS

1. Would you use an "electronic cash" card? Why or why not?
2. Would you expect such cards to be used widely by the public? Why or why not?
3. Some people think that the "cashless society" is *inevitable*, while others think it is *impossible*. Who do you think is right? Why?

into an account from which they could be transferred by cheque or electronically. Similarly, *term deposits* (which the depositor has agreed to leave on deposit for longer periods, such as from one to five years) can be readily converted into chequable deposits, or money. These non-chequable deposits, which are for obvious reasons known as "near money," considerably complicate our attempts to define and measure Canada's money supply.

Money in Canada Today

Basically, there are three forms of "money" in Canada today:

- coins
- bank notes
- deposits (book entries)

While many people associate the word "money" with coins and bank notes, these forms of money are only a small proportion of the total amount of money in circulation, or the money supply. Depending on the types of deposits counted, only about 5 to 8 percent of Canada's money supply consists of coins and bank notes, and 92 to 95 percent is deposits (book entries) of various sorts.

Canada's Money Supply Defined and Measured

In defining and measuring the money supply, we must remember that our main concern is that *the size of the money supply* is closely related to *the level of aggregate demand*, which is a major factor in the performance of the economy. The difficulty is that the vast majority of the money supply consists of bank deposits, and there are many different types of these.

At the one extreme are *demand deposits* (current chequing accounts), which will almost certainly be spent very soon, adding to aggregate demand. At the other extreme are *term deposits*, many of which contain long-term savings that are unlikely to be spent soon—some of these, in fact, will be part of people's savings for retirement. Between these extremes lie a variety of types of accounts with different probabilities of being spent soon. If we are trying to develop a definition of "money" that relates closely to the level of aggregate demand, which types of bank deposits should we include, and which should be excluded?

Table 5-1 shows three different measures of Canada's money supply: M1, M2, and M2+. **M1** is the narrowest definition of money, including only funds that are very likely to be spent very soon—*currency outside the banks* (that is, bank notes and coins in circulation) plus *demand deposits* (current chequing accounts). M1 does not include any accounts that pay interest.

Until 1982, M1 was used as the "official" measure of Canada's money supply, mainly on the grounds that all of the funds in it (cash and chequing accounts) were likely to be spent quite soon, adding to aggregate demand. But as Canadians increasingly used other types of accounts (especially daily interest chequing/savings accounts) for paying regular expenses, M1 failed to include more and more funds that should be counted as money, so its use as the "official" definition of the money supply was discontinued.

M1 The narrowest definition of the money supply, including only currency (bank notes and coins) outside the banks plus demand deposits (current chequing account deposits).

www.statcan.ca/english/
Pgdb/econ07.htm

TABLE 5-1 Canada's Money Supply, June 2002

	Billions of Dollars
Currency Outside Banks	$ 38.0
Demand Deposits	95.1
Total: M1	133.1
Personal Savings Deposits and Non-Personal Notice Deposits	411.6
Total: M2	544.7
Deposits at Trust and Mortgage Loan Companies, Credit Unions and Caisses Populaires and Money Market Mutual Funds, etc.	237.0
Total: M2 +	781.7

Source: Bank of Canada, adapted from *Banking and Financial Statistics,* September 2002.

Since dropping M1 as the official definition of the money supply, Canada's monetary authorities considered alternative measures of the money supply, two of which are shown in Table 5-1. **M2** includes *personal savings deposits* (and thus the daily interest accounts that had acquired such popularity) as well as *non-personal notice accounts* that contain the interest-earning savings deposits of some businesses and other organizations that are often directly connected to chequing accounts to facilitate the spending of such funds. As Table 5-1 shows, these accounts, together with daily interest accounts, contain a large volume of funds, making M2 much larger than M1.

M2 A wider definition of the money supply, including M1 plus personal savings deposits plus non-personal notice deposits.

However, many Canadians have deposits at financial institutions other than chartered banks. These funds are included in **M2+**, a more recent addition to the measures of the money supply. M2+ adds to M2 deposits at trust and mortgage loan companies and credit unions and caisses populaires. In addition, M2+ includes money market mutual funds, which in the 1990s increased rapidly in popularity and size.[1]

M2+ A wider definition of the money supply, including M2 plus deposits at trust and mortgage loan companies, credit unions, and caisses populaires.

The result of these additions is a still larger measure of the money supply—as Table 5-1 shows, M2+ is considerably larger than M2. In addition, there are still other measures of the money supply, such as M3, which is M2 *plus* non-personal fixed-term deposits *plus* foreign currency deposits of residents banked in Canada.

The problem is that as we move farther away from the narrow definition M1, we are including more funds in our definition, but also including more funds that are likely to be *saved* rather than *spent*, at least in the short run. Since a key reason for keeping statistics on the money supply is that the money supply is an important factor in the level of aggregate demand, the real question is which measure of the money supply moves most closely with the level of total spending on goods and services in the economy. M2 and M2+ appear to best suit this purpose: according to Canada's monetary authority, the Bank of Canada, "Among the regularly published aggregates, M2 and M2+ appear to track total spending best over the longer run." However, none of these measures of the money supply is linked sufficiently closely to the level of aggregate demand to have been adopted as *the* official measure of the money supply. As a result, while the money supply is very significant, it is difficult to measure its *actual size*. Nonetheless, by tracking these various measures of the money supply, we can estimate the extent of *changes* in the money supply.

The Acceptability and Value of Money in Canada

As we have seen, the vast majority of Canada's money supply is in the form of bank deposits—only a small proportion consists of coins and bank notes.

---

[1] Money market mutual funds allow smaller investors to "pool" their funds in order to invest in short-term securities such as Treasury Bills, commercial paper, and so on. They offer safety, liquidity, and a reasonable return on short-term funds. Money market mutual funds are available through banks and other investment institutions, which charge a fee for the purchase of them.

Until the 1930s, when a uniform national currency was established, Canada's currency consisted of a variety of coins and notes issued by various private banks.

We have also seen that Canada's money supply is not backed by gold—it functions as money because people have faith in it. People accept money in exchange for goods and services because they believe that can use the money to buy other goods and services of equivalent value. Ultimately, this confidence in money is really confidence in the monetary authority of the country—that it will not issue an excessive amount of money, causing inflation that will reduce the value of money too rapidly. This monetary authority is the Bank of Canada, which is an agency of the federal government and which will be discussed in Chapter 7.

While faith is what gives money its acceptability, the *actual value* of a dollar—what it is worth—depends on its *purchasing power*, or how much it will buy. The purchasing power of the dollar, in turn, depends on the general level of the prices of goods and services. If prices in general rise due to inflation, the value of the dollar will fall because its purchasing power will be reduced.[2]

Conversely, if the prices in general were to fall, the value of the dollar would rise. So the actual value of the dollar is inversely related to the general level of prices—the higher the level of prices, the lower the value of the dollar.

Part B: How Money Is Created

Where does all the money listed in Table 5-1 *come from*? How is it *created*? Coins are manufactured (minted) and bank notes are printed, under close government supervision. But coins and paper bills are a very small proportion of the money supply. Of much greater importance and interest is the vast majority of the money supply that consists of *bank deposits*. Where do these come from? How are they created? These bank deposits are in fact *created by the banking system, when it makes loans*. This process is more complicated, and it requires some explanation.

The Operation of Early Banks

To illustrate the process by which the banking system creates money, we will use the earliest banks, operating in a simple situation in which money consisted only of gold coins and bank notes (paper bills) issued by privately owned banks—in this economy, book entries were not yet used as money.

These early banks accepted deposits of gold coins, and issued receipts, in the form of bank notes. As we have seen, people eventually used the bank notes instead of gold coins for transactions. So relatively few holders of bank notes would redeem them for coinage at the banks. And when gold coins were withdrawn and spent, the recipients would usually deposit them back

---

[2] The value of the dollar referred to here is its value in use *inside Canada*, when used to buy goods and services. The *international value* of the Canadian dollar—its value in terms of other nations' currencies—is a different matter, which will be covered in Chapter 10.

into the banks.

So not much coinage would be withdrawn from the banks, and withdrawals of coinage would tend be offset by deposits of coinage. These two facts enabled the banks to operate quite smoothly with a relatively *small amount of coins backing up a much larger amount of bank notes*. As an illustration, a bank might receive deposits of $100 000 of gold coin, issue $100 000 of bank notes, but only need $10 000 of gold coins on hand to cover withdrawals of coinage.

But in such a bank, there would be considerable amounts of gold coins sitting around doing nothing—in our example, *$90 000* of idle gold coins. At some point, these early bankers realized that they could use these "reserves" of coinage to *make loans*, and earn interest income. While borrowers could take loans in the form of coins, they would generally take *bank notes* instead, such as the bank note shown in Figure 5-4, which were the most common form of money.

FIGURE 5-4 A Typical Early Bank Note

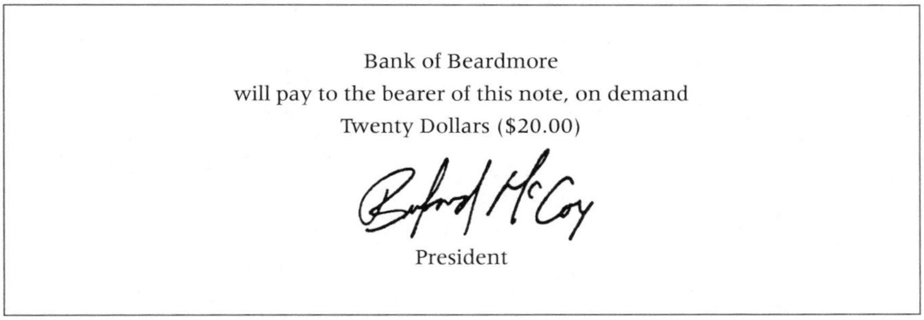

Bank of Beardmore
will pay to the bearer of this note, on demand
Twenty Dollars ($20.00)

Buford McCoy
President

Bank Loans Create Money

The key question is, How much could the bank in our example lend out? The answer lies in the arithmetic of our earlier example, in which $10 000 of gold coins in the bank "covered" $100 000 of bank notes in circulation, meaning that the $90 000 of "idle" gold coins would be able to "cover" *$900 000* of bank notes, which would be put into circulation when the bank made loans.

So when making loans, banks could put into circulation *far more* bank notes than the amount of coinage, or cash, that the banks had on hand to "back" their bank notes. And in doing so, the banking system *increased* the volume of bank-note money in circulation—i.e., the banking system *created money* by making loans.

Cash Reserves and the Cash Reserve Ratio

How many bank notes could a bank put into circulation through loans on the basis of a given level of gold coins? Obviously, the process is not unlimited: if

cash reserves That
amount of cash kept on
hand by a bank to cover
day-to-day withdrawals
of cash.

cash reserve ratio The
percentage of total
deposits that a bank
keeps as cash reserves.

a bank made *too many* loans and issued *too many* notes in this way, it would have so many notes in circulation that there would be a high risk that too many note-holders would redeem their notes for gold coins at one time, causing the bank to run out of gold coins and collapse. (It could also prove personally dangerous for the banker.) While this does not mean that *every one* of its notes must be backed by gold coins, the bank must have the gold coins to back *a certain percentage* of its notes, to ensure that it is able to meet withdrawals of coinage by its customers. The coinage kept on hand to cover withdrawals is called the **cash reserves** of a bank. The percentage of its bank notes outstanding kept as cash reserves is called the bank's **cash reserve ratio**. In our example, the bank had $100 000 of bank notes in circulation, backed by cash reserves of $10 000, so the cash reserve ratio would be 10 percent ($10 000 divided by $100 000). Looked at differently, on the basis of $10 000 of cash reserves, the banking system has expanded the money supply to $100 000, creating money in the process of making loans, as shown in Figure 5-5.

FIGURE 5-5 Creation of Money by Early Banks

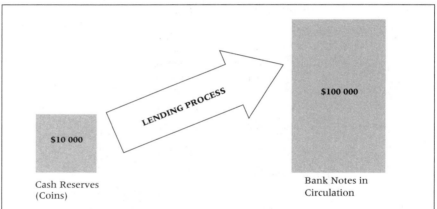

$10 000

Cash Reserves
(Coins)

$100 000

Bank Notes in
Circulation

LENDING PROCESS

The Creation of Money by a Modern Banking System

In a modern banking system, the nature of money is more sophisticated than in our previous example. Bank notes are no longer issued by the banks, but rather by the government, and, as we have seen, over 90 percent of the money supply consists of bank deposits, or book entries, which are transferred between accounts by cheques or electronically. These bank deposits, however, are created in essentially the same way as bank notes were created by the early banks: through the process of making loans. When a modern bank makes a loan, the borrower does not usually get cash (bank notes or coins). Instead, the bank simply increases the balance in the borrower's account, thus giving the borrower more money (book entries) to spend. Using a small amount of cash (bank notes plus coins) as reserves, a modern banking system is able to create a large amount of money (bank deposits), as illustrated in Figure 5-6. In this way, the banking system can create a large volume of money on the basis of a small volume of cash reserves.

FIGURE 5-6 Creation of Money by a Modern Banking System

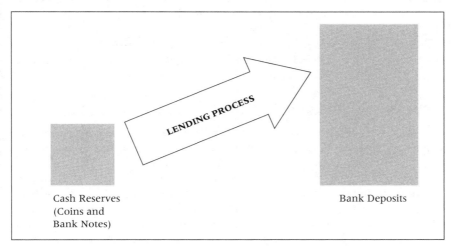

Cash Reserves
(Coins and
Bank Notes)

Bank Deposits

A Formula for Calculating the Creation of Money

How much money can the banking system create in this way? Money creation depends on two factors:

* the volume of *cash reserves* that the banks have, and
* the *cash reserve ratio* that they maintain.

The extent to which the banking system can create money can be calculated from the following formula:

$$\text{Potential Total Deposits} = \frac{\text{Cash Reserves}}{\text{Cash Reserve Ratio}}$$

So, if the banking system had cash reserves of $18 billion and a cash reserve ratio of 3 percent, total deposits could be as large as:

$$\frac{\$18 \text{ billion}}{0.03} = \$600 \text{ billion}$$

Note that $600 billion represents *potential* total deposits: it is not certain that total deposits actually will *reach* $600 billion. In order for the potential to be reached, the banks would have to make every loan that is mathematically possible—they must carry no "excess cash reserves" over and above the 3-percent ratio. Since we cannot know whether this will in fact happen, we must remember that our formula only indicates the *potential* amount of money that can be created by the banking system on the basis of a given amount of cash reserves and a given cash reserve ratio.

The Cash Reserve Ratio and the Money-Creating Process

From our formula, it can be seen that the size of the cash reserve ratio has a large impact on the amount of money that the banking system can create. If the cash reserve ratio had been only 2 percent, total deposits (and therefore the money supply) could have reached $900 billion ($18 billion divided by 0.02)—50 percent larger.

The reason for this relationship is simple: because the banks have to keep *less* cash reserves on hand, they are able to lend *more* money, so that total deposits can rise by more, creating more money.

How Can So Little Cash Back Up So Many Deposits?

How is it possible for banks to operate safely with so little cash to back up their deposits? We have already seen the answer to this question, but it is worth reviewing here. First, in most transactions—over 90 percent by volume—funds are transferred electronically or by cheques so that no cash needs to be taken out of the bank; all that is needed are changes in book entries. This reduces tremendously the need for cash, not only on the part of the public but also on the part of the banks. Second, while people and businesses do make cash withdrawals, they also make cash deposits, and there is a strong tendency for cash deposits to offset cash withdrawals. People take out some cash every payday, and as they spend it over the next two weeks, the stores that receive it deposit it back into the banks.

When a bank has a large number of depositors, it can be confident that while some depositors will be withdrawing cash from the bank at any given time, others will be making deposits of cash that will offset those withdrawals, maintaining the bank's cash on hand.

In one sense, there is an incentive for banks to keep a low level of cash reserves, because the less cash reserves a bank keeps, the more loans it can make, increasing its interest income. On the other hand, banks must not let their reserves get too low because, ultimately, banks rely upon the confidence of their depositors. The worst thing that can happen to a bank is for its depositors to lose confidence in it. The result can be what is known as a "run" on the bank, with many depositors trying to withdraw their deposits in cash at once. In these circumstances, any bank would quickly run out of cash, and would "fail," a polite term for a bank bankruptcy. So there is also an incentive for banks to be sure to keep sufficient cash on hand to meet depositors' needs and maintain their confidence.

Banks must therefore strike a balance between lower cash reserves for interest income and higher cash reserves for safety. Statisticians have estimated that a large bank can operate quite safely with reserves of about 2 percent of its deposits.

Deposit Insurance

All banks are required by law to be members of the *Canada Deposit Insurance Corporation* (CDIC), which provides insurance on depositors' deposits of up to

www.cdic.ca

$60 000 per person per institution.[3] The CDIC is financed by contributions by member institutions that are based on the size of their insured deposits.

Most people see the CDIC's role as compensating depositors in the event that their bank fails, as the CDIC has indeed done on several occasions (see the "In the News" box on p. 118). More basically, though, deposit

---

YOU DECIDE

CASH IN CIRCULATION

The following graph shows currency (bank notes and coins) in circulation as a percentage of GDP. For instance, during most of the 1960s, for every $100 of GDP that was bought, there was about $3.80 to $4.00 of bank notes and coins in circulation.

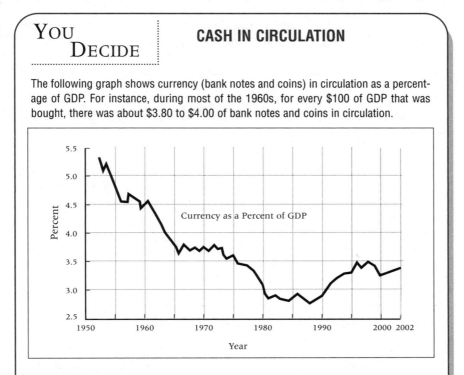

Source: Bank of Canada, adapted from Bank of Canada *Review* and *Banking and Financial Statistics*.

Questions

1. From 1953 to 1990, currency in circulation declined steadily from 5.4 percent of GDP to 2.8 percent of GDP. What would likely account for this trend?

2. This long-term decline reversed itself abruptly in 1991, after which currency in circulation increased sharply to 3.3 percent of GDP, an increase of roughly $3.5 billion in the amount of cash carried by Canadians. What could explain this sudden and sharp reversal of the 37-year trend?

3. After 1995, cash in circulation stabilized at about 3.3 to 3.5 percent of GDP. What might be the significance of this trend?

---

[3] This coverage can be expanded in certain ways. For instance, a Registered Retirement Savings Plan is considered a separate legal "person," as is a joint account. In addition, several financial institutions have set up subsidiary companies that also have CDIC memberships, allowing depositors to double their CDIC coverage by placing deposits with both the parent company and the subsidiary.

insurance is intended to help *prevent* financial institutions from failing, and so keep the financial system stable. The insurance of deposits (or, more properly, the confidence on the part of the public that their deposits are insured) is meant to prevent depositors from panicking and starting a ruinous run on a bank. As we saw earlier, even the soundest bank could not withstand a run because it has deposits far in excess of its cash reserves.

Another safeguard in addition to deposit insurance is that the loans and investments of banks are subject to inspection by audit teams of the Inspector General of Banks. The goal of this inspection process is to ensure that depositors' funds are being invested in an appropriately secure manner.

The Banking System, the Money Supply, and the Economy

We have seen how the banking system, by increasing its lending activities, can cause the nation's money supply to increase. On the other hand, if the banking system were to curtail its lending, the money supply would decrease. As outstanding loans were repaid, a decline in deposits, not offset by new deposit-creating loans, would occur.

This ability of the banking system to create (and destroy) money can greatly affect the money supply and therefore the level of aggregate demand

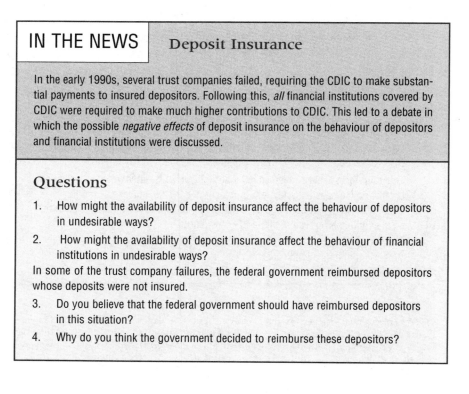

IN THE NEWS   Deposit Insurance

In the early 1990s, several trust companies failed, requiring the CDIC to make substantial payments to insured depositors. Following this, *all* financial institutions covered by CDIC were required to make much higher contributions to CDIC. This led to a debate in which the possible *negative effects* of deposit insurance on the behaviour of depositors and financial institutions were discussed.

Questions

1. How might the availability of deposit insurance affect the behaviour of depositors in undesirable ways?

2. How might the availability of deposit insurance affect the behaviour of financial institutions in undesirable ways?

In some of the trust company failures, the federal government reimbursed depositors whose deposits were not insured.

3. Do you believe that the federal government should have reimbursed depositors in this situation?

4. Why do you think the government decided to reimburse these depositors?

in the economy. Figure 5-7 summarizes how bank lending can affect aggregate demand, and thus output, employment/unemployment, and the rate of inflation.

FIGURE 5-7 The Banking System and the Economy

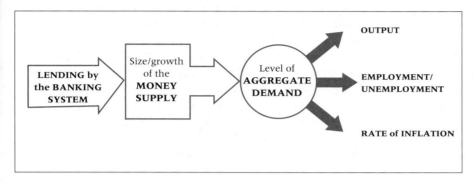

The economy requires an appropriate money supply in order to generate high levels of output and employment without excessive inflation. Too small a money supply can slow down spending and economic activity to the point of causing a *recession*, while if too much money is created, excessive demand will generate a problem of *inflation*.

Because the banking system's lending activities can have such strong effects upon the country's economy, the banking industry is subject to an unusual degree of government regulation and influence, as we will see in Chapter 7.

Chapter Summary

1. The size of the money supply is vitally important to the performance of a nation's economy, since too little money in circulation will cause a recession and too much will cause inflation. (L.O. 1)

2. Money serves three economic functions: as a medium of exchange, a standard of value, and a store of value. (L.O. 2)

3. The one characteristic that money must have is acceptability; other characteristics that help make an item acceptable as money are scarcity, portability, durability, and divisibility. (L.O. 3)

4. Money has evolved over the years, from precious metals long ago to electronically stored and transferred book entries today. The forms of money in use in Canada today are coins, bank notes, and bank deposits (book entries). (L.O. 4)

5. There are various definitions of the money supply, ranging from narrow ones such as M1, which includes only currency plus chequable bank deposits, to wider definitions such as M2 and M2+, which include savings deposits. (L.O. 5)

6. The bank deposits that represent over 90 percent of the money supply are created through the lending activities of the banking system. (L.O. 6)

7. The process of money creation by the banking system is made possible by the fact that banks can operate successfully with cash reserves that represent only a small proportion of their total deposits, which in turn makes it possible to build a large volume of deposits on the basis of relatively small cash reserves. (L.O. 6)

8. The potential level of total deposits, or money, that can be created through the lending activities of the banks is equal to the banks' cash reserves divided by their cash reserve ratio. (L.O. 7)

9. Since the banking system's operations can increase or reduce the nation's money supply, they have a strong influence on the performance of the economy and are therefore subject to various government regulations. (L.O. 8)

Questions

1. The text discusses barter as an antiquated system of exchange. However, in recent years there has been an *increase* in barter transactions in Canada. What could explain this increase?

2. Recent experience has been that automated teller machines were being used extensively by the public for cash *withdrawals*, but relatively little for *deposits*. What could explain this apparent contradiction? Have the banks been successful in overcoming it?

3. An interesting side effect of the growing use of direct debit cards is that more merchants have been refusing to take cheques. Why would this be the case?

4. What effect would a period of rapid inflation likely have on the role of money as a store of value, and on people's attitudes toward money generally? Why?

5. From the data below, calculate:
   (a) M1
   (b) M2
   (c) M2+

Personal savings deposits	$ 45 billion
Deposits at trust and mortgage loan companies	60
Demand deposits	12
Non-personal notice deposits	35
Deposits at credit unions and caisses populaires and money market mutual funds, etc.	10
Currency outside the banks	10

Chapter 6

Booms, Recessions, and Inflation

Learning Objectives

After studying this chapter, you should be able to:

1. Explain why each of the following occurs, and how it contributes to the problem of business cycles:
    (a) fluctuations in investment spending,
    (b) the multiplier effect,
    (c) the accelerator effect, and
    (d) fluctuations in exports.

2. Summarize the major economic forces that lead to each phase of the business cycle, namely,
    (a) the recovery phase,
    (b) the expansion (boom) phase,
    (c) the inflation phase,
    (d) the peak, at which an economic downturn begins, and
    (e) the recession phase.

3. Describe the two major techniques used for economic forecasting.

Since 1950, the Canadian economy has generally grown quite strongly, with real GDP increasing at an average annual rate of over 4 percent. However, this growth has been far from steady. During economic booms, output and employment have increased more rapidly, while in recessions output and employment have actually *decreased*. In fact, a "recession" is defined as two consecutive quarters of shrinking real GDP (a quarter is a three-month period).

The most infamous economic downturn was, of course, the Great Depression of the 1930s. Since then, there have been several recessions: in 1951, in 1953–54, in 1957–58, in 1960–61, in 1970, in 1974–75, in 1981–82, and in 1990–92. Most of these have been relatively mild and brief; however, the recessions of the early 1980s and early 1990s, which can be seen in Figure 6-1, were the two most severe since the Great Depression. The 1981–82 recession brought the sharpest decline in output and the highest unemployment rate since the 1930s, while the recession of the early 1990s was noteworthy for its long duration.

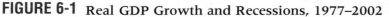

www.statcan.ca/english/
pgdb/econ05.htm

FIGURE 6-1   Real GDP Growth and Recessions, 1977–2002

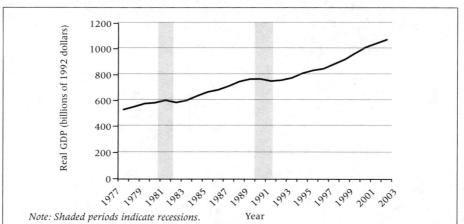

Note: Shaded periods indicate recessions.

Source: Statistics Canada, adapted from *National Income and Expenditure Accounts*, Catalogue 13-001, 2002.

All recessions that have occurred since the Great Depression of the 1930s are mild by comparison to it. During the 1930s, real GDP shrank by 30 percent, the unemployment rate soared from 3 percent to over 20 percent, and real GDP did not recover to its 1929 level for ten years. By comparison, the recession of the early 1990s lasted for less than two years, during which real GDP fell by 2.1 percent and the unemployment rate rose from 7.5 percent to a peak of 11.4 percent.

And, of course, whenever the economy slips into a recession, the unemployment rate increases, partly because some people are laid off and partly because there are not enough new jobs for those who are entering the labour force. Figure 6-2 shows the fluctuations in the unemployment rate over the years, with the Great Depression of the 1930s included for comparison.

www.statcan.ca/english/
Pgdb/econ10.htm

FIGURE 6-2 **Percentage of Labour Force Unemployed, 1926–2002**

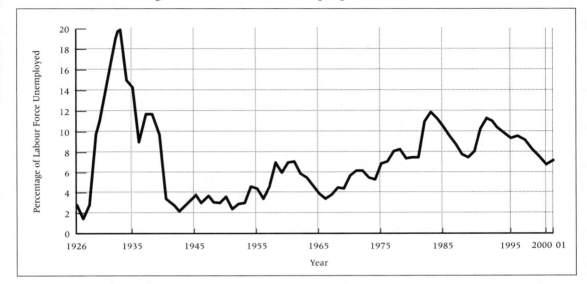

Source: Statistics Canada, adapted from *Historical Labour Force Statistics*, Catalogue 71-201, March 2001.

Phases of the Business Cycle

The term **business cycle** describes the fluctuations of the economy between boom and recession. Figure 6-3 portrays a typical business cycle, with its phases labelled. In the *contraction* phase (commonly known as a recession), output and employment fall, bottoming out in a *trough* when economic activity is at its slowest. This phase is followed by the *recovery* phase, during which economic growth begins to resume. Next comes the *expansion* phase (also known as a "boom"), which usually involves more rapid increases in output and employment as economic conditions improve. This trend continues until the *peak* (which may involve increasingly rapid inflation) is reached, after which the economy goes into a downturn and the cycle repeats itself. Since the Second World War, recessions have occurred, on average, every seven or eight years; however, the period between recessions has varied from one and one-half years to more than twelve years. So, while business cycles tend to recur *periodically*, they do not do so in a regular and predictable manner.

Our economic system is successful in many respects, but its tendency toward periodic recessions with high unemployment has been one of its traditional weaknesses. This fact makes it important for us to try to understand why business cycles occur, so that we can try to take steps to reduce their severity.

business cycle The fluctuation of the economy between booms and recessions.

"We've had expansions last anywhere from one year to 14 years—there's nothing deterministic about these things."

Philip Cross, Statistics Canada

FIGURE 6-3 A Typical Business Cycle

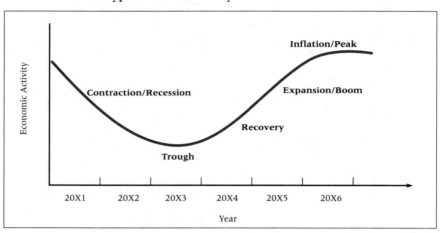

Theories of Business Cycles

Attempts to explain business cycles have brought forward a variety of theories based on various factors that can affect economic activity. Long ago, when gold was used as money, the discovery of *new gold mines* boosted the economy by increasing the money supply. Historically, *wars* have caused high levels of government spending that generated boom-like conditions with high levels of economic activity and low unemployment, although the military output produced did not add to the prosperity of the people as consumer and capital goods do. And certain major *inventions*, such as the railroad, the automobile, and the internet can stimulate the economy by giving rise to surges of capital investment spending.

While factors such as these affect the economy, they tend to occur at random intervals and therefore are not a convincing explanation for business cycles, which tend to occur repeatedly. For the causes of these economic fluctuations, we will have to look elsewhere.

Fluctuations in Aggregate Demand

Business cycles involve periodic fluctuations of output and employment across the entire economy. From our analysis of the operation of the economy in Chapter 4, the most likely source of such widespread swings in economic activity would be *fluctuations in aggregate demand*, or total spending on goods and services in the economy. An upward surge in aggregate demand would boost virtually all sectors of the economy, while a decrease in aggregate demand would be felt across most of the economy.

However, analyzing fluctuations in aggregate demand is not a simple matter, since aggregate demand is a vast and complex force that consists of various diverse but interconnected elements: consumption spending, business investment spending, government spending, and net export spending. So untangling the causes of business cycles is a complex task that requires careful analysis.

In addition, the economy sometimes tends to gain "momentum"; that is, booms can feed on themselves and grow stronger, and recessions can deepen and become more severe. Again, the answer to this tendency seems to lie in the dynamics of the economic system itself, and particularly in the complex interactions between consumption spending and investment spending that can generate such "momentum," either upward or downward.

This chapter deals with the problem of economic instability in two stages. In the first part of this chapter, we will look at what leads to economic instability, namely:

(a) *fluctuations in business investment spending,* the effects of which spread through the economy due to

(b) *the multiplier effect,* whereby fluctuations in investment spending generate fluctuations in consumption spending, and

(c) *the accelerator effect,* through which changes in consumption spending cause changes in business investment spending, and

(d) *fluctuations in exports,* which are a separate and important source of instability in the Canadian economy.

In the second part of this chapter, we will examine the various stages of a typical business cycle, and how the factors listed above interact in ways that generate business cycles.

The Instability of Investment Spending

Business investment spending fluctuates considerably, rising rapidly in some years and decreasing in others. This fluctuation is reflected in Figure 6-4, which shows investment spending since 1976 in real terms—that is, adjusted for inflation.

Another type of investment that fluctuates considerably is *residential construction,* or the home-building industry. Like business investment, the demand for homes varies widely from year to year—at times, home-builders cannot keep up with soaring demand, while at other times they cannot find buyers for houses they have already built. Figure 6-5 illustrates the fluctuations in housing starts caused by these fluctuations in demand.

www.cmhc-schl.gc.ca

Why Does Investment Spending Fluctuate So Much?

As we saw in Chapter 4, the level of business capital-investment spending depends mainly on two factors: (1) businesses' *expectations* concerning the future profitability of investment projects, and (2) the *rate of interest* that businesses must pay on money borrowed to finance such projects. And, since both expectations and interest rates can change considerably from year to year, business investment spending tends to fluctuate considerably. When the

FIGURE 6-4 Real Business Investment Spending, 1976–2002

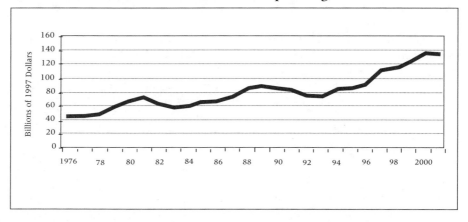

Source: Statistics Canada, adapted from *National Income and Expenditure Accounts*, Catalogue 13-001, 2002.

FIGURE 6-5 Housing Starts, 1977–2002

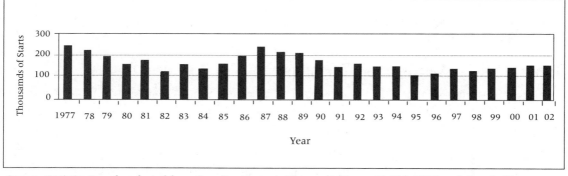

Source: Statistics Canada, adapted from *Canadian Economic Observer*, Catalogue 11-010, 2002, and Canada Mortgage and Housing Corporation (CMHC). Canadian Housing Statistics, 2002. All rights reserved. Reproduced with the consent of CMHC. All other uses and reproductions of this material are expressly prohibited.

economic outlook is favourable and interest rates are low, business investment tends to rise briskly. At other times, uncertain or poor expectations and/or high interest rates can cause businesses to reduce investment spending, in some cases quite sharply.

Expectations and interest rates also explain most of the fluctuations in the residential housing market. When consumer confidence is high and mortgage interest rates are low, activity in this industry can be frantic—buyers want to buy, and they will pay high prices now because they fear that prices will rise again shortly. Builders and suppliers are barely able to keep up with the demand. But periodically, the situation reverses itself—mortgage interest rates become high and people expect an economic slowdown in which interest rates and home prices may actually fall. So, the demand for homes falls sharply, and the residential construction industry goes into a slump.

Businesses' investment in inventories also fluctuates a great deal due to expectations. If retailers and wholesalers expect sales to be strong, they will spend heavily to add to their inventories. On the other hand, if sales are slow, retailers may spend little or nothing on inventory.

How Fluctuations in Investment Spending Affect the Economy

Obviously, such fluctuations in business investment spending will strongly affect the capital goods sector of the economy. High business investment spending will bring prosperity to industries such as construction and machinery and equipment, whereas periodic decreases in investment spending will mean hard times and layoffs in these industries.

But business investment spending and the capital-goods industries associated with it seldom amount to more than one-eighth of the nation's GDP, hardly enough to account for booms and recessions that affect most of the economy. For a fuller understanding of these broad economic fluctuations, we will need to go beyond the capital goods sector, and examine how these variations in investment spending interact with the much larger consumption spending sector. This brings us to the effects known as the "multiplier" and the "accelerator," which are discussed in the following sections.

The Multiplier Effect

Suppose that a new family moves into a town and builds a $200 000 house, using local labour and materials. This will add $200 000 to the *incomes* of the townspeople involved. While some of this increase in incomes will go to taxes and some will be saved, much of it will be spent on consumer goods and services, such as clothes, home repairs, restaurant dinners, and so on. To those who receive this money—the tailor, plumber, and restaurant owner and employees—it represents an increase in *their* income. They will respend a large part of it on a variety of goods and services, generating additional income for the suppliers of those items, who, in turn, will increase *their* spending. This *respending effect* will continue as increases in income are respent again and again; however, it will grow weaker at each stage because not all of the increase in incomes is respent at each stage.

The result is similar to the ripples on a pond caused by throwing a stone: the original $200 000 spent on the new house is the initial splash, and the respending of the increases in income at each stage creates a series of ripples, each smaller than the previous one, spreading out from the centre and through the economy. Just as the stone disturbs the pond by much more than the initial splash, the *total* economic effect of the spending of the $200 000 on the house will be much greater than the original $200 000 because as the money is respent, total spending—and incomes—will increase in a series of stages following the initial spending. In effect, the impact of the

multiplier effect The
effect whereby fluctua-
tions in spending (for
instance, investment
spending) spread by
means of the respending
effect through the econo-
my, with the total impact
on GDP and incomes
being considerably larger
than the initial fluctua-
tions in spending.

original $200 000 will be magnified, or *multiplied*, by this respending effect.
For this reason, the respending effect is known as the **multiplier effect**.

A Numerical Example of the Multiplier

The principle that was shown in the previous illustration can be applied to
the entire economy. Suppose total investment spending in the economy
increases by $100 million over last year's levels, causing the incomes of
people in the capital goods industries to be $100 million higher than last year.
Not all of this $100 million of additional income will be spent on consump-
tion—part will go to taxes, part will be saved, and part will be diverted to
foreign nations through purchases of imports.

Assuming that taxes, saving, and imports absorb one-half of the increase
in incomes, consumption spending will rise by $50 million over last year's
level. This increase in consumer spending represents a $50-million increase
in GDP *and income* to those who receive it. Assuming that they will also
respend half of it, this respending will give rise to a further increase in
consumption spending of $25 million, which boosts GDP and incomes by
another $25 million. Of this $25 million of increased incomes, $12.5 million
would be respent as the cycle continues, increasing *both GDP and total incomes*
at each stage, as shown in Figure 6-6.

FIGURE 6-6 The Respending Effect Underlying the Multiplier

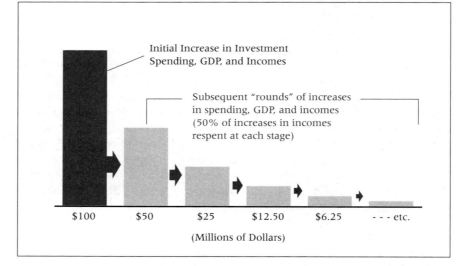

Obviously, the respending effect means that the initial investment
project of $100 million has a much more far-reaching effect on the economy
(that is, on GDP and total incomes) than its size suggests. To calculate the
total impact of the $100 million of investment spending on the economy, we
would have to add together all of the increases in spending, GDP, and
incomes at each stage of the process: $100 million + $50 million + $25 million

+ $12.5 million, etc. And we would find that the $100 million of investment spending caused GDP and total incomes to rise by $200 million, as shown in Figure 6-7. In this example, the size of the multiplier is *2*, because an increase in investment of $100 million caused the GDP to rise by $200 million.

FIGURE 6-7 The Respending Effect with a Multiplier of Two

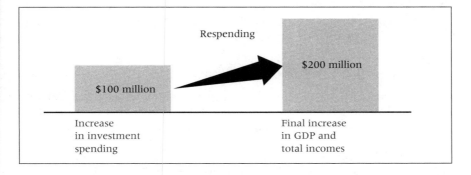

The Canadian Multiplier

In the Canadian economy, the multiplier tends to be smaller than in the previous example (that is, 2), mostly because the respending effect is diminished by Canadians' high spending on imports. Various economic models and studies, using different assumptions, have developed estimates of the size of the Canadian multiplier. It has been estimated that, for government spending on capital formation (such as public works projects), the size of the multiplier is 1.6 over a one-year period. That is, a $1-million increase in expenditures on public works will boost GDP and total incomes by $1.6 million over the next year. Other studies have estimated the multiplier to be as large as 1.8 and as small as 1.0. These studies agree that the multiplier is higher during economic booms, when people are inclined to respend a greater proportion of any increases in their income, and smaller during recessions, when the opposite is true.

The Downward Multiplier

So far, we have applied the multiplier only to *increases* in investment spending. However, the multiplier also works in reverse. Suppose that investment spending *decreased* by $3.0 billion from the previous year's level. This decrease would *reduce* incomes, with the result that consumer spending would be cut back. These spending cuts would reduce other incomes, which would cause further spending cuts, and so on. This process is known as the *downward multiplier*. Obviously, it can make recessions more severe, by increasing the economic impact of reductions in investment spending. For instance, if the multiplier were 1.6, a reduction in investment of $3.0 billion would lead to a $4.8 billion decline in GDP and total incomes.

The Multiplier and Economic Instability

The multiplier effect contributes to economic instability because it magnifies the impact of any fluctuation in spending on the economy. For instance, with a multiplier of 1.6, fluctuations in investment spending of a magnitude of $5 billion will cause the GDP and total incomes to fluctuate by about $8 billion. The multiplier effect also magnifies the impact of changes in other types of spending besides investment: it is through the multiplier effect that the entire Canadian economy feels the effects of seemingly local developments, such as increased exports of British Columbia resource products, falling wheat sales on the Prairies, or an investment boom in central Canada.

The Accelerator Effect

accelerator The effect whereby rising consumption spending causes rapid increases in induced investment, and a slowing down or leveling off of consumption spending causes sharp declines in induced investment.

The multiplier effect shows how changes in investment spending generate changes in consumer spending. The **accelerator** effect operates in the other direction, with changes in *consumption spending* causing changes in *investment spending*.

Specifically, increases in consumer spending can generate increases in investment spending, as businesses spend on plant and equipment to increase capacity to meet rising consumer demand. Rising consumer spending will not always cause investment spending to rise in this way. During a recession, when a business may be operating at only 70 percent of capacity, an increase in consumer demand will not cause it to invest in new plant and equipment because it has idle capacity that can be used to increase output. However, when rising consumer demand pushes output to near-capacity levels, further increases in consumer spending will lead to increased investment spending in order to raise capacity to meet the anticipated demand. When rising consumer spending affects investment spending in this way, the resulting investment is called **induced investment**, and the effect on the economy is called the *accelerator effect*.

induced investment Capital investment spending undertaken by business in response to increases in sales that have brought production to near-capacity levels and that are expected to continue.

So, during an economic boom in which many industries are operating near capacity, rising consumer spending can kick off a *surge* of investment spending, which will create a *strong boom* in the capital goods industries (construction, machinery, steel, building materials, and so on). This is illustrated in year 20X2 in Figure 6-8, and can also be seen in the late 1990s in Figure 6-4.

However, this boom in the capital goods industries may well prove to be temporary. Soon manufacturers will have enough capital equipment for their present level of sales, and they will not order any more new capital equipment unless consumer spending (that is, their sales) *increases further*. Year 20X3 of Figure 6-8 illustrates this point: the slowdown of consumer spending has a drastic effect on manufacturers' orders for new capital equipment, so that a mere *slowdown* in consumer spending causes a *sharp decline* in induced investment. So, induced investment is a particularly fragile component of investment spending—for induced investment to be *sustained*, consumer spending must *keep rising continuously*. And, when consumer spending merely slows down or levels off, induced investment will fall sharply.

FIGURE 6-8 The Operation of the Accelerator

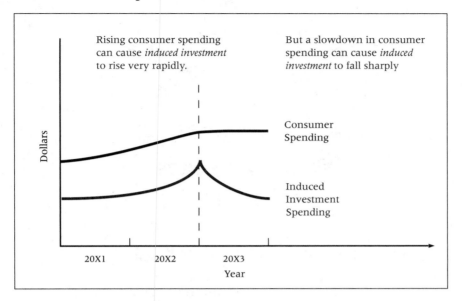

Ironically, in year 20X3 of Figure 6-8, consumer spending, while barely rising, is nonetheless at record-high levels, whereas induced investment has declined sharply from its previous levels. This disparity helps explain why, while the economy in general ("consumer spending" on the graph) is prosperous, there can be a slump in the capital goods industries ("induced investment" on the graph). So, industries such as construction, steel, and machinery can experience slumps *simply because consumption spending isn't rising fast enough.* As a result, induced investment is very unstable, which helps to explain why capital goods industries tend to experience "feast-or-famine" cycles, and also why the economy tends to experience ups and downs. To aggravate the situation even further, the decline in induced investment can drag the level of consumption spending down with it through the multiplier effect.

The Multiplier and Accelerator Effects Combined

We have seen how the multiplier and the accelerator operate separately. But when the multiplier and accelerator *combine*, they can add even greater momentum to a boom.

In Figure 6-9, an economic boom is in progress. Rising investment spending is boosting incomes and consumption spending through the respending effect of the multiplier. And if the rising consumption spending pushes production to near-capacity levels, the accelerator effect will cause induced investment to increase. This further increase in investment spending will boost the economy to even higher levels, as the multiplier and accelerator effects are combined.

FIGURE 6-9 The Multiplier and Accelerator Effects Combined

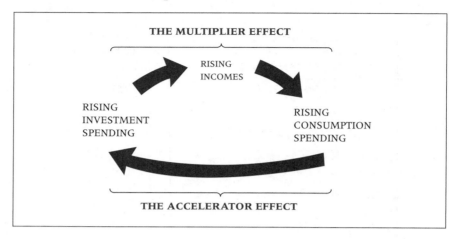

Exports as a Source of Economic Instability

With over two-fifths of its GDP sold in export markets (85 percent of this to the United States alone), Canada is particularly exposed to international economic fluctuations. When other nations, particularly the United States, have economic booms, their demand for Canadian exports adds significantly to aggregate demand in Canada, boosting the economy. And, when these nations experience economic slowdowns, their demand for Canadian products slumps significantly, with serious effects on the Canadian economy.

The effects of such fluctuations in exports are not, however, confined to regions and industries linked directly to Canada's export industries. The multiplier effect spreads their effects throughout the economy, and can contribute to a more general economic boom or slowdown.

So economic trends in other countries, especially the United States, are an important source of economic fluctuations in Canada. Unlike the other causes of instability examined earlier in this chapter, the source of this problem lies outside Canada. We will consider the matter of Canada's international trade more fully in Chapters 9 to 12.

The Dynamics of Business Cycles

We have seen how several factors can cause the economy to swing between boom and recession—fluctuations in investment spending, the multiplier effect, the accelerator effect, and fluctuations in exports. Next, we will examine the *actual dynamics* of economic instability—how these and other factors *interact* in order to cause the economy to undergo swings between booms and recessions, and how those swings, once started, can *gain momentum*, making the fluctuations of the economy more severe. No two booms or slumps are the same, but the following will show the typical kinds of interactions that occur in the economy as it swings upward and downward.

To illustrate the dynamics of business cycles, we will use the "supply side–demand side" model from Chapter 4. This model is shown in Figure 6-10, in which the supply side of the economy is represented by the dotted line, which shows potential (capacity) output rising gradually, and the demand side is represented by the solid line showing the level of aggregate demand in the economy. We will start at the stage of the cycle at which the economy is beginning to recover from a recession.

The Recovery Phase

In year 20X1 in Figure 6-10, aggregate demand is far below the capacity output of the supply side of the economy. Businesses are operating well below their capacity output level, and unemployment is high.

FIGURE 6-10 The Economy in the Recovery Phase

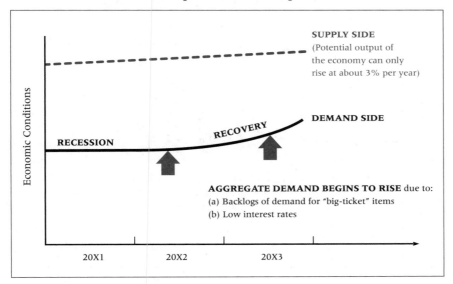

In years 20X2 and 20X3, the economy is in its *recovery* phase from the recession. Aggregate demand has started to rise, causing output and employment to rise slowly. Demand could be rising for various reasons, such as:

- *Backlogs of demand* for certain consumer goods probably exist. In particular, during the recession, consumers have probably postponed purchases of "big-ticket" items such as cars and houses, and the appliances and furniture that are often bought with a new house.
- *Low interest rates* could be making it more attractive to borrow money for such purchases. Interest rates tend to be lower during recessions, to encourage borrowing. To finance such purchases, consumers will take out bank loans. This will speed up the money-creation process described in Chapter 5, causing the money supply to begin to increase and contributing to the growth of aggregate demand.

As aggregate demand slowly increases, output and employment will gradually start to recover from the recession. At this point in the recovery, the rising level of aggregate demand will generate little or no additional inflation in the economy. The supply side of the economy can easily increase output to match demand, because firms have excess plant capacity and ready access to labour and materials.

The Expansion (Boom) Phase

In Figure 6-11, the economy is moving into the *expansion* (or "boom") phase of the business cycle in years 20X3 and 20X4, as rising aggregate demand is driving output and employment toward quite high levels.

FIGURE 6-11 The Economy in the Expansion (Boom) Phase

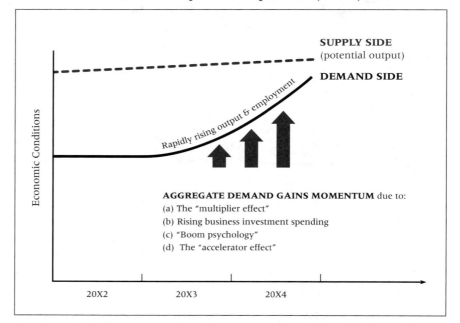

During the boom phase, the increases in demand are gaining momentum, pulling output and employment upward at a faster pace. The economy *gains momentum* in this way for various reasons:

(a) *The multiplier effect.* Through the multiplier effect explained earlier in this chapter, rising spending will generate higher incomes, which will lead to a chain reaction of respending that will boost consumption spending further.

(b) *Rising business investment spending.* As the economic outlook improves, and with interest rates still low, business investment spending can be expected to increase, generating additional increases in employment, incomes, and aggregate demand.

(c) *"Boom psychology."* As the economic boom progresses, consumers and businesspeople will feel more confident about the economic future. This **boom psychology** will make them more willing to borrow money to buy houses, and "big-ticket" consumer durable goods (such as cars, appliances, and furniture) and capital goods for businesses. As bank lending increases to finance these purchases, the money-creation process will speed up further and the money supply will grow at a faster rate, adding momentum to the pace of spending.

boom psychology
People's expectation of a future boom that makes them more willing to borrow to buy big-ticket items and capital goods.

(d) *The accelerator effect.* Later in the boom, when rising consumer spending pushes output to near capacity levels, the accelerator effect will add further to demand. At this point, induced investment spending will push aggregate demand, output, employment, and incomes even higher.

The combined effect of these factors can become quite strong. Together, they can cause aggregate demand, output, and employment to rise rapidly in an economic boom, as shown in years 20X3 and 20X4 in Figure 6-11. However, such high levels of aggregate demand can bring not only an economic boom but also a troublesome side effect—*inflation*.

The Inflation Phase

With aggregate demand gaining momentum and growing at such a rapid pace in the boom phase of the cycle, it is quite possible that demand will rise to the point where it exceeds the economy's ability to produce goods and services. If this happens, the general level of prices of goods and services will increase—and there will be *inflation*.

This situation is shown in Figure 6-12: in years 20X5 and 20X6, aggregate demand has outrun the ability of the supply side of the economy to produce goods and services, and is generating inflation.

Under certain conditions, inflation can *gain momentum*, and become more severe. This problem is partly caused by **inflation psychology**, which is people's expectation that inflation will continue. This expectation will lead people to take actions that are intended to protect themselves against inflation, but that will actually cause inflation to become more severe. Workers who expect higher inflation in the future will press their employers for larger wage increases to protect their living standards against inflation. And if their employers also expect more inflation, they will be more likely to agree to larger wage increases. But these pay raises will also *add to inflation* by increasing businesses' labour costs, forcing product prices up. And if people see prices rising rapidly, they may decide to buy big-ticket items such as houses now, before their prices rise even further, and borrow if necessary to do so. This extra borrowing and spending will add to the money supply and aggregate demand, generating more inflation. So people's expectation of inflation, or inflation psychology, can lead them to do things that make inflation worse, in a sort of spiral.

inflation psychology
People's expectation of future inflation that leads them to seek larger wage increases and to make purchases of some big-ticket items quickly, before prices rise further.

FIGURE 6-12 The Inflation Phase

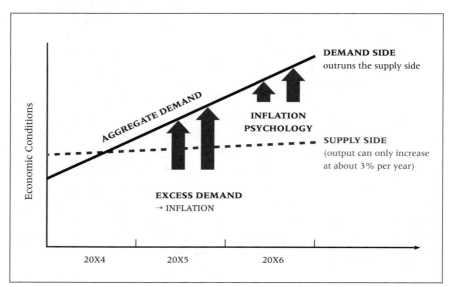

The Peak of the Cycle: How a Boom Can Become a Downturn

Once inflation becomes severe, it has a strong tendency to lead toward an economic downturn, or recession. The main reason for this tendency is that *rapid inflation causes high interest rates.*[1]

If lenders fear that inflation will erode the value of their capital, they will insist upon higher interest rates to compensate for this problem. For instance, suppose that someone offers to borrow $100 from you for one year, and to pay you 6 percent interest for the year. Whether this is an attractive investment for you depends on the *rate of inflation* for the next year.

If the rate of inflation were 3 percent,		
you would gain		
in the interest you receive:	$6	(6% of $100)
while inflation would reduce the		
purchasing power of your $100		
by 3 percent, or $3, causing you to lose:	<u>3</u>	
for a net gain of:	<u>$3</u>	

1 Actually, it is lenders' *expectations* of inflation in the future that leads them to increase interest rates. Usually, however, it is rapid inflation *today* that leads to such fear of inflation *in the future,* so we just say that high rates of inflation cause high interest rates.

On the other hand, if the rate of inflation were 7 percent,
　　you would gain
　　on the interest you receive:　　　　　　　　　　　$ 6
　　while inflation would reduce the
　　purchasing power of your $100
　　by 7 percent, or $7, causing you to lose:　　　　　 _7_
　　　　　　　　　　　　　 for a net <u>loss</u> of:　　$ 1

Clearly, the second case would be unacceptable to lenders. To protect the purchasing power of their savings, they would insist upon a higher rate of interest. For instance, an interest rate of 10 percent would leave lenders with a net gain of 3 percent, the same as in the first example.

And, if the rate of inflation were expected to be 10 percent, lenders might well want an interest rate of 13 percent.

So the higher the rate of inflation is expected to be, the higher interest rates will be. Or, put differently: *High rates of inflation cause high interest rates.*

And if interest rates rise, borrowing and spending in the economy will be slowed down, as will aggregate demand.

This problem is shown in Figure 6-13, in year 20X7. High interest rates are:

(a) depressing (slowing down) consumer spending on "big-ticket" items such as houses and cars because consumers are reluctant to borrow at such high interest rates to buy these things, and

(b) depressing business investment spending, because:

- businesses are reluctant to borrow at high interest rates to finance investment projects, and

FIGURE 6-13 How Inflation Turns to Recession

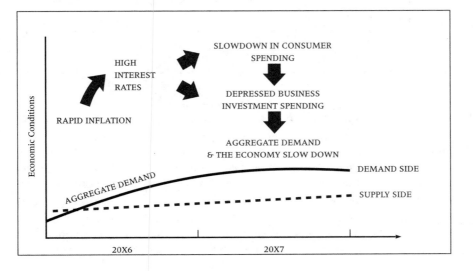

- with consumer spending slowing down due to the reason in (a) above, businesses do not need to expand as they had been doing in the previous few years. Note that the point at which a slow-down in consumer spending leads to a cutback in induced invest-ment is where the accelerator effect, described earlier in the chapter, takes place.

As a result, by the end of year 20X7, aggregate demand begins to weak-en, the period of boom/inflation comes to an end, and the economy hovers on the edge of a recession.

The Recession Phase

Figure 6-14 shows the economy sliding into recession in years 20X8 and 20X9. Aggregate demand is falling, output is decreasing, and unemployment is rising.

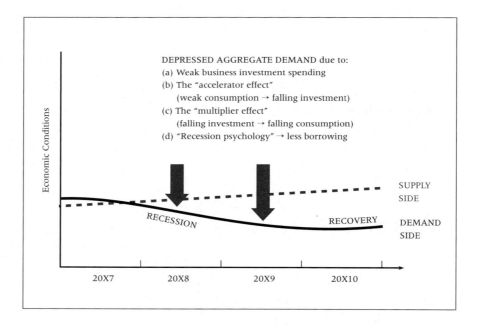

FIGURE 6-14 The Economy in Recession

We have seen how inflation and high interest rates will have already slowed down consumer spending and business investment spending. Once the economy *starts* into a recession, factors tend to come into play that cause the recession to *gain momentum* and become more severe. These are the same factors that operated during an economic boom, but in a recession, they work in the opposite direction:

(a) *Weak business investment spending.* In a recession, business investment spending tends to fall especially rapidly, because expectations and business confidence tend to be particularly low during recessions.

(b) *The accelerator effect.* With consumer spending levelling off, many businesses will not need to buy as much additional new capital equipment as in the recent past. As a result, their purchases of capital goods will tend to decrease. This behaviour is an example of the accelerator effect operating in reverse; that is, depressing investment spending rather than boosting it.

(c) *The multiplier effect.* In a recession, the multiplier effect also operates in reverse. As business investment spending decreases, incomes in the capital goods sector decrease as workers are laid off, which in turn causes reductions in consumer income and depresses consumer spending. Like a chain reaction, these decreases in consumer spending spread through the economy, dragging down incomes and consumer spending.

(d) *"Recession psychology."* Fearing unemployment, consumers tend to borrow and spend less during a recession. Similarly, since businesses expect slow sales, they tend to borrow and spend less because there is no need to expand production capacity or to increase inventory. This **recession psychology** drags aggregate demand down even further, taking with it output, employment, and incomes.

recession psychology People's concerns regarding recession and unemployment that lead them to curtail their spending, especially on big-ticket items that require borrowing.

In addition, many consumers and businesses could by now have become concerned about the high levels of debt that they have accumulated over the previous few years. With already heavy debt loads and interest payments, and facing increasingly uncertain prospects for the economy, both consumers and businesses may decide to avoid further borrowing, and concentrate instead on repaying their debts. This decline in borrowing and new stress on debt repayment will create an additional drag on aggregate demand, slowing the economy further.

The factors discussed above will tend to cause the recession to deepen and become more severe. Finally, the recession will "bottom out" and another recovery can begin. This is shown in year 20X10, when a backlog of consumer spending, with the help of low interest rates, marks the beginning of another cycle.

The Business Cycle in Review

Figure 6-15 on p. 141 shows a typical business cycle such as that covered in this chapter. The gradual rise of the dotted line reflects the fact that the potential output of the economy (the *supply side*) can only grow at about 3 percent per year, as the labour force and output per worker increase each year. But unlike capacity output, aggregate demand fluctuates. Sometimes aggregate demand grows quite rapidly, carrying the economy through a brisk *expansion,* or boom. Such rising demand can gain momentum and can outrun the economy's capacity, or potential output, generating *inflation*. At other times, aggregate demand can actually decrease, gaining momentum as it does so, dragging the economy into a *recession*.

FIGURE 6-15 The Business Cycle in Review

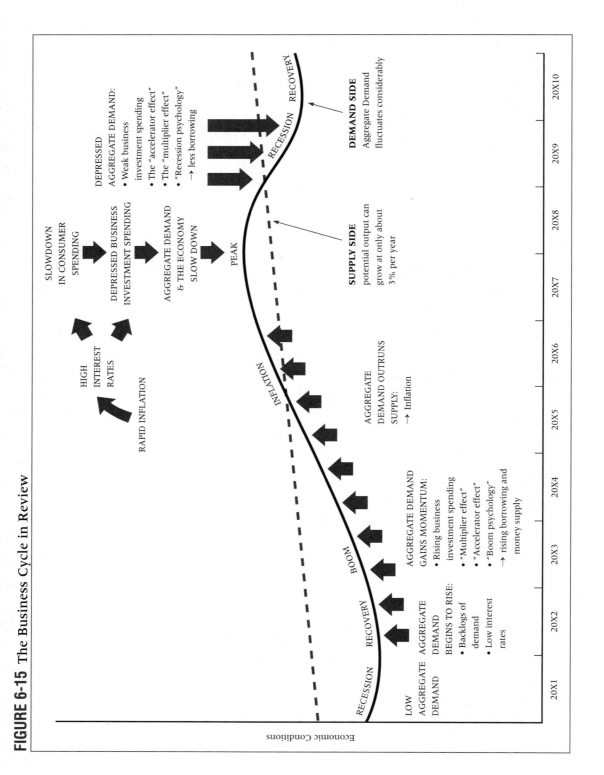

JOBS AND PROFITS

Because financially troubled corporations often lay off employees, many people think that lower employment means higher profits, and that higher employment must therefore mean lower profits. However, when we look at the economy on a macroeconomic scale, the following statistics show that this is clearly not the case—business profits and employment actually tend to *move together*. Generally, in years when employment grows strongly, so do profits, and when employment grows slowly or falls, profits fall.

Profits and Jobs

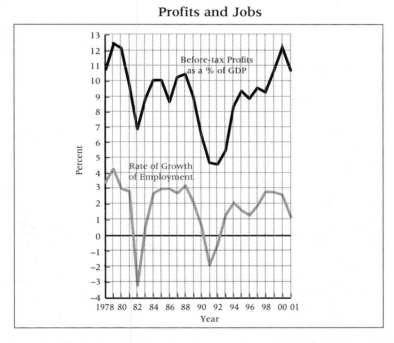

Sources: Statistics Canada, adapted from *National Income and Expenditure Accounts*, Catalogue 13-001, 2002, and *Historical Labour Force Statistics*, Catalogue 71-201, March 2001.

QUESTION

1. What could explain the fact that profits and employment growth tend to move in the same direction so regularly?

Economic Forecasting

Obviously, it would be very useful for strategic economic decision-makers in business and government to have advance notice of future economic conditions, so that they could make timely preparations for them. However, it is easier to *appreciate* the value of accurate economic forecasts than it is to actually *prepare* them.

Economic forecasting is a very challenging task, as it involves attempting to predict the behaviour of millions of consumers and businesses and various levels of government, as well as countless foreign buyers of Canadian exports. Furthermore, the decisions of these various groups are often interrelated (for instance, stronger spending by consumers may induce businesses to increase their capital spending), making the forecasting of the overall situation that much more complex.

> "The experience of being disastrously wrong is salutary. No economist should be denied it, and not many are."
>
> John Kenneth Galbraith

One approach to economic forecasting is to forecast the levels of the various components of aggregate demand—consumer spending, business investment spending, government spending, and net export spending. By considering past trends and likely future developments, forecasters estimate the future levels of these types of spending, and thus of aggregate demand itself, in a sort of gigantic "sales forecast," as shown in Table 6-1. This approach to forecasting generally uses a computer model of the economy that attempts to incorporate into the forecast the numerous interrelationships among the variables in the forecast. Table 6-1 merely shows the results of such a forecast; it does not reveal the complexity of the process by which the forecast was developed.

TABLE 6-1 Forecasting Aggregate Demand

		Forecast 20X1 ($ billions)
Consumer Expenditure		$510
Investment Spending		
Business investment in plant and equipment	$90	
Housing expenditure	40	130
Government Spending on Goods and Services		175
Net Exports		
Exports of goods and services	$310	
Imports of goods and services	290	20
Aggregate Demand		$835

leading economic indicators Economic statistics that tend to increase or decrease in advance of increases or decreases in the pace of economic activity, thus giving advance notice of changes in economic trends.

Another way to gain advance indications of changes in the direction of the economy is through **leading economic indicators**. The values of these economic statistics tend to increase *before* the economy speeds up, and to *decrease* before a downturn begins.

Through a combination of theory and experience, economists have developed several such leading indicators. Some of these are stock prices, money supply data, the average number of hours worked per week, statistics on housing and housing starts, orders for durable goods, and the U.S. leading indicator.

Often, several of these statistics are combined, or averaged, into what is known as a *composite leading indicator*. Because it includes a broader range of data than any one indicator, a composite indicator is considered more reliable. Figure 6-16 shows Statistics Canada's Composite Leading Indicator, which contains ten components, over the 1990–2002 period.

www.statcan.ca
(published monthly with
"The Daily")

FIGURE 6-16 Statistics Canada's Composite Leading Indicator

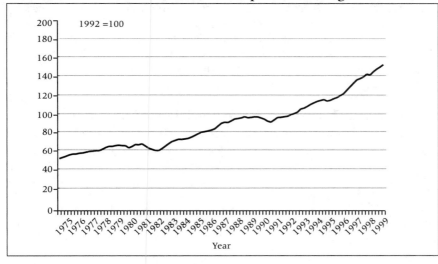

Source: Statistics Canada, adapted from *Canadian Economic Observer*, Catalogue 11-010, 2002.

....

Conclusion

"Market" economies—in which consumers and businesses are free to spend or not spend, as they see fit—have a natural tendency toward instability. At times, consumers and businesses will spend strongly, pushing aggregate demand upward and generating economic booms, while at other times, demand will be weak and the economy will experience recessions. And when these economic fluctuations become severe, they can cause serious problems.

The hardships associated with recessions are well known. In fact, many people have experienced unemployment, or know people who have been unemployed. And, as we will see in Chapter 7, the experience of the Great Depression of the 1930s left a permanent imprint upon government economic policy, in the form of an undertaking in 1945 to maintain "a high and stable level of employment."

The worst experience with inflation was the "Great Inflation" of the 1970s and 1980s, when the rate of inflation reached 12 percent per year at

---

YOU DECIDE

MONITORING THE ECONOMY

Each Monday, the Financial Post section of the *National Post* publishes its "FP Econowatch," which shows many of the economic statistics used in this and other chapters. These statistics include GDP, real GDP, the Composite Leading Indicator, profits, retail sales, housing starts, money supply, bank loans, the consumer price index, disposable income, employment and unemployment, exports and imports, as well as key statistics for the U.S. economy. The statistics are shown for the most recent period (usually month) and the previous month, and the percentage change over the past year is shown. Together, they provide a good basis for monitoring the progress and direction of the economy. Another good source of such information is the TD–Canada Trust website (www.td.com); select "TD Economics," then "Forecasts."

QUESTIONS

1. Check these statistics each week over a period of time, looking for trends.
2. Try to determine the reasons for any apparent trends.
3. Try to forecast the general direction of the economy over the next several months or year.

---

one point. This experience showed that high rates of inflation cause serious economic problems.

- Rapidly rising prices can make a nation's products less competitive internationally. This is a serious concern for a country such as Canada, which exports over 40 percent of its GDP.
- Rapid inflation causes hardship for people who cannot increase their incomes as fast as prices are rising.
- Rapid inflation causes very high interest rates, which can lead to an economic downturn and high unemployment.

The experience of the 1970s and 1980s left its own imprint upon government policy, in the form of an undertaking in 1991 that the rate of inflation would be kept below a maximum of 3 percent per year.

The problem of economic instability has historically been one of the most serious weaknesses of the market system economy. In this chapter, we have examined the causes of this problem; in Chapters 7 and 8, we will see what governments have been able to do to try to correct it.

Chapter Summary

1. Market economies are prone to economic fluctuations, alternating between periods of rapid expansion (booms) and slumps (or

recessions). There are various interrelated factors in the economy that cause these business cycles by generating *fluctuations in aggregate demand*. These include:

(a) fluctuations in investment spending, (L.O. 1a)

(b) the multiplier effect, whereby fluctuations in investment spending cause fluctuations in consumption spending, (L.O. 1b)

(c) the accelerator effect, through which fluctuations in consumption spending cause much sharper fluctuations in induced investment (L.O. 1c), and

(d) fluctuations in exports. (L.O. 1d)

2. In the *recovery phase* of the cycle, the economy is recovering from a recession as aggregate demand is starting to grow, perhaps due to backlogs of demand for big-ticket items and low interest rates. (L.O. 2a)

3. In the *expansion (boom) phase*, aggregate demand is rising and gaining momentum, as consumption spending and investment spending boost each other through the multiplier and accelerator effects, and "boom psychology" encourages higher levels of borrowing and spending. (L.O. 2b)

4. In the *inflation phase*, aggregate demand has begun to outrun the capacity of the economy to produce goods and services, causing the rate of inflation to increase. Inflation psychology may cause inflation to gain momentum. (L.O. 2c)

5. At the peak of the cycle, inflation causes higher interest rates, which depress consumer spending on housing and big-ticket items. Business investment spending is also depressed by higher interest rates and the slowdown in consumer spending, and aggregate demand weakens. (L.O. 2d)

6. In the *recession phase*, aggregate demand falls. The multiplier and accelerator effects operate in reverse, with low consumer spending pulling down investment spending and low investment spending dragging down employment, incomes, and consumer spending. Recession psychology depresses aggregate demand further. (L.O. 2e)

7. Economists attempt to forecast the future direction of the economy by preparing forecasts of the level of aggregate demand and through using leading economic indicators. (L.O. 3)

Questions

1. On the Statistics Canada website (www.statcan.ca), search "The Daily" for recent releases of the Composite Leading Indicator. What does the direction of the indicator suggest about the direction of the Canadian economy?

2. In a recession, which *one* of the following industries would likely suffer the greatest percentage decline in its sales, and why?
   (a) Clothing

(b) Breweries

(c) Steel

(d) Agriculture

(e) Furniture

3. In which *one* of the following industries would you expect annual profits to *vary the most* from year to year, and why?
    (a) Distilling (liquor)

    (b) Construction equipment

    (c) Banking

    (d) Cosmetics

    (e) Retail food stores

4. Which *one* of the following would be most likely to experience *periodic* unemployment (from time to time)? Do not refer to seasonal factors in your explanation.
    (a) Teachers

    (b) Managers

    (c) Employees of insurance companies

    (d) Bricklayers

5. Suppose that there were a growing belief among Canadians that the economy was heading into a serious recession. Explain how and why this belief would likely affect economic developments in Canada.

6. *An Illustration of the Accelerator.* Acme Toy Company needs one machine for every 5000 toys it produces per week. In year 1, as the following table shows, Acme has 20 fully utilized machines producing 100 000 toys per week. We will assume that this production figure exactly matches the number of toys bought weekly by consumers, so that it also represents consumer demand for Acme's toys. In year 2, consumer demand and toy output increase to 105 000, so that Acme needs 21 machines, as shown in column 2. Since it only has 20 machines (column 3), Acme must buy one new machine (column 4). Since this machine was bought in response to increased consumer demand for toys, we can also regard column 4 as "induced investment" spending.

    Now, suppose that in years 3, 4, and 5, consumer demand (toy sales) and toy production are 115 000, 120 000, and 120 000, as shown in column 1.

Year	(1) Toy Sales and Output (000)	(2) No. of Machines Needed	(3) No. of Machines in the Plant	(4) No. of New Machines Bought
1	100	20	20	0
2	105	21	20	1
3	115	—	—	—
4	120	—	—	—
5	120	—	—	—

(a) Complete columns 2, 3, and 4 in the table.

(b) Summarize the results in the following table.

Year	(1) Consumer Spending (= Toy Sales and Output) (000)	% Change From Previous Year	(4) Induced Investment (= Purchases of New Machines)	% Change From Previous Year
1	100	—	0	—
2	105	+5.0%	1	—
3	115	+9.5%	—	—
4	120	—	—	—
5	120	—	—	—

(c) From year 2 to year 3, there was an increase of 9.5 percent in consumer purchases of toys, which induced an increase of ____ percent in purchases of new toy-making machines.

(d) From year 3 to year 4, consumer purchases of toys increased by ____ percent, causing purchases of new toy-making machines to ____ by ____ percent.

(e) From year 4 to year 5, consumer purchases of toys remained stable at 120 000; the result of this was that purchases of new toy-making machines ____ by ____ percent.

(f) Show the figures for *consumer spending* and *induced investment* from the table in part (b) on the following graph.

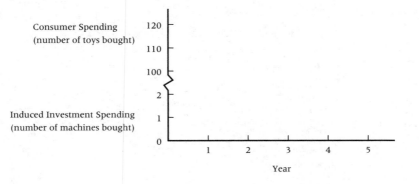

7. Suppose that business inventories increased by $1 billion. How might this statistical fact be interpreted as an indication that:
   (a) economic conditions were deteriorating, and
   (b) economic conditions were improving?

   What might help to determine which of these two possible interpretations was correct?

Chapter 7

Stabilizing the Economy: Government Monetary and Fiscal Policies

Learning Objectives

After studying this chapter, you should be able to:

1. Name the agency that is responsible for monetary policy in Canada and the main policy tools that it uses to influence aggregate demand.

2. State the purpose of an *easy money* policy, and describe how the Bank of Canada implements an easy money policy.

3. Explain how an easy money policy affects the economy.

4. State the purpose of a *tight money* policy, and describe how the Bank of Canada implements a tight money policy.

5. Explain how a tight money policy affects the economy.

6. Name the body that is responsible for fiscal policy in Canada, and list the two main tools of fiscal policy used to influence aggregate demand.

7. Explain the two main components of fiscal policy for combatting a recession.

8. Explain the concept of using fiscal policy to "kick-start" the economy.

9. Define *budget deficit*, and explain the role of deficits in fiscal policy and how deficits are financed.

10. Describe the type of fiscal policy that is appropriate during economic booms and periods of inflation, and state two reasons why such a fiscal policy is considered appropriate.

As we saw in Chapter 6, economic activity in a market economy can fluctuate considerably. During economic booms, output and employment rise rapidly, and inflation can become a concern. And during recessions, output actually falls and unemployment becomes a serious concern.

The most basic cause of these recurrent business cycles is *fluctuations in aggregate demand*. At times, consumers and businesses spend strongly, generating an economic boom, while at other times a decrease in spending will cause declines in output and employment. And the threat of recession or inflation is increased by the tendency of aggregate demand to *gain momentum* at times. During a boom, growing confidence and optimism can cause consumers and businesses to borrow and spend more freely, pushing the money supply and aggregate demand even higher and increasing the danger of inflation. The opposite can happen during recessions, when low confidence and uncertainty reduce borrowing and spending by both consumers and businesses, dragging aggregate demand down further and making the recession worse.

Experience has shown that business cycles can have serious consequences. During the Great Depression of the 1930s, unemployment was very high for a decade. And during the "Great Inflation" of the 1970s, rapidly rising prices and interest rates brought hardship to many people, and eventually led to the second and third most serious recessions of the century.

Because of these problems, a basic goal of government economic policy is to stabilize the economy, by smoothing out business cycles. Government policies seek to stabilize the economy by increasing aggregate demand during recessions and by slowing it down when inflation is a concern. This is no small task: aggregate demand exceeds one trillion (i.e., one thousand billion) dollars and, as we saw in Chapter 6, involves complex interactions between the spending decisions of millions of Canadian households and businesses, as well as the countless foreign buyers of Canadian exports who purchase about two-fifths of our GDP.

To influence the direction of the entire economy on such a broad scale requires some very large economic policy tools that are capable of influencing the spending decisions of millions of buyers, both inside and outside Canada. The main such "policy levers" are *interest rates and the money supply* ("monetary policy") and *government spending and taxes* ("fiscal policy"). In this chapter, we will consider how these policies can be used in order to smooth out economic fluctuations and reduce their impact on Canadians.

Monetary Policy

Monetary policy involves changes in *interest rates* and the *money supply* to influence the level of aggregate demand, and thus the general direction of the economy. In Chapter 5, we saw how the lending activities of the banking system create money, and how this process affects aggregate demand. If borrowing is low, aggregate demand will be low and a recession is likely. On the other hand, high levels of borrowing can boost aggregate demand so high that inflation becomes a problem. During the 1970s and much of the 1980s, inflation was a serious problem in the Canadian economy.

monetary policy The Bank of Canada's use of interest rates and the money supply to influence the level of aggregate demand in the economy.

While implementing monetary policy involves operations that can be quite complex (as we will see in the following sections), the goals of monetary policy are quite straightforward—to reduce interest rates in order to encourage borrowing and spending during recessions, and to raise interest rates in order to discourage borrowing and spending when inflation threatens. The government agency that conducts monetary policy is the *Bank of Canada*.

The Bank of Canada

www.bankofcanada.ca

central bank A government agency with responsibility for monetary policy, as well as other financial functions, on behalf of the government.

The Bank of Canada was established in 1935, when the Great Depression caused increased concern regarding economic and monetary management. Unlike the commercial banks, which are corporations owned by shareholders, the Bank of Canada is an agency of the federal government known as a **central bank**. The Bank of Canada does not deal with the general public as the commercial banks do; rather, it has much broader responsibilities relating to government finances and economic policy.

The Bank of Canada is owned by the Government of Canada and managed by a board of directors that consists of the governor, the senior deputy governor, the deputy minister of finance, and 12 directors. The governor is appointed for a seven-year term by the directors, with the approval of the federal cabinet. The Governor of the Bank of Canada has been described as "the most powerful unelected official in the country."

The Bank of Canada acts as the sole issuer of Canadian bank notes and as the fiscal agent of the federal government. In this latter capacity, the Bank of Canada operates the deposit account through which government revenues and expenditures flow, handles the sale of government securities, and acts as financial adviser to the federal government. In addition, the Bank of Canada has international responsibilities on behalf of the government, particularly with respect to the international value of the Canadian dollar, as we will see in Chapter 10.

settlement balances Deposits (at the Bank of Canada) of the commercial banks and other financial institutions that are used to settle debts and transactions between them.

bankers' deposit rate The rate of interest paid by the Bank of Canada on the chartered banks' deposits at the Bank of Canada.

Bank Rate The rate of interest charged by the Bank of Canada on loans (advances) it makes to banks and other financial institutions.

Another function of the Bank of Canada is to act as a "bank for banks." Each day, millions of cheques written by businesses and individuals are cleared, requiring funds to be transferred between banks. For instance, if your friend writes you a cheque for $100 on her account at the Royal Bank and you cash or deposit her cheque at your branch of the CIBC, it is the CIBC that provides you with $100 of funds. So the Royal Bank owes the CIBC $100 as a result of this transaction. To facilitate this process of transferring funds between banks, the Bank of Canada holds deposits (**settlement balances**) from chartered banks and other financial institutions, and each day transfers funds between their accounts, thus acting as a means of settling debts between the chartered banks. (Your friend's cheque would cause $100 to be transferred from the Royal Bank's account at the Bank of Canada to the CIBC's account at the Bank of Canada at the end of the day.) The Bank of Canada pays the banks interest on these deposits at a rate of interest known as the **bankers' deposit rate**.

If the clearing of these settlements leaves a bank or other financial institution short of funds, it can borrow funds temporarily from the Bank of Canada, at a rate of interest known as the **Bank Rate**. More likely, though, it would borrow from another bank or financial institution that has surplus funds. Such short-term loans are known as **overnight loans**, and the interest rate on them is called the **overnight rate**.

The relationship between these three interest rates is as follows:

- The Bank Rate is the highest (for example, 3.0 percent);
- the overnight rate falls between the Bank Rate and the bankers' deposit rate; and
- the bankers' deposit rate is one-half percentage point below the Bank Rate (in our example, 2.5 percent).

The gap of one-half percentage point between the bankers' deposit rate and the Bank Rate is known as the Bank of Canada's **operating band**.

Monetary Policy

The single most important responsibility of the Bank of Canada is monetary policy, or *controlling the money supply* of the nation, as set out in the preamble of the Bank of Canada Act, which states that the central bank's mandate is to

> ... regulate credit and currency in the best interests of the economic life of the nation ... and to mitigate by its influence fluctuations in the general level of production, trade, prices and employment, so far as may be possible within the scope of monetary action ...

The most visible aspect of the Bank of Canada's monetary policy is its announcements regarding interest rates. On eight predetermined dates each year, the Bank of Canada announces its decision concerning its "target" for its key policy interest rate, which is the overnight rate. The Bank of Canada's target for the overnight rate is in the middle of the operating band between the bankers' deposit rate and the bank rate.

Monetary Policy to Combat Recession: An "Easy Money" Policy

To combat a recession, the Bank of Canada would want to reduce interest rates in order to increase borrowing and spending by consumers and businesses.

A Target for Interest Rates

The Bank of Canada would announce that it was *lowering* its target for the overnight rate (and lowering the operating band and the Bank Rate as well). This announcement would include an explanation for the change in the Bank of Canada's policies, and would be interpreted as a "signal" to Canadians that the Bank of Canada was shifting toward an **"easy money policy"** of lower interest rates and greater availability of credit. An announcement of a lower target for the overnight rate would help to build confidence that action was being taken to combat the recession.

overnight loans Very short-term loans between financial institutions to cover temporary short-falls in areas such as settlement balances.

overnight rate The rate of interest on one-day loans made by banks, investment dealers, and other financial institutions to each other.

operating band The one-half percentage point range established by the Bank of Canada for the overnight rate; the top of the range is the Bank Rate and the bottom of the range is the bankers' deposit rate.

easy money policy Monetary policy directed toward making interest rates lower in order to stimulate aggregate demand.

Reaching the Target

The next step is to actually push the overnight rate downward toward this new target. The Bank of Canada can do this in different ways. One way is for the Bank of Canada to offer overnight loans to banks and other financial institutions at an interest rate that is below the prevailing market rate, which will push the overnight rate downward in the way that the Bank of Canada wants.

The Bank of Canada can also increase the ability of the banks to make loans by *increasing the banks' cash reserves*. To do this, the Bank of Canada can *buy government bonds* from the banks. When the Bank of Canada pays the banks for the bonds, the banks' cash reserves—and their ability to make loans—will increase. The Bank of Canada can also *buy* government bonds from the public. When the public deposits the proceeds from the sale of the bonds into the banking system, the banks' cash reserves will increase. And with more funds to lend, the banks will lower their interest rates on loans, following the trend set by the reduction in the overnight rate.

Another approach is for the Bank of Canada to *shift Government of Canada deposits* from the government's account at the Bank of Canada into its accounts at the banks. This will increase the funds on deposit with the banks. If the banks then invest these surplus funds by lending them out as overnight loans, the increased supply of these funds will push the overnight rate lower, toward the Bank of Canada's new target.

The combination of lower interest rates and increased availability of loanable funds sets the stage for increased borrowing and spending by consumers and businesses.

Easy Money Policies, the Canadian Dollar, and Exports

From 1991 to 2001, the Canadian dollar fell by 26 percent against the U.S. dollar. Over the same period, Canada's exports grew by 107 percent.

An easy money policy can also increase aggregate demand by increasing *foreign demand for Canadian exports*. When Canadian interest rates decrease, Canadian dollar deposits and securities that pay interest become less attractive to foreign investors. Then, foreign investors will reduce their purchases of Canadian dollars for the purpose of making these investments, causing the international price (value) of the Canadian dollar to decrease.

A lower-priced Canadian dollar makes Canadian products more attractive to foreign buyers. For instance, if the Canadian dollar were to decrease from US$0.67 to US$0.63, Canadian goods and services would become about 6 percent cheaper to American buyers. If Americans then buy more Canadian goods and services, Canadian exports would rise, increasing aggregate demand for goods and services in the Canadian economy.

The Effects of an "Easy Money" Policy on the Economy

An easy money policy is intended to stimulate bank lending and spending by consumers and businesses. Consumers will be able to borrow more at lower interest rates to buy houses and cars, and for businesses, the cost of loans for working capital, inventories, and equipment will be lower. As borrowing increases, the money supply and aggregate demand will increase, causing real output to rise and unemployment to decrease, as shown in Figure 7-1. In addition, the lower Canadian dollar should add to exports, further bolstering aggregate demand.

However, lower interest rates are not a "sure fix" for an ailing economy. If the economy is in quite severe recession and confidence is low, consumers and businesses may be reluctant to borrow and spend money, despite reductions in interest rates. This problem has been likened to "pushing on a string," which suggests that easy money by itself may not always be sufficient to lift the economy out of a recession. Japan provides a recent example of this problem, as we will see in Chapter 11.

And even when an easy money policy does work, it is not a "quick fix" for an ailing economy. In fact, the effects of monetary policy occur with quite long *time lags*. There are three such time lags: the *recognition lag*, the *policy lag*, and the *impact lag*.

The *recognition lag* arises because it takes time for economic policy-

> A reduction in interest rates from, say, 3.00 percent to 2.75 percent may not seem significant. However, this decrease reduces the cost of borrowing *by 8.3 percent* (0.25 divided by 3.00).

FIGURE 7-1 The Effects of an "Easy Money" Policy

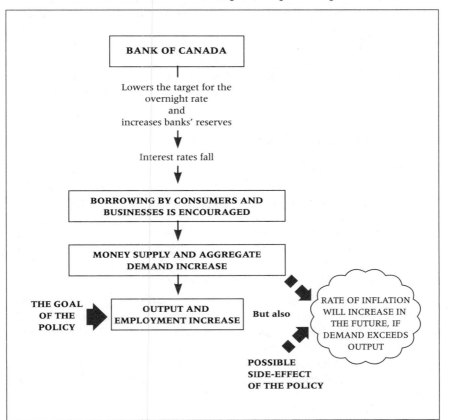

makers to be sure that the economic situation requires action. It may take several months before the available economic statistics make it clear to policy-makers that they should take action.

The *policy lag* occurs due to delays in the implementation of policies by the government. In the case of monetary policy, this lag is short, since the Bank of Canada can move quite quickly to reduce short-term interest rates.

The *impact lag* arises because it takes time for government policies to affect the economy. For monetary policy, the impact lag is long. Lower interest rates will not speed up borrowing and spending immediately—consumers and businesses will need time to reassess their borrowing plans. And many will wait to see if economic conditions are in fact changing in ways that justify changing their plans. As a result, it can take a year or more for an easy money policy to generate a significant increase in aggregate demand.

Together, these time lags can add up to a total of one to two years or more. Such long time lags can create real problems for economic policy-makers, which we will consider in Chapter 8.

When easy money does generate higher aggregate demand, there is another matter that requires the Bank of Canada to be cautious—a side effect of higher aggregate demand could be an increase in the rate of inflation. While this would not be a concern while the economy was in a recession, it could become a problem in the future if aggregate demand were to rise too rapidly and exceed the economy's capacity to produce goods and services. This argument is not against using an easy money policy; rather, it is a caution against using it excessively.

To summarize, an easy money policy is a potentially powerful medicine for an ailing economy, but it does not work rapidly, and it must be used in the right dosage.

Monetary Policy to Control Inflation: A "Tight Money" Policy

If high aggregate demand were threatening to generate too much inflation, the Bank of Canada would want to *increase interest rates* in order to discourage borrowing and spending, and "cool off" the overheated economy. To achieve this, the Bank of Canada would essentially reverse the policies described in the previous sections.

Raising the Target for the Overnight Rate

tight money policy
Monetary policy directed toward making interest rates higher in order to slow the growth of aggregate demand.

To combat inflation, the Bank of Canada would announce that it was *raising* its target for the overnight rate (and raising the operating band and the bank rate as well). The Bank of Canada's announcement would explain the reasons for the increase in interest rates, and it would be regarded as a "signal" to Canadians that the Bank of Canada was shifting toward a **"tight money policy"** of higher interest rates and reduced availability of credit, and that the economy will probably be slowing down.

Reaching the Target

The next step is to actually *push* the overnight rate upward toward this new target. To do this, the Bank of Canada "mops up" some of the reserves of the banking system.

One way of reducing bank reserves is for the Bank of Canada to *sell government bonds* to the banks. When the banks pay the Bank of Canada for the bonds, the banks' cash reserves will decrease. If the Bank of Canada sells government bonds to the public, the public will remove funds from the banking system to pay the Bank of Canada, and the banks' cash reserves will decrease.

The Bank of Canada may also *shift Government of Canada deposits* out of the banks and into the government's account at the Bank of Canada. This will reduce the banks' reserves. If the banks then have to borrow from the overnight loans market to replenish the reserves, the increased demand for these funds will push the overnight rate higher, toward the Bank of Canada's new target.

With the banks having less funds available for lending, the interest rates on loans in general will tend to rise, following the trend set by the increase in the overnight rate. And the combination of higher interest rates and reduced availability of loans sets the stage for decreased borrowing and spending by consumers and businesses.

Tight Money Policies, the Canadian Dollar, and Exports

A tight money policy can also dampen aggregate demand by decreasing *foreign purchases of Canadian exports*. Higher Canadian interest rates make Canadian dollar deposits and securities that pay interest more attractive to foreign

---

IN THE **NEWS**   Bank of Canada Raises Overnight Rate Target

OTTAWA (July 16, 2002)—The Bank of Canada today announced that it is raising its target for the overnight rate by one-quarter of one percentage point to 2¾ percent. The operating band for the overnight rate is correspondingly increased, and the Bank Rate is now 3 percent.

Questions

1. What sorts of developments would have prompted the Bank of Canada to make this announcement?
2. What would be the Bank of Canada's intention in making this policy change?
3. How would this policy change affect the international value of the Canadian dollar?
4. In percentage terms, how much more costly has it become to borrow short-term funds as a result of this policy change?

investors. When foreigners buy more Canadian dollars in order to make these investments, the international price (value) of the Canadian dollar will rise.

A higher-priced Canadian dollar makes Canadian products less attractive to foreign buyers. For instance, if the Canadian dollar were to increase from US$0.63 to US$0.66, American buyers would have to pay 5 percent more for Canadian goods and services. The effect of such an increase would be to depress Canadian exports and aggregate demand in the Canadian economy.

And this in fact happened in the late 1980s, when the Bank of Canada was fighting inflation with high interest rates. At this time, the Canadian dollar rose to US$0.89, slowing the growth of Canadian exports considerably. The effects of slower exports were spread across the economy by the multiplier effect.

The Effects of a "Tight Money" Policy on the Economy

The higher interest rates associated with a tight money policy will discourage borrowing by consumers and businesses, causing aggregate demand to grow more slowly. A higher Canadian dollar will also help to slow down demand, by holding down exports. And, as Figure 7-2 shows, with aggregate demand held in check, the rate of inflation will decrease.

FIGURE 7-2 The Effects of a "Tight Money" Policy

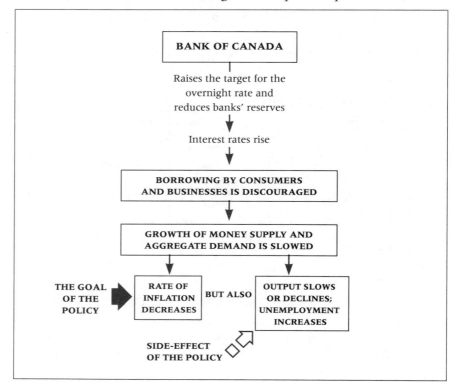

However, the rate of inflation may not fall quickly. If people remain optimistic about the future, or if consumers and businesses expect inflation to drive prices even higher, they may continue to borrow and spend, despite high interest rates.

Also, the effects of a tight money policy are delayed by the same time lags that delay the effects of an easy money policy. Because of the *recognition lag*, policy-makers will take some time to decide that a tight money policy should be implemented. The *policy lag* is short because the Bank of Canada can move quickly to increase short-term interest rates, but the *impact lag* is long. Consumers and businesses will complete major purchases that had already been planned, and the spending on these will continue to ripple through the economy for some time, due to the respending effect of the multiplier that we saw in Chapter 6. Even after borrowing is reduced and the growth of the money supply slows down, the rate of inflation will take about a year to decrease. Such long time lags make economic policy-making a difficult task, as we will see in Chapter 8.

Experience has shown that, eventually, tight money policies will depress aggregate demand, and will slow down inflation. However, a tight money policy will also have the unpleasant side effects of *slower economic growth* and *higher unemployment*.

There are other problems associated with tight money policies. High interest rates affect some sectors of the economy particularly severely. *Construction* is probably the industry that is hardest hit by tight money because high mortgage rates discourage the buying of new homes and the building of commercial and industrial complexes. As you can see in Table 7-1, rising mortgage interest rates have a significant effect upon the monthly mortgage payments faced by homeowners.

TABLE 7-1 Monthly Payments on a 25-Year $100 000 Mortgage at Various Interest Rates

Interest Rate	Monthly Payment[a]
5%	$ 584.59
6%	644.30
7%	706.78
8%	771.82
9%	839.20
10%	908.70
11%	980.11
12%	1053.22
13%	1127.84
14%	1203.76
15%	1280.83
16%	1358.89
17%	1437.80
18%	1517.43
19%	1597.68
20%	1678.45

[a]Assuming interest is compounded monthly.

Because high interest rates will reduce investment spending, tight money also tends to have severe effects on the *capital goods industries,* such as building materials and industrial equipment. In the consumer goods sector, the effects of tight money fall the hardest on the big-ticket items, such as cars and appliances, which involve considerable borrowing to buy and whose sales tend to follow the sales of new houses.

Small businesses are affected more severely by tight money than are big corporations. Because they tend to have smaller profit margins than do large corporations, small businesses tend to be more dependent upon borrowing to finance their operations and less able to afford high interest rates.

So, for various reasons, a tight money policy is a painful policy direction for a government to have to take. Despite these difficulties, a tight money policy is regarded as essential to any successful anti-inflation program. Indeed, most economists believe it to be the *only* really effective anti-inflation policy, because only a tight money policy will attack the basic cause of inflation, which is excessively rapid growth of the money supply generated by high levels of borrowing.

Does the Bank of Canada *Control* Interest Rates?

Sometimes the policy actions of the Bank of Canada are misinterpreted as meaning that the Bank of Canada *controls* interest rates in the Canadian economy. In reality, this is not possible.

Interest rates are a *price*—the price of borrowing money. Interest rates are expressed as a percentage of the loan per annum—for instance, 6 percent per year. Any price must find a middle ground (known to economists as "equilibrium") between the needs of buyers and the sellers. An interest rate of, say, 6 percent represents a balance between the needs of lenders (suppliers of funds) and borrowers ("buyers" of loans). If the government were to try to decree that the rate of interest be only 4 percent, lenders might well prove unwilling to extend loans at such a low rate.

This reality is made more forceful by the fact that money is an internationally "traded" item, in the sense that investors lend money around the world, just as wheat and oil are sold globally. If the world price of oil increases, Canada will have to pay the world price for the oil that it imports. For the same reasons, if interest rates in the United States or in the world generally rise, there will be pressure on Canadian interest rates to rise also. If the government tried to hold Canadian rates too low, lenders would take their funds out of Canada to countries where they could earn a higher return.

For these reasons, the Bank of Canada cannot *control* interest rates in Canada. What it can do, however, is *influence* interest rates by using the policies described in the previous sections to nudge interest rates higher when inflation threatens, and lower when recession and unemployment are the larger concerns. And by doing so in a timely manner, the Bank of Canada can influence aggregate demand and the direction of the Canadian economy.

Monetary Policy in Review

As Figure 7-3 shows, the overnight rate and the rate of growth of the money supply (as measured by M2+) have fluctuated widely over the years. During the 1970s, the money supply grew at very rapid rates of more than 15 percent per year, generating the very high rates of inflation of that period. Since then, money-supply growth has slowed greatly, to less than 5 percent per year. The slowdowns in money-supply growth were concentrated in two periods of strong "tight money" policies. The first of these was in the early 1980s, when anti-inflation policies drove interest rates to extremely high levels, and the second was in the late 1980s and early 1990s, when interest rates increased sharply again in order to curb inflation. After 1991, with the rate of inflation reduced to quite low levels but unemployment high, interest rates were reduced sharply in order to try to stimulate increases in borrowing that would help the economy to recover more strongly from the recession of the early 1990s.

FIGURE 7-3 The Overnight Rate and Money-Supply Growth

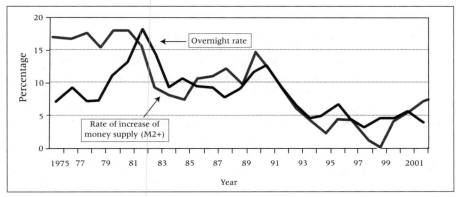

Source: Bank of Canada, adapted from the *Bank of Canada Review* and *Banking and Financial Statistics*.

YOU DECIDE   GOOD NEWS/BAD NEWS?

Late in an economic boom, there often occurs a seemingly peculiar and contradictory sequence of events. First, there are reports of the boom becoming stronger—higher output, lower unemployment and so on. This is followed quickly by a *decline* in the stock market, which is apparently not a random event; in fact, it often seems that *the better* the economic news, *the worse* is its effect on stock prices.

Question

1. Can you explain the reason for this phenomenon?

Fiscal Policy

www.fin.gc.ca

Fiscal policy uses changes in *government spending* and *tax revenues* to influence the level of aggregate demand and the direction of the economy. As we saw in Chapter 6, government spending adds to aggregate demand, either by buying goods and services itself or by providing transfer payments to people who will use the funds to buy goods and services. We also saw in Chapter 6 that taxes have the opposite effect—they reduce aggregate demand, by reducing the purchasing power of households and businesses.

With spending and tax revenues of nearly $190 billion per year, Canada's federal government is in a position either to boost aggregate demand in the economy by increasing spending and/or cutting taxes, or to decrease demand, by doing the opposite. Since government tax revenues and expenditures are contained in the government's budget, the use of fiscal policy (the government's budget) in these ways is sometimes referred to as *budget policy*. Fiscal policy is the responsibility of the federal Department of Finance, under the direction of the Minister of Finance and the federal cabinet.

How Fiscal Policy Combats Recession

In Figure 7-4, the economy has slipped into a recession in year 20X1—aggregate demand has been falling, dragging the levels of output and employment down with it. In 20X2, the government's budget is planned so that government *spending* is larger than the government's *tax revenues*. The purpose of this policy is to boost aggregate demand in order to help the economy out of the recession.

FIGURE 7-4 Fiscal Policy to Combat Recession

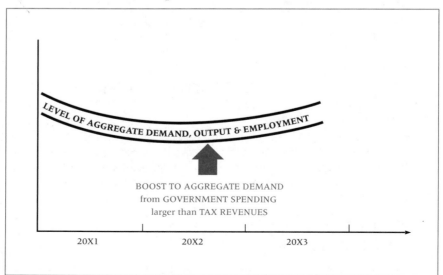

The boost to aggregate demand pictured in Figure 7-4 could be achieved by an increase in government spending (on goods and services, or on transfer payments), by tax reductions, or by some combination of these, as discussed in the following sections.

Increases in Government Expenditures

We have seen how increases in government spending can raise the level of aggregate demand and help to lift the economy out of a recession. Traditionally, governments have used *public works projects* (more recently renamed *infrastructure* projects) for this purpose. These projects involve building or repairing roads, bridges, parks, and public buildings during recessions, when the construction industry is particularly depressed. In addition, government spending on transfer payments to people under the Employment Insurance and welfare programs will increase during a recession, providing more support to the level of aggregate demand.

Reductions in Taxes

Tax reductions during a recession can boost aggregate demand by leaving households and businesses with more after-tax income to spend. The most popular—and most effective—of such policies is a reduction in personal income taxes, because consumers will generally increase their spending when their disposable income rises. Reductions in taxes on business are considered less effective as an anti-recession policy, because, in a recession, businesses would be less likely than consumers to spend their tax savings.

The operation of fiscal policy to combat recessions is summarized and illustrated in Figure 7-5.

Automatic Stabilizers

Some aspects of fiscal policy, such as public works projects, are described as *discretionary* policies because they require decisions by the government. It takes time for a government to implement discretionary fiscal policies. Other aspects of fiscal policy, however, swing into action *automatically* when the economy slips into a recession. For instance, government expenditures on Employment Insurance and welfare benefits rise automatically during recessions, as unemployment rises. In addition to this, many government tax revenues, such as those from income taxes, profits taxes, and sales taxes, tend to be depressed by slower economic activity during recessions. This combination of lower government tax revenues and higher expenditures will provide automatic support to the level of aggregate demand during recessions. For this reason, such programs are described as **automatic stabilizers**.

automatic stabilizers Government spending and taxation programs that have the effect of automatically supporting aggregate demand during recessions and depressing aggregate demand during periods of boom/inflation.

The Multiplier and Fiscal Policy

As we have seen, fiscal policy is used to stabilize the economy in recessions by increasing spending on goods and services by government, consumers, and businesses. The *multiplier effect* will help fiscal policy to work, by spreading

FIGURE 7-5 Anti-Recession Fiscal Policies

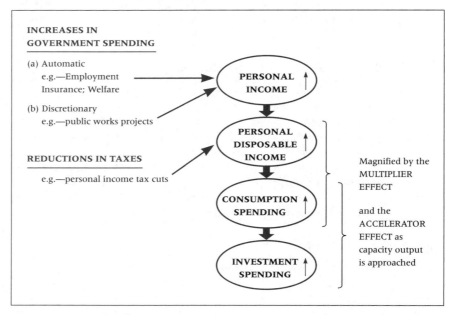

increases in spending through the economy as money is respent. For example, a government road-building program will increase the incomes of construction workers, who will spend part of their increased incomes on consumer goods and services, starting a chain of respending that will increase total incomes and GDP by perhaps 1.6 times the original increase in government spending. Similarly, personal income tax cuts that boost consumer spending will initiate a respending effect that will ripple through the economy. The contribution of the multiplier effect to fiscal policy is also shown in Figure 7-5.

You Decide

HOW MUCH TO INCREASE SPENDING?

Suppose that the GDP were $800 billion and it were forecasted that there would be a recession in which aggregate demand would fall by about 2 percent from its current level over the next year.

Question

1. Assuming a multiplier of 1.6, what amount of increased government spending would be required to keep aggregate demand stable and avoid a recession?

"Kick-starting" the Economy

Fiscal policy that is used to stimulate the economy can also benefit from the *accelerator effect*. Once the level of consumption spending has risen to the point where it is causing induced investment spending by business, the economy should be able to grow again on its own.

In this way, fiscal policy can be used to *kick-start* the economy out of a recession. Just as a motorcycle needs a kick-start to get it moving, the economy can sometimes benefit from a temporary boost. And just as the motorcycle works on its own once kick-started, the economy should be able to grow on its own once boosted onto the path to recovery from a recession. Following a *temporary stimulus* from fiscal policy, the multiplier and accelerator effects should generally be able to carry aggregate demand and the economy into recovery and expansion, as shown at the lower right of Figure 7-5.

Fiscal Policy and Budget Deficits

We have said that using fiscal policy to deal with a recession involves *increasing government spending* and *reducing taxes*, which will require the government to spend more than it collects in tax revenues, or run a **budget deficit**, as shown in Figure 7-6.

budget deficit A government budget in which expenditures exceed tax revenues.

FIGURE 7-6 Illustration of a Government Budget Deficit

If GOVERNMENT SPENDING is	$100 billion
and GOVERNMENT TAX REVENUES are	90 billion
the GOVERNMENT BUDGET DEFICIT is	$ 10 billion

Financing Deficits: Where Will the Money Come From?

In the illustration in Figure 7-6, the government's spending exceeds its tax revenues by $10 billion. Where will the government obtain the $10 billion that it needs?

The government can (and does) raise the necessary funds by *borrowing them*—by *selling government bonds*. These bonds are bought as investments by pension funds, investment funds, banks, insurance companies, other financial institutions, and by investment dealers, who sell them to individuals.

The government also has the power to create new money (the popular term is "print money") to finance its spending and its deficits. The first step in the money-creation process is for the government to sell government bonds to the Bank of Canada, which pays for the bonds by increasing the deposit in the government's account at the Bank of Canada. As the government spends these funds, they flow out into the economy and the banking system, adding to the money supply. "Printing money" like this on a large scale is considered to be very inadvisable, because it risks increasing the money supply *too quickly*. Such a policy would cause *severe inflation*, as the excessive amount of money in circulation pushes aggregate demand up so rapidly that output cannot keep pace. So, while a financially pressed government may find it tempting to "print money" to finance its budget deficits, this method would be inappropriate.

But What About Balancing the Government's Budget? And What About Government Debt?

Two concerns that emerge from the situation described here are that the government is *not balancing its budget* and that *government debt will increase*. In each year that the government has a budget deficit, its borrowing will cause its debt to increase.

Both of these are true for the years in which the government is using deficits to combat a recession. However, when the economy has recovered from the recession and is operating at high levels of output and employment, the situation regarding government finances should change considerably, as the next section shows.

Fiscal Policy for Economic Booms and to Control Inflation

"When prosperity comes, do not use all of it."

Confucius

budget surplus A government budget in which tax revenues exceed expenditures.

As the economy recovers and expands into a boom, the automatic stabilizers described earlier will reduce the government's budget deficits. Government tax revenues will automatically grow as sales, incomes, and profits all increase. In addition, government spending on Employment Insurance and welfare will automatically fall as unemployment decreases. As other temporary antirecession spending programs and tax cuts are ended, the government would have a **budget surplus**—an excess of tax revenues over government expenditures. A budget surplus would serve two important purposes:

- the excess of taxes over government spending would help to *hold down aggregate demand*, reducing the risk of inflation as a result of the economic boom, and
- the funds from the budget surplus could be used to *reduce the government's debt* that it had accumulated while fighting the recession a few years earlier.

Countercyclical Fiscal Policy

Properly timed, budget deficits and surpluses can help to smooth out the economic fluctuations associated with the business cycle. As Figure 7-7 shows, budget deficits can support aggregate demand, output, and employment during recessions, while budget surpluses can help to ease the pressures of excess aggregate demand during the inflationary peaks of the business cycle.

Figure 7-7 also shows how the government debt that will accumulate while budget deficits are being used to combat a recession can be reduced when the economy recovers and moves into a boom. During a boom, the

FIGURE 7-7 Countercyclical Fiscal Policy

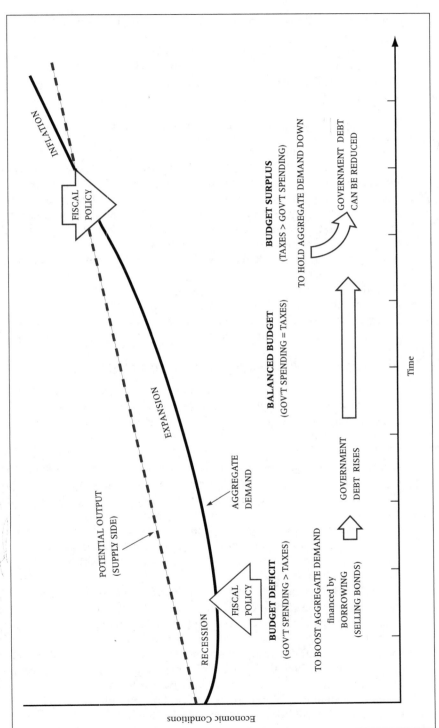

countercyclical fiscal policy A policy of using fiscal policy (budget deficits during recessions and surpluses during periods of inflation) to smooth out the economic fluctuations associated with the business cycle.

balanced budget A government budget in which tax revenues and expenditures are equal.

government will have budget surpluses that can be used to reduce the government's debt.

Economists refer to this as **countercyclical fiscal policy** because the government is deliberately using its budget to offset ("counter") the economic ups and downs of the business cycle, and to smooth out these economic fluctuations.

Should the Government Ever Balance Its Budget, Then?

According to the theory of countercyclical fiscal policy, *in any given year*, it is unlikely that a **balanced budget** (with government spending equal to tax revenues) would be appropriate. As we have seen, if the economy were in a recession, a budget deficit would be in order, while a period of boom/inflation would call for a budget surplus. Only if the economy were operating at a near-ideal balance between these conditions (as in the middle of Figure 7-7) would a balanced budget be appropriate. In these circumstances, a budget that neither stimulated nor depressed aggregate demand would be what the economy needed.

Over the longer run, the budget deficits that are incurred during recessions should be more or less offset by budget surpluses during boom periods, creating a more or less balanced budget *over a period of years*, rather than *in each year*. If this were done, the use of fiscal policy to stabilize the economy would not cause government debt to grow so large as to become a problem.

But This Isn't What Really Happened in Canada, Is It?

No. During the early 1990s, Canadian governments experienced serious problems concerning huge budget deficits and massive government debt. These problems were far removed from the fiscal policies described in the previous sections.

For more than 20 years after the mid-1970s, the federal government had large budget deficits in every year. It did not use surpluses to reduce debt during economic booms. These *continuous annual budget deficits* caused government debt to accumulate steadily, eventually to very high levels. Then *very high interest payments* on the massive debt added to government spending and kept the government's budget deficits high, forcing the government to borrow even more. The borrowing requirements of governments became so great that they had to borrow from foreign lenders, who purchased large volumes of Canadian bonds.

By 1993, the debt of Canadian governments had reached such high levels that foreign lenders became concerned about the risks involved in buying and holding Canadian bonds. This concern forced Canadian governments to reduce their deficits and borrowing requirements through large and painful cuts to spending on social programs such as health care, education, and welfare.

We will consider these government policy decisions and the problems that they generated in more detail in Chapter 8. At this point, it should be noted that while this experience gave budget deficits a "bad name" in Canada, the idea of *periodic* government budget deficits to finance temporary antirecession programs is regarded as sound economic policy.

Monetary and Fiscal Policy in Review

We have seen how the Bank of Canada uses monetary policy and the federal Department of Finance uses fiscal policy to influence the level of aggregate demand in the economy. To conclude this chapter, we should review briefly how monetary and fiscal policies interact to influence the performance of the economy, as shown in Figure 7-8.

FIGURE 7-8 Monetary and Fiscal Policy Combined

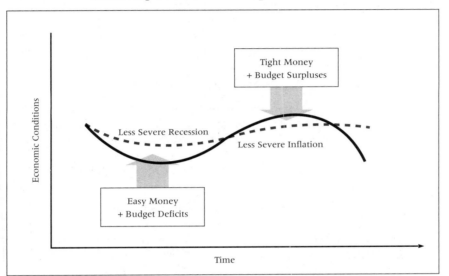

During a recession, when aggregate demand is weak, a *budget deficit* (achieved through increased government spending and/or tax reductions) can be combined with an *easy money policy* consisting of lower interest rates. Both policies will increase the demand for goods and services by households and businesses. This increase in spending will be magnified by the respending effect of the multiplier, and will in part be financed by increases in the money supply resulting from increased bank lending to both consumers and businesses. Also, increased consumer spending may cause businesses to increase their investment spending (the accelerator effect), which would also be financed by bank lending, encouraged by lower interest rates on loans. The overall result would be to stimulate output and employment in the economy through an interaction of monetary and fiscal policies. However, it is important to avoid applying these policies too strongly, as this could push aggregate demand upward with a momentum that would generate inflation in a couple of years or so.

During a period of inflation, rapid growth in the money supply can push aggregate demand for goods and services so high that the supply of them cannot keep pace, causing prices to rise rapidly. The main weapon for fighting inflation is a *tight money policy of high interest rates,* which will attack the high levels of borrowing that are generating such rapid growth of the money supply. The Bank of Canada's tight money policy should be supported by fiscal policy in the form of reductions in government spending and/or higher taxes. The objective of these policies is to depress the demand for goods and services in order to relieve the pressure of excess demand on the supply and on the prices of goods and services. With total demand depressed in these ways, the rate of inflation will tend to decrease. However, as aggregate demand slows down, unemployment will increase. If these policies are applied too strongly, they could push the economy into a recession.

As Figure 7-8 shows, the fiscal policy of the Department of Finance and the monetary policy of the Bank of Canada can be combined to influence the economy's performance. By coordinating the two types of policy, the effect can be made considerably stronger than if either were used by itself.

Coordinating Monetary and Fiscal Policies

Figure 7-9 shows the coordination of fiscal policy, which is conducted by the federal government (the Department of Finance, under the Minister of Finance), and monetary policy, which is conducted by the Bank of Canada.

FIGURE 7-9 Coordinating Monetary and Fiscal Policies

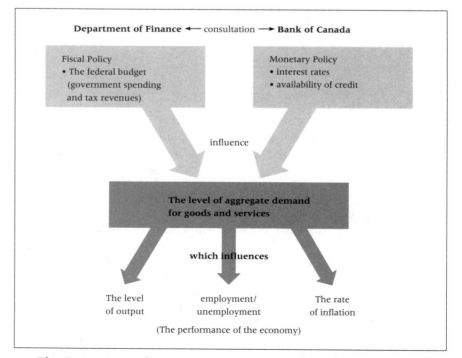

The Department of Finance reports to a federal minister who is a key member of the federal government's cabinet. The cabinet represents an elected government that is ultimately accountable to the public in the next election. On the other hand, few members of the cabinet (or Members of Parliament) have expertise in economic and financial matters.

The Governor of the Bank of Canada and its staff certainly possess great expertise concerning economic and financial issues. However, they are not elected and accountable to the public; they are appointed. And they are appointed for quite long terms—in the case of the Governor and the Senior Deputy Governor, seven years. This enables them to view economic policy from the longer-term perspective.

To provide for coordination between the government and the Bank of Canada, the *Bank of Canada Act* requires regular consultation between the Governor of the Bank of Canada and the Minister of Finance (on behalf of the government). In addition, the Act provides that in the event of a fundamental disagreement, the government can direct the central bank, in writing, as to the monetary policy to be followed; that is, the government can overrule the Governor of the Bank of Canada.

However, it would be very difficult for a government to do so. The law requires that any government directive overruling the Bank of Canada be made public. And it is generally understood that following such a directive, the Governor of the Bank of Canada would resign. Given the respect for the Bank of Canada's expertise, such actions on the part of the government would risk undermining the confidence of the Canadian public and foreign investors in the government's economic policies. So a government would be quite reluctant to overrule the Governor, a fact that gives the appointed experts at the Bank of Canada considerable influence over government economic policy, and helps to explain why the Governor of the Bank of Canada has been described as "the most powerful unelected official in the country."

Looking Ahead

The thoughtful reader will by now be wondering why, if monetary and fiscal policies really work as described in this chapter, Canada has not succeeded in eliminating both unemployment and inflation.

First, there are some "real-world" obstacles that make it impossible to eradicate *both* unemployment *and* inflation; we will consider these in Chapter 8. And, as we will also see in Chapter 8, governments have not always used their economic policies effectively—sometimes their policy decisions have actually caused problems rather than resolved them.

Chapter Summary

1. The Bank of Canada is responsible for monetary policy, which uses changes in interest rates and the money supply to influence the level of aggregate demand. (L.O. 1)

2. To combat a recession, the Bank of Canada would use an *easy money policy*. The Bank of Canada would lower its target for the overnight rate of interest and take actions to increase the reserves of the banking system. (L.O. 2)

3. An easy money policy would reduce interest rates and encourage borrowing and spending by consumers and businesses. It might also reduce the international price of the Canadian dollar, which would stimulate exports and reduce imports. If aggregate demand were increased too rapidly, the rate of inflation could increase in the future. (L.O. 3)

4. To combat inflation, the Bank of Canada would use a *tight money policy*. The Bank of Canada would raise its target for the overnight rate of interest and take actions to reduce the reserves of the banking system. (L.O. 4)

5. A tight money policy would increase interest rates and discourage borrowing and spending by consumers and businesses. It might also increase the international price of the Canadian dollar, which would depress exports and increase imports. As the growth of aggregate demand slowed, unemployment would rise. (L.O. 5)

6. Fiscal policy, which is conducted by the Department of Finance, uses changes in government spending and taxes to influence the level of aggregate demand. (L.O. 6)

7. For combating recessions, fiscal policy involves increased government spending and/or tax reductions, which lead to government budget deficits. (L.O. 7)

8. After being "kick-started" by temporary budget deficits (L.O. 7), the economy should grow on its own as the multiplier and accelerator effects carry aggregate demand to higher levels. (L.O. 8)

9. The budget deficits that arise through implementing fiscal policy designed to combat recessions are financed by government borrowing through bond issues. (L.O. 9)

10. When the economy booms and inflation threatens, the focus of fiscal policy should change to the creation of budget surpluses. A budget surplus will not only slow down aggregate demand but will also provide funds that the government can use to reduce its debt. (L.O. 10)

Questions

1. Visit the Bank of Canada's website (www.bankofcanada.ca) and check the Bank's most recent press release concerning policy announcements involving interest rates and the most recent *Monetary Policy Report* or *Monetary Policy Report Update*. How has the Bank of Canada changed its target for the overnight rate recently, and what were the reasons for its change in the target?

2. What effect would a tight money policy tend to have on
   (a) the price of corporate shares on the stock market?
   (b) the price of outstanding government bonds (bonds that were issued in the past and have not yet matured and can thus still be bought and sold)?

3. Make the strongest possible argument that monetary policy
   (a) should *not* be decided by the federal government alone.
   (b) should *not* be decided by the Bank of Canada alone.

4. "Even apparently pointless make-work programs ('digging holes and filling them up again') run by the government can be of economic value under certain conditions." What is the speaker's reasoning? Do you agree or not?

5. (a) Which of the following do you believe would have a *stronger* stimulative effect on the economy: a $100-million increase in government spending or a $100-million reduction in personal income taxes? Why?
   (b) Which of the two policies in (a) do you believe would have a *faster* effect on the economy? Why?

6.

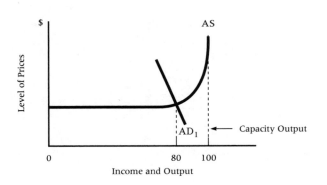

(a) At the level of aggregate demand represented by AD_1, the level of GDP and income is $80 billion, or _____ percent below the economy's potential, and the economy is in a state of _____.

(b) What would be the appropriate action for the government to take regarding its budget?

(c) Draw a new aggregate demand curve (AD_2) to represent the new situation that might result from the government's action in (b), and show on the graph how this new AD curve would affect

   (i) the level of incomes and GDP, and
   (ii) the level of prices.

(d) Explain why the effects referred to in (c) will occur.

7. Why is the Governor of the Bank of Canada described as "the most powerful unelected official in the country"?

8. Suppose you have just heard that the Bank Rate has been increased significantly. How might you expect this to affect you personally?

9. In 2001–02, interest rates in the United States were reduced sharply in an attempt to boost the sluggish U.S. economy. By the end of 2002, some observers were concerned that this policy would not have its intended effect. What might have led to these concerns? Have events since 2002 shown that these concerns were justified or not?

Chapter 8

Perspectives on Macroeconomic Policy

Learning Objectives

After studying this chapter, you should be able to:

1. Explain how monetary and fiscal policies that increase aggregate demand will affect output, employment, and the rate of inflation:
   (a) during a recession, and
   (b) as the economy approaches its capacity output and full employment.

2. State the unemployment rate that is considered to represent "full employment," and explain why this rate is as high as it is, with reference to:
   (a) the trade-off between unemployment and inflation,
   (b) the different types of unemployment, and
   (c) differences in unemployment rates between regions and age groups.

3. Referring to Canada's experience, explain why it is important for government policy-makers to keep the rate of inflation low and relatively stable.

4. State the target range for inflation that has been established by the Bank of Canada and the federal government, and explain the purposes of this target range.

5. Describe two situations in which government borrowing is economically beneficial.

6. Referring to Canada's experience, explain why it is important for government policy-makers to keep government debt under control.

7. Explain how the time lags involved in implementing monetary and fiscal policies can limit the effectiveness of these policies.

8. Explain three ways in which international factors limit the freedom of Canadian economic policy-makers.

The monetary and fiscal policies described in Chapter 7 are impressive in scope, directed toward increasing or decreasing the pace of the entire economy by influencing the behaviour of millions of consumers and businesses. The impact of these policies is measured in terms of tens of billions of dollars of output and hundreds of thousands of jobs.

If these policies worked ideally, we might expect to have very little unemployment or inflation. However, this has not been the case—in the last quarter of the twentieth century, the average unemployment rate was over 9 percent of the labour force, and the average rate of inflation was nearly 6 percent. Also, as Figure 8-1 shows, economic conditions were far from stable, as the rates of both unemployment and inflation fluctuated widely over the period.

Why have we not been able to do better than this? To a large extent, our less-than-ideal economic performance reflects the fact that when monetary and fiscal policies are implemented in the "real world," certain obstacles exist that limit the extent to which unemployment and inflation can be reduced. In addition, these obstacles also reflect the unfortunate effects of some past government policies. To explain the track record in Figure 8-1, we will consider the following five limitations:

1. Obstacles to reducing unemployment.
2. The need to keep inflation in check.
3. The need to keep government debt within limits.
4. Time lags associated with implementing policies.
5. International limitations on Canadian policies.

1. Obstacles to Reducing Unemployment

Figure 8-1 shows that the lowest unemployment rate we have achieved since 1974 has been 6.8 percent, and that the unemployment rate has seldom been below 8 percent. To understand these facts better, we need to consider the matter of unemployment in more detail.

Types of Unemployment

In Chapter 2, we saw that there are various reasons why people become unemployed. An examination of these reasons can provide a better understanding of unemployment and what can be done about it.

cyclical unemployment
Unemployment that is caused by periodic cyclical weaknesses in aggregate demand associated with recessions.

Cyclical unemployment, which arises from the periodic recessions associated with the business cycle, is probably the best-known type of unemployment. Cyclical forces account for the periodic peaks in the unemployment rate that are evident in Figure 8-1, during recessions. And when the economy recovers, cyclical unemployment and the unemployment rate decrease.

However, there are several other factors that also affect the unemployment rate, and these considerably complicate the government's task of reducing unemployment.

FIGURE 8-1 Inflation and Unemployment Rates, 1966–2002

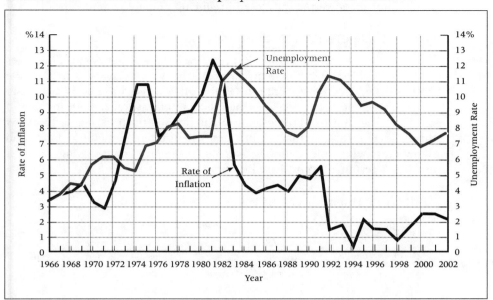

Source: Statistics Canada, adapted from *Historical Labour Force Statistics*, Catalogue 71-201, March 2001, and *The Consumer Price Index*, Catalogue 62-001, 2002.

Frictional unemployment is due to people being temporarily out of work because they are changing from one job to another. Frictional unemployment is considered to be a normal aspect of a free and dynamic economy in which jobs change in response to constant changes in product demand and technology.

Frictional unemployment can be increased by disincentives to work that arise from government income-support programs. For instance, if a recipient of Employment Insurance or welfare earns income by working, his or her benefits are often reduced by so much that there is little or no economic incentive to work. Also, the availability of Employment Insurance benefits can cause recipients to prolong their job searches, adding to unemployment.

Seasonal unemployment is also relatively short-term in nature. Because of the seasonal nature of industries such as agriculture, fishing, forestry, and construction, unemployment is higher in the winter. Seasonal unemployment is an inevitable aspect of Canadian labour markets; however, it has decreased over the past 20 years or so.

Structural unemployment is a much more serious problem for affected workers because of its longer-term nature. Structural unemployment arises from a mismatch between the skills required by employers and those possessed by unemployed workers, which can make it very difficult for the unemployed to find work. The major causes of structural unemployment are changes in *production technology* or *product demand*.

frictional unemployment
Unemployment arising from people being temporarily out of work because they are in the process of changing jobs.

seasonal unemployment
Unemployment arising from seasonal downturns in employment in some industries.

structural unemployment
Unemployment arising from a mismatch between the skills required by employers and those of unemployed people.

As we will see, the existence of these various types of unemployment complicates the government's task of reducing unemployment considerably.

Regional Differences in Unemployment Rates

Statistics Canada collects data on 69 different regional labour markets across Canada.

As Table 8-1 shows, there are large and persistent differences in unemployment rates in the various regions of Canada. Unemployment rates in the Atlantic provinces and Quebec are persistently higher than the national average, while in Ontario and the prairies, the unemployment rate is regularly below the average. British Columbia's unemployment rate is sometimes above and sometimes below the national average, depending upon swings in that province's resource export-based economy.

TABLE 8-1 Unemployment Rates by Region

		Unemployment Rates				
Year	Canada	Atlantic Region	Quebec	Ontario	Prairie Region	British Columbia
1970	5.7%	5.7%	7.0%	4.4%	5.0%	7.7%
1980	7.5	11.1	9.8	6.8	4.3	6.8
1990	8.1	12.7	10.2	6.3	7.1	8.4
1998	8.3	12.9	10.4	7.2	5.7	8.9

Source: Bank of Canada, adapted from the *Bank of Canada Review* and *Banking and Financial Statistics*; Statistics Canada, adapted from *Historical Labour Force Statistics*, Catalogue 71-201, March 2001.

These regional variations in unemployment also complicate the government's efforts to reduce unemployment, because even when an economic boom makes unemployment quite low in Canada as a whole, and very low in some parts of the country, it will still be quite high in other regions.

Age Differences in Unemployment Rates

As Figure 8-2 shows, unemployment rates are particularly high among young people, even when the economy is strong. At the peak of the boom in 2000, when the unemployment rate for people 25 and over was only 5.7 percent, 12.6 percent of the 15–24 age group was unemployed.

There are various reasons why unemployment rates for the young are so high. When the economy slows down, employers reduce or cease hiring, leaving many young people who are trying to enter the labour force unable to find work. Also, layoffs are most commonly done by seniority, so the young are generally laid off first. In addition, frictional unemployment is high among the young, because people move more frequently from job to job early in their careers. Also, Canada's minimum wage laws are believed to contribute to Canada's high rate of youth unemployment. By requiring minimum wage rates for younger workers that are not much less than those for more experienced workers, these laws make it less attractive to employ young people.

FIGURE 8-2 Unemployment Rates by Age, 2001

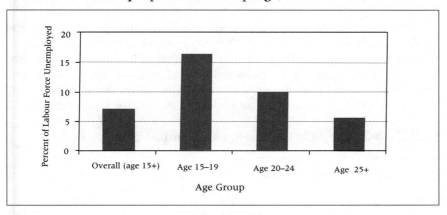

Source: Statistics Canada, adapted from the CANSIM database,
http://cansim2.statcan.ca/cgi-win/CNSMCGI.EXE.

YOU
DECIDE

TWO VIEWS OF CANADA'S PERFORMANCE ON EMPLOYMENT

The unemployment rate measures the percentage of the labour force that is unemployed. By this yardstick, the job performance of the Canadian economy seems weak—Canada's unemployment rate has been among the higher of the major nations.

Another way to measure the employment performance of a nation's economy is through the percentage of the working-age population that is employed, or the **employment-to-population ratio**.

By the standard of the employment-to-population ratio, Canada's performance has been much better—in the middle range among those of major nations.

employment-to-population ratio
The percentage of the working-age population that is employed.

Question

1. What could explain Canada's employment performance being so much better by the yardstick of the employment-to-population ratio than by unemployment rate statistics?

Monetary and Fiscal Policies to Reduce Unemployment

In Chapter 7, we saw how *easy money* (a monetary policy of low interest rates) and *budget deficits* (a fiscal policy of increased government spending and/or lower taxes) can be combined to combat unemployment by increasing aggregate demand. However, since 1981, the number of unemployed Canadians has never been less than one million. To see why lower unemployment rates have not been achieved, we will examine how the economy responds to government policies that boost aggregate demand:

(a) when unemployment is high, and

(b) when unemployment is low.

First, it is helpful to recall that in any market, an increase in demand can have two effects: it can cause an *increase in output* (and employment), an *increase in prices*, or a *combination of these*, as shown in Figure 8-3. And the more that output can rise in response to higher demand, the less prices will rise. On the other hand, if output cannot rise as fast as demand, prices will rise. So, how fast output can increase will be a key to how fast prices will rise.

FIGURE 8-3 The Effect of Higher Demand on a Market

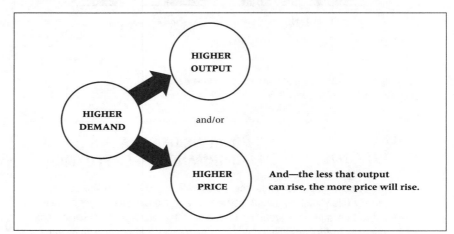

The Effects of Increased Demand When Unemployment Is High

Suppose the economy is in a recession, with cyclical unemployment high and output far below capacity. With aggregate demand this low, the rate of inflation will be very low.

If the government uses its monetary and fiscal policies to increase aggregate demand, the results should be quite favourable. Output and employment will increase, but the rate of inflation will remain low.

First, output and employment can be increased readily in a recession. Businesses will have unused plant capacity and will be able to obtain materials from suppliers who are in a similar position. And with cyclical unemployment high, businesses will be able to recall or hire unemployed workers in order to increase production.

The rate of inflation will remain low for several reasons, the basic one being that output can be increased so readily. Also, with unemployment high, businesses will be able to obtain the workers they need without having to pay higher wages. And as output increases, production costs per unit will actually fall, as production facilities are used more efficiently and fixed costs are spread over more units of output. Furthermore, with the economy still sluggish, businesses and unions will be unlikely to increase prices and wages for fear of jeopardizing their sales and jobs.

In short, when there is a recession, government policies that increase aggregate demand will have very *beneficial effects* on the economy, by causing quite large increases in output without increasing the rate of inflation significantly. And as the economy recovers from the recession, the unemployment rate will decrease as cyclical unemployment falls.

The Effects of Increased Demand When Unemployment is Low

As these expansionary monetary and fiscal policies bring unemployment down, their effects on the economy will gradually change. As output gets nearer to capacity and unemployment becomes quite low, further increases in aggregate demand will have *mixed effects* on the economy. Output will not be able to rise as rapidly as before, and prices will begin to rise more rapidly.

As the economy approaches capacity output, firms will have difficulty increasing output as rapidly as in the past. They may no longer have the unused plant capacity to increase capacity, and/or they may have problems recruiting more workers. With employment now high, cyclical unemployment has nearly vanished. Most of the unemployment that remains will be *structural* unemployment—people who lack the skills or incentives to work at the jobs that are becoming available. This situation will make it considerably more difficult for many businesses to recruit the workers they need to increase output. For instance, in mid-2000, with the national unemployment rate at 6.7 percent, many employers were unable to recruit workers with the skills they required.

Because output cannot increase as readily, prices will begin to rise more rapidly as demand increases. The rate of inflation will increase, for several reasons. Shortages of specific productive inputs (such as skilled labour and certain raw materials) will probably develop, causing their prices and wages to rise even though the economy as a whole has not yet reached its capacity output. Some businesses will have to pay overtime in order to keep up with demand, while others may pay higher wages in order to attract qualified workers from other employers. The price increases resulting from these production *bottlenecks* will force up production costs, contributing to more rapid inflation. Furthermore, as economic conditions improve, higher demand will enable more businesses to raise prices, and labour unions will take advantage of the improved bargaining position that low unemployment rates bring, negotiating larger wage increases that add to employers' labour costs and push prices higher.

In summary, as the economy expands into the boom phase of the cycle, government policies that drive aggregate demand higher will encounter more difficulty in pushing output and employment higher, but will drive the rate of inflation up. And the closer the economy gets to its capacity output, the more severe inflation will become.

The Problem of Inflation

And therein lies the problem. Long before monetary and fiscal policies have eradicated unemployment, they will be generating a problem of inflation. With aggregate demand high enough that inflation is threatening to become a serious problem, unemployment will still be high in some regions, such as the Atlantic provinces and Quebec, and among some groups, such as the young and the structurally unemployed. And if the government attacked this unemployment by using its monetary and fiscal policies to push aggregate demand even higher, it would achieve only small improvements in unemployment at the cost of generating a growing problem of inflation that threatens to accelerate. (The next section will explain the dangers of accelerating inflation.)

At this point, the economy would have reached **"full employment"**; that is, the unemployment rate would be as low as it can go without inflation becoming a problem.

full employment The lowest rate of unemployment that can be achieved without generating unacceptable inflation in the economy.

What Is "Full Employment"?

How low can the unemployment rate go without inflation becoming a problem? There is no "magic number" that is the answer to this question. Rather, the evidence is that the answer can change over time.

In 1989, at the end of the economic boom of the 1980s, the unemployment rate dipped to 7.5 percent, the lowest in almost a decade. However, this unemployment rate of 7.5 percent did not prove to be sustainable, because inflation was beginning to accelerate, to a rate of 5.6 percent. To slow down inflation, the Bank of Canada raised interest rates, causing the economy to slow down and unemployment to rise again. This experience led observers to conclude that "full employment" was an unemployment rate between 7.5 and 8.0 percent.

By the peak of the next boom in 2000, however, things had improved. The unemployment rate fell to a low of *6.7 percent, but the rate of inflation remained low*. What had changed? One explanation was that unemployment had been reduced by changes to Employment Insurance and welfare programs, making it more difficult for people to passively rely on these programs. Another was that in the 1990s, the behaviour of workers and employers was less inflationary. In the late 1980s the fact that they *expected* more inflation had led them to increase both wages and prices more rapidly, which tended to *create* the inflation that they feared. But by the late 1990s, there were no such expectations, so increases in both wages and prices were more moderate.

Following this experience, many observers believed that "full employment" in Canada was probably an unemployment rate of close to 7 percent of the labour force.

2. The Need to Keep Inflation in Check

The previous section explains that the need to restrain inflation limits how far government policies can reduce unemployment. Now, let's consider *why* government policy-makers place such emphasis on keeping inflation in check. The experience of the "Great Inflation" of the 1970s and 1980s demonstrated painfully that if the government does not keep the rate of inflation quite low, inflation can *accelerate*, with serious economic consequences. As a result, much more emphasis is placed today on *preventing* inflation from reaching the point at which it begins to gain momentum.

The "Great Inflation" of the 1970s

The Great Inflation of the 1970s was generated by a very rapid increase in the money supply of Canada and other nations. Subsequently, aggregate demand and the economy also grew rapidly. At first, the increase in the rate of inflation that accompanied these developments seemed to be a small trade-off for the gains in output and employment.

However, after a time lag of about a year, the money-supply growth pushed aggregate demand beyond the economy's capacity, and the rate of inflation soared from less than 3 percent per year in 1971 to nearly 11 percent in 1974.

How Inflation Accelerated

Once inflation got underway, it tended to gather momentum and became more and more rapid, due to *inflation psychology*, or people's behaviour when faced with inflation. As discussed in Chapter 6, in this kind of situation, people came to expect that rapid inflation would continue. To protect themselves against this expected rapid inflation, they sought very large wage and salary increases and spent their money before prices rose further, even borrowing money to do so. This behaviour made inflation more severe, as higher wages pushed up production costs and prices, and higher spending added to inflationary pressures. As a result, rates of inflation of 9 to 12 percent per year became ingrained in the economy for about a decade after 1972, as Figure 8-4 shows.

The Damage Caused by Severe Inflation

Inflation and Exports

If inflation in Canada is more rapid than in other countries, Canadian goods will become more expensive relative to foreign goods, and Canadian producers will become less competitive internationally. Foreigners will buy fewer Canadian exports, and Canadians will buy more foreign imports, causing output and employment in Canada to fall. Because Canada's exports and imports are such a high proportion of its GDP, the potential loss of output and also of employment in such a situation are a serious concern. ⌐

FIGURE 8-4 The Rate of Inflation, 1961–2002

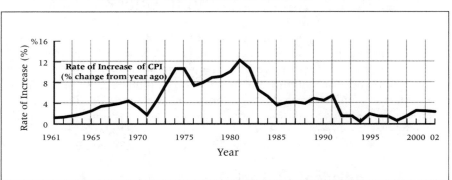

Source: Statistics Canada, adapted from *The Consumer Price Index*, Catalogue 62-001, and *Consumer Prices and Price Indexes*, Catalogue 62-010.

Inflation and the Economically Weak

Another concern is the effect of rapid inflation on the economically weak members of society. With prices rising rapidly, people must obtain large wage increases just to stand still economically. For professionals, skilled workers, and members of strong labour unions, this is generally possible. But economically weak groups such as pensioners, the unskilled, and nonunion workers will not be able to increase their incomes as fast as prices are rising. For them, rapid inflation means that their standard of living will fall.

Inflation and the Saving–Investment Process

Inflation *undermines the saving–investment process*, which is the key to higher productivity and prosperity. The main reason for this problem (as we saw in Chapter 6) is that rapid inflation *causes high interest rates* that discourage business investment spending. Fearing that continuing inflation will erode the real value (purchasing power) of the capital that they loan out, savers/lenders will insist on higher interest rates to offset the declining value of their capital. This situation is shown in Table 8-2. In the low-inflation scenario in the left column, savers/lenders expect inflation to reduce the value of their capital by 2 percent per year, so they accept an interest rate of 5 percent on any loans they make—after inflation, this would leave them with a **real interest rate**, or after-inflation gain, of 3 percent. But in the high-inflation scenario in the right column, they expect inflation of 10 percent, so they will have to earn an interest rate of *13 percent* to earn the same real (after inflation) interest rate of 3 percent. But if rapid inflation forces interest rates too high, businesses may find borrowing for capital investment to be too costly. And less investment means slower growth of productivity and living standards.

real interest rate The rate of return earned by a lender after inflation is taken into account. For instance, if the rate of interest is 6 percent and the rate of inflation is 2 percent, the real interest rate is 4 percent.

TABLE 8-2 Inflation and Incentives to Save and Invest

$100 invested for one year	With Inflation Expected to Be 2%		With Inflation Expected to Be 10%	
Interest rate	5%		13%	
⟶ Interest income	⟶	$5.00	⟶	$13.00
less:				
Loss of purchasing power on the $100 due to inflation	2%	2.00	10%	10.00
equals:				
"Real" return (after inflation)	3%	$3.00	3%	$3.00
less:				
Taxes on interest income (40%)		−2.00		−5.20
equals:				
Return after inflation and taxes		+1.00		−2.20

But Table 8-2 also shows a second problem: *rapid inflation reduces the incentive to save.* In the low-inflation scenario in the left column, on an investment of $100 the saver/investor earns a real return of $3 before taxes, and $1 after taxes of $2 (40 percent of the $5 interest income). But in the high-inflation scenario in the right-hand column, the saver/investor *loses money.* On the $13 of interest income, the taxes will be $5.20 (40 percent of $13), leaving the investor with a *loss* of $2.20 after inflation and taxes. So the incentive to save and invest is actually lower in the high-inflation/high-interest rate situation than in the low-inflation/low-interest rate situation.

In summary, rapid inflation is the enemy of the saving–investment process that is a key to prosperity. Rapid inflation discourages not only capital investment, but also the saving upon which much capital investment depends. By doing so, severe inflation can undermine productivity growth and the supply side of the economy.

Inflation Leads to Recession

Periods of severe inflation tend to end in recessions. Eventually, the problems caused by inflation will force the government to fight inflation. Since inflation is caused by a rapidly rising money supply generated by heavy borrowing, the only really effective anti-inflation policy is a "tight money" policy with very *high interest rates*, to discourage borrowing. Such policies led to mortgage interest rates of over 20 percent in 1981 and a recession in 1981–82. This unhappy experience was repeated in the early 1990s, when mortgage rates exceeded 13 percent and a recession follwed.

So, for a variety of reasons that are summarized in Figure 8-5, we learned in the 1970s and 1980s that rapid inflation will have serious economic consequences. As a result of these experiences, the government decided that keeping inflation under control should be a priority for economic policy in the future.

FIGURE 8-5 The Effects of Inflation

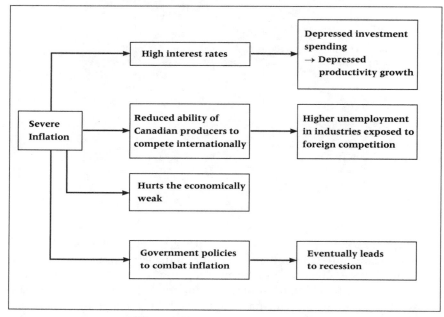

Inflation Targets

In 1993, the federal government and the Bank of Canada announced the objective of keeping the rate of inflation inside a "target range" of 1 to 3 percent per year. This announcement asserted that in the future, the Bank of Canada's primary goal would be to *prevent* inflation from accelerating as it had done in the 1970s and 1980s. Because monetary policy operates with long time lags, this goal would require that the Bank of Canada be ready to take *early action* to increase interest rates if there were signs of inflation accelerating in the economy.[1]

Inflation targets could also help to keep inflation under control by changing expectations concerning inflation. If the public believes that inflation will be kept under control, the public's expectation that causes inflation to

www.bankofcanada.ca/
en/backgrounders/bg–13

---

[1] This does not mean that price stability was to be the *only* goal of the Bank of Canada. When the economy is in a recession and the rate of inflation is very low, the Bank of Canada will reduce short-term interest rates with the intention of stimulating aggregate demand, as described in Chapter 7. This was done in 1994–96 and again in 2001–02, when economic conditions were sufficiently slow that such a policy would not create a danger of inflation.

accelerate (inflation psychology) will be less likely to develop, making it easier for the Bank of Canada to maintain a low rate of inflation.

3. The Need to Keep Government Debt Under Control

The experience of the 1970s and 1980s demonstrated not only the need to keep inflation under control, but also the need to keep government budget deficits and debt under control.

This is not a simple question of government borrowing and debt being "bad." In the right circumstances, government borrowing can bring economic and social benefits. First, we will consider two situations in which government borrowing can be beneficial, then we will examine the problems that Canada experienced with government deficits and debt.

Countercyclical Budget Deficits

As we saw in Chapter 7, periodic government budget deficits can help to boost aggregate demand during recessions, through a combination of higher government spending and lower taxes. These *countercyclical* deficits will, of course, require the government to borrow and increase its debt during recessions. However, after the recession has ended and the economy is booming again, there is an opportunity for the government to pay down its debt by running budget surpluses, as shown in Figure 8-6. Such countercyclical budget deficits are a generally accepted element of government economic policy.

FIGURE 8-6 Borrowing to Combat Recessions and to Finance Assets

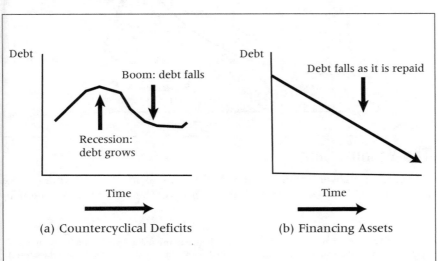

(a) Countercyclical Deficits   (b) Financing Assets

Borrowing to Finance Social Assets

A common reason for borrowing is to *acquire assets*, such as homes and cars for households, and plant and equipment for businesses. Borrowing is necessary because such assets are too costly to purchase out of the current year's income. And since the benefits from the asset will be received over a long period of time, it is quite reasonable to borrow to buy the asset and to pay for it over a period of years, as the loan is repaid.

In a similar manner, it is considered reasonable for governments to borrow to build *social assets*, such as hospitals, schools, transportation systems, and so on. Since these assets will provide long-term benefits to the public, governments typically issue long-term bonds to raise the funds to build them.

What Not to Do

While it is considered reasonable to borrow to pay for large *one-time expenditures* such as assets (or combatting a recession), borrowing to pay *ongoing current operating expenses* is a very different matter. These are not one-time expenditures; rather, they recur regularly, month after month. Borrowing to pay expenses such as these will only lead to regular monthly borrowing, and an ever-increasing debt. And after the debt reaches a certain point, the *rising interest costs* on the debt might well eventually become unmanageable, pushing the debt even *higher* in a sort of spiral, as shown in Figure 8-7.

FIGURE 8-7 **The Consequences of Regular Annual Borrowing**

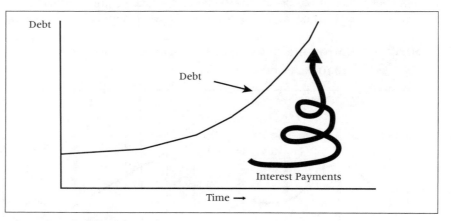

National Debt A measure of the indebtedness of the federal government; specifically, the difference between the government's liabilities (mostly outstanding bonds) and its net recorded assets.

The National Debt

As noted, the government finances its budget deficits by borrowing money, mostly through the sale of government bonds. These bonds are bought by

---

[2] Specifically, the National Debt is the difference between the federal government's liabilities (mostly outstanding bonds) and its net recorded assets (mostly those assets that yield interest, profits, or dividends).

large investment funds such as pension funds and mutual funds, by financial institutions such as banks and insurance companies, and by individuals as part of their investment portfolios. The total amount of federal government debt is called the **National Debt**.[2] In 2002, the National Debt was about $535 billion, or about $17 000 for every Canadian man, woman, and child.

The relationship between the National Debt and the federal government's budget deficits is shown in Table 8-3. The National Debt is the *total*

TABLE 8-3 Federal Budget Deficits and the National Debt

Year	Government Spending	Government Tax Revenues	Budget Deficit	National Debt
		($ Billions)		
20X1	$50	$50	$0	$0
20X2	60	55	5	5
20X3	70	56	14	19
20X4	80	68	12	31
20X5	83	75	8	39

accumulated federal debt as a result of past budget deficits, while each year's budget deficit represents *that year's addition* to the National Debt.

In Table 8-3, it is assumed that the government has no debt at the start of year 20X1, no budget deficit in 20X1, and therefore no debt at the end of 20X1. After that, there are deficits for four years, with the total government debt (National Debt) increasing by the amount of each year's deficit. Note that even after the government manages to *reduce its deficits* in 20X4 and 20X5, the National Debt continues to grow. As long as there is *any* budget deficit, the National Debt will rise. Only by having budget surpluses (revenues larger than spending) such as in year 20X6 can the government *reduce* its debt.

Canada's Experience with Government Deficits and Debt

In the 1950s and 1960s, the federal government had periodic budget deficits, which were quite small and mostly the result of recessions. The size of the National Debt increased over this period, but much less rapidly than the GDP. As a result, the federal government's debt as a percentage of GDP decreased, from 63 percent in 1950 to only 18 percent in 1975.

Beginning in the early 1970s, a very different situation developed concerning the federal government's budget. *In every year* the government had a budget deficit, and these deficits became *much larger* than in the past— as large as $13 billion per year by the late 1970s and about $30 billion per year in the 1980s.

There were various reasons for these deficits. During the 1970s, the federal government made a series of policy decisions that *increased its expenditure commitments* and *depressed its tax revenues*. For instance, the federal government increased benefits under various social programs, such as unemployment insurance and pensions, and made commitments to transfer large amounts of federal funds (in the range of $20 billion per year) to the provincial governments to help finance rapidly rising provincial government spending on programs such as *health care, welfare,* and *post-secondary education.*

Having increased its spending commitments in these areas, the federal government introduced after 1974 a variety of *tax reductions on both personal and business income,* which had the effect of depressing its tax revenues.

These decisions caused a built-in imbalance to develop between government spending and tax revenues, generating what are known as **structural budget deficits**—budget deficits that occur each year, *whether the economy is in a recession or not.* Figure 8-8 shows the budget deficits and the growth of the federal government's debt during this period. The figures are expressed as a percentage of GDP because dollar figures present a distorted picture during a period of rapid inflation such as this.

structural budget deficits Deficits arising from a built-in imbalance between government expenditures and revenues that results in deficits even when the economy is in a period of boom.

FIGURE 8-8 Budget Deficits and the National Debt, 1968–93

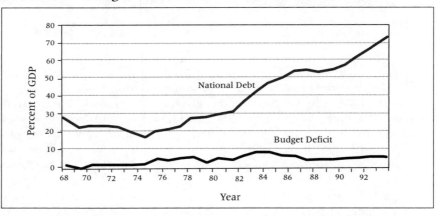

Source: Department of Finance, adapted from *Fiscal Reference Tables,* September 2000. Reproduced with permission of the Minister of Public Works and Government Services Canada, 2003.

This imbalance meant that the federal government was providing Canadians with services (such as health care and education) and transfer payments (such as unemployment insurance and welfare) far in excess of what they were paying for with their taxes, and was borrowing heavily to do so—even in years when the economy was not in a recession.

The recession of the early 1980s increased federal budget deficits sharply. With many more people on unemployment insurance, and government tax revenues depressed by the recession, the deficit increased into the $20 to $25 billion per year range. By 1985, the National Debt was $208 billion, more than eight times its 1973 level of $24 billion.

In the second half of the 1980s, the federal government tried to reduce its deficits by restraining its spending and increasing various taxes. But by this point, another factor was driving the federal budget deficit upward—*interest payments on the government's massive debt*. Interest payments became the second-largest item of current government expenditure, keeping the deficit high and forcing the government to borrow even more. For instance, in the boom year of 1989, the government had a deficit of over $20 billion and interest payments of more than $37 billion. The government was borrowing more in order to pay the interest on its debt.

The recession of the early 1990s drove the federal budget deficit into the $30 billion range. The federal government's debt was over $500 billion, and was being driven higher by annual interest payments of about $40 billion.

The finances of the provincial governments were also deteriorating. To reduce its budget deficits after 1985, the federal government had cut its transfer payments to the provinces for health care, welfare, and post-secondary education. These cuts forced the provincial governments into deficits, and when the recession struck in the early 1990s, the combined deficits of the provincial governments soared to about $24 billion in 1992 and 1993.

Canada's Foreign Debt

These large federal budget deficits led to Canada's having the heaviest *foreign debt* of any major industrialized nation in the world. While the federal government sold most of its own bonds *within* Canada, its borrowings were so large that they absorbed much of Canadians' savings. As a result, provincial governments and corporations often could not obtain the funds they needed to borrow from Canadian lenders, and were forced to sell their bonds to *foreign lenders*. In addition, the federal government itself increasingly turned to selling its bonds to foreign lenders. By 1993, 28 percent of federal debt was owed to foreign lenders, as compared to 3 percent in 1973.

From 1986 to 1994, Canadian governments and corporations increased their debts to foreign lenders by over $140 billion. This brought Canada's total foreign indebtedness to about 45 percent of GDP, by far the largest of any major industrialized nation. To place this foreign debt in perspective, Italy's was second highest at about 10 percent of GDP.

Deficits, Debt, and Interest Rates

Such high government deficits and debt pushed interest rates to very high levels, partly due to governments' high demand for borrowed funds. However, another reason for high interest rates was that foreign lenders were becoming increasingly concerned about the financial condition of Canadian governments. Figure 8-9 shows how the real (after-inflation) interest rate on Government of Canada long-term bonds became very high in the 1990s. By making borrowing very expensive, such high interest rates prolonged the recession of the early 1990s. They also added to governments' interest costs, making their deficits worse. By the mid-1990s, Canada had the highest real interest rates of any major industrialized nation.

FIGURE 8-9 Real Long-Term Interest Rates, 1980–94

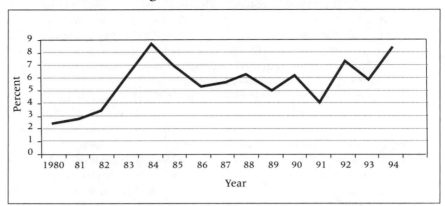

Source: Bank of Canada, adapted from the *Bank of Canada Review* and *Banking and Financial Statistics*.

The Critical Point

> How much is a billion? One billion *seconds* is 31.5 *years*.

By 1993, the situation had become critical. The combined budget deficits of all levels of government in Canada amounted to $58 billion per year. The total net debt of Canadian governments was nearly $700 billion (95 percent of GDP), and interest payments were driving this debt higher, in an upward spiral. Canada's debt to foreign lenders, about half of which was owed by Canadian governments, was by far the largest in the world as a percentage of GDP and was rising rapidly. Canadian governments, especially the provinces, were increasingly dependent upon foreign lenders to finance their public services by buying their bonds.

But foreign lenders were growing concerned about the creditworthiness of Canadian governments, especially some provinces. As their credit ratings deteriorated, some provinces faced having to pay higher interest rates on their bonds in order to attract lenders. These developments intensified the pressure on Canadian governments to deal with their budget problems.

Finally, the federal government made cuts to its spending, particularly its transfer payments to the provinces. This led to a series of cutbacks by provincial governments that cut into all of Canada's key social welfare programs—health care, education, and welfare. In effect, the standard of living of Canadians in the 1990s was being reduced by the government's decision in the 1970s and 1980s to postpone paying for government benefits and services.

This experience with the consequences of excessive debt changed the priorities of governments, by making both government policy-makers and the public more cautious about government borrowing. And for governments trying to deal with the problem of unemployment, this new concern about deficits and debt added another limitation.

4. The Problem of Time Lags

Another limitation on the effectiveness of government monetary and fiscal policies is that they work slowly, or with *time lags*.

The problem of time lags was introduced in Chapter 7. To recap, there are three types of time lags, which are summarized in Figure 8-10. The first is the *recognition lag*, or the time that it takes for policy-makers to clearly recognize that there is a problem of inflation or unemployment that needs to be addressed. Next is the *policy lag*, which occurs because government policies cannot be put in place immediately. The Bank of Canada can move quickly to change short-term interest rates, but changes in fiscal policy involving taxes and government spending take longer, as they may involve budget or legislative changes. Finally, there is the *impact lag*, or the time it takes for the policies to take effect on the economy. Changes in interest rates and government budgets will affect spending by consumers and businesses, but not for six to eighteen months. Monetary policy operates with long time lags, especially policies intended to slow down inflation.

FIGURE 8-10 Time Lags

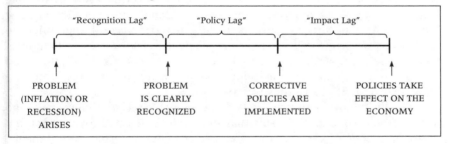

Together, these time lags can add up to a total of *between one and two years*. Such long time lags can create real problems for economic policy-makers. Because of the lags, the problem being attacked (either inflation or recession) can grow considerably more severe and difficult to correct by the time the government's policies take effect.

Taking Aim Carefully

Since the effects of the government's monetary and fiscal policies will not be felt for a year or two, the government should direct its policies toward correcting economic problems that it *expects will exist* in a year or two. Accurate economic forecasts would be particularly helpful to governments in deciding the direction of their policies and in introducing their policies as early as possible. Unfortunately, as we saw in Chapter 6, economic forecasting is an imprecise process at best, adding to the uncertainties of the economic policy-making process.

Driving Carefully

Using monetary and fiscal policies to "steer" the economy is somewhat like handling an oil supertanker. These massive ships move with such momentum that there are major time lags involved in handling them. For instance, after its rudder has been turned, a supertanker will continue to go in the same direction for several kilometres before even *beginning* to turn. So in handling such ships, one must carefully *plan far ahead* and make only *gradual changes* in direction and speed in order to avoid steering in the wrong direction (and maybe at the wrong speed!) and being unable to make corrections for some time.

Trying to "steer" a nation's economy involves time lags like those involved in handling a supertanker, but with some additional complications. A supertanker is trying to reach (or avoid) certain *fixed locations*, such as a port (or a reef!). But macroeconomic policy-makers must direct their policies toward what amounts to a *moving target*—the economic conditions that they *expect will exist* in a year or two. To return to the supertanker analogy, it is somewhat like trying to steer a supertanker past a distant reef that is moving in a direction and at a pace that you can only try to predict.

These problems both complicate the task of economic policy-makers and increase the cost of errors. Like a supertanker, if the economy gets moving in the wrong direction or at the wrong speed, it can get into serious trouble, such as hitting a reef, or its economic equivalent in the form of a recession or inflation. And as with a supertanker, these dangers make it appropriate to take a very *deliberate approach* to economic policy-making—take a long-term perspective, plan well ahead, get all the facts before acting, be cautious and patient, and don't do anything sudden that might get you (and the economy) off course and into dangerous waters.

Finally, following all this good advice is much easier for the captain who is in complete command of a supertanker than for an elected government that faces an impending election, unfavourable economic statistics, critical media, and the opposition party gaining in the polls. So while good economic policy-making requires a long-term perspective, elected governments sometimes have much shorter political time horizons that can influence their decisions.

5. International Limitations on Canadian Policy-Makers

The Canadian economy has an unusually large exposure to international economic forces. Canada is heavily involved in world trade, exporting over two-fifths of its GDP, with about 85 percent of its exports going to the United States. Furthermore, Canada has historically received large inflows of foreign capital, also mostly from the United States, which have financed a significant proportion of Canada's industrial development. This reliance of the Canadian economy on foreigners as both buyers and investors places certain limitations on the economic policies of Canadian governments.

Monetary Policy and Interest Rates

Probably the major international limitation on Canadian policies relates to monetary policy, particularly *interest rates*. In today's globalized world economy, money flows quite freely from country to country, and from one nation's currency into another's. This has created a virtual "world market" for money, with interest rates being the "price" of funds. In order to attract foreign funds that are needed and to keep Canadian funds from leaving Canada, Canadian interest rates must be competitive with interest rates elsewhere, particularly in the United States.

These international considerations can limit the freedom of the Bank of Canada in formulating Canadian monetary policy—when considering its interest rate policy, the Bank of Canada must keep one eye on economic conditions in Canada and the other eye on international interest rates and the concerns of foreign investors and lenders.

Canadian authorities are also generally reluctant to allow Canada's *rate of inflation* to significantly exceed American inflation rates for long. If Canada's prices were to rise faster than American prices, Canada's exports to the huge American market would decrease and imports would increase, threatening Canadian jobs.

Fiscal Policy

International considerations limit the *tax policies* of Canadian governments. If Canadian taxes on profits or investment income such as interest or dividends become too high relative to American taxes, there is a risk that the flow of investment capital into Canada will be reduced, and that Canadian businesses will invest in the United States instead of in Canada.

....

Summary: You Can't Always Get What You Want

Canadians want a great deal from their economic system, including the following:

(a) *Full employment.* Since the Great Depression, a basic objective of government economic policy has been full employment, or the lowest possible rate of unemployment.

(b) *Steady economic growth.* Another key objective of economic policy is a steadily growing economy, in which rising production of goods and services will provide both a higher standard of living for Canadians and jobs for a growing labour force.

(c) *Stable prices.* Economic policy-makers seek the lowest possible rate of inflation in order to avoid the problems experienced with inflation during the 1970s and 1980s.

Over the long term, Canada's economy has been very good at providing rising output and employment and high living standards. However, its growth tends to be irregular due to business cycles, and when the economy stumbles into periodic recessions, unemployment often rises to quite high levels.

Monetary and fiscal policies can help to moderate business cycles and ease their impact on people. However, they can only do so within limits that are imposed by economic realities. For instance, policies that stimulate aggregate demand will reduce unemployment, but beyond a certain point, the danger of accelerating inflation limits what can be done to reduce unemployment. Also, the implementation of fiscal policy is limited by the need to avoid excessive government debt. In addition, the problem of possibly quite long time lags in implementing government policies limits the potential success of these policies. Finally, the fact that Canada is just one small player in a large international economy limits what can be expected of Canadian economic policies.

Chapter Summary

1.   During a recession, monetary and fiscal policies that increase aggregate demand will produce considerable increases in output and employment without increasing inflation significantly. (L.O. 1)

2.   As the economy approaches its capacity output and full employment, monetary and fiscal policies that increase aggregate demand will produce smaller increases in output and employment, and will generate more inflation. (L.O. 1)

3.   "Full employment" is considered to be an unemployment rate of about 7 percent under the conditions prevailing in the early 2000s, because:

   (a) this rate was the lowest unemployment rate that could be sustained without generating a problem of accelerating inflation, (L.O. 2)

   (b) government policies that increase aggregate demand can reduce cyclical unemployment, but they are not as effective at reducing other types of unemployment (L.O. 2), and

   (c) it is particularly difficult to reduce unemployment in provinces east of Ontario and among young people. (L.O. 2)

4.   It is important to keep the rate of inflation low and stable because inflation can accelerate, and high rates of inflation make Canadian producers less competitive internationally, hurt the economically weak, impair the saving–investment process, and eventually lead to recession. (L.O. 3)

5.   In 1993, the federal government and the Bank of Canada established a target range of 1 to 3 percent per year for inflation, to ensure that the

Bank of Canada would take timely action to prevent inflation from gaining momentum as it did in the 1970s. The existence of the target could also reduce inflationary expectations that could add to inflation. (L.O. 4)

6. When governments borrow to combat recessions and to build social assets, this government borrowing is considered to be economically beneficial. (L.O. 5)

7. It is important to keep government deficits under control because a series of deficits can lead to the accumulation of a large government debt that can gain momentum due to heavy interest payments. Such heavy debt can generate very high real interest rates and lead to large cutbacks in government social-welfare spending in order to eliminate the deficits. (L.O. 6)

8. Time lags involved in implementing monetary and fiscal policies make it difficult for governments to use these policies as effectively as we would like. (L.O. 7)

9. In deciding policies that affect interest rates, taxes, inflation, and government borrowing and debt, Canadian governments are limited by the need to keep Canada attractive to foreigners, upon whom Canada relies as both buyers of its output and as investors and lenders. (L.O. 8)

Questions

1. Obtain statistics on unemployment and inflation for the past three years, from either Statistics Canada's website at http://www.statcan.ca or from Statistics Canada's *Canadian Economic Observer* (11-010-XPB), which is in most libraries.

    (a) What do the statistics suggest about the condition of the economy and its direction?

    (b) What appear to be the reasons for the present condition of the economy?

    (c) Would you say that the statistics indicate that the government's monetary and fiscal policies should be used to speed up the economy or slow it down? Why?

2. It was expected that as the federal government's budget deficits were reduced and finally eliminated, long-term interest rates would decrease.

    (a) Why would this be a logical expectation?

    (b) Has this happened?

3. "The reason for Canada's so-called unemployment problem is the laziness of so many people, especially the young. The solution is to make unemployment and welfare benefits so low that people can barely survive on them. That would get these people off the backs of the taxpayers and out working where they belong, and unemployment will cease to be a problem."

Comment on this viewpoint in light of the material in this chapter.

4. The unemployment rate for males has generally tended to be slightly lower than that for females, but *higher* than that for females *during recessions* such as those that occurred in 1982–83 and the early 1990s. What could explain this pattern?

5. (a) There are an estimated 325 000 seasonal workers in Canada, and in the winter, seasonal factors probably add some 200 000 people to the ranks of the unemployed. Can you explain the difference between these numbers?

   (b) What might account for the decline in seasonal unemployment over the past 20 years or so?

6. Suppose that an employer is considering a 5-percent pay reduction for all of its employees in order to avoid layoffs. Assess this proposal from the perspective of:
   (a) junior employees, and
   (b) employees with many years of service.

7. Suppose you are the Minister of Finance. Prepare a statement
   (a) explaining to a group of unemployed young people why the government has decided to implement anti-inflation policies that will have the side effect of increasing unemployment, especially among young Canadians.
   (b) explaining to a group of senior citizens why the government has decided to stimulate aggregate demand to reduce unemployment, when the pensioners fear that these policies will cause more inflation that will reduce the purchasing power of their fixed pensions.

8. Generally when interest rates *rise*, the price of bank shares *falls*. Why would this be the case?

9. In 1973–75, real interest rates were actually *negative*.
   (a) What would a negative real interest rate mean?
   (b) What could explain such an unusual development?

10. In 1993, the federal government's debt was 64 percent of GDP. In 1947, it was nearly *104 percent* of GDP. What would explain this extremely high level of government debt at that time?

11. One Japanese practice that has reduced unemployment rates in that country is that all the employees of a firm take pay cuts (in the form of reduced profit-sharing bonuses) during a recession. With each employee accepting less pay, the employer can avoid laying off workers, or at least lay off fewer workers. Do you think it is likely that Canadians would adopt such a practice?

12. In a boom, would you expect frictional unemployment to decrease? Why or why not?

Chapter 9

International Trade

Learning Objectives

After studying this chapter, you should be able to:

1. Describe the importance of international trade to the economic prosperity of Canadians.

2. Describe how the composition of Canada's exports (the proportion represented by resources and resource-related products and by manufactured goods) has changed over the past quarter-century.

3. Explain three ways in which trade between nations helps to generate higher productivity and living standards.

4. Explain three ways in which tariffs and other restrictions on trade have negative effects on productivity and living standards.

5. Describe the "infant industry" argument for imposing tariffs, and explain the problems associated with such a strategy.

6. Explain why lower wages do not necessarily give a country a competitive advantage over countries where wages are higher.

7. Explain how economic analysis can be used to compare the costs and benefits of tariffs.

8. Explain the meaning of "globalization," and state four reasons for the world economy's trend in this direction.

9. Explain the implications of globalization for the Canadian economy.

International trade is tremendously important to the economic prosperity of Canadians. While Canada is a large country geographically, it is economically quite a small country in a big world, with a domestic market of only about 31 million people and a GDP that is about 3 percent of total world output.

Much of Canada's prosperity comes from its relationship with larger nations. In recent years, over 40 percent of the output of the Canadian economy has been exported, and about one in five Canadian jobs was directly dependent upon exports that amounted to over $15 000 for every Canadian. As a country with a small domestic market, Canada's stake in international trade is much higher than most nations'—Japan, for all its renowned success in world trade, exports roughly 10 percent of its GDP, as does the United States, as Figure 9-1 shows. But despite Canada's export success, there are continuing concerns about the ability of many Canadian manufacturers to compete internationally.

> "Canada is moving away from resources and into manufactured goods, which is really exciting."
>
> Mark Drake, President, Canadian Exporters' Association

FIGURE 9-1 Exports as a Percentage of GDP, 2000–01

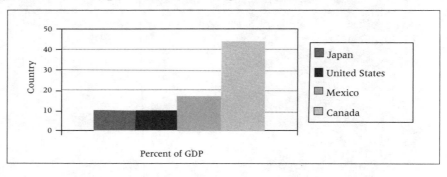

Sources: Statistics Canada, adapted from *National Income and Expenditure Accounts*, Catalogue 13-001, 2002; adapted from Bank of Mexico, Bank of Japan, and U.S. Bureau of Economic Analysis.

Patterns of Canadian Trade

In 2002, the value of Canada's exports of wheat was $3.1 billion. The value of exports of automotive products was $97.1 billion in the same year.

About 200 000 Mexican workers come to Canada annually on temporary work permits, mostly as unskilled labourers on farms and in orchards.

Canada's traditional image is that of a major exporter of natural resources and importer of manufactured goods. Indeed, as Table 9-1 shows, resources and resource-related products do comprise about 38 percent of Canada's merchandise exports, which is higher than most industrialized nations.

On the other hand, Table 9-1 also shows that Canada's exports of goods have been growing, and its traditional reliance on resource exports has been declining. In 2002, over 50 percent of Canada's exports were manufactured goods, as compared to only 36 percent 25 years earlier. In recent years, exports of automobile products alone have been more than

TABLE 9-1 Canada's Major Merchandise Exports, 1971 and 2002

http://stragegis.ic.gc.ca

Commodity Grouping	Percent of Total Exports	
	1971	2002
Agricultural and fishing products		
Wheat	4.7%	0.7%
Other agricultural & fish products	7.3	6.7
Total	12.0	7.4
Energy Products		
Crude petroleum	4.5	4.6
Natural gas	1.4	4.7
Other crude materials	12.6	3.0
Total	18.5	12.3
Fabricated Materials		
(Lumber, sawmill products, pulp & paper,		
chemicals, fertilizers, metals, and minerals)	33.5	25.8
Manufactured Goods		
Motor vehicles and parts	23.4	223.6
Other	13.1	27.3
Total	36.5	50.9
Total Merchandise Exports ($ billions)	$17.8	$410.7
Merchandise Exports as a Percent of GDP	18.3%	35.9%

Source: Department of Finance, *Economic Reference Tables*, August 1996, adapted with the permission of the Minister of Public Works and Government Services Canada; Statistics Canada, adapted from the CANSIM database http://cansim2.statcan.ca/cgi-win/CNSMCGI.EXE, Table 228-001, Table 228-002, and 228-003.

three times as large as exports of agricultural and fish products, and more than twice as large as exports of forest products. Today, manufactured goods comprise a much higher proportion of Canada's exports than many people suppose, which also means that the economic benefits of exporting are no longer concentrated in resource-producing regions, but rather are spread widely across Canada.

The data at the bottom of Table 9-1 show the tremendous growth of Canadian merchandise exports, from 18 percent of GDP in 1971 to 36 percent in 2002. As noted, much of this growth has come from exports of manufactured goods, which increased much faster than exports of resource-related products. And in addition to the merchandise exports shown in Table 9-1, Canada exported $58 billion worth of services in 2002, over 28 percent representing travel and tourism, and another 19 percent representing transportation.

As Figure 9-2 shows, the vast majority of Canada's trade is conducted with one nation—the United States. The importance of the U.S. market to Canada has grown in recent years—in 2002, 85 percent of Canada's merchandise exports went to the United States, up from 71 percent 20 years earlier. The strong link between the two economies was enhanced by the Canada–U.S. Free Trade Agreement of 1989, which evolved five years later into the North American Free Trade Agreement (NAFTA) with the addition of Mexico. In 2002, the value of merchandise trade between Canada and the United States amounted to nearly *$1.7 billion per day.*

In 2001, the value of Canada's exports to Mexico was $2.7 billion. The value of exports to Arizona was $3.1 billion.

FIGURE 9-2 Canada's Exports and Imports by Area, 2002

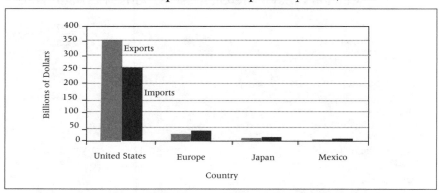

Source: Statistics Canada, adapted from the CANSIM database, http://cansim2.statcan.ca/cgi-win/CNSMCGI.EXE, Table 228-001, 228-0002, and 228-0003.

How Does International Trade Contribute to Prosperity?

The period since the end of the Second World War has seen a remarkable increase in economic prosperity in many nations. Much of this improvement in living standards is attributed to the great expansion of world trade that occurred during that period, and to the trend toward freer trade among nations. Nonetheless, the matter of international trade involves many misunderstandings, myths, misconceptions, and fears. In order to work through these, our examination of this topic will take the form of a discussion between a curious citizen and an economist.

Citizen: Why do economists see international trade as such a major contributor to economic prosperity?

Economist: The key to high living standards is high *productivity*, or output per worker. Nations with high output per worker can enjoy high consumption per person, or high living standards. Trade between nations contributes to higher productivity in three ways: through increased *competition, economies of scale*, and *specialization.*

Citizen: It's easy to see how international trade would increase competition, and how competition from foreign firms would push producers everywhere to become more efficient. But what do you mean by "economies of scale"?

Economist: Economies of scale refer to the fact that in some industries, the most efficient production methods involve mass-production technology that generates high productivity. As a result, "world-class" plants in these industries tend to be very large, and produce a high volume of output. For instance, the Ford plant in Oakville, Ontario, produces 65 vehicles per hour. In turn, these industries must have a *large market* into which to sell all that output. In some mass-production industries, it has been estimated that the minimum market size needed for fully efficient production is about

100 million people. International trade can provide access to the very large markets that can support such plants and the economies of scale that they deliver. This is particularly important for a small country like Canada, with its domestic market of only 31 million people. As an example, Canada's "showpiece" manufacturers such as automobile companies export most of their output.

Citizen: So international trade improves productivity through economies of scale as well as through competition. But you also mentioned *specialization.* How does that work?

Economist: The competition of international trade pushes nations to specialize their production. Instead of trying to be self-sufficient and produce all sorts of products, many of them inefficiently, nations will specialize in what they produce most efficiently, in order to be competitive. And by increasing efficiency throughout the world, specialization makes possible higher living standards.

Citizen: But wouldn't that make us dependent upon other nations for products that are important to us? Wouldn't it be better to be independent, or self-sufficient?

> "It is the maxim of every prudent master of a family, never to attempt to make at home what it will cost him more to make than to buy. The tailor does not attempt to make his own shoes, but buys them of the shoemaker. The shoemaker does not make his own clothes, but employs a tailor .... What is prudence in the conduct of every private family, can scarcely be folly in that of a great kingdom."
>
> Adam Smith, 1776.

Economist: Trade doesn't make nations so much dependent as *interdependent*—nations depend upon each other, and all can gain in the process. The idea of being independent has a certain superficial appeal, but it doesn't stand up well to the test of logic. If you believe that Canada should keep out "foreign" goods, then why shouldn't Ontario or Alberta seek to keep out "outside" goods, too? But then where do you stop with this "us versus them" line of thought? Should British Columbia or Montreal keep out goods produced by "outsiders"? Should your family isolate itself from the rest of the world in a quest for self-sufficiency? Families that actually do this are considered to be eccentric "survivalists" at best, whereas government policies of the same sort are seen by some people as "patriotic."

The answer lies, of course, in the fact that it is *economically beneficial* for people—and regions, and nations—to specialize in things that they do well, to sell those things to others, and to buy from others those things that the others produce more efficiently.

Citizen: It's easy to find examples of this. Alberta is best-suited to oil production, and southern Ontario specializes in manufacturing—obviously the most efficient arrangement at present. And it's obviously best for both Canada and Brazil to specialize in wheat and coffee, respectively, and to trade their products.

Economist: Those examples are accurate enough, but international specialization goes much further than that, and is often much more subtle. Surprisingly, a great deal of trade is not between countries that are dissimilar, but rather between countries that are quite similar—the highly developed and industrialized nations such as the United States, Japan, Canada, Britain, Germany, France, Italy, and others.

Citizen: That seems rather odd. How do you explain that?

Economist: These industrially advanced economies have in many cases pushed specialization to the *n*th degree. For example, the United States exports large, long-range aircraft to Europe but imports smaller, short-range planes from Europe. These high degrees of specialization create even greater opportunities to benefit from trade.

Citizen: I'm having trouble with this. The United States has the highest productivity in the world—it's so advanced technologically that it is more efficient than most other countries in the production of most products. So how can the U.S. *gain anything* through trade with other nations?

Economist: This can be explained by something economists call the **theory of comparative advantage**. It can be illustrated by a simple example on a personal level. Suppose the best lawyer in town is the best typist in town—should she do her own typing?

Citizen: I don't think so. She may be a faster and better typist than her secretary, but her greatest gains come from doing legal work. For every hour she spends typing, she might save $15 on secretarial costs, but she would lose maybe $150 by not using the time for legal work.

Economist: In other words, she can increase her efficiency and her income by specializing in what she does *best of all*?

Citizen: Right. If she does something else, she will lose more than she will gain. She just has better uses for her time. It's that idea of opportunity cost from Chapter 1.

Economist: And the same principle applies to the way nations use *their* productive resources such as labour and capital equipment. To return to your example of the United States, suppose the U.S. is 30 percent more efficient than other nations at producing machinery, and 3 percent more efficient at producing shirts. Then the U.S. would be economically better off to concentrate on producing machinery—it would not make sense to divert scarce productive resources away from producing machinery, where they are most efficiently used, and into producing shirts, where they are less efficiently used. It's the same principle as the lawyer and the typist, but on a much larger scale. And with the U.S. and other nations all specializing in products that they produce best of all, there is an opportunity to increase overall productivity and living standards. And the international competition that we discussed earlier will push nations' economies toward such specialization, because the most efficient producers will be successful and will grow.

Citizen: In summary, then, international trade increases productivity and prosperity through competition, economies of scale, and specialization. (See Figure 9-3.)

theory of comparative advantage The theory that even if one nation is more efficient in the production of all items than another nation, it can still be to the economic advantage of both nations to specialize in what they produce most efficiently (items in which each has a "comparative advantage"), and trade with each other.

FIGURE 9-3 The Economic Benefits of Trade

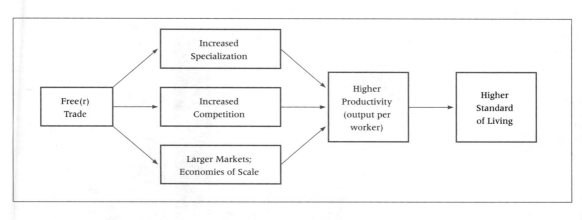

Economist: That's right.

Citizen: Okay—I can see how, *in theory*, international trade increases economic prosperity. But what I see *in the real world* is foreign imports causing trouble for Canadian producers and workers in areas such as appliances, clothing, toys, footwear, and so on.

Economist: The problem with that line of thought is that it only looks at *one part* of the total picture—the import competition. The broader picture takes into account that we have more exports, increased efficiency, more competition, and lower prices and higher living standards for people.

And what's wrong with competition? Isn't that what free enterprise is supposed to be all about? It's interesting how many people instinctively favour competition between firms *within* their country, but also instinctively oppose competition from *outside* it. Sure, it causes problems for some producers, but it also keeps them on their toes, and benefits consumers through lower prices.

Also, international competition works both ways—Canadian producers sell a great deal abroad, you know. In recent years, over 40 percent of Canada's Gross Domestic Product has been exported, and in those markets, *we* are the "foreign competitors," and rather successful ones at that. In fact, as Figure 9-4 shows, exports have been by far the strongest sector of the Canadian economy recently.

Citizen: If free trade is as wonderful as you say it is, then why are there so many trade disputes between nations?

Trade Disputes

Economist: That point is too true to be good. Governments everywhere declare themselves to be in favour of free trade, and sign trade agreements pledging to reduce barriers to trade. The next thing you know, there's a bitter trade dispute between the governments of these "trading partners," accompanied

FIGURE 9-4 Growth of Sectors of the Economy[1], 1989–2001

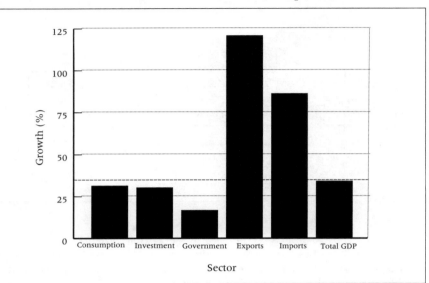

[1] Growth figures based on real GDP data in 1992 dollars.

Source: Statistics Canada, adapted from *National Income and Expenditure Accounts*,
Catalogue No. 13-001.

by accusations and threats of restrictions on imports and retaliation in kind. As just one example, the United States complained for years that the European Union (EU) discriminated against bananas from Latin America and favoured fruit from former French colonies in the Caribbean and Africa. To push the EU into changing its trade practices, the U.S. threatened to impose 100 percent tariffs on various EU imports into the U.S., including champagne and cheese. In response, the EU warned that it would retaliate against U.S. imports, raising concerns that the dispute might escalate into a "trade war."

Citizen: So it seems that in the area of trade, there is often a wide gap between what governments *preach* and what they *practise*.

Economist: That's often true. While officially favouring free trade, many governments act as though their real goal is to gain access to foreign markets for their exporters while protecting their own producers from import competition. However, when another nation places restrictions on their exports, they express righteous outrage and threaten to retaliate. Not surprisingly, this can lead to disputes, usually over whether the foreign competition or trade rules are "unfair."

The economic reality is that trade is a two-way street, but the political reality is that governments like one direction more than the other. The part that they *like* is that freer trade means more *opportunities* for their efficient producers to succeed in foreign markets. The part they *dislike* is that the same

"Governments commit themselves ad nauseum to defend and protect the liberal trading order (free trade). Often, in the same breath, they criticize the 'unfair' practices of their trading partners and threaten to raise barriers in retaliation."

The Economist

freer trade also brings foreign competition that represents a *threat* to their less efficient industries. And this fear of foreign competition can generate insecurity, which explains why the public tends to be less fond of free trade than are economists (who, to be fair, might well have less to fear from foreign competition than do many people). It seems that this has always been the case—in 1824 Lord Macaulay observed that "[f]ree trade, one of the great blessings which a government can confer on a people, is in almost every country unpopular."

In the tough competition of international trade, there will be losers as well as winners, and governments sometimes try to protect their less competitive industries—and the jobs of their workers—against foreign competition. And these restrictions on imports can lead to retaliation by other nations, and to economic hostilities. This is the next matter that we must consider.

Tariffs and Other Barriers to Trade

Citizen: How do governments try to protect their domestic producers from imports?

Economist: The traditional, and most visible, restriction on trade is **tariffs** (or customs duties), which are taxes levied on goods imported into a country. The effect of a tariff is to increase the price of the imports, making it more difficult for them to compete. For instance, Japanese automobiles imported into Canada are subject to a tariff of about 6 percent, and certain Canadian agricultural products such as dairy products and poultry are protected by extremely high tariffs, some of which are over 200 percent.

Another way to protect domestic producers is through **import quotas,** which limit the amount of a product that can be imported into Canada in any one year. Quotas have the effect of reserving the rest of the market for domestic producers.

Citizen: It sounds as though if a government wanted to keep out import competition, tariffs and quotas should be able to do the job.

Economist: They would, except for the fact that most nations have signed trade agreements in which they specifically agree *not* to increase tariffs and quotas (more on this in Chapter 11). Largely because of this, governments that want to restrict imports have in recent years turned to more subtle trade barriers, known loosely as **nontariff barriers**.

Nontariff barriers obstruct imports in various ways, often through the use of rules. Sometimes these are overt, as when governments practice *preferential purchasing policies* by buying only from domestic suppliers, or when they give *subsidies* (financial assistance) that give domestic companies an unfair advantage. However, sometimes nontariff barriers are more subtle. For instance, some nations impose so many bureaucratic *rules and procedures* ("red tape") on would-be importers that they give up trying to do business in those countries. Sometimes nations adopt *product standards* that coincidentally "happen to"

tariffs Taxes, or import duties, levied by a nation on products imported from foreign countries.

import quotas Legal limits on the volume of particular goods that may be imported into a nation.

nontariff barriers Other methods (besides tariffs) of restricting imports, including quotas and licences for imports, preferential purchasing policies, and subsidies for domestic producers.

exclude certain imported products. For instance, for years the European Union have effectively kept Canadian and U.S. beef out of the European market by refusing to allow imports of meat from livestock treated with growth hormones that were used in North America but not in Europe.

Trade agreements between nations can outlaw tariffs and quotas, but nontariff barriers such as these are more difficult to regulate. When the Canadians and Americans complained that Europe was restricting their sales, the Europeans argued that the hormone ban was purely a health concern that had nothing to do with obstructing imports. And when international trade authorities ruled that they were in fact violating trade rules, the Europeans kept the ban in place pending further scientific study of the long-term effects of the hormones on humans, which would take many years.

So despite general agreement that trade is economically beneficial, governments sometimes protect their domestic producers by restricting imports, even when doing this circumvents trade agreements and rules. And disagreements over such trade restrictions periodically lead to threats of retaliation and "trade wars," a far cry indeed from the ideals of harmonious free trade preached by those same governments.

What About Jobs?

Citizen: But wouldn't keeping out imports protect Canadian jobs from foreign competition? Unemployment is an ongoing concern in Canada, and maybe tariffs could help to reduce unemployment.

Economist: Let's do a reality check on this idea. If raising tariffs would reduce unemployment, wouldn't we have solved our unemployment problems long ago? So we need to look into this a little further. Suppose Canada tried to reduce unemployment by increasing tariffs on imports from other countries. What would *those nations* probably do about this?

Citizen: I see—they would retaliate, by increasing their tariffs on our exports to them. Then Canada's exports would fall and jobs would be lost in *our* export industries.

Economist: Exactly. What we might gain in employment in some industries by raising tariffs, we would lose in our export industries when our trading partners retaliated. What many people forget is that Canada is a small nation that counts upon selling about two-fifths of its output to other countries. For us, getting into trade disputes with our trading partners that we should be able to avoid is not a good idea. In the words of Edward Carmichael of the C.D. Howe Institute,

"For a country as dependent on trade as Canada, matching foreign trade restrictions with domestic ones is not a winning strategy. Canadians would be denied access to an international market large enough to sustain efficient scale production, and an important source of improved productivity and living standards would be foreclosed."

www.cdhowe.org

Citizen: Does this explain why Canadian government officials are so frustratingly *patient* so much of the time when dealing with irritating trade matters?

Economist: It's probably one reason—we do have more to lose in trade disputes than most nations. They may also be remembering some lessons from history. During recessions, when people are especially concerned about unemployment, public opinion in all countries can create pressure to raise tariffs. However, governments need to remember that raising tariffs is a dangerous course of action that can actually make unemployment worse. During the Great Depression of the 1930s, governments tried to "export unemployment" by raising tariffs. By the time that everyone had retaliated against everyone else in what became a trade war, tariffs had become so high that international trade had been severely reduced, with large job losses in all nations.

Citizen: The whole matter of tariffs and trade restrictions seems both important and pretty complex. Can we sort it out?

Economist: Let's summarize, using as an illustration tariffs on bicycle imports into Canada. The conclusions we will reach would apply equally to any type of restriction on imports of any product.

Suppose the Canadian government places a tariff on imported bicycles in order to protect Canadian bicycle producers and workers' jobs against competition from more efficient producers in Europe. By sheltering them from foreign competition, this tariff will benefit the Canadian bicycle industry and its workers. Their sales and output will be higher than they would have been, producers' profits will be higher and there will be more jobs and quite possibly higher wages for workers in the bicycle industry.

However, Canadian consumers will have to pay for this through higher prices for bicycles. Obviously, the tariff will increase the price of imported bicycles; however, the effects will not stop there. With competition reduced in the Canadian market, Canadian producers will also be able to charge higher prices. So bicycle prices in general will be higher as a result of the tariff. And if Canadians shop outside Canada for bicycle bargains, they will be stopped at the border and required to pay the tariff ("duty") at that point.

In addition, the tariff on bicycles could have a third important effect, and one that is not so readily seen and understood by the public. The tariff could become part of a trade dispute in which the Europeans retaliate with tariffs on Canadian products such as lumber or steel. To make matters worse, if such retaliation against Canadian exporters became widespread, they could be denied access to the larger international markets that they need in order to achieve economies of scale. And confined to the small Canadian market, they would be less efficient, making their prices in Canada higher.

> "Trade blockades are something our enemies do to us in wartime and we do to ourselves in peacetime."
>
> Henry George

Citizen: So tariffs protect inefficient and uncompetitive producers, and penalize efficient industries that are internationally competitive.

Economist: Yes, which explains why some of our industries (such as resources and large and efficient agricultural and manufacturing industries) are strongly in favour of free trade, while others (such as clothing, footwear and some small manufacturers) want protection against imports. To some, free trade is an *opportunity,* while to others it represents a *threat.*

Citizen: In summary, then, tariffs and other barriers to trade benefit a few of us, but at the cost of lower living standards of the general public.

Economist: Yes, as a general rule that is true. If you were to summarize what we have said, it would be as follows (see Figure 9-5):

(a) Tariffs do benefit the protected industry and its workers. Their sales, employment, profits, and wages will be higher than they would have been if imports were not restricted.

(b) Tariffs reduce the standard of living of the public as a whole, by increasing prices.

(c) Tariffs reduce productivity and prosperity generally, by limiting both competition and the economies of scale available to Canadian producers.

(d) Tariffs also hurt Canadian exporters, who will probably face retaliatory tariffs.

FIGURE 9-5 **The Economic Effects of Trade Restrictions**

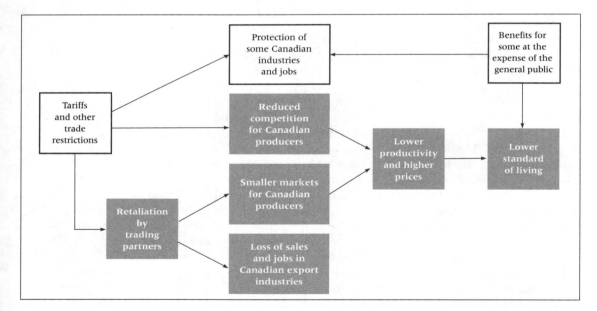

Citizen: It looks like the gains in point (a) are more or less offset by the losses in point (d), leaving on balance points (b) and (c)—a lower standard of living—as the net effect of tariffs.

Economist: Yes, on balance their effect is higher prices, or, if you prefer, lower efficiency and a lower standard of living than we could have had. It's really just two different ways of looking at the same thing. Lower productivity means higher costs and prices, and both mean lower living standards.

Citizen: Then why do governments ever impose tariffs *at all*?

Economist: Sometimes governments impose tariffs for political reasons, in a misguided attempt to protect an industry from foreign competition. I say "misguided" not only because of the negative effects of tariffs we were just discussing, but also because such actions are usually violations of international trade agreements, and as such expose the nation to retaliation from its trading partners under those agreements.

Tariffs as a Stimulus to Industrial Development

Economist: However, many tariffs have their origin in another reason that is known as the infant industry argument. This argument is based on the idea that newly established industries (**infant industries**) could grow to become efficient and internationally competitive, *but only if* they were protected by tariffs during their early years. This protection from well-established foreign competitors would give them a chance to become established, in the same way as an infant child gradually matures into an independent adult.

infant industries
Industries protected by government from foreign competition until they have matured to the point of becoming internationally competitive without protection.

This argument for tariffs is particularly important for nations that desire long-term industrial growth. For instance, both Canada and Mexico have in the past used tariffs to promote the growth of the manufacturing sectors of their economies by protecting them against American competition.

Citizen: I can see why. They wouldn't want to be merely suppliers of raw materials to American industry forever. Developing their own manufacturing industries could benefit them economically.

Economist: True, although the industries that did develop were not always "their own." When some U.S. firms found that tariffs were making it uneconomical to export into Canada from their U.S. plants, they decided to establish **branch plants** in Canada. By setting up branch plants, U.S. companies could avoid Canadian tariffs because their products would no longer be imports; they would be produced in Canada. The branch plants allow the foreign firm to in effect "jump over" the tariff. There are many examples of industrial development through branch plants, from the automobile industry to the building of similar breakfast food plants on either side of the Niagara River.

branch plants
Manufacturing plants established in a nation by a foreign-owned firm in order to avoid tariffs on imports by producing their products inside that nation.

Citizen: So, by protecting domestic producers and by attracting branch plants, tariffs can contribute to a nation's industrial development, diversifying its economy away from dependence on resource extraction and agricultural products, and boosting productivity and employment. All this makes tariffs appear to be good policy, rather than economically negative as you suggested earlier.

Economist: But it's not that simple—you don't get something for nothing, at least not in economics. Tariffs can stimulate the manufacturing sector of the economy, but this development comes at a cost—the consumer must pay higher prices for the products of these industries. In effect, the public is *subsidizing* the protected industries.

Citizen: But the subsidization should be temporary, shouldn't it? Once the infant industries have matured and become efficient, the tariff protection will be removed.

Economist: In theory, that should happen, but in reality, it often doesn't work out that way. Because they are sheltered from competition, such industries tend to *remain* inefficient, and dependent upon continued tariff protection.

Reducing tariff protection is often made more difficult by the politics of the situation. Once protected industries become established and employers of significant numbers of people, they can become effective lobbyists for continued tariff protection. The economic benefits of tariff protection are concentrated in the hands of the protected industries and their workers, who are often well organized through their industry associations and labour unions in order to pressure the government for continued tariff protection. By contrast, the economic costs of tariffs are spread thinly over large numbers of consumers, who are not organized into an effective political lobby. So the political influence of the protected few can outweigh that of consumers, and some infant industries can have a prolonged and sheltered "childhood" at the cost of consumers and the economy in general.

Citizen: So tariffs can help to stimulate industrial development, but there are costs and dangers in doing this. How can we tell whether it's worth protecting an industry from foreign competition or not?

Economist: There's no simple answer to that question; it's a matter of trade-offs, or benefits versus costs. The benefits are obviously the industrial development and the jobs associated with it. There are two types of costs to consider, the first being the costs to consumers, in terms of higher prices.

Suppose that an industry is tariff-protected, inefficient, and has been declining for years. Suppose it were estimated that tariff protection preserved 50 000 jobs in this industry and cost the average family $15 per year in higher prices, for an average cost to consumers of about $3000 per job saved. Many might consider the benefits of tariff protection to outweigh the costs in this simple example. On the other hand, the matter would be quite different if only 10 000 jobs were saved and the cost per family were $100 per year, for an average cost to consumers of $100 000 per job saved. And this is not an outrageous example—before free trade, it was not uncommon for the cost per job saved by trade barriers in various countries to be estimated at $100 000 to $200 000 per year.

Citizen: Sounds simple enough. I'd support the tariff protection in the first case, but not in the second—the cost is out of all proportion to the benefits in that example.

Economist: Unfortunately, it's not that easy—there's another considera-tion. Even when the cost per job saved is not so high, there's another type of cost that has to be considered. Other nations may retaliate against your tar-iffs with tariffs of their own that hurt your export industries and jobs in them.

Let's go back to that first case, with 50 000 jobs saved at a cost of $3000 each. Now suppose that if you removed the tariff protection of your industry, Europe would drop its tariffs on some of your exports, resulting in 25 000 more skilled jobs in your growth-oriented, high-wage export industries. What would you do then?

Citizen: I'm not sure. In the short run, agreeing to the tariff cuts would mean that 50 000 jobs would be lost in the protected industry, but that industry was declining anyway. And there would be 25 000 jobs gained in an efficient, growing sector of the economy, which could well mean many more jobs being created in the longer run. Also, the tariff cuts would save consumers quite a bit of money. That would be a tough call—it would seem heartless to end the protection of the industry and its workers, but I'd be a poor strategist if I didn't give our efficient growth industries better access to larger export markets.

Economist: And that's what government trade policy should be all about—long-term strategy that's in the best interests of the country as a whole, not the short-term interests of particular groups.

What About Low-Wage Foreign Competition?

Citizen: You said that trade policy should be in the best interests of the country as a whole. But Canada is a high-wage nation, so wouldn't it be in the best interests of Canadians to have tariffs to protect their jobs against imports from low-wage countries such as Mexico and Asian countries? How can Canadian producers possibly compete against foreign producers using low-wage labour?

Economist: That's a common viewpoint, but it's not supported by the facts. Let's subject it to a "reality check." First, many high-wage Canadian firms such as auto manufacturers *actually do* compete successfully internationally, so we know that this can be done. Second, if low wage rates were the key to being internationally competitive, you would expect the lowest-wage indus-tries in any country to be its most successful exporters. In actual fact, the opposite tends to be true—it is usually the higher-wage industries such as automobile manufacturing that export the most. And third, if low wage rates were the key to being competitive, nations such as the Dominican Republic would be major manufacturing centres. So low wage rates do not necessarily provide a competitive advantage, nor do high wage rates necessarily mean that an industry or nation cannot compete internationally. The situation is more complex than that.

Citizen: Those facts are interesting. What explains this?

Economist: The key is efficiency, or the productivity of labour—*output per worker per hour*. Suppose a foreign worker receives $3.00 per hour for making pencils and, using simple hand tools, produces 150 pencils per hour. As Table 9-2 shows, the labour cost per pencil is obviously $0.02 ($3.00 divided by 150). Now suppose a Canadian worker earns $15.00 per hour, but using modern machinery, produces 750 pencils per hour. The labour cost of each Canadian-made pencil will also be $0.02 ($15.00 divided by 750, as Table 9-2 also shows). What this example shows is that you must consider *both* wage rates *and* productivity: high wage rates can be offset by high productivity, and low wage rates do not provide a competitive advantage if productivity is also low.

Citizen: So high productivity can more than offset high wage rates.

TABLE 9-2 Productivity and Labour Costs

	Canadian Worker	Foreign Worker
Hourly Wage	$15.00	$3.00
Hourly Output	750	150
Labour Cost per Unit	$0.02	$0.02

Economist: Right. It's sort of ironic—North American workers worry about competition from low-wage foreign workers, but those same foreign workers also protest against free trade because they fear that they will be unable to compete with tremendously efficient North American workers with their capital equipment. For example, it has been estimated that while Mexican workers' wages are on average only about one-fifth of those in North America, the average hourly output of a North American worker is roughly five times that of a Mexican worker.

Citizen: Your example of the pencils was "rigged" to come out in a tie, with the labour cost of the pencils being the same in both cases. Your example of Mexico and North America looked much the same. But in the real world, *who does* have the competitive advantage?

Economist: It depends on the product. So far, we have talked in terms of averages—average wage rates and average productivity. But international competition is on a product-by-product basis, so we have to look at particular products, or at least types of products.

Where production lends itself to mechanization or automation, high-technology/high-productivity nations such as the United States or Canada usually have an advantage. For more manual ("labour-intensive") production tasks such as making clothing or footwear, the lower-wage labour of third-world countries is often more cost-efficient. For some products, companies produce *the parts* in the United States using mass-production technology, then ship the parts to Mexico to be *assembled* by low-wage Mexican labour, then bring back the assembled product to be sold in North America.

Citizen: So the "bottom line" is that some nations are better at some things, and others are better at other things.

Economist: Yes, which is why it pays economically to specialize at what you do best, and then trade. Then, it's possible for everyone to be better off. The "cheap foreign labour" argument is misleading—if it were valid, it would prevent *any* trade from happening, since one nation or the other would fear that it could not compete. And generally, nations with higher wage rates also have higher technology and productivity.

Citizen: But what if third-world nations get our modern production technology—wouldn't they then have *both* high productivity *and* low wages, making it impossible to compete with them? And wouldn't corporations just shift jobs by the millions to those economies, creating massive unemployment in the developed nations?

Economist: I was waiting for that one. That's a more sophisticated concern that requires more detailed explanation. First, try a "reality check" on it—if this is so attractive, why hasn't it already been done on a large scale? Next, let's look at *why* it's not being done as much as one might expect.

One reason is that the potential for labour-cost savings is often much smaller than what people think it is. In industries that use high-technology ("capital-intensive") production methods, direct labour costs (that is, of production workers) are often already quite low. For instance, in industries such as automobile manufacturing and machinery, direct labour costs are often only 10 to 15 percent of total production costs. So saving on labour costs would not be a good reason for relocating this type of industrial firm to a low-wage country. Another reason is that such production methods require a highly skilled workforce, which is often not available in low-wage nations.

Furthermore, major manufacturing businesses know that any labour-cost savings that they did achieve would be short-lived, for two reasons. First, experience has shown that as the skills and productivity of workforces increase, so do their wages. And second, experience has also shown that if a nation's exports increase a great deal, the international price of its currency will increase, as foreigners buy lots of it in order to buy that nation's products (more on this in Chapter 10). But as the price of that nation's currency rises, so will the cost of its exports to foreign buyers, reducing the advantage of locating there.

Finally, such a corporate strategy might well invite trouble from governments in the industrialized nations. Most international trade agreements permit nations to take emergency measures against a "surge" of imports that threatens to seriously disrupt their domestic markets, and corporations know this.

Together, these considerations make it less likely that major corporations would risk moving extremely costly high-technology production facilities into low-wage countries on a large scale.

Citizen: So all the concerns about free trade are unfounded, then? Everyone benefits?

Economist: Not quite. There are some legitimate concerns about the effects of free trade, although these are more subtle than the simplistic ones we have been discussing.

In labour-intensive industries such as clothing and footwear, where labour costs may be one-third or more of total production costs, there certainly is an incentive to shift production to lower-wage countries. Not only are the prospective labour-cost savings greater, but also the skills required are usually lower, making it easier to find the workers needed. This process has been going on for decades, and is really only one aspect of the specialization we discussed earlier. Nonetheless, it does result in reduced employment opportunities for low-skilled workers in the industrialized nations, and the reduced demand for these workers seems to have held down their wages. In recent years, the gap between the incomes of lower-skilled and higher-skilled people has been widening. Most economists believe that the main reason for this is technology that replaces less-skilled jobs; however, imports would have a similar effect. Two of the most fundamental economic forces in recent years have been technological change and freer trade, and it seems that the combined effect of these forces has been twofold: to increase productivity and the average level of living standards, and to shift the distribution of income in favour of the more skilled, and away from the less skilled.

The "Globalization" of the World's Economy

Citizen: This seems to have something to do with all the talk about "globalization" that we've been hearing. Everyone talks about it, but just what does it *mean*?

globalization The trend toward more international trade and investment that has characterized the world economy since the early 1980s.

Economist: Since the early 1980s, the structure of the world's economy has undergone a major transformation. Increasingly, more trade and investment is being conducted *between* countries, rather than *within* countries' borders. This extremely important economic development, which is known as **globalization,** has been the result of several factors, which are summarized in Figure 9-6.

FIGURE 9-6 Globalization

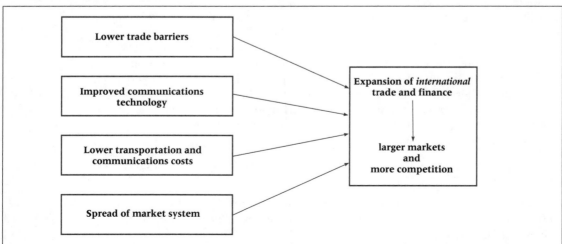

Probably the most important cause has been *tariff reductions* negotiated by nations over the years through various trade agreements (which are covered in more detail in Chapter 11). Another key factor has been improved *communications technology* that facilitates communications between buyers and sellers around the globe. As an illustration, years ago a buyer of fashion clothing for a Toronto department store might have sought bids on an order of dresses from a list of a limited number of designers/suppliers in Canada and perhaps the United States. Today, the same buyer can use computer and telecommunications technology to scan the offerings of many more designers and to communicate with them anywhere around the world. Within an hour of the order being placed, the designer can send the drawings and specifications for making the garments via satellite to a fibre-optic link in, say, Hong Kong, where they appear on a high-resolution computer monitor, ready for a manufacturing engineer to transform them into prototype garments. The prototypes might then be reproduced in a Chinese factory, with the factory supervisor, the engineer, and the designer working out the details via a video teleconference. The finished garments could arrive in Toronto less than six weeks after the order was placed.

The economic implications of this combination of freer trade and communications technology are tremendous. By allowing buyers and sellers to communicate quickly and effectively all around the world, the very concept of a "market" is expanded dramatically, from your local area to the entire globe. The number of sellers that buyers can choose from (and buyers to whom sellers can sell) are also greatly increased, extending markets to a global basis and intensifying competition.

In addition to freer trade and improved communications technology, *falling transportation and communications costs* have also contributed to globalization. In particular, transporting goods in "containers" and lower prices for oil and fuel have made it more economical for producers to compete from greater distances than in the past. Finally, in recent years more countries have entered into world trade, such as Mexico, China, and former Communist countries, following the collapse of the former Soviet Union at the start of the 1990s.

Globalization has tremendous implications for a nation such as Canada, which is small and widely exposed to international economic forces. Many Canadian producers faced *stronger competition* as globalization brought more players into the marketplace. On the one side, Canada faced strong competition in high-technology industries from the advanced Western economies such as the United States, Japan, and Western Europe. On the other side, the newly industrialized countries such as Mexico, Brazil, and various Asian countries such as Taiwan, Hong Kong, Singapore, Korea, Indonesia, Malaysia, the Philippines, and Thailand provided strong competition in labour-intensive industries such as footwear and clothing and in assembly activities such as electronics.

However, globalization means not only *more competition*, but also *larger markets* for Canadian producers. As noted earlier, Canada is a small country economically and the rich, advanced economies of the United States and

Europe provide very large markets for a wide variety of Canadian exports. In addition, the emerging nations provide smaller but growing markets for the infrastructure and capital goods they need to build. As a world leader in some of these fields (such as telecommunications, engineering services, transportation equipment, and mining), Canada's opportunities for exports to these countries will grow considerably as these nations develop.

Globalization is considered to be one of the most powerful economic forces in the world over the last two decades of the twentieth century. The globalization of the world's economy, and its implications for Canada, will be considered more fully in Chapters 11 and 12.

In Conclusion

The second half of the twentieth century saw major improvements in living standards, for which the growth of international trade has received much of the credit. On the other hand, with the growth of world trade, trade disputes between nations take on added importance, as trade wars would be potentially disastrous in a world grown so dependent upon trade. This makes it more important than ever that nations establish and maintain a stable environment for trade, through *trade agreements* that provide rules for international trade that will be followed by all concerned. This will be one of the two main topics of Chapter 11, where we return to the matter of globalization.

Chapter Summary

1.   International trade is very important to Canada, which exports over two-fifths of its GDP, over 85 percent of which goes to the United States. (L.O. 1)

2.   Canada's exports of manufactured goods have increased considerably in importance over the past quarter-century, and now comprise over half of Canada's exports. (L.O. 2)

3.   Trade between nations promotes economies of scale, international specialization, and competition, all of which increase productivity, making higher living standards possible. (L.O. 3)

4.   The results of tariffs and other barriers to trade are: reduced economies of scale, specialization and competition; lower productivity; higher prices; and lower living standards. (L.O. 4)

5.   "Infant industry" tariffs are meant to protect new industries from competition while they develop. However, such industries often remain inefficient and uncompetitive. (L.O. 5)

6.   Low wage rates may not give a country or industry a competitive advantage, if labour productivity is also low. (L.O. 6)

7. One way to measure the costs of tariffs as compared to their benefits is to estimate how much each job that is preserved by a tariff costs consumers through higher prices. (L.O. 7)

8. "Globalization" refers to the increasingly international character of business (trade) and investment. It is the result of freer trade, improved communications technology, lower transportation and communications costs, and the entry into world markets of more countries. (L.O. 8)

9. Globalization has great implications for Canada, which is a small country with much international exposure. These implications include both increased foreign competition and increased opportunities in export markets for Canadian producers. (L.O. 9)

Questions

1. During the 1990s, the strongest sector on the demand side of the Canadian economy was exports. Is Canada's export sector still performing well? Why or why not? (You can check the recent growth of the various sectors of the economy in Statistics Canada's *Canadian Economic Observer* [11-010-XPB], which is available in most libraries, or at http://www.statcan.ca/english/Pgdb/econ05.htm.)

2. There is an old saying of politicians that you should never talk about free trade during a recession or an election year. What is the reasoning behind this advice?

3. What could Canada's labour-intensive industries such as footwear and clothing do in order to compete more successfully with imported goods?

4. The text notes that many people seem to instinctively favour competition between businesses *within* their own country, but instinctively oppose competition from foreign producers *outside* their country. What might explain this apparent inconsistency?

5. Suppose that you are the Minister of Trade, and an industry that has had tariff protection for 50 years holds a press conference at which its spokesperson states that unless you increase its tariff protection, foreign competition is likely to result in the loss of thousands of Canadian jobs within two years. Write a response to this statement that explains fully to the industry and the public why you will *not* agree to their request.

6. Since 1989, Canada has reduced its tariffs considerably under two trade agreements—the Canada–U.S. Free Trade Agreement of 1989 (which became the North American Free Trade Agreement with the addition of Mexico in 1994), and the World Trade Organization's 1995 agreement. Following these agreements, both Canada's exports and its imports increased sharply. What do you think would have been the consequences for Canadians if Canada had *not* been part of these agreements to reduce tariffs?

Chapter 10

The Canadian Dollar in Foreign Exchange Markets

Learning Objectives

After studying this chapter, you should be able to:

1. Explain how the international value of the Canadian dollar is determined in foreign exchange markets.

2. Define the term Balance of Payments *deficit*, and explain how, under a "floating" exchange rate system, a Balance of Payments *deficit* will affect the exchange rate, and how this change in the exchange rate will affect the nation's Balance of Payments.

3. Define the term Balance of Payments *surplus,* and explain how, under a "floating" exchange rate system, a Balance of Payments *surplus* will affect the exchange rate, and how this change in the exchange rate will affect the nation's Balance of Payments.

4. Explain how a rapid increase or a rapid decrease in a nation's exchange rate could create economic problems.

5. Explain how the activities of foreign currency speculators can add to the economic problems associated with fluctuations in exchange rates.

6. Describe two ways in which a government operating under a "dirty float" system can try to prevent its exchange rate from increasing or decreasing too rapidly.

7. Explain how the Bank of Canada's exchange rate policy interacts with monetary and fiscal policies to influence the direction of the economy.

As we have seen, Canada's ability to compete internationally is extremely important to the prosperity of Canadians. One key to Canada's international competitiveness is *productivity*, or efficiency, since this affects the price that foreign buyers must pay for Canadian goods and services. But before they buy Canadian *exports*, foreign buyers must buy *Canadian dollars*. So Canada's international competitiveness is also affected by the price that foreigners must pay for Canadian dollars. This is the international value of the Canadian dollar, also known as Canada's **exchange rate**. For instance, it was easy for Canadian exporters to sell to the United States in 1986, when it only cost Americans about $0.72 in U.S. currency to buy $1.00 Canadian. But by 1991, Americans had to pay US$0.89 for a Canadian dollar, making it much more difficult for Canadian exporters to sell their goods to American buyers. By the late 1990s and early 2000s, however, the Canadian dollar was back down to below US$0.65, and Canadian exports were booming.

> **exchange rate** The international price, or value, of a currency in foreign exchange markets.

Why does the international value of the Canadian dollar fluctuate so much, and what do these fluctuations mean to Canadians? These matters are obviously important, but to many people they seem mysterious. In fact, they can be readily explained and understood in terms of the economic basics involved. In this chapter, we will examine the basic economic forces that determine the international value of the Canadian dollar. In the following two chapters, we will expand our examination of these international matters to a global scale.

Markets for Currencies

International transactions, such as trade, investment, and tourism between nations, require that there be some mechanism for exchanging various nations' currencies. For example, a Canadian importer of French wine must be able to exchange Canadian dollars for French francs to pay for the wine, and a Japanese firm buying Canadian pork must be able to convert its Japanese yen into Canadian dollars to complete the purchase.

These transactions take place in **foreign exchange markets** in which various currencies can be bought and sold. For instance, the Japanese importer of Canadian pork is in fact *buying Canadian dollars* and selling Japanese yen, and the Canadian importer of French wine is really *selling Canadian dollars* and buying French francs. On any given day, vast amounts of various currencies are bought and sold for a wide number of reasons, including imports and exports, investment, tourism, and the payment of interest and dividends between nations. These transactions are conducted through banks in each country that have arrangements with banks in other countries for exchanging various nations' currencies.

> **foreign exchange markets** Markets, conducted through banks, in which currencies of different nations are bought and sold (exchanged for each other).

In short, just as there are markets for goods and services, there are *markets for currencies*. The marketplace for international currency transactions consists of banks, where currencies are bought and sold. Most people have participated in this market at least in some small way at one time or another—for example, by converting Canadian dollars to U.S. dollars before

> On an average day in 2002, CDN$37 billion was bought and sold on international currency markets.

travelling to the United States. While we describe such a transaction in terms of "exchanging" or "converting currencies," the reality is that we are *selling* Canadian dollars and *buying* U.S. dollars.

International Exchange Rates

If currencies are to be bought and sold, there must be *prices* for them. For instance, when the Canadian tourist exchanges Canadian dollars for U.S. dollars, will he or she get 70 U.S. cents for each Canadian dollar? Or 60 U.S. cents? Or 80 U.S. cents? Similarly, how much is a Canadian dollar worth in terms of Japanese yen, British pounds, or euros? There are no fixed answers to these questions—exchange rates, or the international values of currencies, are prices that fluctuate on a day-to-day basis. Table 10-1 shows the international price (or value) of the Canadian dollar on one day (April 10, 2003), but the price of the Canadian dollar fluctuates considerably, as can be seen from Figure 10-1.

TABLE 10-1 International Price (Value) of $1.00 Canadian, April 10, 2003

$1.00 Canadian = 0.6879 U.S. dollars
= 0.6373 euros
= 82.30 Japanese yen
= 7.3749 Mexican pesos
= 0.4374 British pounds

These figures can be interpreted in two ways:

(a) If you were *buying* Canadian dollars on April 10, 2003, the price you had to *pay* for each Canadian dollar was 0.6879 U.S. dollars, 0.6373 euros, 82.30 Japanese yen, 7.3749 Mexican pesos, or 0.4374 British pounds.

(b) If you were *selling* Canadian dollars on April 10, 2003, the value you *received* for each Canadian dollar was 0.6879 U.S. dollars, 0.6373 euros, 82.30 Japanese yen, 7.3749 Mexican pesos, or 0.4374 British pounds, as shown in Table 10-1.

What *Determines* Exchange Rates?

So on April 10, 2003, it took US$0.6879 to buy $1.00 Canadian (or CDN$1.00). What actually *decided* this value of the Canadian dollar? Why was it not US$1.03, as it had been in 1976, or US$0.62, as it was at one point in 2002?

Simply stated, the international price of the Canadian dollar, like the price of anything, depends on *supply and demand*. In this market, "supply" means the volume of Canadian dollars being offered for sale in foreign exchange markets, and "demand" refers to the volume of offers to purchase Canadian dollars. It is the balance between the supply of, and the demand for, the Canadian dollar in foreign exchange markets that determines its value, or price.

www.statcan.ca/english/
Pgdb/econ07.htm

FIGURE 10-1 The International Value of the Canadian Dollar

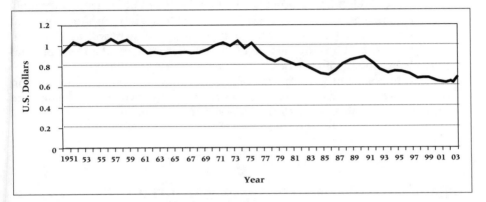

Source: Bank of Canada, adapted from *Public Information Service*.

For instance, in the early 1970s, strong foreign demand for Canadian exports generated increased buying of Canadian dollars, which rose significantly in value from US$0.925 to over US$1.03. After 1976, the international price of the Canadian dollar declined sharply, in part due to increased selling of Canadian dollars by corporations and investors wanting to invest outside of Canada. In the second half of the 1980s, high Canadian interest rates attracted foreign lenders who bought large volumes of bonds issued by Canadian governments and corporations. This buying activity increased the demand for the Canadian dollar and drove it as high as US$0.89. In the early 1990s, this trend was reversed as large volumes of Canadian dollars were sold in order to pay the interest on Canada's large and rising foreign debt, and the international value of the Canadian dollar fell considerably. These fluctuations in the Canadian dollar can be seen in Figure 10-1.

> The highest-ever international value of the Canadian dollar was US$1.0613, on August 20, 1957.

Receipts and Payments

A useful way to summarize a nation's international transactions (and thus the demand for and supply of its currency) is to classify transactions as either **receipts** or **payments**. For example, Canadian exports of lumber to Japan cause Canada to *receive* foreign currency, so exports are classified as a "receipt" to Canada. Conversely, the winter vacations spent by Canadian tourists in Florida are classified as "payments," because they involve *payments* from Canadians to a foreign nation. Receipts generate a *demand* for the Canadian dollar because foreigners must *buy* Canadian dollars in order to pay Canada, whereas payments generate a *supply* of Canadian dollars, or offers by

receipts International transactions in which a nation receives funds from other countries, causing the foreign countries to buy that nation's currency.

payments International transactions in which a nation pays funds to other countries, causing that nation to sell its currency.

Canadians to *sell* Canadian dollars in order to pay foreign nations.

In summary, Canada's international transactions can be classified as:

- *receipts* (money flowing *into* Canada), which generate *buying* of Canadian dollars that *increases* the international price of the dollar, and
- *payments* (money flowing *out* of Canada), which generate *selling* of Canadian dollars that *decreases* the international price of the dollar.

These receipts and payments generate the forces of demand and supply in the market for the Canadian dollar. Receipts (demand) push the Canadian dollar upward, while payments (supply) push it downward, as shown in Figure 10-2. And it is the balance of these forces of demand and supply that will determine the international value of the Canadian dollar.

A summary of Canada's major receipts and payments is presented in Table 10-2. As the balance of Canada's receipts and payments fluctuates, the international value of the Canadian dollar will rise and fall.

FIGURE 10-2 The Market for Canadian Dollars (CDN$)

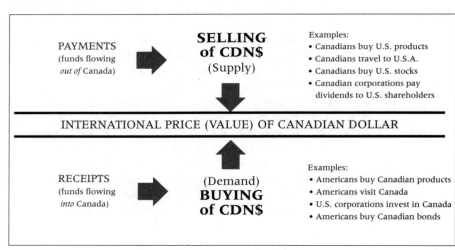

TABLE 10-2 A Summary of Canada's Major International "Receipts" and "Payments"

Canadian Receipts	Canadian Payments
(Transactions generating **offers to buy** Canadian dollars, and thus increasing the international price of the Canadian dollar.)	(Transactions generating **offers to sell** Canadian dollars, and thus depressing the international price of the Canadian dollar.)
1. Exports of Merchandise (Foreigners must buy Canadian dollars to pay for Canadian goods.)	**1. Imports of Merchandise** (Canadians must sell Canadian dollars to buy foreign currencies to pay for imports.)
2. Foreign Tourists Visiting Canada (Foreigners must buy Canadian dollars to spend while in Canada.)	**2. Canadian Tourists Visiting Other Countries** (Canadians must sell Canadian dollars to buy foreign currencies to spend abroad.)
3. Interest and Dividends Received (Foreigners must buy Canadian dollars to pay interest and dividends to Canadian lenders and investors.)	**3. Interest and Dividend Payments** (Canadian businesses and governments must sell Canadian dollars to buy foreign currencies to pay interest and dividends to foreign lenders and investors.)
4. Foreign Investment in/Loans to Canada (When foreign funds are invested in or loaned to Canada, they must first be converted into—that is, used to buy—Canadian dollars.)	**4. Investment by Canadians in Foreign Countries** (Canadian citizens and businesses investing in other countries must first sell Canadian dollars in order to buy foreign currencies with which to make such investments.)

YOU DECIDE   HOW MUCH WILL IT COST ME?

The spring study week is approaching and you are planning to go to Myrtle Beach to study, which means you need to buy some U.S. dollars. You have heard that the international value of the *Canadian* dollar is presently US$0.65, but you have not heard what it costs to buy a *U.S. dollar*.

Questions

1. With the Canadian dollar at US$0.65, how many Canadian dollars will you need in order to buy US$400?

Your economics teacher mentions that the Canadian dollar is likely to rise in value over the next few months, so you postpone buying your US$400 until the last minute. Unfortunately, by that time the value of the Canadian dollar has *fallen* by one-half cent to US$0.645.

2. How much more will you have to pay for your US$400 because of this decline in the Canadian dollar?

Balance of Payments A summary of all of a nation's receipts and payments for a given year.

current account Balance of Payments items relating to day-to-day transactions in goods and services, including interest and dividends.

capital account Balance of Payments items involving flows of investment funds (capital), both long-term and short-term, between countries.

www.statcan.ca/english/Pgdb/econ01a.htm

direct investment Officially defined as "those investments in business enterprises which are sufficiently concentrated to constitute control of the concern," this term usually refers to investment by foreign firms in plant and equipment for their Canadian subsidiaries; it also includes provision of working capital for Canadian subsidiaries by foreign parent firms, and mergers in which the assets of Canadian firms are purchased by foreign firms.

Canada's Balance of Payments

The **Balance of Payments** is an annual summary of all of Canada's international financial transactions, classed as receipts or payments. These items, as Table 10-3 shows, are divided into **current account** and **capital account** transactions. Current account transactions include mostly day-to-day transactions in goods and services, and capital account transactions refer to flows of investment funds, both long-term and short-term, into and out of Canada.

TABLE 10-3 Major Categories of Canada's Balance of Payments

Receipts	Payments
Current Account	**Current Account**
Merchandise Exports	Merchandise Imports
Travel and Tourism	Travel and Tourism
Interest and Dividends	Interest and Dividends
Freight and Shipping	Freight and Shipping
Inheritances and Immigrants' Funds	Inheritances and Immigrants' Funds
Capital Account	**Capital Account**
Foreign Direct Investment in Canada	Canadian Direct Investment Abroad
Foreign Purchases of Canadian Stocks and Bonds	Canadian Purchases of Foreign Stocks and Bonds
Foreign Purchases of Canadian Short-Term Deposits and Securities	Canadian Purchases of Foreign Short-Term Deposits and Securities

The left side of Table 10-3 shows all of Canada's international receipts. These receipts include earnings from the various current account items shown, plus inflows of capital into Canada, including foreign **direct investment** [1] into Canada, foreign purchases of Canadian stocks and bonds (including bonds issued by both corporations and governments), and foreign purchases of Canadian bank deposits and short-term securities. The right side of Table 10-3 shows Canada's payments, which comprise payments for the various current account items, plus outflows of capital from Canada, as Canadian businesses and citizens invest in long-term capital and short-term funds of other nations.

---

[1] "Direct investment" is defined by Statistics Canada as "those investments in business enterprises which are sufficiently concentrated to constitute control of the concern." More specifically, such investments include new plants and equipment built by foreign firms, as well as the provision of working capital for Canadian subsidiaries by foreign parent firms, and mergers in which the assets of Canadian firms are purchased by foreign firms.

The Balance of Payments and the Exchange Rate

As we have seen, foreign exchange markets, in which the currencies of various nations are bought and sold, resemble a "tug of war" between each nation's receipts (which push the international price of its currency up) and its payments (which push the international price of its currency down). There are three possible situations regarding a nation's Balance of Payments and the international value of its currency:

(a) a **Balance of Payments deficit**, when payments exceed receipts,

(b) a **Balance of Payments surplus**, when receipts exceed payments, and

(c) **Balance of Payments equilibrium** with payments equal to receipts.

Using Canada as an example, we will examine the results of each of these situations.

A Balance of Payments Deficit

If Canada has a Balance of Payments "deficit," Canada's payments (offers to sell Canadian dollars) exceed its receipts (offers to buy Canadian dollars). So the supply of Canadian dollars in foreign exchange markets will exceed the demand for Canadian dollars, and the international price of the Canadian dollar will *fall*, as shown in Figure 10-3. An example of such a situation is the 1990s, when outflows of investment funds and interest payments contributed to a considerable decline in the exchange rate.

Balance of Payments deficit A situation in which a nation's payments exceed its receipts.

Balance of Payments surplus A situation in which a nation's receipts exceed its payments.

Balance of Payments equilibrium A situation in which a nation's receipts and payments are equal to each other.

FIGURE 10-3 Balance of Payments Deficits and the Exchange Rate

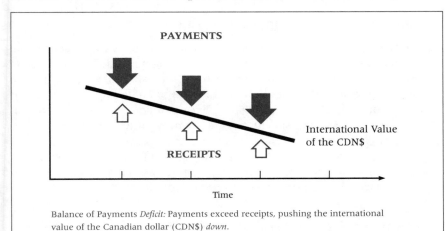

Balance of Payments *Deficit:* Payments exceed receipts, pushing the international value of the Canadian dollar (CDN$) *down*.

A Balance of Payments Surplus

If Canada has a Balance of Payments "surplus," Canada's receipts will exceed its payments, so that the demand for the Canadian dollar will exceed the supply of it, causing the international price of the Canadian dollar to rise, as shown in Figure 10-4. Such a situation occurred in the early 1970s, when strong exports created a surplus on current account, boosting the international value of the Canadian dollar. After 1985, the dollar rose strongly for a different reason: growing surpluses on capital account, due to inflows of foreign capital into Canada as foreign lenders bought large volumes of Canadian bonds.

FIGURE 10-4 Balance of Payments Surpluses and the
                 Exchange Rate

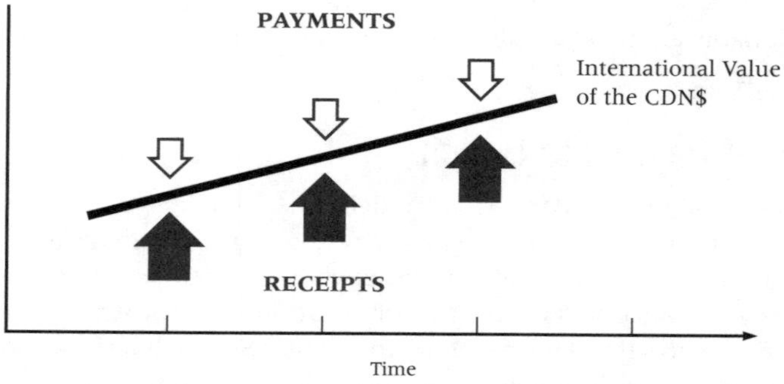

Balance of Payments *Surplus:* Receipts exceed payments, pushing the international value of the Canadian dollar (CDN$) *up.*

Equilibrium in the Balance of Payments

If Canada's Balance of Payments were "in equilibrium," with receipts equal to payments, the supply of and demand for the Canadian dollar would be in balance, and the international value of the Canadian dollar would tend to remain stable at its present level. It is important to appreciate, however, that this does not mean that the Canadian dollar has found its "proper" value, at which it will remain—this stability would last only until receipts and/or payments changed, causing a Balance of Payments surplus or deficit to develop. Given the dynamic nature of international trade and investment flows, such stability is rare and short-lived. In fact, day-to-day fluctuations in currency values in response to market fluctuations are normal.

A Floating Exchange Rate System

We have been examining how the international prices (values) of currencies can rise and fall in response to changes in international receipts and payments. When a nation permits the international value of its currency to move up and down as the supply of and demand for it change, it is said to be operating on a **floating exchange rate** system.

In the following sections, we will examine how a system of floating exchange rates, or currency prices, operates under conditions of (a) a Balance of Payments surplus, and (b) a Balance of Payments deficit.

floating exchange rate A situation in which the international value of a currency is allowed to fluctuate freely with the supply of and demand for it.

How a Floating Exchange Rate Operates with a Balance of Payments Surplus

Suppose Canada is operating on a floating exchange rate system, with the international value of the Canadian dollar at US$1.00, when Canada develops a Balance of Payments surplus (say, due to increased exports). As noted earlier, the Balance of Payments surplus will cause the international price of the Canadian dollar to rise, say, to US$1.04.

The increase in the price of the Canadian dollar will set into motion an *automatic adjustment mechanism*, which will work to eliminate the Balance of Payments surplus. Because the Canadian dollar is more costly to foreigners, Canada's receipts will fall as foreigners buy fewer Canadian goods and travel less to Canada. Also, because the international value of the Canadian dollar has risen, it will be less costly for Canadians to buy imports and travel to other nations. As Canadians increase their purchases of foreign goods and services, Canada's payments will rise. With receipts falling and payments rising, the original Balance of Payments surplus will tend to disappear, with the international value of the Canadian dollar having moved to a new higher equilibrium level that is more consistent with the high demand for Canadian exports. Such changes in exchange rates help to keep imports and exports in balance (see the "In the News" box on p. 228).

This tendency to move automatically toward equilibrium is illustrated in Figure 10-5. It shows a Balance of Payments surplus causing an increase in the price of the Canadian dollar, which in turn tends to eliminate the surplus.

How a Floating Exchange Rate Operates with a Balance of Payments Deficit

In the case of a Balance of Payments deficit, the adjustments are the opposite of those described above. Suppose Canada develops a Balance of Payments deficit, due to increased imports of foreign goods. The deficit will cause the international value of the Canadian dollar to fall from its original level of US$1.00, say, to US$0.98.

This decrease in the price of the Canadian dollar will cause the automatic adjustment mechanism described earlier to operate in the opposite direction, as shown in Figure 10-6. With the Canadian dollar less costly to them, foreigners will buy more Canadian goods and travel to Canada more, so Canada's receipts will rise. And with other nations' currencies now costing Canadians more, they will buy fewer foreign goods and services, causing Canada's international payments to decline. As a result of the increased

FIGURE 10-5 Adjustment of a Floating Exchange Rate to a Balance of Payments Surplus

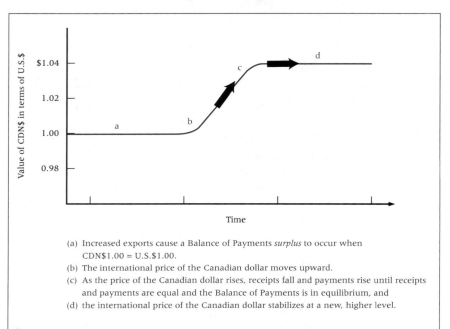

(a) Increased exports cause a Balance of Payments *surplus* to occur when
    CDN$1.00 = U.S.$1.00.
(b) The international price of the Canadian dollar moves upward.
(c) As the price of the Canadian dollar rises, receipts fall and payments rise until receipts
    and payments are equal and the Balance of Payments is in equilibrium, and
(d) the international price of the Canadian dollar stabilizes at a new, higher level.

IN THE **NEWS**   Exchange Rate Changes and Competitive Balance

When NAFTA brought Mexico into free trade with Canada and the United States, some people feared that Canadian and U.S. industries would be totally unable to compete with low-wage Mexican industries, and that a flood of Mexican imports would take over U.S. and Canadian markets.

Question

1. Under a system of floating exchange rates, would it be possible for one nation to flood another nation's markets to the extent that these people feared?

receipts and reduced payments, Canada's Balance of Payments deficit will tend to disappear, and the Balance of Payments will move toward an equilibrium situation with the Canadian dollar at a new, lower equilibrium level.

FIGURE 10-6 Adjustment of a Floating Exchange Rate to a Balance of Payments Deficit

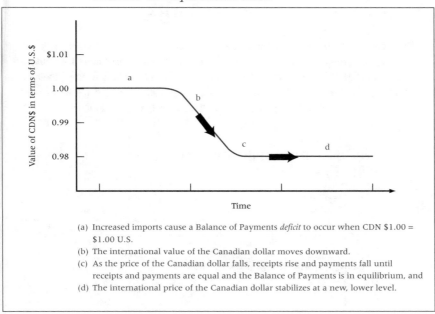

(a) Increased imports cause a Balance of Payments *deficit* to occur when CDN $1.00 = $1.00 U.S.

(b) The international value of the Canadian dollar moves downward.

(c) As the price of the Canadian dollar falls, receipts rise and payments fall until receipts and payments are equal and the Balance of Payments is in equilibrium, and

(d) The international price of the Canadian dollar stabilizes at a new, lower level.

So a Balance of Payments deficit will cause the international price of the Canadian dollar to fall, which will increase receipts and reduce payments, moving the Balance of Payments toward equilibrium, but at a lower exchange rate. And these changes in the international price of the Canadian dollar will affect the Canadian economy, as the *In the News* item on p. 230 shows.

....

Summary

Under a system of floating exchange rates, a nation's Balance of Payments will tend to move toward equilibrium because of the relationship between the Balance of Payments and the exchange rate (or international price of the currency). This is a two-way street—the Balance of Payments affects the exchange rate, but the exchange rate also affects the Balance of Payments.

If a Balance of Payments deficit develops, it will tend to be removed by a reduction in the exchange rate, which will increase receipts and reduce payments. Conversely, a Balance of Payments surplus tends to be eliminated by an increase in the exchange rate, which reduces receipts and increases payments. In both cases, the Balance of Payments tends to return to equilibrium through changes in the international price of the currency.

But there is no single level that represents *the* equilibrium price for the Canadian dollar, toward which the exchange rate will always move. Nor, having reached its equilibrium level, will the price of the Canadian dollar *stay*

IN THE **NEWS**

The Floating Exchange Rate as a "Shock Absorber"

For a country such as Canada that exports a large proportion of its GDP, a floating exchange rate can act as a sort of "shock absorber" during a recession. If a recession in the United States were spreading to Canada by reducing Canada's exports, the international price of the Canadian dollar would probably decrease. And the lower dollar would have a positive effect on Canada's exports, somewhat softening the impact of the recession on Canadians.

Exports, the GDP, and the Exchange Rate in the Early 1990s

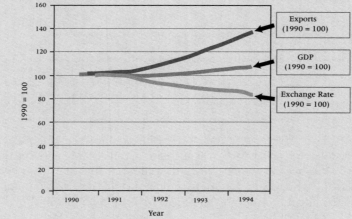

Source: Bank of Canada, adapted from *Banking and Financial Statistics*.

The figure shows what happened in the recession of the early 1990s, when the falling Canadian dollar helped to generate an export-led recovery from the recession. In the figure, the statistics have all been adjusted to start at 100 in 1990 in order to focus on *the changes* that occurred over the period shown.

Questions

1. Why might a relatively small decrease in the Canadian dollar (say, 3 or 4 percent) have a significant effect on exports?

2. What negative effect would such a decrease in the international value of their dollar have on Canadians?

3. Has a similar effect occurred since the recession of the early 1990s?

at that level. As international trade and investment patterns change, causing shifts in payments and receipts, the supply of and demand for the Canadian dollar—and its equilibrium value—constantly change. The equilibrium price of the Canadian dollar is a moving target, toward which the value of the dollar will tend to move under a floating exchange rate system. Table 10-4 presents a summary of the operation of a floating exchange rate in the three contexts that we have discussed.

TABLE 10-4 Summary of the Operation of a Floating Exchange Rate

Situation	Effect on Foreign Exchange Markets	Effect on the Balance of Payments
1. Canada's PAYMENTS exceed RECEIPTS (a Balance of Payments deficit)	The supply of CDN$ exceeds the demand for CDN$; the price of the CDN$ falls.	As the CDN$ falls, receipts will increase and payments will decrease until they are equal and the CDN$ stabilizes at a new, lower equilibrium level.
2. Canada's RECEIPTS exceed PAYMENTS (a Balance of Payments surplus)	The demand for CDN$ exceeds the supply of CDN$; the price of the CDN$ rises.	As the CDN$ rises, payments will increase and receipts will decrease until they are equal and the CDN$ stabilizes at a new, higher level.
3. Canada's PAYMENTS and RECEIPTS are equal (the Balance of Payments is in equilibrium)	The supply of and demand for CDN$ are equal; the price of the CDN$ remains stable.	Payments and receipts remain equal; CDN$ remains at equilibrium level until payments or receipts change.

Exchange Rate Changes and Trade Balances

Changes in exchange rates such as we have been discussing have played a very important and valuable role in maintaining balanced trade among nations. This can be illustrated by two of the more dramatic adjustments to exchange rates over the past few decades—the Japanese yen and the British pound.

After 1970, Japanese exports became very successful in world markets. This generated such a high demand for Japanese yen that by 1995 the yen was nearly *four times* its value in 1970 in terms of U.S. dollars. Such a dramatic adjustment of the yen's value had major economic consequences for the Japanese. First, their currency's purchasing power in foreign markets was dramatically greater, giving the Japanese a higher standard of living that amounted to an international *economic reward* for being so successful at building and exporting their products. (The Japanese enjoy their strong international purchasing power more through travel and tourism than through buying imports of foreign products.) On the other hand, the higher value of the yen made Japanese exports more expensive to foreigners. This served as a *limiting factor* on Japanese success, since it had the effect of limiting the further growth of Japanese exports, and prevented Japan from dominating world markets, as some people had feared it would. From another perspective, the higher yen made it possible for other nations to compete with Japan, and so "saved" some manufacturers and jobs in other countries from Japanese competition.

An example of the opposite situation is provided by Great Britain, which found itself relatively uncompetitive after the Second World War ended in 1945. A combination of low exports and high imports gave Britain large annual Balance of Payments deficits. With the supply of pounds on currency markets outweighing the demand, the pound lost more than half of its value in terms of the U.S. dollar. This large-scale depreciation of the pound made import prices in Britain much higher, reducing the standard of living of the British—a sort of *economic penalty* for not keeping up with the international competition. On the other hand, the decrease in the pound's international value also served as a *protective factor* for British industry and jobs. With the pound much cheaper for foreigners to buy, the ability of many British industries to compete in international markets was protected, as were some British jobs. For the British, it was similar to a nation taking a pay cut (a lower standard of living) in order to protect jobs.

Exchange rate adjustments such as those of the yen and the pound reflect basic economic forces such as the changing competitiveness of nations. They take effect over long periods of time and to help maintain a competitive balance among nations, as noted above. And because they occur gradually, nations and their industries have time to adjust to the changes they create in international competitiveness.

A quite different situation is presented, however, by *rapid short-term fluctuations* in exchange rates as discussed in the next two sections. When these occur, their effects on a nation's economy can be more disruptive.

Foreign Exchange Speculation

The international values of currencies, including the Canadian dollar, fluctuate considerably over time, sometimes quite suddenly and dramatically.

speculation The buying of an asset (here, a currency) with the objective of reselling it for a higher price in the future.

These fluctuations introduce the possibility of making profits through **speculation** in currencies—that is, buying a currency when its value is low and selling it after its value has risen. For instance, there was an opportunity to buy Canadian dollars in early 1986 for US$0.69 and sell them five years later for US$0.89 for a gain of nearly 30 percent. And a person who anticipated the rapid decline of the Canadian dollar from US$0.89 to US$0.75 after late 1991 could have converted CDN$10 000 into US$8900 in October 1991 and converted this back into nearly CDN$12 000 just two years later, for a gain of nearly 20 percent.

Of course, hindsight makes this all seem so easy. At the time that such decisions have to be made, however, the outcome is not at all certain. And, while quick gains can be made through foreign exchange speculation, equally quick losses can be incurred if the currency does not move as the speculator anticipated it would. In spite of these risks, speculators will often move considerable volumes of short-term capital out of currencies seen as "weak" (likely to fall in value) and into currencies believed to be "strong" (likely to rise), hoping to make a quick profit by anticipating exchange rate fluctuations arising from economic or political developments.

As a result, there exists a considerable volume of speculative short-term funds, known as "**hot money**," that are capable of moving very rapidly from currency to currency. Such speculative purchases and sales of currencies can cause their values to fluctuate more dramatically, by forcing "strong" currencies higher and "weak" currencies lower. And such rapid exchange rate fluctuations can cause difficulties for the economies of the nations involved, as we will see in the next section.

hot money Short-term funds that can be moved readily from one currency to another.

Problems Concerning Currency Fluctuations

If the international value of a nation's currency changes *excessively rapidly*, that nation's economy can be adversely affected. A rapid increase in the international value of the Canadian dollar could threaten the competitive position of Canadian producers (and jobs) by suddenly making Canadian exports more expensive and foreign imports cheaper. On the other hand, a sharp decline in the value of the Canadian dollar would cause import prices to rise quickly, which would reduce Canadians' living standards.

As a result, governments are often reluctant to allow the international value of their currencies to change too rapidly, either upward (known as **appreciation of a currency**) or downward (called **depreciation of a currency**). So governments sometimes seek to *moderate* the currency fluctuations associated with floating exchange rates. When they do so, the situation is referred to as a **dirty float**, because while the exchange rate is floating, it is also being influenced by the government. Government policies that influence the exchange rate are also known as **exchange rate management**.

appreciation of a currency Increases in the international value of a currency.

depreciation of a currency Decreases in the international value of a currency.

dirty float A situation in which a government influences the exchange rate by purchases and sales of currencies in foreign exchange markets, and changes in interest rates.

Exchange Rate Management

Purchases and Sales of Currencies

To influence the international value of currencies, governments can *buy and sell currencies* in foreign exchange markets. By buying a weak currency,

exchange rate management Government policies to moderate fluctuations in exchange rates. See **dirty float**.

> "Movements in the exchange rate are of concern because of their potential impact on domestic prices, output, and income. Exaggerated changes in the exchange rate that are not consistent with market fundamentals and that threaten domestic objectives may require corrective action."
>
> John W. Crow, past Governor
> of the Bank of Canada.

foreign exchange reserves Holdings of foreign currencies and gold maintained by governments for the purpose of stabilizing their exchange rates through purchases and sales of their currencies.

governments can hold its price up, or support it. And governments can hold down the value of a strong currency by selling it in foreign exchange markets.

In Canada, exchange rate management is the responsibility of the Bank of Canada. If the Canadian dollar is rising too rapidly as a result of heavy foreign demand, the Bank of Canada may slow down the rise of the dollar by *selling Canadian dollars* to foreign buyers in foreign exchange markets. In the process of selling Canadian dollars to foreign buyers, the Bank of Canada also *buys foreign currencies*, mostly U.S. dollars. The Bank of Canada holds these foreign currencies as part of Canada's **foreign exchange reserves**, or official international reserves, as shown in Figure 10-7. The sharp increase in Canada's international reserves in 1986–90 reflects the fact that the Bank of Canada was trying to restrain the rapidly rising Canadian dollar during this period, by selling Canadian dollars and buying U.S. dollars.

FIGURE 10–7 Canada's Official International Reserves, 1978–2002

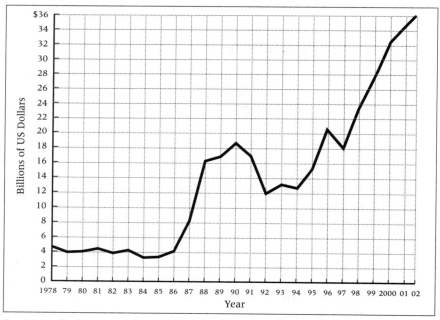

Source: Bank of Canada, adapted from *Bank of Canada Review* and *Banking and Financial Statistics*.

www.bankofcanada.ca/en/interven.htm

These official international reserves are useful when the Bank of Canada wishes to prevent an excessively rapid decline in the exchange rate. If the exchange rate declines too rapidly, the Bank of Canada can *buy Canadian dollars* in foreign exchange markets in order to support its price. Buying Canadian dollars requires that the Bank of Canada *sell foreign currencies* from its official international reserves, which will reduce its reserves. The decline in Canada's international reserves in 1992–93 reflects the Bank of Canada's attempts to support the dollar during this period by buying Canadian dollars and selling its reserves.

By selling and buying Canadian dollars (and adding to and decreasing its official international reserves in the process), the Bank of Canada can, within limits, prevent excessive fluctuations in the exchange rate and their possibly disruptive effects on the economy.

Changes in Interest Rates

The Bank of Canada can also influence the exchange rate through its *interest rate policies*. If the Canadian dollar is declining too rapidly, the Bank of Canada can increase interest rates in Canada. Higher interest rates make Canadian dollar deposits and securities more attractive to foreign investors. And when foreign investors buy Canadian dollars in order to obtain Canadian dollar deposits and securities, the international value of the Canadian dollar is supported. This interest rate policy can also be used in the other direction: if the Canadian dollar were rising rapidly, the Bank of Canada could hold the Canadian dollar down by reducing Canadian interest rates.

FIGURE 10-8 Interest Rates and the Canadian Dollar

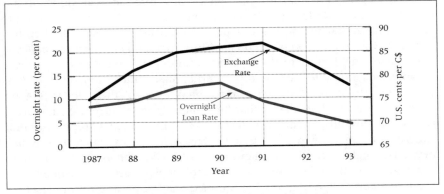

Source: Bank of Canada, adapted from *Banking and Financial Statistics*.

Governments tend to be cautious in raising or lowering interest rates to stabilize the values of their currencies because changes in interest rates can have significant effects upon not just the exchange rate, but also the entire economy. An increase in interest rates will support the Canadian dollar, but it will also depress borrowing and aggregate demand in the economy. In a period of high demand and inflation, this effect may be welcome, but at other times it could tilt the economy toward a recession. Conversely, a reduction in interest rates will hold the Canadian dollar down, but it will also increase borrowing and demand in the economy. During a recession, this effect would be helpful, but during a boom it could add to inflationary pressures by increasing borrowing and demand. As a result, the Bank of Canada and the central banks of other countries tend to use purchases and sales of currencies as their first line of defence to stabilize exchange rates, and to fall back on interest rate changes when economic conditions warrant these or when the problem with the exchange rate is sufficiently large that stronger measures are required.

In summary, as Figure 10-8 shows, by increasing Canadian interest rates, the Bank of Canada can support the international value of the Canadian dollar, and by holding Canadian interest rates down, it can depress the exchange rate. Such changes in interest rates represent another tool for the Bank of Canada for influencing the exchange rate, in addition to purchases and sales of currencies.

Since 1998, the Bank of Canada no longer intervenes in foreign exchange markets frequently in order to smooth changes in the exchange rate. Rather, the Bank intervenes only on those occasions when international events threaten a major change in the exchange rate.

Objectives of Exchange Rate Policy—More Trade-offs

What is better for Canadians—a high or low international value of the Canadian dollar? While a higher international value of their currency sounds better to many Canadians, the situation is not nearly so simple. Rather, the answer to this question depends on *one's perspective* and on *economic conditions*.

In part, the answer to this question also depends on whether one is a consumer or a producer exposed to international competition. To Canadian consumers, an increase in the international value of their dollar is good news. Because the Canadian dollar buys more foreign currencies, imported goods and trips outside Canada will cost less. But to Canadian businesses that export or compete with imports, an increase in the exchange rate is bad news. The higher-priced Canadian dollar will make Canadian exports more expensive, and the relatively lower value of foreign currencies will encourage Canadians to buy imports instead of Canadian products. Conversely, a reduction in the exchange rate would be welcomed by businesses that export or compete with imports, but it would mean higher prices for consumers. As a result, exchange rate policy involves a degree of balancing "trade-offs" between the interests of consumers and the interests of producers.

The answer also depends on the *economic conditions in Canada* at the time. If Canada is in a recession, a lower international value of the Canadian dollar will help to boost the demand for Canadian exports, and so help reduce unemployment. On the other hand, if inflation were the main problem in the economy, a falling exchange rate would only make matters worse, by increasing the price of imports. Instead, a rising Canadian dollar would help contain inflation by keeping import prices down.

Exchange Rate Policy and Monetary and Fiscal Policies

From the foregoing, it can be seen that the Bank of Canada's exchange rate policy is linked to its monetary policy and interest rate policy, and to the whole question of "demand management" that we saw in Chapters 7 and 8. As Figure 10-9 shows, government policies to combat recession could include a government budget deficit and lower interest rates to boost spending by Canadian consumers and businesses, with lower interest rates contributing to a lower exchange rate that could also boost foreign demand for Canadian exports. This was essentially the direction of Canadian policy in 1992–93.

FIGURE 10-9 Government Policies to Combat Recession

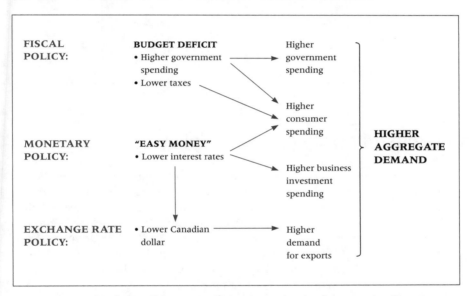

Figure 10-10 shows the same policies operating in the opposite direction, to slow down inflation. Budgets surplus, and higher interest rates can depress spending by Canadian consumers and businesses, and higher interest rates could push the price of the Canadian dollar higher, depressing both export demand and the price of imports. In 2002–2003, this was the general thrust of Canadian policy.

The late 1980s and early 1990s provide a good illustration of how the Bank of Canada's interest rate policies affect the Canadian dollar. In the late 1980s, the Bank of Canada was fighting inflation by increasing interest rates. As Figure 10-8 shows, the exchange rate increased over the same period, as interest rates were increased. And when recession struck in the early 1990s, the Bank of Canada reduced interest rates, and the international value of the Canadian dollar decreased.

FIGURE 10-10 Government Policies to Combat Inflation

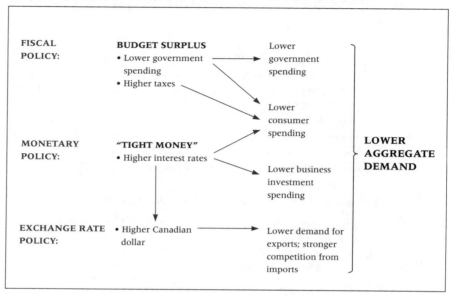

Limits on Exchange Rate Policy

In determining its exchange rate policy, a government cannot ignore the fact that there is at any point in time an *equilibrium international value* for its currency. If a government tries to maintain the value of its currency *too far* below its equilibrium level to assist its exporters, it would have to sell vast amounts of its own currency in foreign exchange markets. To sell such quantities of its currency, it would have to borrow (or even print) such large volumes of money that it would damage its own economy through high interest rates and perhaps severe inflation. For example, Japan and Germany resisted the upward movement of the yen and deutschemark for fear it would depress their export industries; however, both nations finally found it impossible to prevent their exchange rates from rising.

Similarly, a nation that seeks to keep its exchange rate too far above its equilibrium level will encounter difficulties. To achieve this, the government would have to continually purchase its own currency on a large scale, using its foreign exchange reserves to do so. Such a policy would eventually deplete its reserves, and force the government to allow the value of its currency to decrease. The only other way to keep a currency at a level well above its equilibrium would be through interest rates so high that they would depress the nation's entire economy.

So when we speak of a government "managing" its exchange rate, we do not mean that the government *controls* the international value of its currency.

A government can *influence* its exchange rate, but only to prevent excessively rapid fluctuations around its equilibrium level—it cannot succeed for long in keeping its exchange rate much above or much below its equilibrium level.

Summary

In summary, the international value of the Canadian dollar is determined in foreign exchange markets by the buying and selling of the Canadian dollar that is generated by:

- regular day-to-day international transactions such as those in the current account of the Balance of Payments,
- flows of investment funds such as those in the capital account of the Balance of Payments,
- flows of short-term funds ("hot money," often speculative in nature) into and out of Canadian dollars, and
- occasional purchases and sales of Canadian dollars by the Bank of Canada, seeking to moderate the fluctuations in the exchange rate.

Fluctuations in the Canadian dollar can have major effects upon Canadians. When the Canadian dollar was as high as US$0.89 in the late 1980s, Canadian consumers benefited from cheap imports, but many Canadian exporters had difficulty competing internationally, and jobs were lost. On the other hand, when the Canadian dollar plunged to below US$0.63 in 2002, Canadian exporters enjoyed great success, while consumers had to pay more for U.S. dollars and imported goods and services. And the dollar's rapid rise in 2003 pleased consumers but concerned many businesses.

Looking Ahead

This chapter has stressed the importance of the exchange rate of the Canadian dollar to the international competitiveness of Canadian businesses and to the economic prosperity of Canadians. It also emphasized that rapid changes in the exchange rate can have negative effects upon an economy that is as exposed to international economic forces as Canada's.

On a broader scale, a reasonably stable system of worldwide exchange rates is also economically beneficial. Excessive fluctuations in the prices of nations' currencies create an uncertain climate that discourages international trade and investment. On the other hand, a reasonably stable world exchange-rate system can contribute to world economic prosperity by encouraging international trade and investment. For this reason, governments generally try to maintain reasonably stable currency prices, partly by using the exchange-rate management policies described in this chapter.

Sometimes these efforts are successful, while at other times exchange rates fluctuate suddenly and sharply, with disruptive effects. In Chapters 11 and 12, we will examine these matters further.

Chapter Summary

1. The international value of the Canadian dollar is determined by the supply of and demand for it in foreign exchange markets, with Canadian receipts from other nations generating a demand for Canadian dollars, and Canadian payments to other nations generating a supply of Canadian dollars. (L.O. 1)

2. The Balance of Payments summarizes Canada's international receipts and payments for a given year, classifying them into current and capital accounts. If receipts exceed payments, there is a Balance of Payments *surplus,* and if payments exceed receipts, there is a Balance of Payments *deficit.* (L.O. 2)

3. Under a "floating" exchange rate, a Balance of Payments deficit will cause the exchange rate to fall, and a surplus will cause the exchange rate to rise. These adjustments will bring the Balance of Payments and the exchange rate automatically toward equilibrium. (L.O. 2, 3)

4. A rapidly rising exchange rate can increase unemployment by making a nation's goods and services less competitive internationally, while a rapid decline in its exchange rate can make inflation worse by generating increases in import prices. (L.O. 4)

5. Foreign currency speculation can add to these problems, as speculators buy currencies that are "strong," forcing their values even higher, and sell currencies that are "weak," driving their values down farther and faster. (L.O. 5)

6. Under a "dirty float" system, the government influences the exchange rate so as to prevent excessively rapid fluctuations. To support a "weak" currency, the government can buy its own currency and/or increase interest rates, and to hold down a "strong" currency, the government can do the opposite. (L.O. 6)

7. To combat a recession, a monetary policy of lower interest rates and a fiscal policy of budget deficits can be combined with an exchange rate policy of a lower international value of the Canadian dollar to stimulate aggregate demand. (L.O. 7)

8. To combat inflation, a monetary policy of higher interest rates and a fiscal policy of budget surpluses can be combined with an exchange rate policy of a higher international value of the Canadian dollar to slow down aggregate demand. (L.O. 7)

Questions

1. Classify each of the following transactions as either a *receipt* or a *payment* for Canada, on either *current account* or *capital account,* and state whether it would cause the international value of the Canadian dollar to *increase* or *decrease*.

(a) Canada exports mining equipment to Russia.

(b) Canadian tourists visit Florida.

(c) A Canadian corporation establishes a branch plant in South Carolina.

(d) An American investor buys shares in a Canadian oil exploration company.

(e) An American business ships its products on a Canadian Great Lakes freighter.

(f) The Canadian subsidiary of a U.S. corporation pays dividends to its U.S. parent company.

(g) American pension funds buy bonds issued by the Government of Ontario.

(h) A Canadian company contracts to use computer services supplied by a U.S. firm.

(i) Canadian provincial governments pay interest to American holders of their bonds.

(j) American foreign-exchange speculators transfer large amounts of money from U.S. dollar accounts into Canadian-dollar short-term bank deposits.

2. In what ways was Canada's exchange rate situation in the 1990s similar to that of Great Britain in the years after the Second World War, as described in the text?

3. Has the Bank of Canada intervened in foreign exchange markets to influence Canada's exchange rate recently? If so, what were the purposes of the intervention and why was it necessary? (See www.bankofcanada.ca/en/interven.htm.)

4. Do you think that the Canadian economy would benefit more from an increase or a decrease in the international value of the Canadian dollar at this time? Why?

5. Has Canada's merchandise trade surplus increased or decreased recently? Why? (See http://www.statcan.ca/english/Pgdb/econ01a.htm.)

6. What is the current international value/price of the Canadian dollar? If you wanted to buy US$400, how much would it cost you in Canadian dollars? How much would 200 British pounds cost you in Canadian dollars? The international value of the Canadian dollar can be found in any newspaper, in the "Financial Markets" section of Statistics Canada's *Canadian Economic Observer* (11-010-XPB), or at one of the following websites: http://www.statcan.ca/english/Pgdb/econ07.htm and http://www.bankofcanada.ca/en/exchange.htm.

Chapter 11

The Global Economy

Learning Objectives

After studying this chapter, you should be able to:

1. Explain the lessons learned from two types of destructive economic policies used by governments during the Great Depression.

2. Summarize the goals and achievements of the General Agreement on Tariffs and Trade (GATT), which was renamed the World Trade Organization (WTO) in 1995.

3. Explain why the GATT/WTO encountered problems in promoting freer trade among nations in the 1980s and 1990s.

4. Describe the exchange rate system that was established in 1945, explain why this type of system was adopted, and why it was eventually abandoned in 1973.

5. Describe the exchange rate system that emerged after 1973, and explain the importance of capital flows in this system.

6. Describe the recent economic developments concerning
   (a) the United States
   (b) Japan
   (c) Europe

7. Explain the meaning of *deflation*, why deflation is a serious economic condition, and why as of 2002 there were concerns about deflation in the global economy.

8. Summarize the main objectives of the Doha Round of World Trade Organization trade negotiations, and obstacles to the success of these negotiations.

9. Define *trading bloc*, describe three such blocs, and summarize the view that the world might be evolving into three major economic power blocs.

Over the course of the twentieth century, the world changed dramatically. The first half of the century was often characterized by *conflict* between nations in the tradition of the aggressively nationalistic attitudes of the previous century. In the sphere of economic policy as well as foreign policy, these conflicts proved to be mutually destructive for all concerned. Largely as a result of these experiences, the second half of the century saw more attempts to reduce conflict and increase *cooperation* among nations, especially concerning their economic policies.

First, we will review briefly the conflicts of the first half of the century; then we will consider the economic changes since then that have contributed to the *globalization* of the world's economy.

The First Half of the Twentieth Century

In the first half of the twentieth century, the dominant influence was the *nationalism* that had characterized the nineteenth century and often led to conflict between nations. The most dramatic examples of this conflict were of course the two world wars, the first from 1914 to 1918 and the second from 1939 to 1945. However, the nationalism that bred military conflict also extended into economic policy. As a result, much of the period between the two wars was characterized by economic conflict between nations.

This international economic conflict was intensified by the Great Depression of the 1930s, and involved both tariffs and exchange rates—the topics of the previous two chapters. Confronted with high unemployment during the Depression, governments resorted to two types of aggressive economic policies aimed at reducing unemployment in their own countries at the expense of their trading partners. The first such policy involved countries *increasing tariffs* so as to keep out imports and thus "save jobs" of workers in industries facing foreign competition. Unfortunately, this policy merely led to retaliatory tariffs on the part of their trading partners that in turn led to even higher tariffs being imposed by all concerned. The result was a **trade war**, in which tariff barriers became so high that world trade was reduced considerably, forcing layoffs in export industries in all nations and making the Depression even worse.

trade war Retaliatory escalation of trade barriers by nations against each other's exports.

The second type of aggressive economic policy was equally destructive, for the same reasons. Some nations deliberately manipulated the prices of their currencies downward, in an attempt to gain a competitive advantage over their trading partners by making their exports cheaper. Their goal was to "export unemployment" by increasing their exports to other countries. But their intended victims retaliated by taking similar steps to reduce the price of their own currencies. As these actions escalated, currency prices became unstable and unpredictable, adding new risks to international business transactions. This increasing level of risk discouraged international trade even further, increasing unemployment in export industries everywhere and making the Depression more severe. From 1929 to 1932, the value of international trade fell *by 63 percent*, throwing millions of people out of work around the globe.

The Great Depression was ended by the Second World War, which forced governments to spend so heavily on the military effort that jobs were created on a massive scale for more than half a decade. As the war neared its end in 1945, nations realized that they could not return to the mutually destructive economic policies of the 1930s.

The Second Half of the Twentieth Century

As a result, the second half of the twentieth century witnessed the rise of *internationalism* in the area of economic policy. After the Second World War, governments of the world's major nations made substantial changes to their economic policies that were intended to create a more stable environment in which international trade and investment would be encouraged, rather than discouraged as in the 1930s. Specifically, governments agreed to:

- reduce tariffs so as to move in the direction of freer trade, through the *General Agreement on Tariffs and Trade* (GATT), since renamed the World Trade Organization (WTO), and
- cooperate so as to make exchange rates more stable, through the *International Monetary Fund* (IMF).

Much of the world's economic history since the end of the Second World War has consisted of a search among nations, through the GATT/WTO and the IMF, for cooperation and stability in the area of international economic relations that would promote international trade, investment, and prosperity. These efforts have met with considerable success—overall, as we will see, there has been substantial improvement over the past. But as we will also see, there have been setbacks, opposition, and threats to the progress that has been made over the past half-century.

www.wto.org

First, we will consider developments in the area of international trade, and then the efforts of nations to maintain a more stable exchange rate system. Finally, we will review the condition of the global economy as of early 2003.

General Agreement on Tariffs and Trade (GATT)
An international agreement under which many nations, following 1947, negotiated reductions in tariffs in order to promote freer trade.

World Trade Organization (WTO)
Successor to the GATT as of 1995.

Part A: International Trade: The General Agreement on Tariffs and Trade (GATT) and The World Trade Organization (WTO)

The **General Agreement on Tariffs and Trade (GATT)**, which was in 1995 renamed the **World Trade Organization (WTO)**, is one of the most significant international economic developments of the twentieth century.

The half-century following the GATT's establishment in 1947 saw an unprecedented growth of world trade. Indeed, much of the improvement in world economic prosperity in the second half of the twentieth century is attributed to this tremendous expansion of international trade.

The GATT was established when 23 countries, including Canada, signed the original agreement in 1947. The basic purpose of the GATT was to prevent a recurrence of the trade wars in the 1930s. Participating countries agreed to negotiate reductions in tariffs, with the objective of increasing world trade and prosperity for all concerned. The negotiations are *multilateral*, which means that all parties to the agreement negotiate mutual tariff reductions, as distinct from trade agreements between specific nations, such as the North American Free Trade Agreement between Canada, the United States, and Mexico. The 1947 GATT agreement represented a major change in policy and the start of a long trend toward freer international trade.

Since 1947, the members of the GATT/WTO have met in a series of "rounds" of talks to negotiate tariff reductions, as shown in Table 11-1. The focus of the earlier rounds was reducing tariffs on goods, but in the seventh round (the "Tokyo Round," 1973–79), nontariff barriers to trade were also addressed. The eighth round (the "Uruguay Round," 1986–93) included about 116 nations, a great increase from the original 23. The ambitious agenda of the Uruguay Round included trade in services, which had grown to almost 30 percent of world trade, and represented a further broadening of the GATT's focus, which had traditionally been on trade in goods. It was at the conclusion of the Uruguay Round that the GATT was renamed the *World Trade Organization (WTO)*. As Figure 11-1 shows, these rounds of negotiations over many years resulted in large reductions in tariffs, from an average level of 40 percent in 1940 to less than 5 percent by 2000.

TABLE 11-1 GATT/WTO Rounds of Multilateral Trade Negotiations

Order	Date	Location
1st	1947	Geneva (Switzerland)
2nd	1949	Annecy (France)
3rd	1951	Torquay (England)
4th	1956	Geneva
5th	1960–1962	Geneva
6th	1964–1967	Geneva[a]
7th	1973–1979	Geneva[b]
8th	1986–1993	Geneva[c]
9th	2001–2005	Doha

[a]Kennedy Round.
[b]Tokyo Round.
[c]Uruguay Round.

FIGURE 11-1 Tariff Levels, 1940–2000

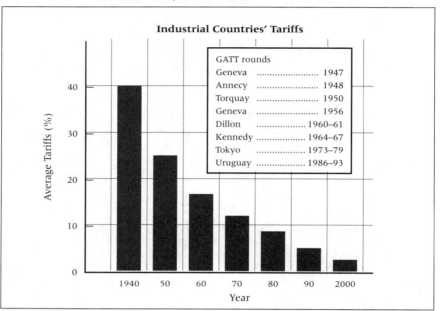

Source: Centre for International Economics; IMF.

In addition to reducing tariffs, the GATT/WTO has sought to establish *rules for fair competition* in international trade. For instance, one *unfair* practice is **dumping**, or exporting a product at a price that is below the cost of producing it or below the price in your home market. It is also considered unfair for a government to give **subsidies**, such as grants or tax breaks, to its industries in order to give them an advantage in international competition by making it possible for them to sell at prices below their real production costs.

To make the WTO more flexible, certain exceptions are allowed. Probably the most important exception is permitting the creation of trade agreements among **trading blocs**, which are specific groups of nations such as the European Union and the North American Free Trade Agreement. The nations involved in such agreements are not required to extend the benefits of their agreements to all other WTO members. Also, nations can restrict imports that are required for their national security, and less developed countries are permitted to restrict imports to protect and encourage developing ("infant") industries.

dumping The practice of exporting a product at a price below the cost of producing it, or below the price charged in the country in which it is produced.

subsidies Government financial assistance to a firm or industry, through measures such as grants, loans, or special tax treatment.

trading blocs Groups of nations that have a trade agreement among themselves outside of the WTO agreement.

Settlement of Trade Disputes

As we saw in Chapter 9, freer trade economically benefits consumers and creates opportunities for efficient producers, but it also threatens less competitive producers due to increased competition from imports. Sometimes foreign competition is alleged to be *unfair*, and these allegations lead to trade disputes between nations. And in trade disputes, there is always the danger that nations will retaliate against each other, escalating the dispute and extending its damaging effects into other industries—the opposite of the WTO's goal of freer trade. So it is important that trade disputes be resolved, rather than allowed to escalate.

The WTO requires that trade disputes between its members be settled in an impartial manner. If the countries involved in a trade dispute (such as whether one country was unfairly restricting imports from the other country) are unable to resolve the problem by themselves, the dispute will ultimately be decided by a "panel" of experts who are knowledgeable about trade, and neutral with respect to the parties to the dispute.

> "The world would be a dismal place without GATT. The major countries would have made their own deals, and smaller countries like Canada would have been exposed. Certainly there would be less trade. The world would be poorer."
>
> Frank Stone, Institute for Research on Public Policy.

Successes and Challenges

By many standards, the GATT/WTO has been successful. As noted earlier, in the second half of the twentieth century large reductions in tariffs were achieved, and world trade expanded tremendously.

However, progress toward freer trade has not been smooth and steady. One major problem faced by the GATT since the early 1980s has been *protectionism*, especially in the United States and Europe. As trade became freer, established industries in the U.S. and Europe faced increasingly strong competition from Japan in high-technology sectors such as automobiles and electronic equipment, and from less developed countries in labour-intensive products such as clothing and footwear. Fear of job losses and allegations that the import competition was "unfair" pushed the American and European governments to restrict imports. Often, these restrictions took the form of *nontariff barriers* to imports. These trade restrictions violated the intent of the GATT, but nations could claim that the restrictions were justified on non-trade grounds such as consumer protection, health standards, product standards, and so on.

And these new trade barriers were substantial. While average *tariff* levels in the 1980s were down to about 10 percent, several of the new *nontariff* barriers were roughly equivalent to a 25-percent tariff—which had been common 30 years earlier. And nontariff barriers are difficult to police, since the nation using them can argue that their purpose is not to restrict imports but rather to maintain product standards, protect consumers, and so on. Sometimes, the U.S. or Europe would simply assert that particular imports were "unfair," because they involved subsidies or dumping, then sidestep the GATT's dispute resolution process by unilaterally restricting those imports. And because such tactics tend to breed retaliation that could escalate into a trade war, the situation was potentially dangerous.

The Uruguay Round (1986–93)

The "Uruguay Round"—the eighth in the series of GATT negotiations that had started in 1947—was intended to reduce trade tensions and to promote the resumption of progress toward freer trade. The Uruguay Round was by far the most complex and difficult round of GATT negotiations ever. The larger number of participants (116 by the end of the talks) complicated the negotiation process, making it more difficult to reach agreements. In addition, the negotiations included the complex matter of nontariff barriers, which had become a substitute for tariffs. A third complicating factor was the complex question of trade in services, which had grown to about 30 percent of all world trade. Finally, there was a long-standing dispute over trade in textiles and a bitter dispute between the U.S. and Europe over Europe's subsidies for farm products that at one point had escalated to such an extent that the U.S. threatened to bar French champagne from the U.S. market.

Finally, a new agreement was reached—a 25 000-page document that became effective in 1995, at which time the GATT was renamed the World Trade Organization (WTO). Under, this agreement, the developed countries were to reduce tariffs on industrial goods by 38 percent over six years. For farm products, the troublesome agricultural subsidies and trade barriers were to be reduced. New rules covering trade in services were established, and long-established barriers to trade in textiles were to be phased out over a period of ten years. In addition, clearer definitions of *subsidies* and *dumping* were established, making the rules for international trade clearer.

Concerning the enforcement of the rules, the new agreement provided for a new system for settling trade disputes between nations. In more definitive terms than before, the agreement stated that "members shall not themselves make determinations of violations or suspend concessions, but shall make use of the dispute settlement rules and procedures."

The WTO system was designed to encourage the parties to resolve the matter on their own if at all possible. The first stage in the process is a "consultation period," during which the parties discuss the issues. If after 60 days there is no settlement, the plaintiff can ask that the dispute be referred to a panel that would make a decision. The members of the panel would be drawn from a list of international law experts. If the nations involved in the dispute could not agree on who should serve as members of the panel, the WTO would appoint the panel. A panel's decision could be appealed to a seven-member appellate body for a final decision, usually within six months. For each step in the process, there are clear deadlines. If a nation is found by a neutral panel to have violated trade rules, it must either change its practices or the plaintiff nation can demand compensation. If that fails, the plaintiff nation can impose its own trade sanctions on the offender, which usually means retaliatory measures against the offender's exporters. The most common such measure is a **countervailing tariff** on one or more of the offender's exports.

countervailing tariff
A tariff imposed in response to a tariff or other restriction on imports imposed by another nation.

The WTO Since the Uruguay Round

Even after all the efforts at the Uruguay Round, the road to freer trade in the years after 1995 was a rocky one. In the political environment fostered by concerns about unemployment in its slowing economy, the United States introduced several protectionist measures that led to several major trade disputes, mostly with Europe. It was against this backdrop of protectionist actions and disputes that the ninth round of WTO negotiations was launched in late 2001—the "Doha Round," in Doha, Qatar.

> On December 11, 2001, China joined the WTO.

Part B: Exchange Rates: The International Monetary Fund (IMF)

International trade agreements alone are not enough to foster increased international trade and investment. It is also important to have a system of exchange rates that is reasonably stable and predictable, so that trade and investment will not be disrupted by uncertainties concerning exchange rate fluctuations. Such a system will also allow governments and businesses to plan trade agreements, investments, and exports without undue fear of these being damaged or even ruined by sudden and sharp changes in exchange rates.

The Experience of the 1930s

During the 1930s, exchange rates became unstable during the Great Depression. Desperately seeking to reduce unemployment, some nations deliberately reduced the international value of their currencies in order to increase employment in their export industries, at the expense of their trading partners. But other nations retaliated by reducing their own exchange rates, the result being a period of unstable exchange rates and uncertainty that further reduced international trade and investment, and made the Depression even worse. The 1930s showed the nations of the world that concerning exchange rates, it would be beneficial for countries to be cooperative rather than combative.

Following the Second World War, nations took steps to prevent a recurrence of the problems of the 1930s. We have seen how in the area of trade and tariffs, they established an international organization (GATT, later the WTO), which was intended to promote the expansion of trade. In the area of exchange rates, there were similar developments: an international organization (The **International Monetary Fund (IMF)**) was established, with the goal of stabilizing countries' exchange rates and so creating a better environment for international trade and investment.

International Monetary Fund (IMF) An international agency established to oversee and maintain the system of pegged exchange rates set up in 1945.

The International Monetary Fund (IMF)

In 1944, 39 nations founded the International Monetary Fund (IMF), which began operations in 1946. The IMF is a large international organization with many responsibilities. We will focus here on its role in stabilizing the exchange rates of nations.

www.imf.org

The Postwar System of "Pegged" Exchange Rates

After the Second World War, the nations of the world resolved to avoid a recurrence of the exchange rate chaos of the 1930s. In 1945, they set up a system of **pegged exchange rates**, in which each nation would establish a "par value" for its currency and its government would keep the currency's price within 1 percent of this par value. The U.S. dollar stood at the centre of the system, with the value of each currency "pegged" to the U.S. dollar. And with each currency "pegged" to the U.S. dollar, the value of each currency was "pegged" relative to the value of other currencies in a rigid system.

To keep exchange rates at their "pegged" levels, governments would *buy and sell currencies* in foreign exchange markets. For instance, if the British pound was losing value relative to the French franc, the British and French governments would buy pounds and sell francs in foreign exchange markets in order to support the price of the pound relative to the franc within 1 percent of its "pegged" level. To enable them to buy their own currencies, governments held deposits of foreign currencies and gold (*foreign exchange reserves*).

In effect, this system was a sort of extreme *dirty float* as described in Chapter 10, but with the objective of not merely moderating fluctuations in exchange rates, but rather of almost *preventing them altogether*. In reaction to the exchange rate chaos of the 1930s, IMF members went to the opposite extreme of establishing a very rigid exchange rate system.

Role of the IMF

It was the IMF's task to help preserve the system of pegged exchange rates established in 1945. The IMF conducted *annual consultations* with member nations. These consultations were intended to encourage nations to follow stable economic policies, and to keep IMF members informed of developments in each others' countries. In its own words, "The IMF is the enemy of surprise."

In addition, the IMF can *lend foreign exchange reserves* to member nations that need them to maintain their exchange rates at their pegged level. Member nations contribute money to the IMF, with richer nations required to make larger contributions. These funds form a pool of money that the IMF can use to make loans to members in financial difficulty.

Strains on the Pegged Exchange Rate System

Despite the efforts of the IMF, it proved impossible to freeze the international prices of currencies indefinitely. Economic conditions changed in ways that made it inevitable that some nations would have Balance of Payments surpluses (which pushed their exchange rates up) and others would have deficits (which pushed their exchange rates down). Governments could offset small, short-term surpluses and deficits by buying or selling currencies, with IMF help if needed. But in the case of large and persistent deficits or surpluses, it proved impossible to peg the currency values for long, because doing so would have required buying or selling impossibly large amounts of currencies in foreign exchange markets.

Upward pressures on currencies were experienced by nations whose strong internationally competitive positions put their currencies in high demand on foreign exchange markets. For example, West German and Japanese exports grew strongly as these nations benefited from a combination of rising industrial efficiency, low inflation rates, and currency values that were pegged at low levels in 1945. So there was upward pressure on the prices of the Japanese yen and the West German deutschemark.

A greater problem was posed by the downward pressures on the currencies of nations whose weak competitive positions caused their currencies to be in relatively low demand and high supply in foreign exchange markets. For example, Great Britain suffered from a combination of high inflation rates, lagging industrial efficiency, and a currency that was pegged at an unrealistically high value.

These factors combined to make Britain's goods uncompetitive in both domestic markets and export markets, generating large trade deficits that continually pushed the price of the pound downward. To maintain the pound at its pegged level, Britain had to buy large volumes of pounds, selling off its reserves of foreign currencies to do so. Eventually, Britain ran out of foreign currencies, and the pound fell suddenly and sharply in value relative to other currencies—a process known as **devaluation** of a currency. The devaluation of a major currency could prove disruptive to both trade and exchange rates, by suddenly altering the prices of currencies relative to each other.

devaluation A reduction in the level of a pegged exchange rate.

Despite attempts to peg exchange rates, a considerable number of devaluations did occur, including that of the British pound, French franc, Italian lira, and Canadian dollar. Under a floating exchange rate system, these adjustments would have occurred gradually as deficits pushed a currency downward, but under the pegged system, governments delayed the adjustment as long as possible. So when the decline in the value of the currency occurred, it happened all at once.

By the 1960s, the U.S. dollar—the key currency in the system—was pegged at a price about 25 percent higher than would have occurred under a floating exchange rate system. This over-valuation of its currency made it even more difficult for the United States to compete with Japan, Germany, and other nations in world trade. Finally, in 1973, the United States "floated" its dollar, effectively bringing the system of pegged exchange rates to an end.

The Pegged Exchange Rate System in Perspective

In one sense, the pegged exchange rate system represented a need to *attempt the necessary*—that is, to stabilize currencies in order to avoid a repetition of the problems of the 1930s. In another sense, it represented an attempt to *achieve the impossible*—that is, to freeze the prices of nations' currencies despite major changes in the economic circumstances of those nations. By buying and selling currencies, governments were able to hold currencies at their pegged values, but only for so long. At that point, there would be a major change in the relative values of currencies, usually occasioned by the devaluation of one or more of them. So it could be said that the actual effect of the pegged exchange rate system was to *postpone* exchange rate changes rather than to *prevent* them. However, it can also be said that between these periodic adjustments, the pegged system did succeed in creating periods when exchange rates were stable.

The Evolving IMF

After the collapse of the pegged exchange rate system, the IMF adapted to the new circumstances. It amended its Articles to give legal sanction to "floating" exchange rates, but it also gave itself a mandate to "exercise firm surveillance over the exchange rate policies of its members" in order to continue to promote exchange rate stability in the new and potentially unstable world of floating exchange rates. Furthermore, the IMF adapted to meet the needs of developing countries, which have become the major users of its resources, by increasing its loan limits and extending its repayment periods. In 2002, these changes in the IMF's mandate were apparent in the IMF's website, which featured articles on poverty reduction and debt relief for developing nations.

By 2002, the IMF's membership had grown to 184 nations from the original 39. Interestingly, the IMF has no authority over its members: it describes itself as "a cooperative institution that 184 countries have voluntarily joined" because they see the advantages of working together to promote international financial stability. Nonetheless, the IMF is regarded as an important international organization.

After the Pegged Exchange Rate System

In 1973, the pegged system of exchange rates was dismantled. In its place there emerged no single exchange-rate system; rather, each IMF member could choose its own approach. Today, probably the most common is the "*dirty float*" system as described in Chapter 10, in which exchange rates can move up and down with market forces, but with governments intervening (usually by buying or selling their currency) to prevent such fluctuations from occurring too rapidly. Other nations allow their currencies to "float" freely, while some currencies are "pegged" to another currency or group of currencies, or only allowed to change in price to a certain extent from a group of other currencies.

There had been fears that the end of the pegged exchange rate system would lead to a return to the exchange rate instability of the 1930s. But this did not happen—nations generally managed their exchange rates quite responsibly, resisting the temptation to manipulate their currency values downward to gain a quick (but almost certainly temporary) competitive advantage.

Capital Flows and Exchange Rates

However, exchange rate fluctuations would continue to be a major factor in international economic developments, as we will see in the following sections. And a new factor was becoming a major force in exchange rate fluctuations—not exports and imports as in the past, but rather *flows of capital* between nations and currencies.

In the globalized world economy, international flows of private capital increased tremendously. These capital flows included bank loans, investment by corporations, purchases and sales of stocks and bonds, and speculative short-term funds, as described in Chapter 10. When large amounts of capital flowed into a nation, the international price of its currency could increase to high levels, as happened with the U.S. dollar. And when investors and lenders pulled funds out of a country on a large scale, as they did in Asia in the late 1990s, the values of those currencies could fall sharply.

In the following sections, we will review the major recent global economic developments, including the role played by capital flows in some of them.

> "Capital flows have been central both to the tremendous advances of the past decade as well as the crises."
>
> Michel Camdessus,
> Managing Director
> of the IMF.

Part C: Recent Developments in the Global Economy

The United States

The outstanding aspects of the United States' position in the global economy in the late 1990s and early 2000s were

1. The very high international value of the U.S. dollar,
2. The very high trade deficits of the United States, and
3. American restrictions on imports that embroiled the United States in trade disputes.

Underlying these developments was the very large *inflow of foreign capital* into the United States in recent years. The net inflow of capital into the U.S. in 2000 was *$399 billion*, as compared to $60 billion ten years earlier. For several years, much of the inflow arose from the foreign buying of shares of U.S. companies as American stock markets soared to giddy (and unrealistic) heights. Even after the stock-market collapse in 2001 and the terrorist attacks in New York, foreign funds continued to flow into the U.S., this time into U.S. bonds. Funds from around the world flowed into the U.S. dollar, which was viewed as the safest haven for capital in an unstable world.

This vast inflow of capital into the United States pushed the international value of the U.S. dollar to very high levels against other currencies such as the Canadian dollar and the Japanese yen. As the U.S. dollar rose, Americans bought more and more imports. At the same time, the strength of the U.S. dollar made it more difficult for American exporters to compete internationally. The result, as Figure 11-2 shows, was growing trade deficits for the U.S.A., which reached a record-high $435 billion U.S. in 2002.

FIGURE 11-2 U.S. Balance of Trade in Goods and Services, 1992–2002

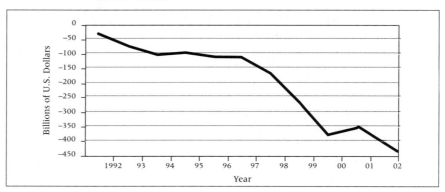

Source: U.S. Census Bureau, Foreign Trade Division, adapted from *U.S. Trade in Goods* (Exhibit 5).

American industries complained about the growing flow of imports into U.S. markets, which led the U.S. government to take various actions to restrict imports. These actions embroiled the United States in trade disputes with various countries, which filed complaints with the World Trade Organization that alleged that the U.S. was violating the WTO agreement.

In 2002, the WTO ruled against the United States in a massive judgment that levied its largest sanctions ever. The WTO ruled that the European Union could impose up to $4 billion of trade sanctions against the United States in retaliation for an American tax law that exempted part of corporations' export income from U.S. taxes. And a long list of countries, including Canada, complained successfully to the WTO about another U.S. law that allowed American firms to initiate complaints about imports and then *keep the proceeds from antidumping duties* imposed by the U.S. against those imports. In addition, both Europe and Japan were threatening in mid-2002 to retaliate against new U.S. tariffs on steel by imposing their own tariffs on U.S. products.

As these trade disputes continued, concern grew around the world that the combination of an overvalued U.S. dollar, trade deficits, and domestic politics might be leading the United States to create policies that would undermine the progress toward freer trade that had been achieved over the years.

Japan

Japan is the world's second-largest economy, and a major international trader, investor, and lender. Until the 1990s, Japan enjoyed tremendous export success and rapid economic growth that averaged 4 percent a year in the 1980s.

But in 2002, Japan was struggling through its third recession in ten years. In the 1990s, its economy had stagnated, with an average growth rate of only 1 percent per year, and by 2002, unemployment was at historically high levels and rising.

Japan's spectacular export-driven economic growth of the 1970s and 1980s was reflected in, and symbolized by, a tremendous increase in the international value of its currency, the yen. As foreigners bought yen with which to buy Japan's outstanding manufactured goods, the price of the yen increased steadily—by about 65 percent in the 1970s, then by another 75 percent in the 1980s, as Figure 11-3 shows. At one point in 1995, the yen was nearly four times as valuable as it had been 25 years earlier.

FIGURE 11-3 Value of the Yen in U.S. Dollars, 1960–2002

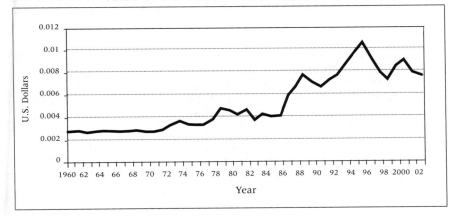

Source: Department of Finance, adapted from *Economic Reference Tables*, August 1996; Bank of Canada, *Banking and Financial Statistics*.

In this environment of rapid growth, the prices of the shares of Japanese corporations soared, as Figure 11-4 shows. Property values also increased dramatically as wealthy investors bought up Japanese assets. And as the value of their assets grew, many people borrowed heavily against those assets in order to buy more stocks and property.

FIGURE 11-4 Nikkei 225 Stock Index, 1982–2002

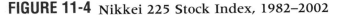

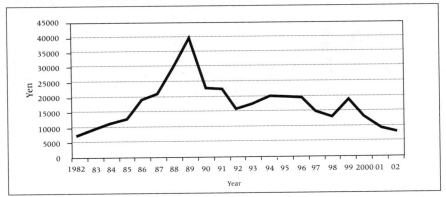

Source: Bank of Japan.

The soaring yen was not only reflected Japan's export success but also contributed to the end of that success. Finally, the yen became so costly to foreigners that Japan's exports stagnated, and the economy lost momentum. The U.S. recession of the early 1990s worsened the situation by cutting further into Japan's exports.

Investors lost confidence and sold off their shares of Japanese companies. From 1990 to 1992, the Japanese stock market (the Nikkei) crashed, losing 57 percent of its value, as can be seen in Figure 11-4. Property values plummeted, too. Many people and businesses were left with heavy debt that they could not repay, and the stocks and property that had been used as collateral for loans had lost much of their value. Japanese banks were stuck with many bad loans, and several banks were in serious trouble by the mid-1990s.

The Japanese economy had excess production capacity, but the banks kept many inefficient, money-losing, and debt-ridden companies operating in the hope that they could recover and repay their loans. When these efforts undermined the financial position of the banks, the government began propping up the banks financially. But the government's own finances were deteriorating badly due to its deficit spending to try to boost the economy. By 2002, government debt was extremely high at 140 percent of GDP. By comparison, the debt of all levels of Canadian governments had peaked at about 90 percent of GDP during Canada's financial crisis of the early 1990s.

deflation A decrease in the general level of the prices of goods and services.

Japan's combination of excess production capacity and low aggregate demand led to recession in some years and very slow growth in others. But it also generated a potentially more serious problem known as **deflation**, or a condition of falling prices—the opposite of inflation. Figure 11-5 shows the gradual decrease in consumer prices in Japan after 1998.

FIGURE 11-5 Change in Japanese Consumer Prices, 1990–2002

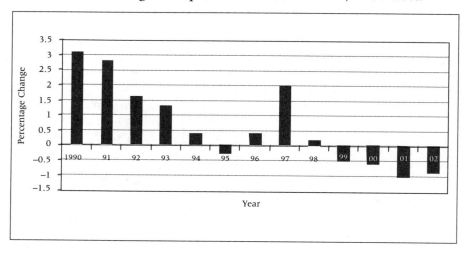

Source: Bank of Japan.

The Japanese economy needed Japan's banking system to "create money" and to boost aggregate demand, but the banks were so burdened with bad loans that they had become more cautious about lending. To make matters worse, debt-ridden consumers and businesses were often unwilling to borrow more.

With excess capacity in many industries and falling prices, Japan's economy was badly in need of higher demand. But government policy-makers seemed unable to generate an increase in aggregate demand, in large part due to deflation. Deflation encourages people to postpone borrowing and spending, because they expect prices to continue to fall in the future. So despite the dramatic decrease in interest rates by the Bank of Japan shown in Figure 11-6, borrowing and spending did not recover as intended.

FIGURE 11-6 Japanese Overnight Interest Rates, 1985–2002

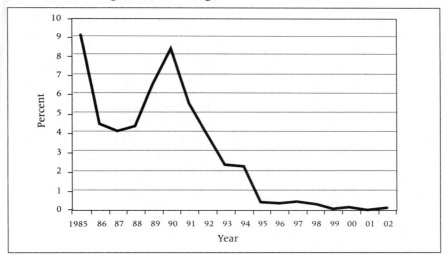

Source: Bank of Japan.

To make matters worse, the government's use of fiscal policy was becoming limited by its debt. Previous (mostly unsuccessful) efforts at using budget deficits to stimulate the economy had left the government with such massive debt (140 percent of GDP, as noted earlier) that more aggressive government borrowing and spending seemed unlikely.

By 2000–03, many observers believed that the only solution to Japan's deflation was a large depreciation of the yen of about *25 percent* (from about 0.8 U.S. cents to about 0.6 U.S. cents). A sharply lower yen would boost Japan's exports and aggregate demand, and could help to reverse deflation through a combination of higher demand and higher prices for imports.

But this solution would be far from simple—such a large depreciation of the currency of the world's second-largest economy could be very disruptive for its trading partners. It would make Japanese exports much less costly to foreigners, perhaps spreading both unemployment and deflationary pressures to other nations such as the United States and Europe as their people bought low-cost Japanese products. And by 2002, both the United States and Europe were becoming concerned about deflation in their own economies.

Europe

The European Union (EU) unites 15 European countries into a very large single market that gives European producers economies of scale and promotes trade and higher productivity. Twelve of the EU countries share a common currency (the euro), which further promotes trade and investment by reducing transactions costs and eliminating uncertainties regarding currency values. This combination of a large free-trade area and a common currency is widely regarded as an excellent basis for economic prosperity.

But in the early 2000s, domestic demand in the EU was stagnant, and there were growing concerns that a deflation problem similar to Japan's might develop. In addition, the EU's own rules limited the ability of the governments of EU nations to deal with these problems.

In order to harmonize the economic policies of the diverse members of the EU so that they could function as a single market with a single currency, the EU had established rules for its members. One key rule is the European Central Bank's inflation target of less than 2 percent per year. There was concern that such a low target might cause the central bank to become preoccupied with combating inflation, and tilt the EU's monetary policy in the direction of either recession or deflation. Also, the EU's rules for government finances limit governments' budget deficits to 3 percent of GDP. So if an EU country were in a recession and its government's budget deficit exceeded 3 percent of GDP, that government would be expected to cut spending and/or increase taxes, despite the recession. This rule further limits the ability of the governments of EU nations to stimulate demand when the economy is floundering, adding to the risk of deflation.

> Canada's trade links with Europe are relatively modest, amounting to 5 to 6 percent of Canada's exports and 10 percent of imports.

The Threat of Deflation

By the early 2000s, deflation was a reality in Japan and a concern in Europe. And by late 2002, it became evident that monetary authorities in the United States were also concerned about the risk of deflation. In late 2002, U.S. interest rates were again reduced aggressively, in an effort to prevent deflation from setting in.

Deflation can be dangerous because like inflation, deflation can feed on itself and grow worse. Falling prices can lead people to expect that prices will continue to fall. And if people expect prices to fall in the future, they will be more likely to postpone borrowing and spending, which will reduce demand further and put additional downward pressure on prices.

As prices fall under deflation, the real burden of the debts of consumers and businesses increases. Recall that inflation makes it *easier* for borrowers to pay off their debts because people's incomes and the prices firms receive for

> "History suggests that central banks should do everything they can to avoid deflation, which is far more harmful than inflation, especially when economies are awash with debt."
>
> *The Economist*,
> September 28, 2002.

goods and services each year are rising, so the real burden of their debt is falling. But deflation has the opposite effect—as prices and incomes decrease, the debt of consumers and firms grows *more burdensome* in real terms. Such a prospect discourages borrowing and drags aggregate demand even lower, increasing downward pressures on prices and forcing employers to lay off more workers.

Worse yet, deflation can make it difficult for government policy-makers to engineer an increase in aggregate demand. The standard prescription for boosting demand is a monetary policy of lower interest rates; however, deflation encourages people to postpone borrowing and spending. And while a country's central bank can try to encourage borrowing by reducing interest rates, *it can only reduce interest rates so far*. Interest rates cannot go below zero.

This dilemma is illustrated in Table 11-2, which shows an extreme case in which the central bank reduces the interest rate to zero. The left column portrays an economy in which the rate of inflation is 2 percent per year. In this situation, the "real" (after-inflation) rate of interest is −2 percent. Borrowers can borrow $100 now at zero percent interest and repay the loan in a year with $100 that will by then have a purchasing power of $98. Such terms would certainly make borrowing attractive—and saving unattractive!

TABLE 11-2 Deflation and Real Interest Rates

	2% Inflation	2% Deflation
Interest rate	0%	0%
minus		
Rate of inflation	2%	−2%
equals		
Real interest rate	−2%	+2%

But if there is deflation instead of inflation, the same monetary policy is less likely to work. The right column in Table 11-2 shows an economy in which there is deflation, with prices falling at a rate of 2 percent per year. Even with an interest rate of zero, the real interest rate (the after-inflation cost of borrowing) is 2 percent. Borrowers can borrow $100 now at zero percent interest and repay the loan in a year with $100. However, in a year, falling prices will have increased the purchasing power of that $100 to $102! So even though the interest rate is zero percent, borrowing now is not all that attractive—it still involves a cost to the borrower of 2 percent per year. So people may decide not to borrow and spend now, but rather to wait for prices to fall. In Japan, this did become a problem after 1995—despite interest rates being very close to zero, monetary policy failed to encourage borrowing and spending as intended.

There is also a risk that deflation can spread from one major economy to other economies. The most likely anti-deflation policy is a very sharp reduction in interest rates. This policy would be intended not only to boost domestic demand but also to *reduce the international value of the country's currency* considerably. A sharp reduction in a country's exchange rate would boost exports and aggregate demand, and it might also combat deflation by increasing the prices of imports. The problem is that this policy would unleash low-priced exports from that country into other nations' economies, increasing unemployment in those countries while putting downward pressure on *their* prices. In short, deflation could spread to other countries through the international trade and currency mechanisms described in this chapter.

Such a scenario is uncomfortably similar to the disastrous policies of the 1930s as described earlier in this chapter, when nations manipulated the values of their currencies downward in attempts to gain a competitive

---

IN THE **NEWS**   The Diving U.S. Dollar

As noted on page 253, the international value of the U.S. dollar increased sharply after 1997 due to massive inflows of foreign funds into American investments. But in early 2003 the U.S. dollar fell sharply, all the way back to its 1997 level. Troubled by the poor condition of the U.S. economy, its huge trade deficits and budget deficits and the low interest rates available on U.S. investments, investors moved funds out of American investments and into other currencies, including the Canadian dollar. While the graph shows the decline in the U.S. dollar relative to the Canadian dollar, the U.S. dollar declined to a similar extent against most major currencies.

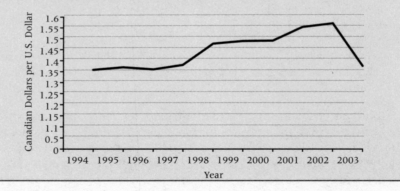

Questions

1. How would such a large decrease in the international value of the U.S. dollar affect
   * Canadian consumers?
   * employment and unemployment in Canada?
   * the problem of deflation in Japan and Europe?
   * the risk of deflation in the United States?
2. Has the international value of the U.S. dollar continued to decrease?

advantage over each other. To avert this risk would require that the governments of *all* the major global economies—the United States, Europe, and Japan—boost their domestic demand not only aggressively, but also *simultaneously*. But with Japan already mired in deflation and Europe's actions limited by its own rules, many observers believed that the United States had by default become the key to global economic recovery. A strongly growing U.S. economy that was also once again open to imports from around the world seemed the best prospect for a global economic recovery.

The Doha Round of WTO Trade Negotiations

As noted earlier, the "Doha Round" of WTO negotiations—the ninth in the history of the GATT/WTO—was launched in late 2001, in Doha, Qatar. One of the basic objectives of the Doha Round was to help developing countries by opening up the markets of the rich countries to their products. In particular, it was hoped that the rich countries would open their markets to developing countries' agricultural products and textiles—two areas in which the rich countries' trade barriers had historically been very high.

The Doha Round did not get underway under the best of circumstances. In the environment of the global economic slowdown described above, governments tended to be more concerned with protecting their industries and jobs than with opening up their markets. And as we have seen, American protectionism had been on the rise, leading to several major trade disputes that nations had been unable to resolve themselves, and had referred to the WTO for rulings.

In addition, the United States introduced in 2002 massive new agricultural subsidies that would increase government spending on agriculture by 80 percent. These subsidies represented a serious threat to one of the basic objectives of Doha, which was to use trade to help developing countries by opening up the markets of the wealthy developed countries to their agricultural products.

As of 2003, the outlook for the Doha Round was uncertain. Pessimists were concerned that the United States might be losing its commitment to free trade. They feared that under the pressures of an overvalued U.S. dollar that was making American industries less internationally competitive, politics in the United States might militate in favour of protectionism. Optimists took a quite different view. They believed that the U.S. government had been temporarily pushed into its protectionist stance by the 2002 elections and recession, and that as the U.S. economy recovered in 2003 and beyond, the United States would once again become a leader toward freer trade.

The Future: Globalization or Regionalism?

To some observers, the problems of the Doha Round were evidence that the WTO's multilateral or "global" approach to freer trade had gone as far as it could. They believed that the complexities of negotiating worldwide trade agreements among so many diverse nations had become overwhelming, and that the future would see more emphasis on *regional* trade agreements,

> "The single market [has given] EC (now EU) companies a large home market to match the domestic markets of the United States and Japan that have enabled their companies to benefit from enormous economies of scale."
>
> Bruce Barnard, Brussels, correspondent for *The Journal of Commerce*.

known as *trading blocs*. These are separate trade agreements negotiated outside of the GATT/WTO, usually among nations in a particular region. The most noteworthy ones are the European Union (EU) and the North American Free Trade Agreement (NAFTA). There are several other regional trading arrangements in the Pacific area, Southeast Asia, Australia and New Zealand, Latin America, Africa, the Caribbean, and the Middle East.

European Union A major free trade area comprising most of the countries of Europe.

The **European Union** is the last step in the long process of the economic unification of many European countries, including Germany, Italy, France, Belgium, the Netherlands, Luxembourg, the United Kingdom, Ireland, Denmark, Greece, Spain, Portugal, Austria, Sweden, and Finland, with several others being considered for membership. It is regarded as a major achievement because of the political complexities of creating a free trade agreement among such a large number of nations with such diverse economic, cultural, political, linguistic, and historical characteristics.

euro A common currency adopted in 1999 by 12 of the 15 countries of the European Union.

The final step in the economic unification of Europe was the introduction of a common currency (the **euro**) for 12 of the 15 members of the EU (Germany, France, Italy, Spain, Portugal, Austria, Belgium, the Netherlands, Finland, Ireland, Luxembourg, and Greece). In 2002, the national currencies of these 12 nations were replaced by the euro. Each of these nations surrendered control of its monetary policy to a supranational institution, the European Central Bank (ECB).

The European Union comprises a very large market with over 350 million consumers, with goods, services, and capital moving easily across national borders, and with all of the associated advantages in terms of economies of scale. The euro was intended to make the European market even more integrated, by reducing currency conversion costs and by eliminating uncertainties regarding currency values. Supporters of the EU hope that it will challenge, or even surpass, the United States as the world's most powerful economic centre.

North American Free Trade Agreement (NAFTA) Free trade agreement between Canada, the United States, and Mexico.

The **North American Free Trade Agreement (NAFTA)** is discussed in more detail in Chapter 12, so we will only sketch the outlines of it here. In 1989, Canada and the United States signed the Canada–U.S. Free Trade Agreement, which, with the addition of Mexico in 1994, became NAFTA.

In some ways, NAFTA was North America's (and particularly the United States') response to the European Union—the economic unification of North America into a single vast market, with similar advantages and economic power like that of the EU. Eventually, the goal is to create a Western Hemisphere trade bloc of 34 or 35 countries with about 850 million consumers. However, the achievement of this goal is complicated by the number and the diversity of the nations involved, plus the fact that there are already six other regional trade agreements in place in the Western Hemisphere in addition to NAFTA.

Asia–Pacific Economic Co-operation (APEC) A group of 21 nations that border the Pacific Ocean and intend to form a free trade area by 2010.

Asia–Pacific Economic Co-operation (APEC) includes Canada, the United States, Japan, South Korea, China, Australia, and 15 other nations of the Pacific area. It is considerably less fully structured than the other trading blocs that we have discussed. It consists of a very diverse group of nations and, therefore, has much farther to go to become a free trade area. APEC's "action agenda" calls upon its industrialized member nations, such as the

United States, Canada, Japan, and Australia, to join a free trade pact by 2010, with less developed countries expected to join by 2020.

Trade, Currencies, and Global Economic Power

Since the Second World War, the degree of international economic cooperation has improved considerably, if not always steadily. Most of this progress was achieved through the two major global institutions of the GATT/WTO and the IMF that operate on a nearly worldwide scale. However, there was growing speculation that the world could be evolving into three major trade and currency areas: a Western Hemisphere bloc centred on the United States, the European Union, and an Asian bloc with Japan as its focal point.

For many years, the United States and the U.S. dollar played a dominant role in the world economy, largely because of the dominance of the U.S. economy internationally—the U.S. is the most productive, prosperous, and powerful single nation in the world. But Europe's plans for its own huge united market and its own unified currency posed a challenge to American dominance. In response, the United States entered into its own free trade agreements, first with Canada, then with Mexico. The long-term American goal was for a Free Trade Area of the Americas, embracing the entire Western Hemisphere and matching or surpassing the European Union in size and prosperity. However, progress toward this broader goal had stalled by the late 1990s.

The position of Japan and Asia in this global economic chess match was less clear. While Asia had great potential for economic development, it was at the turn of the century no match for the EU or the NAFTA blocs. Furthermore, APEC's plans did not envision a full Asia–Pacific free trade area until 2020, and two key players in APEC were the United States and Canada, themselves both members of NAFTA. Only time will tell how the various trade and currency blocs will evolve, and how APEC will fit into the global picture.

Chapter Summary

1. The Great Depression of the 1930s showed the dangers of government policies that try to protect their domestic industries by increasing tariffs and manipulating their exchange rates. (L.O. 1)

2. The General Agreement on Tariffs and Trade (GATT, renamed the World Trade Organization (WTO) in 1995) made great progress in reducing tariffs and promoting increased international trade through multilateral negotiations. (L.O. 2)

3. During the 1980s, the GATT's progress toward freer trade slowed for various reasons, including the growing number of participants and issues, the growing complexity of issues, and growing protectionism on the part of key players, including the United States and Europe. (L.O. 3)

4. In 1945, the major nations of the world established a system of pegged exchange rates under the supervision of the International Monetary

Fund. However, it proved impossible to freeze exchange rates, and the pegged system was abandoned in 1973. (L.O. 4)

5. In place of the pegged system, nations adopted various exchange rate systems, the most common of which was the "dirty float." Under this system, capital flows between nations became a key factor in exchange rate fluctuations. (L.O. 5)

6. As of 2002, capital inflows into the United States were pushing the value of the U.S. dollar to high levels and generating trade deficits and protectionist policies. Japan had been suffering from economic stagnation and deflation for several years. The European economy was sluggish, and there was concern that the European Union's rules for monetary and fiscal policies would limit its prospects for recovery. (L.O. 6)

7. Deflation is a condition of falling prices and economic stagnation that can grow worse. As of 2002, there was deflation in Japan and concerns of deflation occurring in Europe and the United States. (L.O. 7)

8. In 2001, the Doha Round of WTO trade negotiations was launched, with the main objective of helping developing countries by opening up the markets of rich countries to their products. However, its success was made uncertain by growing protectionism in the sluggish economic environment of the early 2000s. (L.O. 8)

9. In addition to GATT/WTO's multilateral approach, there are separate trade agreements (trading blocs) between groups of nations. Some observers believe that the world might evolve into three major regional trade and currency blocs: Europe, the Americas, and Asia. (L.O. 9)

Questions

1. Following are the values of the world's three major currencies in terms of each other in late 2002:

Currency	Value in U.S. dollars	Value in yen	Value in euros
the U.S. dollar	1.00	120.44	0.997
the yen	0.00830	1.00	0.008 27
the euro	1.003	120.86	1.00

(a) What changes have occurred in the values of these currencies since late 2002? (For exchange rates can be found at www.bankofcanada.ca.)

(b) What might explain any changes in exchange rates that have occurred?

(c) How might these changes affect each of these three major economies?

2. Since late 2002, what developments have there been with respect to *deflation* in

(a) Japan?

(b) the United States?

(c) the European Union?

3. How successful has the Doha Round of World Trade Organization negotiations been? What accounts for the success (or lack thereof) of the negotiations?

4. Keep a newspaper file of major international trade disputes. What are the main sources of nations' complaints against each other? Do the WTO's dispute resolution processes (neutral panels) seem to be working effectively?

5. What would a large increase in the value of the yen mean to:
   (a) Japanese automobile manufacturers?
   (b) Japanese consumers?
   (c) North American consumers?
   (d) North American automobile manufacturers?

6. "The higher the yen went, the more likely it was to stop rising." Explain the reasoning behind this statement.

7. Newfoundland and Labrador has chronically high unemployment rates. Would Newfoundland and Labrador be better off if it were a separate country with its own currency, and were able to lower interest rates and increase its money supply in order to stimulate its economy and reduce unemployment?

8. Some observers expected that a united Europe would overtake the United States in terms of global economic power. But there is an interesting difference between Europe and the United States in the area of demographics. Europe's fertility rates fell sharply after the 1950s, so Europe's population is growing slowly and will be aging. In contrast, the American fertility rate reversed its decline in the 1980s, so the United States has a population that is growing faster than was expected and will stay much younger than Europe's. What impact will these demographic differences have on the future prospects for these two economies?

Chapter 12

Canada in the Global Economy

Learning Objectives

After studying this chapter, you should be able to:

1. State the purpose and the main features of Canada's National Policy of 1879, and explain its various effects upon the Canadian economy.

2. Explain why the productivity of Canada's manufacturing sector tended to be low, and why it fell farther behind other nations' productivity in the 1980s.

3. State four factors that pressed Canada in the 1980s to change its traditional trade policy of protecting its manufacturing sector.

4. Describe the major terms of the Canada–U.S. Free Trade Agreement of 1989 regarding tariffs and settlement of trade disputes.

5. Describe the strategic significance of the North American Free Trade Agreement (NAFTA) for the U.S., and the expected economic effect of NAFTA on Canada.

6. Explain the business strategies known as *world product mandating* and *niche marketing* for Canadian firms in the highly competitive world economy.

7. Explain why the international value of the Canadian dollar has decreased since 1975 by such a large amount.

8. Explain the effects on Canadians of this decrease in the international value of the Canadian dollar.

9. Explain what is meant by "dollarization," and the arguments in favour of and against dollarization for Canada.

Economically, Canada is a small country in a big world, with one-half of one percent of the world's population and a GDP that is only about 3 percent of total world output. Canada's market of 31 million people is smaller than the state of California, and not large enough to support the economies of scale achievable in large markets such as the U.S. and Europe.

Canadians are made to feel even smaller by the fact that their nearest neighbour, the United States, has the largest, most productive, and richest economy in the world. On the other hand, Canadians enjoy a high standard of living, which has been made higher by Canada's very active economic relationship with other countries, especially the United States. This relationship includes very high levels of both exports and imports, and large amounts of investment flowing in both directions.

Being situated next to the United States has always presented Canada with something of a dilemma. To Canada, the U.S. has always seemed to represent *both*

- an economic *opportunity*, in the form of the vast market that the U.S. provides to Canadian firms, and
- an economic *threat*, in the form of competition from the U.S.'s highly efficient producers.

For Canadian governments, the threat of U.S. competition has presented an argument for *trade restrictions*, to protect Canadian producers from U.S. competition. On the other hand, the proximity of the large U.S. market has argued in favour of a policy of *freer trade*, to give Canadian firms access to that market. Efficient Canadian exporters have urged the government to adopt free trade, while industries threatened by imports have argued that protectionism is in Canada's interests. Obviously, this has placed Canadian policymakers in a contradictory position between protectionism and free trade, and for many years Canada's trade policy consisted of a search for a balance between these two positions. As we will see, for many years the nation's trade policy emphasized protection of Canadian industries; however, it shifted gradually toward freer trade over time, and has moved much more rapidly in that direction recently.

Part A: Trade and Trade Policy

A Brief Historical Background

National Policy A set of nation-building policies introduced in Canada in 1879, the key economic aspect of which was protective tariffs to foster the development of Canadian industry.

In 1854, the British colonies that were to become Canada were given access to the U.S. market through a trade treaty with the U.S. However, the Americans cancelled that treaty in 1866, leaving these colonies in a difficult position economically. In 1879, the government of the new nation of Canada introduced a nation-building program known as the **National Policy**, the key economic component of which was a system of protective tariffs.

The National Policy (1879)

The tariffs of the National Policy were of the "infant industry" type described in Chapter 9—they were meant to protect Canada's manufacturing industries, which were just starting to develop at this time. By placing a tariff barrier along the Canada–U.S. border, the National Policy intended not only to develop a Canadian manufacturing sector but also to shape trade links along east–west lines rather than the north–south links with the United States that would otherwise have prevailed. The tariffs also provided the government with tax revenue that was used to finance the building of the railroad that was crucial to the forging of east–west links. For over a century, Canadian manufacturers would enjoy considerable tariff protection against competition from imports, and the railroad would be the symbol of Canada's nationhood.

Effects of Tariff Protection

The tariff protection initiated under the National Policy would shape the Canadian economy for over a century. Unquestionably, the tariffs fostered the development of a *larger manufacturing sector* than would otherwise have existed in many industries, from breakfast foods to footwear to automobiles. And this manufacturing sector grew into a major employer, especially in Ontario and Quebec. In this sense, the tariff policy achieved its basic objective.

On the other hand, the tariff protection meant *higher prices* for Canadian consumers. The tariffs not only added to the prices of imported products, but also allowed Canadian firms to charge higher prices for their products. In effect, the protected manufacturers were being subsidized by consumers. This situation was intended to be temporary—as the infant industries matured and became more efficient, less tariff protection would be needed.

In addition, Canada's tariff policy led many foreign manufacturers, especially American firms, to establish *branch plants* in Canada in order to avoid paying the Canadian tariffs. As a result, *foreign ownership* of Canadian industry became very high. These various effects of Canada's tariff policy are summarized in Figure 12-1.

The Manufacturing Productivity Problem

Figure 12-1 shows another problem that would become more serious with the passage of time—much of the manufacturing sector that developed under tariff protection was relatively inefficient and not competitive internationally. Two factors were limiting the productivity of Canadian manufacturers—Canada's own policy of tariff protection and the small size of the Canadian market.

For many years, tariffs protected much of Canada's manufacturing sector from foreign competition and from pressures to become more efficient. And due to Canada's tariffs and its lack of a free trade agreement with other nations (until 1989), many Canadian manufacturers and foreign-owned branch plants were producing mostly for the Canadian market, which is very small by international standards. By the mid-1980s, with international trade

FIGURE 12-1 Effects of Canada's Tariff Policy

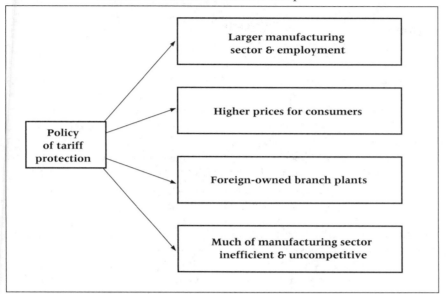

and competition increasing rapidly, Canada was the only high-income country in the Northern Hemisphere that did not have something approximating secure tariff-free access to markets of 100 million people or more, either domestically or through trade.

The small market available to many Canadian manufacturers restricted their use of modern mass-production technology. Since the average Canadian manufacturing plant was significantly smaller than its counterparts in the United States, Europe, and Japan, it was less able to develop the productive efficiency associated with large-scale operations (economies of scale). While this was not a problem in all industries, it was a disadvantage in many.

But the problems of Canadian manufacturing went beyond small plant size. Whereas a plant producing for the vast U.S. market could specialize in mass-producing a single product very efficiently, plants (often branch plants) producing only for the small Canadian market had to produce an entire range of products, each on a small scale. This required that the Canadian plants switch from producing one product to another several times in a year, a costly process that reduced efficiency. Studies indicated that this problem of *short production runs* was often a greater source of inefficiency in Canadian manufacturing than the problem of small plant size.

The Problem of Lagging Productivity

According to the infant industry theory, the efficiency of the tariff-protected "infants" is supposed to improve over time as the infants grow and mature. Eventually, they should become efficient enough to compete internationally without any tariff protection.

Since 1947, through GATT negotiations, Canada had been gradually reducing its tariff protection. Canadian policy-makers recognized that freer international trade was in Canada's long-run best interests, and that in order to gain access to larger foreign markets, Canada would have to gradually reduce its own tariff protection, forcing "infant" Canadian manufacturers to become more efficient and internationally competitive.

And, until the 1980s, the infant industry theory seemed to be working well—Canada's manufacturing productivity was gaining on its American counterpart. Figure 12-2 shows how Canadian manufacturing productivity increased from only 59 percent of the U.S. level in 1950 to 81 percent in 1980. The Canadian "infants" appeared to be maturing as intended.

However, after 1980, Canadian manufacturing productivity did not increase as rapidly as U.S. productivity, falling back to only 69 percent of the U.S. level by 1990. Canada's manufacturing sector was becoming less competitive relative to the United States and to the rest of the world.

The most basic reason for this problem is believed to lie in the phenomenon of *globalization* described at the end of Chapter 9. The expansion of international trade during the 1980s resulted in a combination of increased competition and larger markets, which increased productivity in many industries around the world. But many Canadian manufacturers were still operating on a small scale in the tariff-protected Canadian market. The basic problem was that the world was changing, but Canada was not keeping up; in fact, Canadian manufacturers were falling farther behind, as Figure 12-2 shows.

FIGURE 12-2 Canadian Manufacturing Productivity as a Percentage of American Manufacturing Productivity, 1950–90

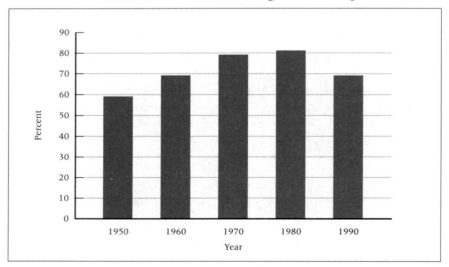

Source: *Pulling Together: Productivity, Innovation and Trade*, Industry Canada, 1992. Reproduced with the permission of the Minister of Public Works and Government Services, 2003.

Research identified several other reasons for the low productivity of Canadian manufacturing. One of these was Canadians' *aversion to change*. Canadian managers were found to be slow to develop and adopt new technology, often taking a short-term, cost-cutting approach to managing rather than taking the more long-term strategic approach of their Japanese and European counterparts. The result was often underinvestment in new technology, research and development (R&D), and employee training. Researchers often concluded that Canadian managers were simply unaccustomed to working in a highly competitive environment.

Another factor has been Canada's *weak performance in science and technology*. Spending by business on research and development has been low, and many firms lack qualified scientific and technical staff. Despite this deficiency, relatively few young people take an interest in careers in science and engineering. Canada's *educational system* has also been criticized for its large number of dropouts and the lack of job-related skills of many high-school graduates.

> "The competitiveness of the Canadian economy... has deteriorated markedly during the past two decades.... [P]roductivity growth fell sharply in the 1970s and virtually halted in the 1980s. While most OECD countries also experienced a sharp drop in productivity growth, Canada's performance is among the worst."
>
> *Report of the Organization for Economic Cooperation and Development, 1992.*

The Automobile Industry—A Noteworthy Exception

The automobile industry was an interesting exception to the tendency of Canadian manufacturers to be inefficient. After 1965, the auto industry operated under a sort of "free trade" agreement between Canada and the United States, known as the **Auto Pact**. Under the Auto Pact, the Canadian and U.S. governments encouraged and supported continent-wide specialization of auto plants, to increase efficiency, and the Canadian auto industry was transformed from a relatively inefficient branch-plant industry to a world-class industry—in fact, one of the showpieces of the Canadian economy. Canadian auto plants now specialize in the production of a few cars, most of which are exported to the United States. On the other hand, many cars bought in Canada are imported from similarly specialized plants in the United States. The Auto Pact showed that Canadian industry could succeed in international competition, and it provided a model that other industries would follow in future years.

Auto Pact The 1965 agreement between Canada and the United States that provided for free trade in automotive vehicles, products, and parts.

In 2001, 68% of Ford of Canada's sales revenues came from exports. For Honda Canada, exports represented 65% of sales.

Consequences of Uncompetitiveness

As the 1980s progressed, the costs of Canada's weakness in productivity and competitive performance became apparent. Canada's share of world trade was declining, and economic studies indicated that this was almost entirely because of a deterioration in Canada's ability to compete. The studies indicated that Canada enjoyed the opportunity for export success by being so close to the vast American market and producing an appropriate range of manufactured goods, but had not taken advantage of that opportunity.

Pressures for Changes to Canadian Trade Policy

In this new, globalized international environment, the following factors were pressing Canada to change from its traditional policy of protecting its manufacturing sector:

- the declining competitiveness of much of Canadian manufacturing,
- the growing costs to consumers and exporters of protecting uncompetitive manufacturers,
- outflows of Canadian business investment capital, and
- growing protectionism in the United States.

In the following sections, each of these four factors is examined in more detail.

The Declining Competitiveness of Much of Canadian Manufacturing

As outlined above, much of the Canadian manufacturing sector lost competitive ground relative to the rest of the world during the 1980s. In the view of most economists, access to larger foreign markets and exposure to foreign competition were needed in order to improve the productivity of Canada's manufacturers.

The Growing Costs of Protecting Uncompetitive Manufacturers

As productivity fell further behind other nations', the costs to Canadians of protecting Canada's manufacturing sector increased. These costs took two forms—the costs to consumers of having to pay high tariff-supported prices for goods, and the costs to Canadian exporters of retaliatory measures by other nations.

Costs to consumers consisted of higher prices due to tariffs. By the mid-1980s, these costs were estimated to be as high as $200 000 for each job saved by tariffs. Such figures raised the question of whether continued protection of some Canadian industries was economically justifiable, particularly when those industries were losing ground to foreign competition even with such costly protection.

Costs to exporters were more difficult to estimate, but were considered to be large. Canada's more efficient and successful industries needed more access to larger foreign markets in order to grow and realize their potential. However, it was difficult to gain this access as long as Canada maintained its protection of many of its own industries, often through questionable trade restrictions. For instance, GATT found Canada's protection of its wine, beer, and some food-processing industries to be in violation of international trade agreements, exposing Canada to retaliatory action by other nations and making it more difficult for Canada to negotiate reductions in other countries' tariffs. The "You Decide" box on p. 273 provides an example of the kind of difficult decision that was being forced upon the Canadian government by its policy of protecting its rather aged "infants," in this case the footwear industry.

YOU **DECIDE**

TRADE POLICY CHOICES

Suppose that import quotas on footwear, which have been in effect for eight years, are scheduled to expire in one month. The Canadian Import Tribunal (a government agency) has recommended that the government should drop import quotas on all footwear except women's and girls' casual footwear, and that quotas on these should be phased out over the next three years. The Import Tribunal bases its recommendation in part on estimates that shoe import quotas are costing Canadian consumers $100 million annually, and that perhaps 350 to 700 jobs have been saved by quotas at an annual cost to consumers of $120 000 to $240 000 per job saved. The Consumers Association of Canada and the Canadian Shoe Retailers Association have both argued that the quotas should be removed, pointing out that even without quotas, footwear imports are subject to a tariff of approximately 20 percent—the highest Canadian tariff.

The Shoe Manufacturers Association of Canada claims that domestic manufacturers' share of the market has declined over the past four years from 47 percent to 33 percent. It has asked the government to extend the quotas for a minimum period of five more years and to reserve 50 percent of the Canadian market for Canadian producers. The industry employs about 15 000 people, mainly in Ontario and Quebec. Over the past few years, the federal government has invested quite heavily in financial support for the industry. Political support for the government in Quebec and Ontario, which was crucial to its success in the last election, has been weakening lately. The labour union movement has clearly stated its opposition to any move that would threaten jobs, and a recent public opinion poll indicates that Canadians are nervous about foreign competition.

Finally, Europe has warned that if the Canadian footwear quotas are extended, it will retaliate against Canadian exports, including methanol, styrene, polyethylene, acetate, kraft paper, wire rod, steel coils, and cold-rolled sheets and plates. The value of these exports is about $170 million per year.

Question

1. If you were the government of Canada, what would you decide?

Outflows of Business Investment Capital

Partly because they could not gain secure access to larger foreign markets, a growing number of Canadian firms turned to establishing branch operations in foreign countries. Historically, Canada had experienced a net inflow of business investment capital; however, after the mid-1970s this turned into a net outflow, mainly due to increased investment abroad by Canadian firms. And with the outflow of investment capital along went the associated jobs.

Growing Protectionism in the United States

In the mid-1980s the United States, the market for about three-quarters of Canada's exports, was becoming more *protectionist*. Faced with stronger foreign competition from various quarters, American authorities moved toward restrictions on imports—including imports from Canada—as a means of protecting American industries and jobs.

Under U.S. law, American industries could obtain government protection from foreign competition by filing complaints with U.S. authorities. Several American industries used this law to obtain government action against Canadian imports, using questionable statistics and economic arguments in the process. Canada could only appeal such actions through U.S. courts, with very little chance of success.

These practices affected only a small proportion of Canada's exports, but they were threatening, and created uncertainty for Canadian firms. Also, fear of American import restrictions was leading a growing number of Canadian firms to build branch operations in the United States, rather than in Canada. This outflow of Canadian business capital—and jobs—was a growing concern in Canada.

Figure 12-3 summarizes these pressures for change to Canadian trade policy. As a result of these factors, Canada in 1985 announced its interest in negotiating a free trade agreement with the United States, and in 1989, the Canada–U.S. Free Trade Agreement (FTA) came into effect.

FIGURE 12-3 Pressures for Change to Canadian Trade Policy

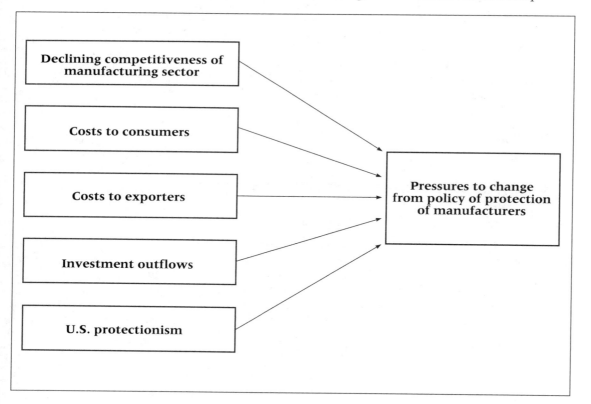

The 1989 Canada–U.S. Free Trade Agreement (FTA)

Contrary to common belief, the FTA did not represent a sudden break-through to free trade between the two nations. Tariffs between Canada and the U.S. had been gradually coming down for decades, and at the time the FTA came into effect, three-quarters of Canada–U.S. trade was already tariff-free and the average tariff was only 12 percent.

From the Canadian perspective, the main features of the agreement were as follows:

- Tariffs between the two countries were to be eliminated—about 15 per-cent of them immediately and the rest over the next 5 to10 years. The highest tariffs, which applied mainly to the more heavily protected consumer goods, were to be phased out over 10 years in 10 equal stages.

- Canada obtained more secure access to the U.S. market, mainly through better protection against the sorts of arbitrary restrictions on Canadian exports described earlier. Under the FTA, such actions by the U.S. could be appealed by Canada to a neutral board ("panel") consisting of five members drawn from a roster of international trade experts. These neu-tral experts can review and overturn decisions by the American (or Canadian) government if American (or Canadian) law has been applied incorrectly or unfairly. Because of the increasing use of such measures by the United States, many observers considered this appeal mechanism to be the key feature of the FTA from Canada's viewpoint.

- Canada relaxed its restrictions on foreign investment, and provided assurances that in the event of energy shortages, Canada would not discriminate against American users of Canadian energy with respect to either price or supply.

Both countries would continue to maintain existing restrictions on foreign ownership in the communications sector (broadcasting) and trans-portation. In Canadian cultural industries, such as publishing, proposed takeovers by foreign firms must be reviewed, regardless of the size of the company being taken over. If an American company wants to establish a publishing business, Canadians must have control of the business. But are Canadian cultural industries truly different from others, and should different rules apply? See the "You Decide" box on p. 276.

On the face of it, most of the economic gains under the FTA went to Canada. The U.S. market is roughly 10 times the size of the Canadian market, and the neutral panels would limit the U.S.'s ability to restrict Canadian exports to the U.S. market that was so vital to the Canadian economy.

However, to the United States, free trade with Canada was only the first part of a much broader strategy. The U.S. saw its world economic leadership being challenged by Europe's plan to establish a vast free trade area by 1992 and to adopt a common currency. To counter the European challenge for global economic leadership, the U.S. wanted to eventually establish an equally large free trade zone in the Western Hemisphere—a "Free Trade Area

YOU DECIDE

CANADIAN CULTURE—A SPECIAL CASE?

In the interests of preserving Canadian culture and identity, Canada has placed restrictions on foreign activity in fields such as television and radio programming and publishing. Such regulations limit the choices available to Canadian consumers, but expand the opportunities for Canadians in these fields.

Question

1. With which of the following views do you agree, and why?

    (a) Without these protections, Canadian culture will be swamped by an influx of mass-produced American competition and will eventually disappear. This loss of our heritage would be too great for Canada to risk in exchange for the supposed economic benefits of free trade.

    (b) Culture is no different from other inefficient Canadian industries that want protection against foreign competition. If Canadian culture is as worthwhile as the nationalists say, it will be able to survive in open competition: if it can't survive, it will be because most Canadians liked something else better. Why should Canadian consumers be forced to support something just because it's Canadian?

of the Americas," with the U.S. at its centre. To the U.S., free trade with Canada was the first step toward this goal; Mexico would be the second.

The North American Free Trade Agreement (NAFTA)

In 1994, Canada, the United States, and Mexico entered into the North American Free Trade Agreement (NAFTA), which in effect extended the Canada–U.S. free trade area to include Mexico. This agreement created the world's largest free trade zone, with a market of about 360 million people.

Background on Mexico

Compared to Canada, Mexico has a much larger population (about 103 million to Canada's 31 million), but this country is only about one-quarter as economically wealthy as Canada, as measured by GDP per person. Unlike Canada, however, Mexico was until quite recently relatively isolated from the broader international economy.

Like Canada, Mexico had traditionally used high tariffs to protect its infant industries from foreign competition, especially from the United States. Unlike Canada, however, Mexico did this in the context of a socialist state, with what is regarded as the world's first socialist constitution (1917).

The result was an economic system that was not only highly protected from foreign competition but also highly regulated by its government. Much of Mexican industry was either government-owned or heavily regulated; in many cases, government regulations prevented competition, leaving many key industries under the control of monopolies. With so little competition and so much regulation, productivity and living standards in the Mexican economy were very low.

Not having joined the General Agreement on Tariffs and Trade (GATT), Mexico remained quite isolated from the globalization trend of the 1980s. It staked most of its hopes for economic prosperity on oil exports, and reaped considerable benefits when oil prices were very high from 1979 to 1985. But the collapse of world oil prices in 1986 sharply reduced Mexico's oil-export revenues and left it in near-bankruptcy from its huge foreign debt, mostly loans made by international banks that had counted on high oil prices.

At this point, Mexico's government decided upon a basic change in strategic economic direction, from an inward-looking, protected, and regulated economy to one that was market-oriented and an active participant in the world economy. The Mexican government privatized and deregulated many of the nation's industries in order to improve their efficiency. In 1987, Mexico signalled its intention of participating in the world economy by taking the very large step of joining the GATT.

From 1987 to 1993, Mexico's average tariff on imports dropped from 45 percent to 9 percent, and Mexico's international trade grew rapidly, especially with the United States. Mexico signed an agreement with five Central American nations to form a regional free trade zone, and in 1991, sought a free trade agreement with the United States and Canada—the North American Free Trade Agreement (NAFTA).

Key Terms of NAFTA

Under NAFTA, tariffs were to be eliminated over periods of up to 15 years; however, virtually all of the tariffs between Canada and Mexico were to be phased out over a maximum of 10 years. On some products, tariffs were to be eliminated immediately, while tariffs on sectors that were more vulnerable to import competition (such as Canada's apparel, footwear, toys, and miscellaneous manufactured articles) would be phased out over 10 years. Both Canada and Mexico have the right to take safeguard measures that allow them to re-impose tariffs to protect producers from surges of imports, should these occur.

Most restrictions on investment were also to be phased out over a period of time, although Canada would retain the right to review foreign takeovers of larger Canadian companies as it had the right to do so under the FTA. Canada would retain its exemption for its cultural industries under the FTA, and its social and health services would be protected, also as it had the right to do so under the FTA.

Finally, the mechanism for resolving trade disputes would be essentially the same as under the FTA. Disputes could be referred to a panel of neutral trade experts that would have the power to overturn a country's decisions that were contrary to its trade laws and NAFTA. As the In the News box shows, there is reason to believe that these panels have worked to the advantage of Canada.

The Economic Impact of NAFTA on Canada

Canada's two-way trade with Mexico is very small—only 2 to 3 percent of its trade with the United States. For this reason, it was expected that the effect of NAFTA on Canada would not be large, at least in the short-to-medium term.

According to the International Trade Commission, Mexico would gain the most from NAFTA, Canada would gain slightly, and the United States would gain the least. Canada's gains would be small for a variety of reasons, the most important of which was that Canada already had a free trade agreement involving the large U.S. market, while its trade with Mexico was much smaller.

In addition, about 85 percent of Canada's imports from Mexico were already tariff-free, and the tariffs on the remaining 15 percent were on average not very high. And Mexico's low wages did not give it a general competitive advantage, since productivity in Mexico was only about one-sixth of Canadian productivity.

NAFTA would increase export opportunities for a number of Canadian industries, mostly those that could provide goods and services related to the modernization of Mexico, such as telecommunications, engineering consulting and construction, transportation, and financial institutions. In addition, under NAFTA Mexico would open up the growing Mexican market to imports of Canadian- and U.S.-built cars. On the other side of the picture, Canada could expect increased competition from Mexico in labour-intensive industries such as apparel, auto parts, textiles, and various manufactured goods, and Mexico could provide Canada with competition for American and foreign business investment.

While the prospective economic gains for Canada under NAFTA were not large, it was considered strategically important for Canada to be part of the deal. If the United States had separate free trade agreements with Canada and Mexico, only companies located in the United States would have had free access to the markets of *all three* countries, giving the United States a significant advantage in attracting business investment capital. So while being in NAFTA would not bring large economic gains for Canada, *not* being in it could have resulted in significant losses in terms of investment and jobs. According to the C.D. Howe Institute, "The overall macro-economic impact of NAFTA is not going to be big for Canada, but we would have lost a lot if we were not in it."

The Chile Free Trade Pact

In late 1996, Canada and Chile concluded a trade agreement that provided for the elimination of tariffs on 80 percent of Canadian exports to Chile. Remaining tariffs were to be phased out over the 1997–2002 period. Chile is a small country of 16 million, and Canada trades more with the United States in a single day than it does with Chile annually. However, Canadian mining companies see opportunities in Chile, and Canada is one of the largest foreign investors in Chile.

On a strategic level, signing a trade agreement with Chile was seen as one more step in extending NAFTA throughout the Western Hemisphere. However, the United States was not part of this agreement, as political opposition there had stalled that nation's progress toward a broader free trade zone in the Americas.

> "The world sometimes still sees the 1948 model rather than the 1998 model of the new Canadian economy."
>
> *Federal Trade Minister Sergio Marchi, 1998.*

Canada Enters the Global Economy: Adjusting to Change

The 1990s saw great changes in Canada's trade policy from its traditional stance of protectionism. The most dramatic change was the Canada–U.S. Free Trade Agreement, which was followed by NAFTA in 1994 and the agreement with Chile in 1996. In the meantime, the GATT/WTO Uruguay Round agreement came into effect in 1995.

The more rapid movement toward free trade would have significant economic effects on Canadians. There would be an *acceleration of change* in the Canadian economy, as some industries expanded and others contracted more rapidly than they otherwise would have. As an illustration of the extent of this change, in real terms (measured in 1997 dollars):

- Canada's GDP grew by 32 percent from 1989 to 2000,
- Canada's exports grew by 125 percent, and
- Canada's imports grew by 96 percent.

Canadian banks are
large "exporters" that
generated 49 percent
of their earnings out-
side Canada in 2001.

From 1989 to 2001, exports increased from 25 percent of GDP to 43 percent, and imports from nearly 26 percent of GDP to 38 percent. As these
changes happened, some industries had to cope with unprecedented foreign
competition, while others enjoyed unprecedented export success.

Such changes involved a substantial adjustment process for both workers and industries, as product lines, production methods, and skill requirements were affected. Some export industries would thrive and grow, while
other industries impacted by imports would rationalize, downsize, or disappear. Production technologies would change, and workers would have to
move to new industries, jobs, or locations.

The most basic adjustment provision in the trade agreements was the fact
that tariffs were to be eliminated gradually, generally over a period of five to
fifteen years. This was intended to give companies and workers adequate time
to adapt to free trade, which presented dangers for some and opportunities for
others. In addition, various retraining programs were available in Canada, and
a retraining element was added to the Employment Insurance program.

Strategies for Success I—World Product Mandating

One of the concerns about free trade was the fate of Canada's foreign-owned
branch plants. As we have seen, the small size of the Canadian market meant
that these branch plants were often much less efficient than the plants of
their parent in the United States. The original reason for American parent
firms establishing and operating branch plants in Canada was to avoid paying Canadian tariffs. This fact raised concerns that free trade would mean the
closing of many Canadian branch plants and the shifting of production back
to the United States. These dire consequences would be much less likely if the
Canadian plants were *specialized* in the production of one or a few products
so that they could be fully efficient; however, the small size of the Canadian
market had precluded that for most companies.

world product mandating
An arrangement whereby
a branch plant acquires a
mandate from its foreign
parent company to
design, manufacture, and
market a particular prod-
uct or products for the
world market.

An interesting approach to making branch plants more specialized and
efficient is **world product mandating**. Under such an arrangement, a
Canadian branch plant acquires a mandate to design, manufacture, and
market a particular product for the world market, on behalf of the parent
company. That is, branch plants would no longer produce, on an inefficiently small scale, the full range of their parents' product lines. Instead, they
would concentrate on one or a few selected products for a wider market.
With greater specialization and longer production runs, Canadian manufacturers could become more efficient and internationally competitive.

The automobile industry provides the best example of a successful world
product mandating strategy, as described earlier in this chapter. But world product mandating has also been successful for a number of companies that have utilized it, including Westinghouse Canada, Du Pont, Kodak, Procter and Gamble,
Garrett Manufacturing, Litton Systems Canada, Gandalf Technologies, GTE
Sylvania, Heron Cable, Hughes Aircraft, Polymer International and others.

World product mandating provides a way to channel the economic
resources of foreign multinational corporations into the development of a

more specialized manufacturing sector that is better able to compete in both Canadian and export markets.

Strategies for Success II—Niche Marketing

Another concern regarding free trade was that smaller Canadian manufacturers could not succeed in head-to-head competition with large U.S. mass-production manufacturers. Under a strategy of **niche marketing**, this would not be necessary. Instead, Canadian producers could target smaller volumes of production into relatively small segments, or niches, of the market. The "market" for many consumer products is not really a single market, but rather consists of several segments, with a large segment for medium-quality mass-produced products at the centre of the market, and various relatively small segments (niches), such as "high-end" products targeted at specific buyer groups. In a small market such as Canada's, such niches are often very small indeed, but in a vast market such as the United States, they can be large enough to offer significant opportunities to niche producers. In addition, the above-average prices in such niche markets can offset the higher production costs of Canadian producers.

niche marketing
Marketing to small segments of a market.

Because the American market is approximately 10 times the size of the Canadian market, a 1-percent share of the American market involves as many sales as a 10-percent share of the Canadian market. For example, in the apparel industry, Canadian firms have done very well by producing high-quality men's suits and high-fashion women's wear for the American market, where they enjoy healthy demand and high prices. Another example is provided by Sleeman Brewing of Guelph, Ontario, a niche brewer of premium-quality beer. After signing an agreement with Stroh Brewing of the United States under which Stroh would distribute Sleeman's beer in Michigan, John Sleeman was quoted as saying, "All we have to do is get 1 percent of the Michigan market and we've got to build a couple more breweries."

Over half of Canada's exports are produced by just 50 companies.

Canada's Trade Since the Agreements

Canada's export performance since the free trade agreements has been more impressive than many had expected. In 2001, exports were 43 percent of Canada's GDP, as compared to 26 percent in 1988, the last year before the FTA. Exports to the United States grew especially rapidly, as reflected in Figure 12-4, nearing 85 percent of total Canadian exports in 2001.

Certainly, Canada's economy became more closely *tied to the United States'*, as two-way trade between the two nations reached $1.7 billion per day and U.S.-bound Canadian exports grew to over 35 percent of all the output of the Canadian economy (45 percent of Ontario's). An interesting measure of the links between the two economies is that in 2001 it was estimated that 60 percent of the bilateral trade between the two countries was intracompany trade conducted between parent companies and their subsidiaries.

On the other hand, the *productivity performance* of Canadian industry continued to be disappointing. Canadian firms did improve their productivity, but less rapidly than their counterparts in other countries, so Canadian firms

FIGURE 12-4 Canada's Merchandise Trade Balance with the
United States and the Rest of the World, 1982–2001

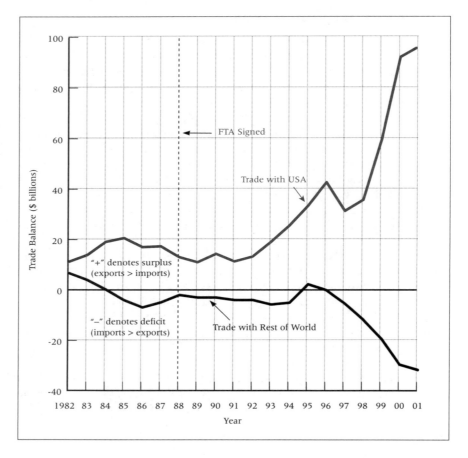

Source: Bank of Canada, adapted from the *Bank of Canada Review* and *Banking and Financial Statistics*.

still lagged in this important area. The main reason for Canada's export success lay in the low international price of the Canadian dollar, a matter we will consider later in this chapter.

Part B: The Canadian Dollar in the Global Economy

One of the most notable aspects of the Canadian economy in recent years has been the decline in the exchange rate of the Canadian dollar. From 1991 to

2002, the international value of the Canadian dollar decreased by 26 percent, from 87.3 U.S. cents to 63.7 U.S. cents, as Figure 12-5 shows.

FIGURE 12-5 The International Value of the Canadian Dollar, 1975–2002

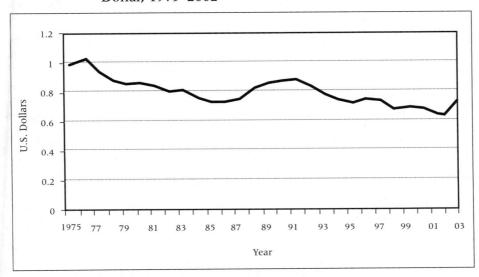

Source: Bank of Canada, adapted from the *Bank of Canada Review* and *Banking and Financial Statistics*.

However, Figure 12-5 also shows that the decline of the Canadian dollar has actually been a longer-term event that started in the mid-1970s. And with the exception of a period in the late 1980s, the decline has been fairly steady. What *caused* such a large decrease in the international value of Canada's currency?

Causes of the Decline in the Canadian Dollar

Most studies of the decline of the Canadian dollar point to three major factors: productivity, commodity prices, and capital flows.

Canada's productivity performance is viewed by many as the most basic reason for the dollar's decline. Generally, the currencies of high-productivity nations such as Japan have a high price because of high demand for their goods. For low-productivity nations, the opposite is the case—lower demand for their goods means lower values for their currencies. So as Canada fell farther behind other nations in productivity, the Canadian dollar gradually lost value relative to other currencies over the past 25 years.

Weak commodity prices on world markets are often cited as a factor in the weakness of the Canadian dollar. To a much greater extent than other industrialized countries', Canada's exports consist of commodities or raw materials such as agricultural products, forest products, and minerals. For some time, the prices of most of these commodities on world markets have risen only

"… with the globalization of financial markets, which have exploded in the last 10 to 15 years, it's financial flows which drive the currency."

James Frank, Chief Economist, the Conference Board of Canada.

slowly or even fallen, due to a high supply of them. So lower prices for commodities over the past two decades have meant lower resource export earnings for Canada—and less demand for Canadian dollars.

Capital flows were a more recent cause of the Canadian dollar's decline relative to the value of the U.S. dollar. We saw in Chapter 11 how the U.S. dollar was pushed to high levels by heavy inflows of foreign capital into the U.S. stock market in the second half of the 1990s. Over this period, Canadians bought large volumes of shares on U.S. stock markets—almost $95 billion from 1998 to 2000 alone. This large outflow of capital from Canada put downward pressure on the Canadian dollar while adding to the upward pressure on the U.S. currency.

So the decrease in the value of the Canadian dollar relative to the value of the U.S. dollar after the mid-1990s was in large part due to the remarkable surge in the value of the U.S. dollar that was described in Chapter 11. This relationship can been seen in Figure 12-6, which shows that while the Canadian dollar fell by about 13 percent in terms of the U.S. dollar from 1995 to 2002, the Canadian dollar actually *increased* in value relative to the values of most other currencies. In other words, the driving force in the decrease of the Canadian dollar was that the U.S. dollar increased sharply in value against the values of most currencies over this period, with its increase against the Canadian dollar being relatively small.

FIGURE 12-6 Change in Value of Canadian Dollar Against Various Currencies, 1995–2001

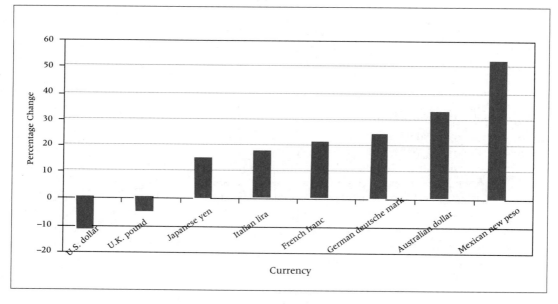

Source: Bank of Canada, adapted from the *Bank of Canada Review* and *Banking and Financial Statistics*.

In summary, the Canadian dollar's 25-year decline relative to the U.S. dollar was the result of various factors, including lagging productivity, low commodity prices, and capital outflows. Other factors were believed to have played a part in the dollar's decline. Some observers argue that Canada's high taxes have contributed to the weakness of the Canadian dollar by discouraging inflows of investment capital into the Canadian economy. Also, in the 1990s many Canadian corporations listed their shares on the New York Stock Exchange, so foreigners who wished to invest in Canadian companies could often do so, and still do so, in U.S. dollars—and *without* buying Canadian dollars.

Another factor behind the weakness of the Canadian dollar in the 1990s was the outflow of interest payments on Canada's very heavy debt to foreign lenders. During the late 1980s and early 1990s, Canada's foreign debt had increased sharply, due to the massive government budget deficits, as described in Chapter 8. The federal government's borrowing was absorbing so much of Canadians' savings that provincial governments and corporations had to do much of their borrowing outside Canada. By the early 1990s, Canada's debt to foreign lenders was by far the heaviest of all major nations, and by 1995, the outflow of interest payments on this debt was about $30 billion per year, twice as high as in 1987. Then, when the federal government eliminated its budget deficits in the late 1990s, the inflow of borrowed foreign funds stopped, which also contributed to the dollar's decline. (Somewhat ironically, the only sustained *increase* in the Canadian dollar since 1975 had also been the result of government actions. In the late 1980s and early 1990s, there was a large inflow of capital into Canada due to heavy government borrowing and high interest rates associated with the Bank of Canada's anti-inflation policies.)

So from 1974 to 2002, the international value of the Canadian dollar went from US$1.02 to US$0.64, a decline of almost 37 percent. What did this mean for Canadians?

Effects of the Low Dollar on Canadians

The low international value of their dollar had two major consequences for Canadians. The bad news was that it depressed Canadians' living standards, by increasing the cost of imports. The good news was that, because the Canadian dollar was so inexpensive to foreigners, Canadian exports increased as never before.

From 1990 to 2002, exports grew by 111 percent in real terms, more than three times the 34-percent growth in the economy as a whole (GDP). Over the same period, exports increased from 27 percent of GDP to 43 percent. In addition, as we have seen, a growing proportion of Canada's exports consisted of manufactured goods.

It was the growth in exports that led Canada out of the recession of the early 1990s and into a long economic boom. During this boom, the unemployment rate reached its lowest point in 26 years—6.7 percent in mid-2000.

However, there was a "trade-off" for these gains in jobs—the lower Canadian dollar meant higher prices for imports, which depressed the standard of living of Canadian consumers.[1] In a sense, it was as if Canadians had taken a pay cut in order to save jobs, as the employees of a financially troubled company will sometimes do.

The 2002–03 *Global Competitiveness Report* of the World Economic Forum ranked Canada eighth in the world in terms of international competitiveness and growth potential. This was Canada's lowest ranking since 1996, mainly due to a decline in Canada's ranking regarding technology.

www.weforum.org/
publications/gcr

Nonetheless, all seemed well with the export sector of the Canadian economy, and with Canada's international competitiveness. But beneath the surface, there was reason for concern. The main reason for Canada's export success was not that Canadian industry was highly productive and competitive, but rather *the low international value of the Canadian dollar*. In effect, the low dollar was "papering over" the weak productivity performance of much of its manufacturing sector.

There had been some concern that foreign takeovers of Canadian businesses would increase because the low Canadian dollar would make Canadian firms bargain-basement takeover targets. However, according to a 2002 study by the C.D. Howe Institute, this did not happen. Canadian firms took over 1,963 foreign companies from 1995 to 2001, while foreigners took over 1,761 Canadian companies. And in terms of dollar value, the takeovers by Canadians would have exceeded foreign takeovers of Canadian firms if not for one huge takeover involving Seagram Ltd.

To Dollarize or Not To Dollarize?

"The fact is, globalization spells the demise of peripheral currencies like the Canadian dollar."

Sherry Cooper, Global Economic Strategist and Executive Vice-President, Bank of Montreal Group of Companies.

As the Canadian dollar drifted lower against the U.S. dollar in the second half of the 1990s, it was proposed that Canada should adopt the U.S. dollar as its currency—a plan known as "dollarization." The idea appealed to many Canadians who had grown weary of seeing the purchasing power of their currency decrease in the United States marketplace; however, there were other economic arguments for dollarization.

The simplest point was that having the same currency as the United States would eliminate the transaction costs of converting one currency to another whenever international transactions occurred. Another argument was that the instability of the Canadian dollar discouraged business investment in Canada, by adding the risk that an investment could be made unprofitable by an unanticipated change in the value of the Canadian dollar.

A more sophisticated—and controversial—theory was that a falling Canadian dollar protects inefficient Canadian producers, much as tariffs used to do. According to this argument, the decline in the Canadian dollar was adding to the price of imports, and by doing so, was *causing inefficiency*, by protecting Canadian producers and thus reducing their incentive to become

---

1. And for Canadian businesses that imported capital equipment, the lower dollar meant higher costs.

more efficient. The conclusion was that having a separate currency was undermining the standard of living of Canadians—that if the Canadian dollar had not decreased in value, Canada would have developed a more efficient and prosperous economy.

Others disagreed, arguing that the cause of Canada's low productivity was not the falling value of the Canadian dollar, but rather other factors. To them, the decline in the dollar had *helped* Canadian industry to cope with the fact that Canadian productivity was not growing as fast as American productivity. The C.D. Howe Institute concluded that if the Canadian dollar had not decreased in value, the economy's performance would have been worse, not better.

The Bank of Canada defended Canada's having its own currency on the grounds that the Canadian and American economies have significantly different structures. In particular, Canada is a large exporter of resource commodities, while the United States is an importer of these. So swings in world commodity prices would tend to have opposite effects on the Canadian and American currencies—for instance, falling world resource prices would push downward on the Canadian dollar and probably upward on the U.S. dollar.

The Bank of Canada also argued that a floating Canadian dollar acts as a "shock absorber" for the Canadian economy when world resource prices tumble, as they did during the Asian crisis of 1997–98. Under these conditions, as Canada's export earnings fall, the price of the Canadian dollar decreases. The lower Canadian dollar then helps to support exports, and so cushions the negative effect of lower resource export prices on the economy. This "shock absorber" effect of a floating exchange rate is especially important in an economy such as Canada's, in which exports are over 40 percent of GDP and resource exports are large. For the United States, exports are only about 10 percent of GDP, and resource exports are very small.

Another argument for Canada's having its own currency is that Canada can control its own monetary policy—an important consideration in view of Canada's much greater exposure, compared to that of the U.S., to international economic fluctuations. By contrast, if Canada's currency were the U.S. dollar, Canada would have virtually no voice in monetary policy—on the basis of population, Canada would have only about 10-percent representation in the monetary policy decision-making process.

On the other hand, in the discussions concerning "dollarization" the Bank of Canada did not rule out a change in the future. The Governor of the Bank of Canada was quoted as saying "… it may well be that in a decade or two decades or three decades, the structure of our (the Canadian and U.S.) economies will look much more similar, and in that case the advantages of a floating currency from a strictly economic point of view go down and the costs remain—and there are costs of having a separate currency."

Finally, it should be noted that Canada is already partly "dollarized." Many Canadian multinational corporations use the U.S. dollar as the unit of account, which is a common practice around the world. And roughly 10 percent of Canadians' total bank deposits are in foreign currency (mostly U.S. dollars), which also reflects the international nature of the Canadian economy.

In 2002, Canadian National—a railway symbol of Canadian nationhood—earned more revenue from its operations in the United States than it did in Canada.

www.cn.ca

A Final Trade Question: Will We Ever Have Free Trade *Within* Canada?

As the world moved toward globalization, Canada was still far from having free trade among its own provinces. The movement of goods, workers, and investment capital between provinces was restricted by a complex web of hundreds of provincial government regulations designed to protect each province's producers and workers against out-of-province competition. The most common such restrictions required governments and their agencies to buy only from suppliers located in that province, often at higher costs to the taxpayer. Other examples of restrictions are Quebec's refusal to allow the sale of coloured margarine and Prince Edward Island's prevention of the sale of milk from Nova Scotia. Other restrictions included standards and rules that excluded out-of-province products or workers.

According to various studies, these restrictions cost Canadians as much as $6.5 billion annually. A more subtle cost of these restrictions was that they subdivided the already small Canadian market into even smaller regional segments, making Canadian producers even more inefficient and less competitive internationally. In the words of a GATT report in 1994, "Inter-provincial trade barriers have become a major problem for Canada, hampering economic growth and job creation, as well as reducing competitiveness of Canadian-based firms."

In 1995, the Agreement on Internal Trade (AIT) between the federal, provincial, and territorial governments came into effect. The goal of the AIT is to reduce interprovincial trade barriers; however, as of 2002, the AIT had not been very successful. The main obstacle to the development of free trade within Canada was simply that many of the provinces were not interested in giving up their protectionist measures. While the AIT provided for neutral panels to settle disputes, their rulings were not binding, so provinces just ignored them. Also, under the AIT just one province could veto a measure, which prevented the introduction of valuable changes. This left Canada in the bizarre position of being a major trading nation that has freer trade *with other nations* than *between its own provinces*.

Chapter Summary

1. Under Canada's National Policy (1879), infant industry tariffs led to the development of a larger manufacturing sector, but also higher prices for Canadian consumers, considerable foreign ownership, and inefficiency in the manufacturing sector. (L.O. 1)

2. Because they operated under tariff protection and on a small scale, Canada's manufacturers fell further behind their foreign competitors in productivity when globalization increased international trade, competition, and productivity in the 1980s. (L.O. 2)

3. Pressures for change in Canadian trade policy arose from the decreasing international competitiveness of much of Canadian manufacturing, the growing costs to Canadian consumers and exporters of protecting uncompetitive manufacturing, outflows of business investment capital, and rising protectionism in the United States. (L.O. 3)

4. In 1989, the Canada–U.S. Free Trade Agreement eliminated tariffs between Canada and the United States over a period of time and established a dispute-settlement process that would provide Canada with more secure access to the U.S. market. (L.O. 4)

5. In 1994, the North American Free Trade Agreement (NAFTA) extended the Canada–U.S. free trade area to Mexico. This was strategically important to the U.S.'s plan for a much wider free trade area to counter the European Union; however, its short-run economic effect on Canada was expected to be quite small. (L.O. 5)

6. Two business strategies for succeeding in highly competitive international markets are world product mandating and niche marketing. (L.O. 6)

7. The international value of the Canadian dollar decreased by nearly 40 percent from 1974 to 2002, mainly due to a combination of low productivity, low commodity prices, and outflows of capital. (L.O. 7)

8. The low dollar depressed Canadians' living standards, but helped to strongly increase exports and to generate low unemployment. (L.O. 8)

9. The dollar's decline led to proposals that Canada should adopt the U.S. dollar as its currency. The Bank of Canada disagreed on the grounds that the different structures of the Canadian and U.S. economies at the current time made it appropriate that Canada continue to have its own currency. (L.O. 9)

Questions

1. The text notes that in its 2002–03 *Global Competitiveness Report*, the World Economic Forum ranked Canada eighth in the world in competitiveness.
   (a) How does the most recent *Global Competitiveness Report* rank Canada, and what strengths and weaknesses does it note? The report comes out each spring and is covered in the media; the address of the World Economic Forum's website is www.weforum.org.

   (b) What government policies would you suggest in order to remedy Canada's weaknesses and take advantage of its strengths as identified in the *Global Competitiveness Report*?

2. Over the past few years, what have been the trends regarding
   (a) Canada's exports to the United States?
   (b) Canada's exports to the rest of the world?

   What seem to be the reasons for these trends?

Current statistics on Canada's trade with the U.S. and the rest of the world can be found on Statistics Canada's website. Go to "Canadian Statistics," then "International Trade,": or access www.statcan.ca/english/Pgdb/gblec02a.htm. You can also find these statistics in Statistics Canada's *Canadian Economic Observer* (11-010-XPB), in the Merchandise Trade, Balance of Payments section.

3. The following table shows the flows of direct business investment into and out of Canada from 1998 to 2002:

Year	Canadian Direct Investment Abroad	Foreign Direct Investment in Canada	Net Flow of Direct Investment
1997	−31 937	+15 958	−15 979
1998	−50 957	+33 828	−17 129
1999	−23 182	+36 306	+13 124
2000	−70 545	+98 940	+28 395
2001	−54 924	+42 527	−12 397
2002	−43 862	+33 604	−10 258

"+" indicates flows of funds into Canada
"−" indicates flows of funds out of Canada

Update these statistics, using data from Statistics Canada's website. Go to *Canadian Statistics*, then *Economic Conditions*, then *National Accounts*, then *Canada's Balance of International Payments*, or access www.statcan.ca/english/Pgdb/econ01b.htm.

Do the statistics since 2002 show any trend in flows of direct investment into and out of Canada? If so, what might explain these trends?

4. Suppose, due to concerns about inflation in its own economy, the U.S. government increased American interest rates.
   (a) How would this probably affect the international value of the Canadian dollar?
   (b) What two basic choices would the Bank of Canada have in these circumstances?
   (c) What would be the consequences for the Canadian economy of each of these choices?
   (d) What would probably decide which choice the Bank of Canada would make?

5. Suppose a Canadian family spends $3000 per month, 20 percent of which is spent on imports. Suppose also that the Canadian dollar were to fall over a period of time from US$0.78 to US$0.65.
   (a) Estimate the cost of the lower Canadian dollar to this family, both in dollars per month and as a percentage of its total consumption.
   (b) What economic benefits for Canada could be claimed as an offset to this reduction in living standards?
   (c) What could this family do to reduce the effect of the lower Canadian dollar on its standard of living?

6. The decrease in the international value of the Canadian dollar during the 1990s led to proposals that the Bank of Canada "fix" or "peg" the value of the Canadian dollar relative to the that of the United States dollar. Suppose that the Bank of Canada had been committed to keeping the Canadian dollar at 75 U.S. cents after 1993.

   (a) How could the Bank of Canada have fixed the Canadian exchange rate in this way?

   (b) What would have been the effects of such a policy upon Canadians and the Canadian economy?

7. Suppose that Canada and the United States were considering adopting a common currency. What would be some of the key questions that would have to be worked out, and what obstacles would there be to such a measure?

8. The 2002–03 *Global Competitiveness Report* of the World Economic Forum that ranked Canada eighth in the world in competitiveness ranked the United States first.

   (a) What do you think were the qualities of the United States that earned it the top ranking?

   (b) Does the difference between the rankings of Canada and the United States make it more or less likely that the two countries will adopt a common currency in the next few years?

9. Have there been any recent developments in the debate over "dollarization," or Canada's adoption of the U.S. dollar as its currency? (A search of the internet will provide a good indication.)

10. From October 2002 to May 2003, the international value of the Canadian dollar increased rapidly, from $0.63 U.S. to $0.73 U.S.

    (a) Why were Canadians initially pleased by this development?

    (b) Why did Canadians begin to express concern as their dollar passed $0.70 U.S.?

    (c) Did the Canadian dollar continue to rise?

Chapter 13

Into the Future

Learning Objectives

After studying this chapter, you should be able to:

1. Define the term *resource wealth mentality* and explain how this mentality could apply to Canada and to its government policies in the past.

2. State four characteristics that help to make a nation's economy attractive to investment in high-technology industries in the globalized world economy.

3. Explain three ways in which Canada was not well-prepared for the globalization trend of the 1980s.

4. Describe four basic changes in Canadian government economic policy since the late 1980s, and explain the purpose of each of these changes.

5. Explain four ways in which the 1990s were a period of difficult transition for Canadians.

6. Explain four ways in which Canada emerged from the 1990s in a stronger economic condition.

7. Explain why Canada's productivity performance was a continuing matter of concern.

During much of the 1990s, Canada had to deal with several major economic challenges and changes. The main driving force behind these changes was the phenomenon known as *globalization,* which was creating a more competitive environment for the international trade and investment that is so important to Canada's economic prosperity. The most visible effect of these international forces was to push many Canadian industries to become more efficient and competitive. For many Canadian industries, this was a difficult process.

In addition, the 1990s saw the following two major changes in government macroeconomic policy:

* the "downshift" from an environment of high inflation rates to one of low inflation rates, and
* the end of a 20-year period of government spending programs financed by borrowing that led to escalating government debt.

Together, these changes forced upon Canadians some difficult adjustments, all of which converged in the 1990s.

In the longer run, these changes were expected to bring significant economic benefits to Canadians in the form of lower inflation rates, sound government finances, increased productivity, and improved international competitiveness. But for much of the 1990s, the transition to these new conditions was a difficult one. To understand why this transition was so challenging, we need to review the nature of the Canadian economy and the orientation of the government policy that existed prior to these changes.

The Way We Were

Professor Michael Porter describes a Canada that had traditionally relied upon exports of natural resources and resource products as its basic source of economic prosperity. These exports, together with substantial inflows of foreign (mainly American) business capital investment, provided Canadians with the foreign currency with which they purchased the imported goods and services that supported their high living standards. By making Canadians among the most prosperous people in the world, these advantages also made it possible for them to "support" a relatively inefficient tariff-protected manufacturing sector, by paying high prices for its products.

With economic wealth so readily provided by resource exports and foreign investment, government policy tended to be relatively unconcerned with *creating wealth*. Rather, government policies focused on promoting a *fair distribution of wealth* by providing assistance to individuals, businesses, and regions that needed it. Over the years, governments established a wide variety of social welfare programs for individuals and families (from education and health care to

> "Traditionally, Canadians have lived in a relatively insulated environment brought about by paternalistic government policies, a history of market protection, and the accumulated attitudes and experiences of both individuals and businesses.
>
> This old economic order, as we call it, was a system where many prospered. However, because the old order generally provided insulation from external pressures and fostered limited internal pressures, many of the critical requirements for upgrading to more sophisticated and sustainable competitive advantages in Canadian industry have been missing or are only weakly present."
>
> Professor Michael E. Porter, *Canada at the Crossroads: The Reality of a New Competitive Environment* (October 1991; a study prepared for the Business Council on National Issues and the Government of Canada).

income support systems such as unemployment insurance, welfare, and pensions), an extensive support system for weaker and less efficient producers (including tariff protection for manufacturers, subsidies for farmers, and assistance of various sorts to corporations in difficulty), and various forms of assistance to economically weaker regions (including equalization payments, regional development grants, and subsidies to people and businesses in those regions).

resource wealth mentality The view that society's economic wealth is derived mainly from the sale of natural resources, as opposed to efficiency in the production of goods and services.

According to some critical observers, Canada had developed a **"resource wealth mentality"**—the view that economic wealth is not something that you *create* so much as something that *happens to you* through possessing and selling resources. With wealth seemingly so easily available that it could be taken for granted, the main role of government became to ensure that the nation's wealth was distributed fairly among all of its people. As a result, government policy became more concerned with the *distribution* of economic welfare than with incentives for the efficiency that *creates* wealth. So while Canadians were generally quite *prosperous* economically, they were not (with the exception of their natural resource sector and certain other industries) particularly efficient or competitive internationally.

Pressures for Change: Globalization and Competition

During the 1980s, a variety of factors combined to generate such a major increase in international trade, competition, and investment that this phenomenon came to be known as the *globalization* of markets. Some of the factors that contributed to this change were lower tariff barriers and improved computer, communications, and transportation technology that facilitated trade and investment on a global scale. Also, there were increasing numbers of "players" in the marketplace as less developed countries entered into world markets. With globalization came increased international competition, which increased productivity and pushed costs and prices downward.

These changes were especially significant to Canada, which relies very heavily upon trade and exports for its economic prosperity. To some Canadian industries, the opening of world markets meant opportunities to export, while to others, it meant foreign competition that presented serious threats.

Canada was slow to respond to the situation as globalization spread during the 1980s. As we saw in Chapter 12, after decades of operating in the small Canadian market behind tariff protection, much of Canada's manufacturing sector was not very efficient and was ill-prepared for stronger international competition. And, despite the importance of trade to its economy, Canada was slow to adapt to this new, more competitive international environment. Rather than look outward to the opportunities presented by the global economy, Canada sought to maintain the "old order" described by Professor Porter, by continuing to protect its less efficient producers against competition with tariffs and government subsidies. So during the 1980s, the efficiency of Canadian industry failed to keep pace with improvements in other nations, and Canada became less internationally competitive, especially in manufacturing.

And as the 1980s unfolded, the costs of Canada's policy of protecting its producers against foreign competition became higher and higher. These included costs to consumers (in the form of higher prices), costs to Canadian exporters (as foreign nations retaliated against Canadian protectionism with barriers against Canadian exports), and lost business investment (as a grow-ing number of successful Canadian businesses expanded into other countries in order to gain access to larger markets). In short, Canada was slow to adapt to the new realities of globalization by becoming more efficient and compet-itive, and the costs of this failure were mounting as the decade went on.

The Challenge of Globalization

In this new, globalized world economy, multinational corporations search the world for the most economical locations for their investment capital and operations. If a country can attract business investment and the jobs and pro-duction that it brings, that country will prosper economically. If it fails to attract investment, it will lag behind economically.

What makes a country an attractive location for business investment? Many people think that the answer is "cheap labour," but the matter is not nearly as simple as that. Cheap labour is only important for labour-intensive manufacturing industries such as clothing and footwear; however, in most industries, such low-wage, semi-skilled labour has been replaced to a great extent by technology. To modern, high-technology industries, the key attrac-tion is not *cheap* labour, but rather *skilled people* with *specialized knowledge*. In addition, a nation needs to have excellent *transportation and communication links* to the rest of the world in order to function effectively as part of the new world economy. According to this view, a nation's key strategic assets eco-nomically are now its *education and training systems and its transportation and communications infrastructure*—the knowledge and skills of its people and the support systems for bringing the productive use of those skills into play in the global economy.

If a country has a skilled labour force and a sound infrastructure, it will tend to gain business investment and prosper economically. Its skilled work-force will earn high incomes, and its economy will provide its government with a strong tax base, which can be used to invest further in better schools, research, and transportation and communications systems. These features will attract more investment, and the cycle of prosperity can be continued.

In addition, it is advantageous for a country to provide a *stable macroeco-nomic environment* of solid government finances, low inflation, and low inter-est rates. Such an environment is more likely to develop a strong saving–investment process and the business confidence (of both domestic and foreign investors) that will generate investment, rising productivity,

> "We are using Russian engineers living in Israel to design (computer micro) chips that are made in America and then assembled in Asia."
>
> Peter J. Sprague,
> Chairman,
> National Semiconductor
> Corporation.

competitiveness, and prosperity. By contrast, economies with problems of large government deficits and debt, high inflation, and high interest rates are not as attractive a location for business investment, and tend to fall behind in both productivity and competitiveness. So the globalization of the world economy puts pressure upon governments to pursue moderate and stable macroeconomic policies.

Canada in the 1980s

> "The outstanding question at the beginning of 1985 is whether Canada will ride the wave of change or be swamped by it."
>
> Edward Carmichael, C.D. Howe Institute.

During the 1980s, Canada's economic environment and policies were not well-suited to the challenges of globalization. Canadian manufacturers were still protected against import competition by relatively high tariffs, and were falling further behind their foreign counterparts. Canada's rate of inflation was higher than most of its trading partners', and by the late 1980s it was increasing again. And Canada's federal and provincial governments had very large budget deficits and high and rising debt. These problems made Canada less likely as a base for successful businesses in the globalized world economy, and a less attractive destination for investment by multinational corporations.

The Shift in Policy

> "For the first 100 years after Confederation, Canada lived off its resources. For the past 16 years, we have lived off our credit. Now we must live off our skills, our wits, our energy and our initiative."
>
> Michael Wilson, Minister of Finance, 1984.

By the late 1980s, the changing international economic situation was forcing Canada to make some fundamental changes to its economic policies. The first—and most symbolic—such change was to Canada's *trade policy*, with the conclusion in 1989 of the *Canada–U.S. Free Trade Agreement*. This change was a landmark in that it signalled Canada's intention to participate more fully in the increasingly globalized markets of the world. As such, it also signalled a basic shift in Canadian policy toward an emphasis on productivity, competitiveness, and an outward-looking internationalism, rather than on the more inward-looking nationalistic policies that had for many years sheltered Canadian industries and workers from international competition. The Free Trade Agreement was regarded as just the first step in Canada becoming more productive and competitive on a global scale. The expansion of the agreement to include Mexico in the North American Free Trade Agreement continued this process, as did the 1995 World Trade Organization agreement. In all of these agreements, Canada gained wider and more secure access to large foreign markets, but had to reduce its own protection of Canadian producers. Figure 13-1 shows the decrease in tariffs levied on imports into Canada from 1988 to 2001.

FIGURE 13-1 Import Duties as a Percentage of Imports

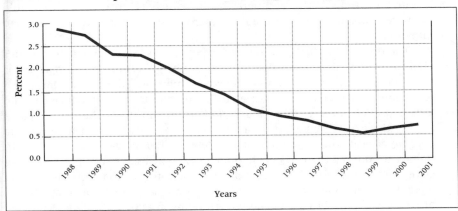

Source: Statistics Canada, adapted from *National Income and Expenditure Accounts*, Catalogue 13-001, 2002; Department of Finance, *Fiscal Reference Tables*, October 2002, and reproduced with the permission of the Minister of Public Works and Government Services Canada, 2003.

To improve Canada's international competitiveness and to make Canada more attractive to investors, much more emphasis was placed on *keeping inflation in check* than had been the case in the past. During the late 1980s and early 1990s, the Bank of Canada determinedly pursued an anti-inflation policy of high interest rates, the effects of which can be seen in the decrease in the rate of inflation in Figure 13-2.

FIGURE 13-2 Rate of Inflation, 1960–2002

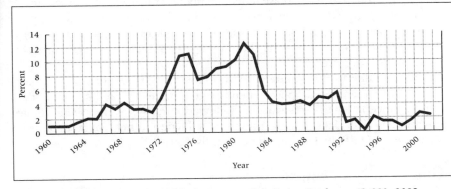

Source: Statistics Canada, adapted from *Consumer Price Index*, Catalogue 62-001, 2002.

And after this "tight money" policy had pushed the rate of inflation down to about 2 percent, the federal government and the Bank of Canada announced in 1993 their intention to *keep* the rate of inflation below 3 percent per year. This was a signal that Canada was committed to maintaining a low-inflation environment, in which more stability and *lower interest rates*

"What we've learned is that you have to keep your inflation rate low. That's the only way you're going to keep your interest rates low."

Gordon Thiessen, Governor of the Bank of Canada, November 1996.

"Maintaining these (inflation) targets will allow markets and investors to plan with confidence, knowing that Canada will remain a low-inflation environment."

Finance Minister Paul Martin, May 2001.

could be expected in the future. Such an environment would be more favourable to business investment and productivity growth, which would improve Canada's international competitiveness and attractiveness to investors.

The third basic change in economic policy was the federal government's plan to *eliminate its budget deficits*. Setting out its plans in a similar manner as it had done concerning inflation, the government stated its targets for deficit reduction over several years, so as to build confidence that Canada would indeed provide a more stable financial environment than it had in the past.

By the early 1990s, the situation concerning government finances had become critical. The combined budget deficits of all levels of government in Canada amounted to over $50 billion per year. The total net debt of Canadian governments was over 90 percent of GDP, and interest payments on the debt were driving it higher, in an upward spiral. Canada's foreign debt, about half of which was owed by Canadian governments, was by far the largest in the world and rising rapidly. And foreign lenders were beginning to demand higher interest rates because of the risks associated with the financial condition of Canadian governments.

The federal government's budget of 1995 announced large reductions in federal spending over a period of several years. Most of the cuts were to *federal transfer payments to the provinces* for health care, post-secondary education, and welfare. This reduction in provincial revenues led to a series of major spending cuts by the provincial governments on their own programs. Hospital services were reduced, grants to colleges and universities were cut (which led to substantial increases in tuition costs for many students), and welfare benefits were reduced, in some cases by more than 20 percent.

At the same time as federal spending was being cut, federal tax revenues increased strongly. This increase in federal tax revenues was mainly the result of economic growth, which generated rising tax revenues from taxes on incomes, profits, and sales. The result of this combination of spending cuts and rising tax revenues was the sharp reduction in federal budget deficits, as can be seen in Figure 13-3.

Largely due to this strong growth of government revenues, the federal deficit was eliminated in 1997, when the government posted its first budget surplus since 1970. In each year that followed, surpluses were used to reduce government debt. Figure 13-4 shows this reduction in net federal debt, from 71 percent of GDP in 1995 to 49 percent by 2001–02.

Other Policy Changes

Since the mid-1980s, governments had been introducing a variety of economic policy changes that had the common objective of *increasing the productivity and competitiveness* of the Canadian economy. Many of these were microeconomic in nature, in that they affected specific sectors of the economy; however, taken together, their impact was on more of a macroeconomic scale. Following are a few examples of the change in direction of government economic policy since the mid-1980s.

"For years, govern-ments have been promising more than they can deliver, and delivering more than they can afford. That has to end. We are ending it."

Finance Minister Paul Martin, 1994.

"Canadians must recapture the pioneering spirit that built our nation and apply it to the challenges that confront us: not merely to survive the new global economy, but to thrive in it; not to turn from competi-tion but to engage it; not to fear the future but to invent it."

Steering Group on Prosperity, *Inventing our Future: An Action Plan for Canada's Prosperity* (1992).

FIGURE 13-3 Federal Government Budgets, 1970–2002

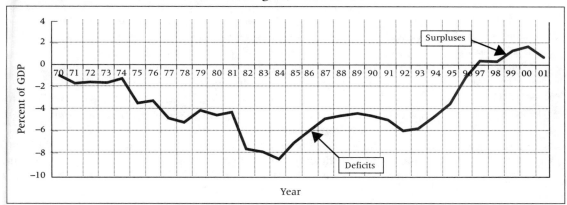

Source: Department of Finance, *Fiscal Reference Tables*, October 2002. Reproduced with the permission of the Minister of Public Works and Government Services Canada, 2003.

FIGURE 13-4 Net Federal Government Debt as a Percentage of GDP, 1970–2002

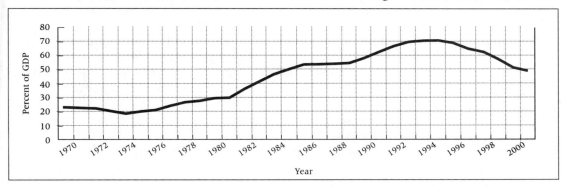

Source: Department of Finance, *Fiscal Reference Tables*, October 2002. Reproduced with the permission of the Minister of Public Works and Government Services Canada, 2003.

One such change involved Canada's *competition legislation*—the legislation intended to promote competition between businesses. Under the new law, it became more difficult for businesses to reduce competition through mergers with competitors or price-fixing, whereby firms agree not to compete regarding prices. And, of course, foreign competition would intensify as tariffs came down under the Canada–U.S. Free Trade Agreement and NAFTA and the GATT/WTO.

Another aspect of the new policy direction was the deregulation of some industries. Over the years, Canada had accumulated a large body of government regulations on business, many of which controlled prices and production and restricted the entry of new competitors into some industries. Many of these regulations had the unintended effect of reducing competition and

deregulation Policies to reduce the extent of regulation of business by government, with the intention of promoting efficiency through increased competition.

www.aircanada.ca
www.cn.ca

efficiency in the regulated industries. To improve productivity performance, the government deregulated some industries. The most notable examples of such **deregulation** were the dismantling of the Foreign Investment Review Act, which had restricted foreign investment, and the National Energy Program, which had regulated the operation of the oil industry. Other important areas of deregulation and increased competition were financial services and communications, most notably long-distance telephone service.

Along with deregulation came *reductions in government subsidies* to business, which forced businesses to improve efficiency rather than rely on government assistance. Several Crown corporations, such as Air Canada and Canadian National, were *privatized*, or sold to private interests, forcing them to operate more efficiently without government subsidies. Changes to unemployment insurance and welfare increased the incentives for people receiving these benefits to work or engage in retraining.

Government policy-makers also increasingly emphasized encouraging the *small business sector* of the economy, which had become a major source of job creation and was expected to play a larger role in the future. Unlike resource and heavy manufacturing industries, the emerging high-tech and service industries are not dominated by giant corporations; in fact, small size, innovation, and flexibility are seen as advantages in these fields.

These new policies represented a significant shift in Canadian economic and social policy. Government policies had in the past been directed largely toward *redistributing economic wealth* through an extensive social welfare system. But to improve productivity and competitiveness, the new Canadian policies emphasized the *creation of wealth*, as well as its redistribution. This change required incentives for work, enterprise, entrepreneurship, and investment, as well as increased emphasis on competition and efficiency.

The 1990s—A Difficult Period of Transition

While the transition from the "old order" described earlier to the new economic environment and policy direction began in the mid-1980s, its main impact occurred during the 1990s. During this period, several major economic changes coincided and interacted in ways that created difficulties and uncertainty for many Canadians.

First, the decade began with a *recession* during which the number of unemployed Canadians increased by nearly 600 000. The recession was prolonged by several factors, especially weak consumer spending. In part, this was due to the high levels of debt that consumers had accumulated during the 1980s; however, consumer confidence was also undermined by other factors.

One such problem was *high interest rates*. The recession was partly caused by and also prolonged by the Bank of Canada's policy objective of "downshifting" the Canadian economy from high inflation to more stable prices. Until inflationary pressures eased, this policy objective required high interest rates that dampened demand and slowed the recovery from the recession. And because of the time lags involved in monetary policy, the effects of these high interest rates lingered for some time, slowing the economy's recovery.

The recovery from the recession was also slowed by the *weak financial condition of Canadian governments*. Ordinarily, the government would have been expected to boost the recovery with budget deficits to stimulate demand. But the large budget deficits and rising debt of both the federal and provincial governments was forcing them to *cut* their spending, which prolonged the period of high unemployment.

Finally, it was at this time that Canada also had to adjust to changes in the *international economic environment*. While globalization and freer trade brought opportunities for Canadian producers, they also brought increased foreign competition. For some firms, this meant restructuring and downsizing that eliminated jobs. Ideally, such adjustments would occur when a booming economy provided plentiful alternative job opportunities. However, in Canada in the early 1990s, the opposite was the case, so many employees displaced by these changes had difficulty finding work.

As a result of these changes and the interactions between them, much of the 1990s was a period of considerable economic change and uncertainty for Canadians, accompanied by persistently high unemployment rates until quite late in the decade.

The extent of these changes is illustrated in Figure 13-5, which shows the growth of the entire economy (real GDP) and each sector of the economy from 1989 to 1998. The growth rate of 18.1 percent for the economy as a whole establishes a "benchmark" to which the growth of each sector can be compared. Consumption spending grew by 19 percent, which was about the same pace as the GDP. This is not surprising, since consumption represents about three-fifths of the GDP. However, consumption was the only sector to grow at about the same rate as GDP.

FIGURE 13-5 Growth of Real GDP and Its Components, 1989–98

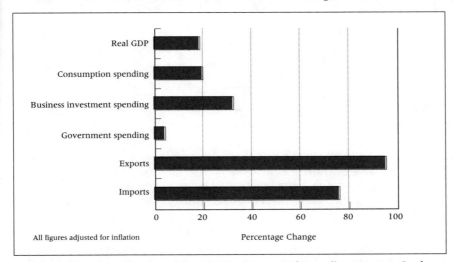

Source: Statistics Canada, adapted from *National Income and Expenditure Accounts*, Catalogue 13-001, 1998.

Government spending grew by only 3.9 percent, reflecting the cutbacks in government spending of the mid-1990s. Investment spending by business increased by more than 32 percent, almost all of which was on machinery and equipment rather than on construction. But the most dramatic changes were in the international trade sector, with exports growing by over 95 percent and imports by more than 76 percent.

All in all, Figure 13-5 portrays an economy undergoing a great deal of change in a brief period, on a scale and at a pace to which Canadians were unaccustomed. Established government spending programs were cut, imports penetrated the Canadian market at a greatly increased pace, and exports grew at the fastest rate of all, nearly doubling.

Through the Transition

By the late 1990s, economic conditions were improving considerably. With the rate of inflation down and government deficits eliminated, interest rates decreased considerably—for instance, the interest rate on a 5-year mortgage in 1998 was 7 percent, as compared to over 13 percent in 1990. Figure 13-6 shows real (after-inflation) long-term interest rates, which decreased by more than half in five years.

FIGURE 13-6 Real Interest Rates, 1960–2002

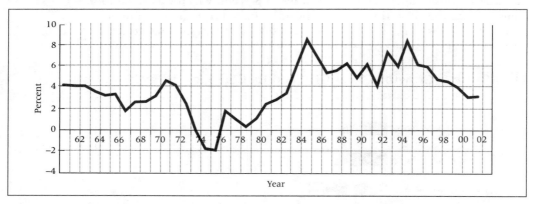

Source: Bank of Canada, adapted from *Banking and Financial Statistics*.

By 2002, "new economy" industries accounted for 8 percent of Canada's GDP, and the associated technology was spreading throughout the entire economy.

Led by rapidly growing exports to the booming U.S. economy, the Canadian economy recovered strongly in the late 1990s. In this more stable and positive economic environment, consumer and business confidence recovered, and aggregate demand gradually gained momentum. Unemployment was the area in which improvement was slowest, but by mid-2000, the unemployment rate was down to 6.7 percent, the lowest in 26 years.

This low unemployment rate, combined with the lowest rates of inflation since the 1960s, marked a major change in the performance of the economy. This change is reflected in Figure 13-7, which shows an unusual statistic called a "discomfort index," which is the sum of the unemployment rate and the rate of inflation. The significance of the discomfort index as an economic indicator is rather debatable; however, this index tends to increase when the economy is unstable, and troubled by unusually high rates of inflation and/or unemployment. Its return in the late 1990s to its lowest level since the early 1970s was an indication that the economic instability of the previous 25 years had passed—at least for the time being.

FIGURE 13-7 Discomfort Index, 1966–2002

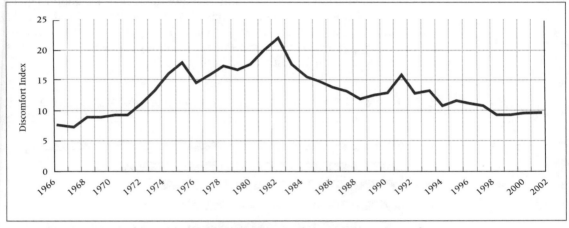

Source: Statistics Canada, adapted from *The Labour Force*, Catalogue, 71-001, 2002, and *Consumer Prices and Price Indexes*, Catalogue 62-010, 2002.

The Unresolved Problem of Productivity

By 2000, Canadians could take much satisfaction from having successfully tackled three major economic challenges in less than a decade:

- bringing the rate of inflation down after a long period of high inflation rates,
- ending a 25-year period of government budget deficits and escalating debt, and
- adjusting from a regime of tariff protection to one of freer trade.

Perhaps the most notable development in the 1990s was the dramatic increase in Canada's exports, especially to the United States. Despite this success, there were continuing concerns about Canada's productivity and international competitiveness. Canada was exporting more than 40 percent of its GDP, but this export success was mainly the result of the low Canadian dollar rather than improved productivity. In fact, Canada continued to lag behind its international competitors in the key area of productivity growth, raising additional concerns about both international competitiveness and Canadians' future living standards.

In the 13 years following the signing of the Canada–U.S. Free Trade Agreement, the productivity of American manufacturers increased at an average annual rate of 3.2 percent per year, compared to 2.0 percent per year for Canadian manufacturers. Over time, such seemingly small differences in productivity growth accumulate into a significant competitive disadvantage for Canadian producers—from 1988 to 2001, productivity in U.S. manufacturing increased by 50 percent, as compared to only 30 percent for Canadian manufacturers.

In the World Economic Forum's 2002–03 *Global Competitiveness Report*, Canada ranked eighth. As Figure 13-8 shows, this ranking placed Canada among the higher-ranked nations, and ahead of the United Kingdom, Japan, and Germany. However, Canada's ranking had slipped from third to eighth, mainly due to its low ranking in the area of *technology*, which is a key to productivity and competitiveness. And Canada's ranking was well below that of the United States, our largest trading partner by far.

FIGURE 13-8 World Economic Forum Competitiveness Index, 2002

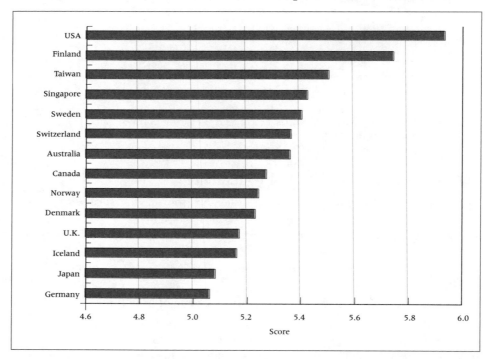

Source: World Economic Forum.

Looking ahead, Canada's persistently slow productivity growth was also raising concerns about the country's economic future. In late 2002, a Conference Board of Canada report noted that Canada's average per capita income in 2000 was US$29,000, which was US$6,000 (17 percent) below the American average per capita income of US$35,000. These figures are represented by the bars at the left side in Figure 13-9.

FIGURE 13-9 Canada–U.S. Income per Capita

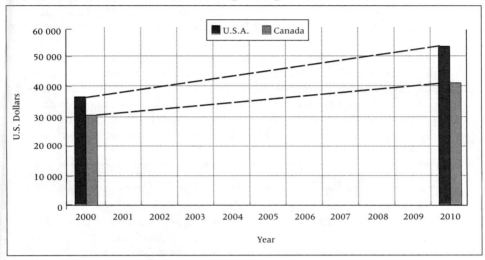

Source: The Conference Board of Canada.

The Conference Board's report went on to project that if past trends continued, the U.S.'s faster productivity growth would increase this gap to US$12,000 by 2010, leaving Canadians' average income 23 percent lower than Americans' average income, as shown by the bars at the right side in Figure 13-9. Such slow growth of real income would limit not only Canadians' standard of living but also the ability of the nation to provide the first-class health, education, and social services that Canadians value so highly. In the words of the president of the Conference Board, "Our position in the world is at risk of deteriorating," and "Canada in 2010 is a comfortable place to live, but in gentle decline."

Productivity as a National Priority

By the late 1990s, there was a growing consensus that the single most important economic priority for Canada was to improve the productivity of its industry. Productivity as a national priority takes us all the way back to Chapter 3, which emphasized productivity as the single most basic key to a society's economic prosperity. The unusually low Canadian dollar of the 1990s had given Canada an export-led boom, but for Canada's prosperity and living standards to progress over the longer term, the productivity of the Canadian economy will have to improve.

....

In Conclusion

Canadians want a great deal from their economic system. They want prosperity for themselves in the form of high levels of private personal consumption, high levels of government services (including a strong social welfare system, health care, and education), economic security, and protection of the environment. To provide all these, the Canadian economy must be productive, competitive, and prosperous. In the long run, it is only by becoming more productive, more efficient, and more competitive that Canadians will find it possible to achieve all of their economic and social goals. The challenge in this situation is to find an effective balance between the consumption (including private consumption and government services) that Canadians want in the present and the investment in not only capital goods, but also human resources, that are essential for their longer-term economic prosperity.

IN THE NEWS   What to Do with Those Surpluses?

The federal budget surpluses of the late 1990s were the first surpluses in nearly a quarter of a century. Not surprisingly, the surpluses generated considerable public interest, and there was no shortage of ideas for how the government should use those surpluses.

Questions

1. What are the three different types of ways in which the budget surpluses could be used?

2. What are the arguments in favour of each of these three uses of the surpluses?

3. Which of these do you believe would be of most benefit to Canadians?

Chapter Summary

1. Traditionally, Canada relied on natural resource exports for economic wealth, while government policies were more concerned with redistributing income and providing social welfare programs than with promoting productivity and competitiveness. (L.O. 1)

2. In the globalized world economy, business investment tends to be attracted by a high-quality labour force, strong communication and transportation links to the rest of the world, and a stable economic environment in terms of low inflation rates, low interest rates, and sound government finances. (L.O. 2)

3. Canada was not well prepared for globalization in the 1980s because its industries were protected by tariffs, and it had a high inflation rate and a problem of large government budget deficits and debt. (L.O. 3)

4. In response to globalization, Canada made the following basic changes to its economic policies:

   (a) a commitment to freer trade,

   (b) a commitment to lower inflation,

   (c) a commitment to end federal budget deficits, and

   (d) a variety of other changes intended to strengthen incentives, competition, and productivity. (L.O. 4)

5. The 1990s were a difficult period of transition during which the following developments interacted: a recession, the adjustment to freer trade, the Bank of Canada's anti-inflation policies, and the federal government's spending cuts to end its budget deficits. (L.O. 5)

6. Canada emerged from this transition with a low rate of inflation, sound federal government finances, much lower interest rates, and stronger consumer and business confidence. (L.O. 6)

7. On the negative side, there were continuing concerns about how Canada's weak productivity performance would affect living standards and Canada's international competitiveness in the future. (L.O. 7)

Questions

1. Update the statistics in Figure 13-5 to monitor trends in the economy since 1998, and try to determine the reasons for any changes that are evident. Regular updates can be obtained from Statistics Canada's *Canadian Economic Observer* (11-010-XPB) or from Statistics Canada's website (www.statcan.ca).

2. What has been the condition of the federal government's budget recently? Has the government used any surpluses to increase program spending, to cut taxes, or to pay down its debt? Regular updates can be obtained from Statistics Canada's *Canadian Economic Observer* (11-010-XPB) or from Statistics Canada's website (www.statcan.ca/english/Pgdb/govt02b.htm).

3. If the federal government began to have very large budget deficits again, how would you expect this to affect:

   (a) the international value of the Canadian dollar, and

   (b) interest rates in Canada?

4. (a) Fill in the columns in the following table for budget deficit/surplus and government debt for each year through 20X4. (Assume that the government's debt at the start of 20X1 was $300 billion.)

| | (BILLIONS OF DOLLARS) | | | |
Year	Government Revenues	Government Spending	Budget Deficit (−) or Surplus (+)	Government Debt
20X1	$100	$100	$_____	$_____
20X2	105	117	_____	_____
20X3	110	125	_____	_____
20X4	114	132	_____	_____
20X5	_____	_____	_____	_____
20X6	_____	_____	_____	_____

    (b) Develop a combination of spending reductions and/or tax increases for 20X5 and 20X6 that eliminates the deficits (balances the budget) by 20X6.

    (c) If the budget were to remain balanced in each year after 20X6, what would happen to the level of government debt?

5. In Figure 13-6, real interest rates were actually *negative* in 1973–75.
    (a) What would a negative real interest rate mean?
    (b) Why might such an unusual development occur?

6. Figure 13-5 shows that business investment spending increased by more than 32 percent from 1989 to 1998. What might explain the fact that over 88 percent of this increase was spending on machinery and equipment rather than on construction?

7. In 2000–01, the federal government began a five-year series of cuts to personal and corporate income that by 2004–05 was projected to reduce personal income taxes by $22.3 billion and corporate income taxes by $4.4 billion. Explain how these tax cuts could be viewed as part of a strategy for improving the performance of the Canadian economy.

8. How has productivity growth in Canada's manufacturing sector compared to its U.S. counterpart in recent years? Statistics are available on the website for the U.S. Bureau of Labor Statistics at www.bls.gov. In this website, select "Productivity," then "International Comparisons."

9. Is it your impression that Canada is in a slow but rather comfortable decline relative to the United States economically, or do you feel that Canada is doing better than that? Why?

APPENDIX
Answers to Boxed Questions

Chapter 1: What Is Economics?

YOU DECIDE: Opportunity Cost

1. Four kilograms of fruit per day. To produce three more kilograms per day of fish would require the transfer of one person from fruit production, where average output per worker was 4 kg per day.

2. Your car will not be fixed.

3. Your mother will be *very* disappointed ... which may involve more severe consequences than a broken-down car.

Chapter 3: Sources of Economic Prosperity: The Supply Side

YOU DECIDE: The "Taxman"

1. Excessively high tax rates can be self-defeating, in the sense that the government's tax revenues can actually be *reduced* by them, as people find ways to avoid paying such high taxes. In the extreme, people may leave the high-tax jurisdiction, as the Rolling Stones did. Or people may evade the taxes, by not declaring income or by engaging in black market activity. Canada experienced this in the early 1990s, when high taxes on cigarettes led to a sharp increase in smuggling from the United States.

Chapter 4: Sources of Economic Prosperity: The Demand Side

IN THE NEWS: Investment in the 1990s

1. The purpose of most business investment was not the construction of *increased capacity*; the economy was growing relatively slowly, so not much expansion was needed. Rather, the goal was to *improve efficiency*, so as to become more competitive in the new environment of freer international trade, which meant more competition from imports but also greater opportunities for exporting, *if* a producer was efficient and competitive enough. This meant more investment in technology and equipment, especially computers and computer-assisted industrial equipment.

IN THE NEWS: Recent Demand Trends

1. Consumption spending increased relatively gradually in the first half of the 1990s due to the recession, high interest rates, and low consumer confidence. After about 1996, all of these restraints on consumer spending eased, and consumer spending grew more rapidly.

    Spending on exports increased more rapidly than any other type of spending. This was due to a combination of the low and falling international price of the Canadian dollar, the Canada–U.S. Free Trade Agreement, and the booming U.S. economy.

Imports were the second fastest-growing sector, mainly due to trade agreements that gave foreign products more access to the Canadian market.

Business investment spending decreased during the recession of the early 1990s, as it usually does in recessions. After that, business investment spending recovered quite strongly for the reasons outlined in the previous case ("In the News: Investment in the 1990s").

Government spending on goods and services increased more slowly than on other types of spending, and was virtually flat for about five years. This reflected the weak financial condition of governments, as their large budget deficits were forcing them to restrain their spending.

In summary, the graph reflects some of the major economic events of the 1990s: the recession early in the decade, the free trade agreements into which Canada entered, the decreasing international value/price of the Canadian dollar, and the financial crisis of Canadian governments around 1993.

YOU DECIDE: What Will Happen to Aggregate Demand?

1. Aggregate demand would increase, mainly because consumers would be more willing to borrow and spend.

2. Aggregate demand would probably increase, as businesses would have both more money to reinvest and a greater incentive to invest. Business confidence would improve.

3. Aggregate demand would probably be depressed as households reduced borrowing and spending in order to control their debt.

4. Aggregate demand would be increased as the government spending added to spending and incomes in the economy.

5. Aggregate demand would be reduced, as businesses and consumers cut back on their borrowing.

6. Aggregate demand would probably be depressed, assuming that the forecasts had negative effects on consumer and business confidence.

7. Aggregate demand would be increased, as consumers would have more disposable income.

YOU DECIDE: What Will Happen?

1. Aggregate demand would increase. This would cause output and employment to increase. However, the rate of inflation would remain low, for at least three reasons. First, output (supply) would be able to keep up with rising demand, as producers would have no problems increasing production. Second, producers' production costs per unit would fall as output increased. Third, most businesses would be reluctant to jeopardize their newfound sales by increasing prices at this point in time.

2. Aggregate demand would increase. However, output and employment could not increase as readily as they would in response to a reduction in interest rates when the economy is in a recession, because the economy is near capacity. As a result, output (supply) would probably

have trouble keeping up with aggregate demand, so an increase in the rate of inflation would be likely.

3. Aggregate demand would decrease. This would drag output and employment down even further, making the recession worse. The rate of inflation would already have been low, and with lower demand, may become even lower.

Chapter 5: Money and the Economic System

YOU DECIDE: Electronic Cash?

1. Consider your own spending patterns and estimate the advantages and disadvantages *for you* of using a cash card. The cost (service charge) was estimated to be around $3 per month.

2. It has been reported that the cash cards were not as widely used as had been hoped by the banks. One possible reason is that people still found cash more convenient for the large number of small purchases they make in a day. Another is that for larger purchases, they simply used their debit cards, which most people already had.

3. Those who view the "cashless society" as inevitable see it as the final step in the long evolution of money as described in this chapter. Some who see it as impossible stress the *technical difficulties*—would every bubblegum machine, pay toilet, and babysitter in the country have a computer terminal? Others who see it as impossible focus on *psychological obstacles*—many people like the feel of "hard money" in their pocket, and quite a few others might not be keen on having every transaction they ever made recorded on a computer somewhere. Cash is a conveniently private form of payment for various transactions that are frowned upon by the law and others.

YOU DECIDE: Cash in Circulation

1. This trend reflects the growing use of noncash forms of money, such as cheques, credit cards, and debit cards.

2. Why did Canadians start carrying more cash around on their person? Most observers believe that this trend reflects the growth of the "underground economy," especially after the introduction of the Goods and Services Tax in 1991.

3. This trend could signify that the underground economy had stopped growing. On the other hand, the underground economy might have continued to increase its use of cash, while the "above ground" economy was reducing its use of cash even further, the net result being the stabilized use of cash shown in the graph.

IN THE NEWS: Deposit Insurance

1. Deposit insurance encourages depositors to seek the highest possible returns on their funds without concerning themselves with whether their money is being invested wisely. The worst possible outcome for

them is that after the bank or other financial institution fails, they get their money back. So deposit insurance can encourage people to deposit their money into institutions whose investments involve higher risks.

2.   Deposit insurance can encourage financial institutions to make more high-risk loans and investments than they otherwise would have. If successful, this investment strategy will generate high income that will permit them to pay higher interest rates on deposits and attract more deposits to invest. And if it is unsuccessful, the worst-case scenario is that any losses will be covered by deposit insurance.

3.   This is a very debatable practice. The message it sends to both investors and financial institutions is that they will not be held responsible for their actions or neglect—the government will bail them out. Also, such bailouts come at the expense of taxpayers, meaning that Canadians who behave responsibly wind up paying for bailouts of those who do not behave responsibly.

4.   Politics. Had the depositors not been covered, the opposition parties could have alleged that government authorities failed to supervise these financial institutions adequately, placing depositors at risk.

Chapter 6: Booms, Recessions, and Inflation

YOU DECIDE: Jobs and Profits

1.   The answer lies in the connection between the level of aggregate demand and *both* employment *and* profits. In a boom, high aggregate demand boosts output *and* employment *and* profits, so *both* employment *and* profits increase. In a recession, the opposite happens—lower aggregate demand causes decreases in both profits and employment, as financially troubled employers lay off employees.

YOU DECIDE: Monitoring the Economy

1.   *Standing alone,* the statistics for any one particular week are not very meaningful. Rather, the key is to *look for trends and patterns* in the data. Which statistics are going up and which are going down, and what is the *overall picture* conveyed by the data? Also, don't be thrown off by the fact that any particular statistic might temporarily head off in an unexpected direction due to special circumstances, such as a strike or other random factor.

2.   What might *explain* any trends that you see? Watch for articles in the paper that might help to explain why trends are happening. Ask yourself whether a scenario of rising or falling aggregate demand "fits" with the statistics.

3.   Many forecasters start by projecting the past year's trends forward for another year in what is called a "naive forecast" that essentially assumes that what *has happened* in the past *will continue to happen* in the future. This may not be true, so the next step is to "guesstimate" changes that are likely in the future, and adjust the forecast accordingly. Watch the newspaper for the monthly publication of Statistics

Canada's *Composite Leading Indicator*, and for articles related to it or any other predictions. Tarot cards or reading of tea leaves should be used only as a last resort.

Chapter 7: Stabilizing the Economy: Government Monetary and Fiscal Policies

IN THE NEWS: Bank of Canada raises overnight rate target

1. An increase in the overnight rate indicates that the Bank of Canada is concerned about inflation. Such concern tends to become stronger, as the economy gets closer to its capacity output, which happens during economic booms when aggregate demand is high. Specific indicators that the economy is getting closer to capacity output could be some combination of a high rate of growth of real GDP, a low and falling unemployment rate, continued increases in the Composite Leading Indicator, and, of course, more rapid increases in the Consumer Price Index or other price indexes.

2. The Bank of Canada's intention would be to slow down the growth of aggregate demand so that demand would not "outrun" capacity. Higher interest rates would help to achieve this by slowing borrowing and spending by consumers and businesses.

3. All other things being equal, an increase in Canadian interest rates would increase the international value of the Canadian dollar. Higher interest rates would attract more short-term deposits, which would mean more buying of Canadian dollars and a higher value/price of the dollar. (This would slow down Canadian exports, which would also contribute to the Bank of Canada's objective of slowing aggregate demand.)

4. The overnight rate has increased from 2.50 percent to 2.75 percent. This increase makes it 10 percent more costly to borrow short-term funds. The increase is 0.25 from a base of 2.50, which in percentage terms is 10 percent.

YOU DECIDE: Good News/Bad News

1. The key to this phenomenon is that when making their decisions, stock buyers do not look *at the present,* but rather *at the future*. Seeing the boom grow even stronger can lead them to expect *higher interest rates* in the near future. Higher interest rates would drive stock prices lower, for two reasons. First, higher interest rates increase the probability of an economic slowdown, in which business profits would fall. Second, people's savings can be invested in two basic ways: in shares of companies or in interest-earning investments such as bonds. Higher interest rates make bonds relatively more attractive as an investment. This pulls more savings toward bonds as an investment, leaving less for the buying of stocks, which in turn depresses the demand for stocks, causing their prices to fall. As a result, the stock market often falls *before* a boom turns into a slowdown/recession, making stock prices one of the "leading indicators" described in Chapter 6. The opposite tends to happen late in a recession, as lower interest rates lead to higher stock prices before the economy has really recovered.

YOU DECIDE: How Much to Increase Spending?

1. About $10 billion, calculated as follows: with aggregate demand at
    $800 billion, a 2-percent decline would mean a loss of about $16 bil-
    lion in demand (2 percent of $800 billion). If the government injected
    $10 billion of additional spending into the economy, a multiplier of 1.6
    would magnify its effect to $16 billion in about one year, filling the
    shortfall in demand. The amount of spending needed would be calcu-
    lated as follows:

    Increase in spending × 1.6 = 16 billion
    Increase in spending = $16 billion/1.6 = $10 billion

Chapter 8: Perspectives on Macroeconomic Policy

YOU DECIDE: Two Views of Canada's Performance on Employment

1. The answer lies in the fact that Canada has an unusually *high labour-
    force participation rate*. This means that even when the Canadian econo-
    my has been quite successful at creating more jobs, there were still
    even more people wanting to work than there were jobs, leaving a
    relatively high number of people unemployed. Another factor is that
    when the economy booms and unemployment falls, the participation
    rate rises even higher, as more people are drawn into the labour force
    seeking work. This tends to keep the unemployment rate relatively
    high even when many new jobs are being created. With such a high
    participation rate, it is possible that there will be *both* high employment
    rates *and* high unemployment rates.

Chapter 10: The Canadian Dollar in Foreign Exchange Markets

YOU DECIDE: How Much Will It Cost Me?

1. $615.20 Canadian, based on $1.538 Canadian for each $1.00 U.S.

    ($400 × $1.538 = $615.20) The cost of U.S. $1.00 as $1.538 Canadian
    is calculated as follows:
    U.S. $0.65 = CDN$1.00
    To get the cost of U.S.$1.00, divide both sides by 0.65.
    so U.S.$1.00 = $1.00/0.65 = CDN$1.538

2. With the Canadian dollar at U.S.$0.645, U.S.$1.00 would cost $1.550
    Canadian ($1.00/0.645). So your U.S.$400 would now cost you
    CDN$620.00, or $4.80 more. Moral: don't sweat the small stuff.

IN THE NEWS: Exchange Rate Changes and Competitive Balance

1. Not for long—the high demand for that nation's currency in order to
    buy its exports would drive the price of the currency up, making its
    exports less attractive.

Chapter 11: The Global Economy

IN THE NEWS: THE Diving U.S. Dollar

1. (a) A decline in the international value of the U.S. dollar from $1.57 Canadian to $1.37 Canadian would mean that the international value of the Canadian dollar had increased from about 64 U.S. cents to about 73 U.S. cents—an increase of over 14 percent. For Canadian consumers, this would be good news, since U.S. dollars, and thus U.S. goods and services, would be 14 percent less costly for them.

    (b) Americans would be less likely to buy Canadian goods and services than before, since the Canadian dollar was now more costly to them. This would depress Canadian exports of both goods (such as industrial products) and services (such as tourism). Furthermore, Canadians would tend to buy more imported goods and services, which would become less costly. Both of these effects would reduce employment in Canada, and increase unemployment.

    (c) The lower U.S. dollar would worsen Japan's and Europe's problems with deflation. Output and employment would be further depressed by the fact that their consumers would tend to buy more U.S. goods and services rather than domestic items—the same effect as in the case of Canada in part (b). The lower U.S. dollar would put additional downward pressure on prices (inflation) in Japan and Europe, by introducing cheaper U.S. goods and services into their markets.

    (d) The opposite effect would occur in the United States. The risk of deflation would be reduced for two reasons. First, as the international value of the U.S. dollar fell, the price of imports would increase, reducing the pressure of import competition on U.S. producers and allowing them more leeway for increasing prices. And second, with import prices higher, Americans would tend to buy more U.S. goods and services, boosting output and employment in the U.S. economy, and also making it easier for U.S. producers to increase prices.

2. Up-to-date information on exchange rates is available in newspapers, or online at the home page of the Bank of Canada (http://www.bankof-canada.ca/en/).

Chapter 12: Canada in the Global Economy

YOU DECIDE: Trade Policy Choices

1. The decision you must make is whether to continue to protect the interests of an industry that is in decline in Canada or to promote the interests of industries that are growing. It's similar to the decisions that sports managers have to make: whether to keep the older players around for another year or bring in the up-and-coming young play-ers—your heart leans one way and your head leans the other way.

YOU DECIDE: Canadian Culture—A Special Case?

1. To clarify the issues here, ask yourself whether there really *is* a "Canadian culture" that we need to protect against foreign competition and influences, or whether this argument is really just an attempt by producers of various "cultural" services to secure special status and protection for themselves at the expense of the Canadian public.

IN THE NEWS: NAFTA Has Helped Curb U.S. Protectionism

1. The "short answer" is that in the case of most Canadian appeals, the U.S. has been in the wrong, but the real question is *why* this has so often been the case. A key reason is that U.S. law almost encourages American industries to file complaints of unfair import competition, as a tactic to harass successful foreign competitors. And once such a complaint has been filed, U.S. authorities have tended to pursue it without much critical examination. Even if the complaint is thrown out when appealed to a neutral panel, this process can take a long time, during which obstacles are put in the way of the imports. Canadians have protested this as a "hit and run" tactic, and neutral panels have often agreed with them.

2. The neutral parties who sit on the panels that hear these appeals are members of a relatively small community of respected experts in their field. They are aware of the sort of problems described in the answer to the previous question, and would not want to tarnish their reputation for objective neutrality by taking the side of their own country when that country is clearly in the wrong.

Chapter 13: Into the Future

IN THE NEWS: What To Do With Those Surpluses?

1.

    (a) to pay down government debt, or

    (b) to increase government spending, or

    (c) to reduce taxes.

2.

    (a) Government debt is very high.

    (b) Government spending on major programs such as health care, education, and income support (welfare and Employment Insurance) was reduced considerably during the 1990s as part of the government's deficit elimination program.

    (c) Canada's tax burden on both persons and businesses is high, and higher than in the United States. These high taxes are considered to be an obstacle to increasing productivity, which is a basic weakness of the Canadian economy.

GLOSSARY

accelerator The effect whereby rising consumption spending causes rapid increases in induced investment, and a slowing down or leveling off of consumption spending causes sharp declines in induced investment.

aggregate demand Total spending on goods and services, consisting of consumption spending, investment spending, government spending, and net exports $(C + I + G + X - M)$.

aggregate supply curve A graphical representation of the supply side of the economy showing how production cost per unit changes as the level of output is increased toward its potential.

appreciation of a currency Increases in the international value of a currency.

Asia–Pacific Economic Co-operation (APEC) A group of 21 nations that border the Pacific Ocean and intend to form a free trade area by 2010.

Auto Pact The 1965 agreement between Canada and the United States that provided for free trade in automotive vehicles, products, and parts.

automatic stabilizers Government spending and taxation programs that have the effect of automatically supporting aggregate demand during recessions and depressing aggregate demand during periods of boom/inflation.

balance of payments A summary of all of a nation's receipts and payments for a given year.

balance of payments deficit A situation in which a nation's payments exceed its receipts.

balance of payments surplus A situation in which a nation's receipts exceed its payments.

balanced budget A government budget in which tax revenues and expenditures are equal.

Bank Rate The rate of interest charged by the Bank of Canada on loans (advances) it makes to banks and other financial institutions.

bankers' deposit rate The rate of interest paid by the Bank of Canada on the chartered banks' deposits at the Bank of Canada.

boom psychology People's expectation of a future boom that leads them to be more willing to borrow to buy big-ticket items and capital goods.

branch plants Manufacturing plants established in a nation by a foreign-owned firm in order to avoid tariffs on imports by producing their products inside that nation.

budget deficit A government budget in which expenditures exceed tax revenues.

budget surplus A government budget in which tax revenues exceed expenditures.

business cycle The fluctuation of the economy between prosperity and recession.

business savings Profits retained in a business after taxes have been paid and dividends have been paid to shareholders. Another source of capital for real investment. (Also known as **retained earnings**.)

capacity output The maximum real output that the economy is capable of producing in any given year.

capital account Balance of Payments items involving flows of investment funds (capital), both long-term and short-term, between countries.

capital equipment The tools, equipment, machinery, and factories used to increase production per worker, and thus improve living standards.

capital taxes Taxes levied on the amount of a corporation's assets, or its capital.

cash reserve ratio The percentage of total deposits that a bank keeps as cash reserves.

cash reserves That amount of cash kept on hand by a bank to cover day-to-day withdrawals of cash.

central bank A government agency with responsibility for monetary policy, as well as other financial functions, on behalf of the government.

consumer confidence The degree to which consumers feel optimistic (or pessimistic) about their future economic prospects.

consumer indebtedness Consumer debt as a percentage of disposable income; affects consumers' willingness to spend.

Consumer Price Index (CPI) A weighted average of the prices of a "basket" of goods and services purchased by a typical urban family.

consumption Consumer goods and services that are used up by consumers for present enjoyment.

countercyclical fiscal policy A policy of using fiscal policy (budget deficits during recessions and surpluses during periods of inflation) to smooth out the economic fluctuations associated with the business cycle.

countervailing tariff A tariff imposed in response to a tariff or other restriction on imports imposed by another nation.

current account Balance of Payments items relating to day-to-day transactions in goods and services, including interest and dividends.

cyclical unemployment Unemployment that is caused by periodic cyclical weaknesses in aggregate demand associated with recessions.

deflation A decrease in the general level of the prices of goods and services.

demand side The purchasers of society's output of goods and services.

depreciation of a currency Decreases in the international value of a currency.

deregulated Policies to reduce the extent of regulation of business by government, with the intention of promoting efficiency through increased competition.

devaluation A reduction in the level of a pegged exchange rate.

direct investment Officially defined as "those investments in business enterprises which are sufficiently concentrated to constitute control of the concern." This term usually refers to investment by foreign firms in plant and equipment for their Canadian subsidiaries. It also includes provision of working capital for Canadian subsidiaries by foreign parent firms, and mergers in which the assets of Canadian firms are purchased by foreign firms.

dirty float A situation in which a government influences the exchange rate by purchases and sales of currencies in foreign exchange markets, and changes in interest rates.

dumping The practice of exporting a product at a price below the cost of producing it, or below the price charged in the country in which it is produced.

easy money policy Monetary policy directed toward making interest rates lower in order to stimulate aggregate demand.

economic boom A condition of higher demand in the economy as a whole, bringing output and employment to high levels.

economic resources Labour, capital equipment, and natural resources that are used to produce goods and services.

economies of scale The achievement of increased efficiency as a result of larger-scale productive operations and reductions in production costs per unit made possible by large-scale production.

effectiveness A measure of how well an economy performs in terms of producing goods and services that meet the needs and wants of people.

efficiency A measure of how well an economy performs in terms of producing high volumes of goods and services at a low cost per item.

employment-to-population ratio The percentage of the working-age population that is employed.

equilibrium A situation, in the Balance of Payments, in which a nation's receipts and payments are equal to each other.

euro A common currency adopted in 1999 by 11 of the 15 countries of the European Union.

European Union A major free trade area comprised of most of the countries of Europe.

exchange rate The international price, or value, of a currency in foreign exchange markets.

exchange rate management Government policies to moderate fluctuations in exchange rates. See **dirty float**.

floating exchange rate A situation in which the international value of a currency is allowed to fluctuate freely with the supply of and demand for it.

foreign exchange markets Markets, conducted through banks, in which currencies of different nations are bought and sold (exchanged for each other).

foreign exchange reserves Holdings of foreign currencies and gold maintained by governments for the purpose of stabilizing their exchange rates through purchases and sales of their currencies.

frictional unemployment Unemployment arising from people being temporarily out of work because they are in the process of changing jobs.

full employment The lowest rate of unemployment that can be achieved without generating unacceptable inflation in the economy.

General Agreement on Tariffs and Trade (GATT) An international agreement under which many nations, following 1947, negotiated reductions in tariffs in order to promote freer trade.

globalization The trend toward more international trade and investment that has characterized the world economy since the early 1980s.

Gross Domestic Product (GDP) A measure of the total value of goods and services produced and incomes earned in a country in one year.

hidden unemployment People who are unemployed but are not counted in the unemployment statistics because they have given up looking for work.

hot money Short-term funds that are used to speculate in currencies by being moved rapidly from currencies that are perceived as "weak" to currencies that are perceived as "strong."

import quotas Legal limits on the volume of particular goods that may be imported into a nation.

induced investment Capital investment spending undertaken by business in response to increases in sales that have brought production to near-capacity levels and that are expected to continue.

infant industries Industries protected by government from foreign competition until they have matured to the point of becoming internationally competitive without protection.

inflation An increase in the general level of the prices of goods and services.

inflation psychology People's expectation of future inflation that leads them to seek larger wage increases and to make purchases of some big-ticket items quickly, before prices rise further.

inputs These are the same as economic resources.

interest rates Percentages of borrowed money paid by a borrower (and received by a creditor) annually.

International Monetary Fund (IMF) An international agency established to oversee and maintain the system of pegged exchange rates set up in 1945.

investment Refers to the production of capital goods that make possible increased production in the future.

labour The largest single productive input available to any economy, labour includes all of the productive talents of the people of a society, mental as well as physical.

labour force Those Canadians who are either employed or are unemployed and both available for work and seeking work.

land Short form for all the natural resources available to a society's economy as economic inputs.

leading economic indicators Economic statistics that tend to increase or decrease in advance of increases or decreases in the pace of economic activity, thus giving advance notice of changes in economic trends.

M1 The narrowest definition of the money supply, including only currency (bank notes and coins) outside the banks plus demand deposits (current chequing account deposits).

M2 A wider definition of the money supply, including M1 plus personal savings deposits plus non-personal notice deposits.

market power The ability to raise one's price. Usually associated with a dominant or monopolistic position in a market.

market system An economic system in which economic decisions are made mainly by consumers and privately-owned producers in a decentralized manner.

monetary policy Where the Bank of Canada uses interest rates and the money supply to influence the level of aggregate demand in the economy.

money GDP GDP in current dollar terms; that is, including any price increases due to inflation.

money supply The total volume of money in circulation, defined variously as M1, M2, and M2+.

multiplier effect The effect whereby fluctuations in spending (for instance, investment spending) spread by means of the respending effect through the economy, with the total impact on GDP and incomes being considerably larger than the initial fluctuations in spending.

National Debt A measure of the indebtedness of the federal government. Specifically, the difference between the government's liabilities (mostly outstanding bonds) and its net recorded assets.

National Policy A set of nation-building policies introduced in Canada in 1879, the key economic aspect of which was protective tariffs to foster the development of Canadian industry.

niche marketing Marketing to small segments of a market.

non-tariff barriers Other methods (besides tariffs) of restricting imports, including quotas and licences for imports, preferential purchasing policies, and subsidies for domestic producers.

North American Free Trade Agreement (NAFTA) Free trade agreement between Canada, the United States, and Mexico.

operating band The one-half percentage point range established by the Bank of Canada for the overnight rate. The top of the range is the Bank Rate and the bottom of the range is the bankers' deposit rate.

opportunity cost The concept that the real economic cost of producing something is the forgone opportunity to produce something else that could have been produced with the same inputs.

output The goods and services produced by a society using its productive inputs.

output per worker The goods and services produced by a worker using productive inputs.

overnight loans Very short-term loans between financial institutions to cover temporary shortfalls in areas such as settlement balances.

overnight rate The rate of interest on one-day loans made by banks, investment dealers, and other financial institutions to each other.

participation rate The percentage of the population of working age that is working or seeking work.

payments International transactions in which a nation pays funds to other countries, causing that nation to sell its currency.

pegged exchange rates Exchange rates that are prevented by governments from moving from their fixed levels in relation to each other.

personal disposable income Personal income less personal taxes, or after-tax personal income that may be spent or saved.

personal saving Personal disposable income not spent on consumption.

personal saving rate The percentage of personal disposable income that is saved.

productivity A measure of productive efficiency, usually measured in terms of labour, as output per worker-hour or output per employee.

profits Those funds left from a business's sales revenues after all expenses have been paid. Such funds are therefore available (after taxes have been paid) for dividends to shareholders and reinvestment in the business.

real GDP GDP statistics that have been adjusted to eliminate the effects of price increases, the result being a statistic that measures only changes in real output. Also called "GDP in constant dollars" or "GDP at 1992 prices."

real income The purchasing power of income (as distinct from its dollar value).

real interest rate The rate of return earned by a lender after inflation is taken into account. For instance, if the rate of interest is 6 percent and the rate of inflation is 2 percent, the real interest rate is 4 percent.

receipts International transactions in which a nation receives funds from other countries, causing the foreign countries to buy that nation's currency.

recession A situation in which the economy is producing considerably less than its potential output, and unemployment is high. Formally defined as two consecutive quarters (a quarter being three months) of declining real output.

recession psychology People's concerns regarding recession and unemployment that lead them to curtail their spending, especially on big-ticket items that require borrowing.

resource wealth mentality The view that society's economic wealth is derived mainly from the sale of natural resources, as opposed to efficiency in the production of goods and services.

retained earnings Profits retained in a business after taxes have been paid and dividends have been paid to shareholders. Another source of capital for real investment. (Also known as **business savings**.)

saving Doing without (forgoing) consumer goods; disposable income not spent on consumption.

scarcity The problem that, while economic inputs (and thus potential ouput) are limited in availability, people's wants and needs are apparently unlimited.

seasonal unemployment Unemployment arising from seasonal downturns in employment in some industries.

settlement balances Deposits (at the Bank of Canada) of the commercial banks and other financial institutions that are used to settle debts and transactions between each other.

speculation The buying of an asset (here, a currency) with the objective of reselling it for a higher price in the future.

standard of living A measure of the economic prosperity of the people of a society, usually expressed in terms of the volume of goods and services consumed per person per year.

structural budget deficits Deficits arising from a built-in imbalance between government expenditures and revenues that results in deficits even when the economy is in a period of boom.

structural unemployment Unemployment arising from a mismatch between the skills required by employers and those of unemployed people.

subsidies Government financial assistance to a firm or industry, through measures such as grants, loans, or special tax treatment.

supply side The ability of the economy to use its productive resources efficiently to produce goods and services.

tariffs Taxes, or import duties, levied by a nation on products imported from foreign countries.

theory of comparative advantage The theory that even if one nation is more efficient in the production of all items than another nation, it can still be to the economic advantage of both nations to specialize in what they produce most efficiently (items in which each has a "comparative advantage"), and trade with each other.

tight money policy Monetary policy directed toward making interest rates higher in order to slow the growth of aggregate demand.

trade war Retaliatory escalation of trade barriers by nations against each others' exports.

trading blocs Groups of nations that have a trade agreement among themselves outside of the WTO agreement.

unemployment rate The percentage of the labour force that is unemployed.

world product mandating An arrangement whereby a branch plant acquires a mandate from its foreign parent company to design, manufacture, and market a particular product or products for the world market, as opposed to producing only for the domestic market of the country in which it is located.

World Trade Organization (WTO) Successor to the GATT as of 1995.

INDEX